French Entrée

Bed and Breakfast in France

The guide to the best
chambres d'hôtes in France

---

third edition

The French Entrée series of travel guides provides independent reviews and opinions on the best local restaurants and hotels in the regions of France. Unlike many other guides, no charge is made and the reviews are the author's own opinions.

To see our complete range of travel books, menu guides and themed phrse books for independent travellers, visit our **www.aspectguides.com**

In the French Entrée series:
Bed and Breakfast in France (1-904012-04-3)
Brittany (1-904012-03-5)
Calais, Bolougne and the North of France (1-904012-00-0)
Normandy (1-904012-02-7)

Menu Companion (1-904012-05-1)
Business French Phrase Book (1-904012-10-8)
Family French Phrase Book (1-904012-09-4)
Young Traveller's French Phrase Book (1-904012-11-6)

French Entrée

Bed and Breakfast in France

The guide to the best chambres d'hôtes in France

---

third edition

by Rosemary Gower-Jones

Aspect Guides

Third edition published in Great Britain 2002
second edition published 2000
first edition published 1998

Published by Aspect Guides, an imprint of Peter Collin Publishing
32-34 Great Peter Street, London, SW1P 2DB

British Library Cataloguing-in-Publication Data
A catalogue record for this book is available from the British Library
ISBN 1-904012-04-3

Design and Production by Book Production Services, Norfolk

Printed and bound in Italy by Legoprint

*Every effort has been made to ensure that the information in this guide is
accurate and up-to-date and the advice is given in good faith. However, neither
the publisher nor the author is responsible for any problems or disappointments
encountered before or during your travels.*

Contents

Introduction

Welcome to this new edition of the French Entrée guide to Bed and Breakfast in France. As with previous editions, and quite unlike our competitors, the publisher does not charge the establishments included. Instead, I have visited each one and provide you with a personal, independent view.

If your idea of a holiday is a hotel with room service, an ever-open bar and restaurant, and not having to chat to strangers, you're reading the wrong book.

If on the other hand you wish to take a leisurely holiday exploring France, then B&B or *Chambres d'Hôtes*, as they are called in France, are for you. What better way of getting to know the people, than staying in the comfort of their private homes, be it château or farmhouse. Most owners speak basic English, many fluently. New friendships will be forged, your French will improve, and you will be introduced to the attractions of the region. Many places offer evening meals. Sceptics will be surprised to find that *chambres d'hôtes*, are often more comfortable, more friendly and have more secure parking than a hotel, at a fraction of the cost.

In this new edition of the guide, I have selected the most popular B&Bs of the last three books (with the help of reader-feedback), added nearly 50 new places, visited every one, and tried to paint a true picture of each home; **you** decide if it is right for you.

Making a selection was difficult, the main criteria were good value and *accueil* (welcome), into whichever category they fell. Looking for new places, I kept my ear finely tuned to the *chambres d'hôtes* grape-vine in France, checked out readers suggestions and followed up requests for inclusion from *chambres d'hôtes* owners.

As always, I would be delighted to hear from you with your views and opinions on the entries in this edition, or suggestions for new entries. Please send comments by post, email or using our website suggestion book.

WELCOME TO NEW READERS

The words 'Bed and Breakfast' tend to conjure up memories of seaside boarding houses where rooms have to be vacated from 10a.m. to supper time. Not so in France, you become private guests of the family.

Chambres d'Hôtes are guest rooms in private homes, the number varies from one to five, occasionally more, breakfast is included in the price. Rooms may be in simple farmhouses, elegant manors or luxurious châteaux. Most are situated in the country – a few in towns. Their owners normally have mastered some English, often speak it well, but for those who have no French, I have included a fair sprinkling of English owned B&Bs to help you break the ice.

Ask yourselves why your hosts started B&B in the first place. To augment their income for sure, but also because they like people. The French seldom take their holidays abroad, (France has so much to offer), but they enjoy meeting foreigners and what better way than entertaining them at home.

I have tried to include places in every region and in all categories. Some close to major roads, for that journey south, others near well-known sites and historical monuments. **Every one has been visited by me** accompanied by my long-suffering husband, who luckily loves France, drives, translates when necessary, and is for ever rescuing me from tangles on the computer.

ROOMS

You may have the choice of double or single beds, bath or shower, so specify when booking. Your room is yours for the duration of your stay, only rarely is it entered by your hostess, to be cleaned if you are staying more than a couple of nights, so don't expect your bed to be made daily, though this does happen in a few places. It is just like staying in a friend's house. Decor varies with every room, some are heavily beamed others have elegant high ceilings, others more modern. Furnished with anything from real antiques, beautifully hand-embroidered bed-linen to family hand-me-downs and *brocante*, or so modern you think you are in the Ideal Home exhibition. Bed-side lamps are always included. Extra pillows are usually in the wardrobe. Cots for babies and an extra bed for a child in your room are usually available, but check when booking.

BATHROOMS

In this guide, private bathrooms or shower rooms with loos, come with 99% of all rooms, most are adjoining the room, but not all (this is noted in the text). Family suites of two rooms share a bathroom. Soap, towels, flannels are provided and often shampoo, hairdryers, tissues and many other luxuries. Those who prefer showers fare better than bath-lovers, as all baths tend to have overhead showers; baths are more likely to be found in the medium to luxury class. Water is metered in France and expensive.

BREAKFASTS

Continental – forget those bacon and egg fry-ups.
A choice of tea, coffee or hot chocolate is always offered.

Basic breakfast at the worst consists of yesterday's bread toasted, butter and jam. Luckily, this is now rare.

Standard breakfast consists of orange juice, fresh bread, usually *baguettes* and *croissants*, with plentiful butter, and a choice of home-made jams, sometimes supplemented by home-made gâteau.

Copious breakfasts offer fruit juice, (often freshly squeezed) cereal, yoghurts, a selection of fresh bread, *croissants,* cheese, ham and fresh fruit, even an egg if on a farm. Surprisingly, the best breakfasts are sometimes found at the less expensive chambres d'hôtes. Where breakfasts are unexpectedly good or poor I have mentioned it in the text.

EVENING MEALS

These must be booked each morning, and can be very good value, consisting of four courses, local *apéritif,* and wine, coffee or *tisane* included in the price. They are rarely obligatory, giving you a chance to try out local restaurants.

SALONS/GARDENS
Sitting rooms may be private, shared with other guests or the host family, and gardens are usually large with plentiful plastic furniture, often swings for children and in many cases with the luxury of loungers round a swimming pool.

KITCHENS
You may be surprised to hear some rooms have kitchen corners enabling you to self-cater. A great saving if you have small children or babies, who wouldn't want to eat a full blown evening meal. Others have a separate kitchen shared by all guests, rarely is everyone clamouring for it at the same time. Normally included in the price of the room., but not always.

PARKING
One of the big pluses – safe, free and enclosed unless stated otherwise. Occasionally a locked garage is available.

LAUNDRY
Washing lines are always available, but take your own soap powder, there are often ironing facilities, and it is sometimes possible to use a washing machine for a small fee, if staying many days. Laundrettes are few and far between, found only in large towns.

BOOKING
It does pay to book ahead, essential in school holidays. With only a few rooms to allocate, the more popular beds are grabbed early. Basic telephone English has usually been mastered. However, ringing up before April you may encounter the dreaded answer-phone, as this is the time owners tend to be away. Don't even think of turning up on spec on busy weekends and *fêtes*. Have the courtesy to phone again if you are delayed, thus strengthening the entente cordiale. Don't bank on an evening meal unless it's pre-booked.

The ideal time to turn up is late afternoon, giving Madame a chance to do her chores and shopping and allow you to get your bearings and relax, Odds are you'll get a welcome cuppa.

Sometimes a deposit is asked for if booked well ahead. An English cheque will do, it is usually returned to you when paying, as it costs at least 8€ to change in a French bank, so be prepared to pay the whole amount.

If booking by letter always use the 5 figure post code number before the name of the town (given after the name in the text). Example:

M. Pompon,
'La Grande Poterie'
03000 Coulandon
France

PRICES

Prices given in this guide are always for **two** people for one night including breakfasts. Single guests usually pay the same for a room, **less** one breakfast.

Evening meals: prices are always quoted for **one** person.

Prices in Euros: this subject is worth a short note. When updating this edition, many of the smaller establishments had not yet decided on a tariff in Euros. In these cases, we have converted the (old) French-franc prices into Euros at the rate in December 2001. However, we also found that some establishments used the change to Euros to round-up their prices. (However, this type of price-increase seems to be true across many different types of service!) When you telephone or write to book your stay, make sure to ask for the current prices.

PAYMENT

Preferably by cash. Credit cards occasionally in the **L** class.

As we, the customers, have demanded higher standards, so have prices risen accordingly. But not much. The present current exchange rate is still favourable but with the introduction of the Euro, you will be paying a little more than last year.

OPENING TIMES

Year-round unless stated. On the other hand owners do sometimes take holidays at slack times, and just close down for a week or two, so it is always wise to ring ahead.

DIRECTIONS

I aim to save you the hassle of bumping down the wrong cart track by giving clear and detailed directions, if I've got them wrong please let me know.

The 5 figure number after the name of each place is the post code.

Symbols

RECOMMENDED

A ☆ indicates a specially recommended entry. They are the paragons, tried and tested, they fulfil at least three of the criteria – good value, welcome, comfort, special situation, preferably all of them.

CATEGORIES

(L) = Luxury. (M) = Medium.(S) = Small.

The **L** group probably means a château or manor house. Expect to pay 64-160€ for B&B for two. You will be getting an inside view of a stunning building, meeting charming, well-educated, probably English speaking hosts, enjoying spacious rooms, tennis court and pool in surrounding grounds, for a fraction of what you would pay in a similar hotel. Furniture will probably be family heirlooms. Dinner (rarely obligatory), will be elegantly served and you will be abusing the hospitality if you turn up in a T shirt and trainers. Count on upwards of 40€ each. The owners, often busily preparing the meal, try to join you for an *apéritif*, though I notice the trend is increasingly to opt out of the communal meal. Breakfast should be of the copious variety. You could economise on lunch.

The **M** group covers the majority of entries. Expect to pay 40-64€ for B&B for two. These could be houses currently too big for their owners, old farmhouses full of character, modern villas in a particularly attractive situation, mills, monasteries, or town houses. Some with swimming pools. The rooms and bathrooms are likely to have been contrived out of existing bedrooms, so rooms will differ in size and price. Evening meals will not always be on offer – but good nearby restaurants will be recommended. Hosts often dine with their guests, and you can count on paying 13-20€. each including wine. Breakfasts are usually standard to copious.

The **S** group represents the budget range and very popular they are as everyone loves a bargain. Expect to pay 32-40€ for B&B for two. Sometimes they are in converted farm buildings, or just those spare rooms brought into use. The rooms can be artistically decorated and furnished, or custom built without a great deal of character, but clean and wholesome with modern shower and loo. Particularly suitable for families, some even have swimming pools. You could get lucky with communal evening meals with quantities to satisfy rustic appetites, astonishing value at 9-15€. Breakfasts are normally standard.

THE REGIONS AND DEPARTMENTS OF FRANCE

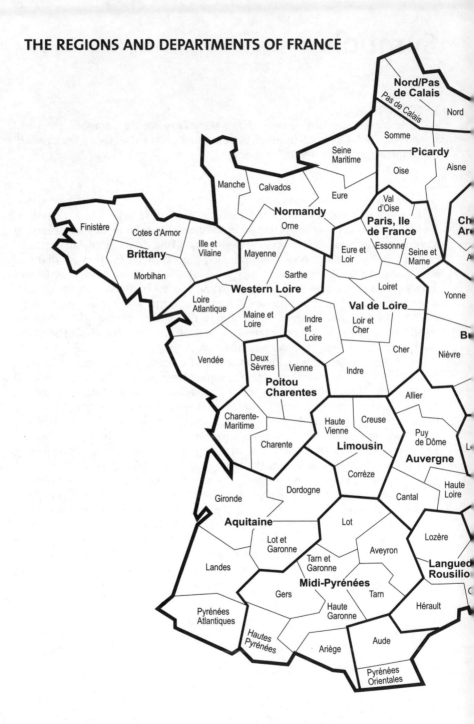

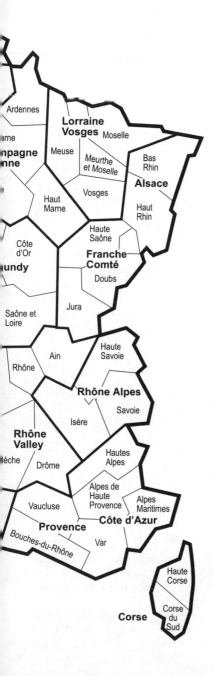

Ardennes

arne

npagne
nne

Lorraine
Vosges Moselle

Meuse

Meurthe
et Moselle

Bas
Rhin

Alsace

Vosges

Haut
Marne

Haut
Rhin

Côte
d'Or

Haute
Saône

Franche
Comté

undy

Doubs

Saône et
Loire

Jura

Ain

Haute
Savoie

Rhône

Rhône Alpes

Savoie

Isère

Rhône
Valley

Hautes
Alpes

lèche

Drôme

Alpes de
Haute
Provence

Vaucluse

Alpes
Maritimes

Provence

Côte d'Azur

Bouches-du-Rhône

Var

Haute
Corse

Corse

Corse
du
Sud

Tips for beginners

HOW TO FIND AN ENTRY
1. Find the area you wish to visit on the map of France on page xii.
2. Note the name of the region and the department you have chosen.
3. Turn to the contents page and you will find the regions listed alphabetically with their departments, and the pages you need.

HOW TO GET THERE
By air to major airports Paris, Nice ,Toulouse or Tarbes etc..
By rail London to Paris or Lille then onwards. Handy for walkers.
Tunnel, the fastest route, about 35 minutes.
By Ferry. Principal ferries:
> P & O Stena Ferries: Dover/Calais. Under two hours.
> P &O European Ferries: Portsmouth to Le Havre or Cherbourg. About 6 hours. To Bilbao about 30 hours. The 'Superstar Express' does the Cherbourg crossing in 2 hours. Weather permitting.
> Club class lounges includes free tea and coffee and newspapers.
> Day and night services. Cabins are vastly improved most are en suite. P & O Club class include breakfast in bed.
> Brittany Ferries: Portsmouth to St. Malo and Ouistreham. From Plymouth to Roscoff, and Santander, luxury cabins are superb.

Bilbao and Santander crossings to Northern Spain are virtually cruises, cutting out a long drive if you are heading for the south-west corner of France. With the Euro you will on longer need pesetas for the autoroute up to France. Shop around, prices vary tremendously, with many special offers.

FRENCH PUBLIC HOLIDAYS
> New Year's Day
> Easter Sunday and Monday
> Labour Day, 1st May
> VE Day 8th May
> Ascension Day
> Whit Sunday and Monday
> France's National Day, 14th July
> The Assumption, 15th August
> All Saints Day (*Toussaint*) 1st November
> Armistice Day, 11th November
> Christmas Day

CLOSING TIMES
Accept that not a cat stirs between 12 noon and 2.30p.m. If you need to drive through a large town this is the time to do it. Even the markets snap abruptly shut – forget impulse picnics after midday. Restaurants and bars stay open. At the other end of the day it's a joy to find shops open until 7 p.m.

Sunday lunch is the Meal of the Week, when several generations settle down together to enjoy an orgy of eating, drinking and conversation that can well last till teatime. You should certainly book then and on *fête* days. Mondays are almost as dead as Sundays, most banks are closed, so if it's a long weekend you're planning, try and add on the Friday instead. Sunday evening meal in restaurants and both meals on Monday can be a real problem.

SUPERMARKETS
These are outside many towns and most have fuel stations. These are rarely open from 12-2 30p.m. or on Sunday. It pays to fill up on Saturday.

MAPS
Good maps are essential. Those in this book are intended only to indicate the whereabouts of the entries. If driving the length and breath of France the hard-back 'Michelin Road Atlas France' is quite the best; expensive but worth its weight in gold. It can be bought in soft back at half the price, but is more cumbersome. The regional Michelin maps are excellent if intending to visit just one area. Armed with these you will be able to avoid busy towns and enjoy the utter peace of the yellow and white roads, discovering all manner of lovely villages missed by those tearing down the Autoroutes.

TOURIST OFFICES
Sometimes called the *SYNDICAT D'INITIATIVE*, usually closed from 12 to 2-30p.m.. These can be found in all large towns and most small ones. Make good use of them, you should find English spoken. Let them do the booking for you if you have problems. This is the place to pick up local maps and brochures.

TELEPHONES
To save using cash, buy a *télécarte* from a post office or *librairie* (bookshop). To dial **within** France use the **ten** figures given in the guide, e.g. **Châtillon-la-Borde** – 01.60.66.60.54.
> *To dial France from UK:*
> 00 33 followed by the 9 figure number given in the guide (omitting the first 0 in the number), e.g. **Châtillon-la-Borde** 00 33 1.60.66.60.54.
> *To dial UK from France:*
> Dial 00 44 then the STD code minus the leading 0, then the number.

EMERGENCY TELEPHONE NUMBERS
Fire 18
Police 17
Operator 13
Directory Enquiries 12

TAKE WITH YOU
Always take your own swimming towels, you will be surprised how many establishments have pools, and they don't appreciate bathroom towels being used beside the pool.
Bedroom clocks are rare, though they are beginning to appear.

BRING HOME
The list of Best Buys doesn't change much. Obviously wine – you should be able to buy it for half the price you pay back home if you stick to the cheapos and the medium-priced bottles. There is far less differential on the vintage wines and sometimes they are cheaper in the UK.

Alsace

ALSACE

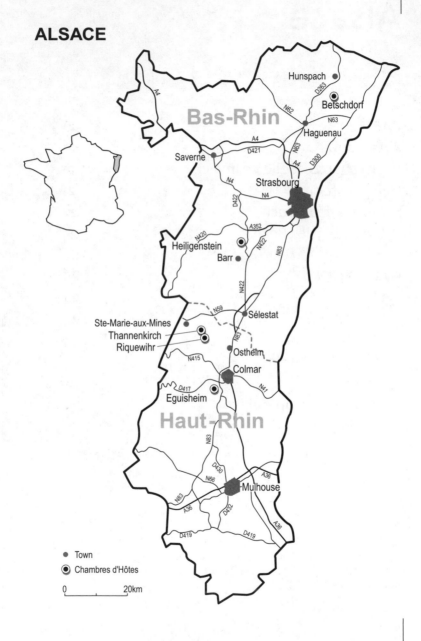

Town
Chambres d'Hôtes
0 — 20km

Alsace

Situated in the north-east corner of France, this region is separated from Germany by the river Rhine. The German influence is still very strong, noticeably in the architecture, the language and the food. The houses are more like Swiss chalets, heavily timbered and everyone speaks not only German and French but a tongue of their own, Alsatian.

All Alsace and part of Lorraine, the sister region, belonged to Germany from the Franco-Prussian war of 1870 until after the 1914/18 war. Again in 1940 Alsace became totally German, not just occupied.

The Vosges mountains in the west form a natural boundary with Lorraine.

The region is divided into two *départements*, Bas-Rhin and Haut-Rhin. The former, in the north, is on low-lying land. The *Préfecture* of Strasbourg, once a tiny island on the river Ill in 800 BC, is now a vast city, housing part of the European parliament.

Hops are grown in the neighbouring flat lands, and very good beer is produced both here and further north at Hochfelden. Don't miss a visit to the lovely little town of Saverne north-west of Strasbourg. At the foot of the town the Marne-au-Rhine canal runs past the Château-de-Rohan. Once owned by the well-known Rohan family, taken over by Napoleon III and now belonging to the State, the château has black railings still surmounted by large gilt 'N's. The town is twinned with Leominster and for the homesick, a gift of a red British telephone box in working order is outside the *boulangerie*.

The southern department of Haut-Rhin has the attractive city of Colmar as the county town. The great wealth of Alsace comes from the vineyards covering the eastern slopes of the Vosges. The Wine Route begins at Marlenheim in Bas-Rhin and extends south, running west of the main roads and railways, to Thann, south of Colmar. Extremely pretty little medieval villages, decked with flowers, line the route, and many happy days can be spent exploring them, and tasting their products. Mostly white wines are produced, a choice of seven different varieties, named after the grapes of their origin. A small amount of eau-de-vie and fruit liqueurs are produced in the Dieffenbach valley.

Food-wise, Alsace is famous for copious dishes of *choucroute*, based on pork sausage and cabbage and *Baeckeoffe*, a stew of beef and lamb with potatoes, but the crowning glory is the *tarte flambé*, savoury or sweet and the *tarte à l'oignon* a close second. There are rich varieties of *charcuterie*, and of course the *Kugelhopf*, a light yeast cake with a scattering of raisins and almonds, always baked in a fluted mould. The only cheese of note is Munster, common to both regions. The sheep, producing the necessary milk, graze on the high slopes of the Vosges.

The emblem of Alsace is the stork. To have one nesting on your roof is a sure sign of good luck. Many buildings have cart-wheels fixed on their chimneys to encourage them to nest. Alsace is at its best in September and October during the *vendage*. The villages are a riot of colour from the hanging geraniums and the streets pleasantly alive with tourists. The Alsatians, though busy with the *vendage*, still welcome tourists, unlike some parts of France where chambres d'hôtes close at grape picking time.

In Alsace hardly any chambres d'hôtes serve evening meals. Restaurants are plentiful and often busy with visitors from across the Rhine.

BAS-RHIN

BETSCHDORF. 67660.
44 km NE of Strasbourg. From Haguenau N of Strasbourg take the D263 northwards; in 10 km turn right to Betschdorf.

Christian & Joelle Krumeich
23 rue des Potiers.
category: (M)
tel: 03.88.54.40.56.
fax: 03.88.54.47.67.
B&B: 46/51€ for two.

Tucked up in the north of Alsace, the village of Betschdorf, noted for its pottery since the beginning of the 18th century, is a far cry from the better known wine villages along the river Rhine. The trade has been handed down over the generations. The grey pots with strong cobalt blue highly glazed designs appear in many a tourist shop further south. Now three kilometres in length, the village is lined with typical half-timbered Alsatian houses. Stop off near the beginning of the main street at:

The house and pottery stand well back from the main road in a garden filled with bushes and flowers. Christian's family goes back through nine generations of potters and they offer not only lessons in pot-making, but also attractive accommodation. Three rooms have been tastefully and interestingly furnished, one has its own kitchenette. Choose this if you prefer self-catering, but there are good local restaurants. Breakfast is, of course, served on their own pottery. Your hosts are such natural and charming people that even if you arrive with no interest in pottery you will find yourself succumbing to their charm and having a go at 'throwing a pot'. Highly recommended in an area where there are few chambres d'hôtes. The price of rooms varies according to size and amenities. 4.5€ extra for use of the kitchenette.

Joelle speaks English, and credit cards are accepted.

HEILIGENSTEIN. 67140.
20 km SW of Strasbourg. 17 km N of Sélestat.

Within easy distance of Strasbourg. However much you may dislike towns, you will regret it if you don't make the effort to visit the city.

For *centre ville* there is a good underground car park in the Place Gutenberg within easy walking distance of the cathedral, tourist office and museums, all in the same square. There are some very old houses here, like the Maison Kammerzell, now a restaurant, and also the oldest pharmacy in France.

The great crowd-puller is *l'Horloge Astronomique'* in the cathedral; it chimes daily at 12:30p.m. because the clock is half an hour slow. The body of the cathedral closes at noon and admission to see the clock in action is by ticket only. Figures of the twelve disciples pass the Christ figure and bow, a cock crows three times at St. Peter's turn, various other things happen, but you need to be six feet tall or take your stilts along to get a good view – the small area of the cathedral by the clock is jam-packed, so get there early even out of season.

It is a lovely cathedral. It was here that Marie Leszczynska married Louis XV by proxy. The colourful windows, an ornate carved pulpit and a sculpture of the Mount of Olives are all interesting. It is a pity the noise of voices and the constant loudspeaker reminders to 'watch your handbags and wallets' detract from it all. Afterwards take a stroll down the side streets from Place Gutenberg to La Petite France where the small tributaries of the river criss-cross the tiny streets, and the medieval houses dip into the water. There are plenty of restaurants to choose from here in the prettiest part of Strasbourg. It was the Mayor of Strasbourg who suggested to a young officer, Rouget de Lisle, that he should compose a rousing song for the army of the Rhine in 1792. The result was what is now the *Marseillaise.*

Head south for Heiligenstein, passing through the pretty little town of Obernai. Heiligenstein is noted for its 'Klevener', a white wine made only on these slopes.

Look for a chambres d'hôtes sign at the northern end of the village, on your right if travelling south.

Mme. Frieda Boch
4, rue Principale.
category: (S)
tel: 03.88.08.97.30.
B&B: 41€ for two. No Dinner

Frieda Boch has been hosting guests in her home for over twenty years, and rarely has a room free, so popular has she become. In a chalet-type house, backed by vineyards, furnishings in the five rooms are of superb quality, from velvet curtains to monogrammed white linen sheets, way above the normal standard for this price chambres d'hôtes. There is even a bed with electric elevations.

There are two rooms on the *rez-de-chaussée* and three above. All have washbasins and private facilities, but only two are adjoining. Two rooms have access to the balcony and one to a large terrace overlooking the Alsace plain to the Black Forest in Germany.

Breakfast is in a room adjoining the summer terrace where there are kitchen facilities for picnics. Madame is noted for her copious breakfasts; the long table is laden with ham, cheese, cakes, biscuits of every variety as well as the normal supply of bread and home-made jams, one made from eglantine berries. You must stay not less than two nights – no great hardship as there are so many places to visit from here. Parking in the garden is locked at night. A recommended restaurant for evening meals which caters for people with small appetites as well as large (perhaps a necessity in Alsace where portions are hefty), is a few steps down the road. Madame is a great character – the matriarch of the family. The *dégustation* next door belongs to her son, above which is another chambres d'hôtes.

Mme. Charles Boch
6, rue Principale.
category: (S)
tel: 03.88.08.41.26.
fax: 03.88.08.58.25.
B&B: 41€ for two.

A useful place to stay if next door is *complet*, when you will still be part of the same family. The modern house is over a smart *dégustation*. Through the salon, which has a kitchen corner, there is a guest room with a large shower room. Patio doors lead to a pleasant terrace overlooking the vineyards and hills behind to Sainte Odile.

Two other rooms on the first floor are equally modern, with shower rooms. Tiled floors throughout, but centrally heated.

HAUT-RHIN

EGUISHEIM. 68420.
6 km SW of Colmar.

A turning off the N83 south of the Colmar by pass. The prettiest of all the villages at the southern end of the *Route-de-Vin* and one of the most important. Well worth staying in, both for itself and nearness to Colmar the *Préfecture* of the *Département*.

Mme. Hertz
3 rue de Riesling.
category: (M)
tel: 03.89.23.67.74.
fax: 03.89.23.99.23.
B&B: 48€ for two. No Dinner

Madame Hertz is a formidable lady, who has been in command of her chambres d'hôtes for over 25 years. The lovely old house with tower is near the centre of the village, but has a delightful large garden where vines intermingle with rosebeds and there is ample safe parking for guests.

Three rooms with good, sturdy family furniture in the old house are very pleasant, two for two people and one for three. I liked the one for two with dual aspect windows.

Two smaller rooms with independent entry in an annexe have less character; but each has a kitchen, which you can use for weekends for 8¤ extra. These are normally let by the week in the summer, but are sometimes used as overflow chambres d'hôtes rooms, out of season. Breakfast, served in a very pleasant verandah-room overlooking the garden includes croissants but don't count on fruit juice.

A comfortable place to stay for a prolonged visit to a village you will find most entertaining. No problems about evening meals – there are 14 restaurants, all within easy walking distance. *Le Dagscourt* is the nearest and probably the best for *Alsacienne* menus.

RIQUEWIHR. 68340.
16 km NW of Colmar. 18 km SW of Sélestat.

Known as the 'pearl' of the *Route du Vin* it certainly is a honey-pot for tourists. One can't help liking its walled centre and prettily coloured old houses. The main street leading down from the gate tower, where there is a museum, is heavily cobbled and usually thronged with people.

Follow the ring road left outside the walls, past the bus-parking etc. until the Chemin des Vignes forks left near the tower.

Mme. J. J. Schmidt
5, Chemin des Vignes.
category: (M)
tel: 03.89.47.96.29 or
03.89.47.86.52.
B&B: 48€ for two.

This one was recommended to me by a reader, and it certainly is in a lovely position above the town but only a few paces away. Young Madame Schmidt is delightful and has two guest rooms on the ground floor, which are very convenient and comfortable but have no great view. One has a luxurious bathroom, the other has the loo along the corridor.

An even better choice is one of the two apartments on the second floor, for two to four people. In season these are let by the week with a kitchen; but out of season let for three nights with a kitchen, or on a daily basis without. Extra bed 15€.

In warm weather breakfast is served on a flower-decked terrace, otherwise in your room. Madame also runs 'Le Cerf' restaurant in the village and can offer a demi-pension rate, which includes a room in the chambres d'hôtes and dinner in her restaurant, within easy walking distance. Wine is not *compris*.

Prices seem high, but real pearls don't come cheap!

THANNENKIRCH. 68590.

16 km SW of Sélestat. 30 km NW of Colmar. 10 km N of Ribeauvillé.

Ribeauvillé I think is one of the most fascinating towns along the wine route. Situated at the foot of the Vosges mountains, it has delightful nooks and crannies leading off the main pedestrian precinct in the centre. Shops and pleasant restaurants line the street. From the 13th-century *Tour-des-Bouchers* near the *Mairie*, there is a good view of the three castles, now ruins, ancient homes of the Ribeaupierre family, whose Counts once owned vast lands around here. The town is noted for its festival of strolling players at the end of August. The shops often stay open from noon to 2 p.m.. and the parking is excellent, under shady trees at the entrance to the town.

If you have had enough of the pretty wine villages on the *Route du Vin*, a night up on the mountainside at Thannenkirch would be most refreshing. This alpine type village looks down over the vineyards of Alsace, and across the Rhine to the Schwartzwald (Black Forest) of Germany. As you drive up the thickly wooded mountain road, the air is noticeably fresher at 600 metres high.

Five kilometres along this road is the famous Château of Haut Königsbourg restored by Kaiser Wilhelm II – all too perfectly restored, but the armoury is interesting and the views from the fifteen windows of one of the towers is riveting. It's a long haul up from the car park, and you'll be glad to slip back to your mountain retreat.

M. & Mme. Dumoulin.
'La Maze d'Eugénie'
15, rue Sainte-Anne.
category: (S)
tel: 03.89.73.12.07.
B&B: 41€ for two. No Dinner

Madame once owned the Logis along the road but on retirement missed it so much she started her own chambres d'hôtes. The house beside the road is only a few steps away from the many hotel restaurants. There are four guests rooms, 'Nasturtium', a very small one, has a bath. The others have showers. 'Waterlily' is for two, 'Hydrangea', with a small glassed-in balcony overlooking the street and hillside, I liked; 'Tulip' likewise. Duvets and matching curtains pick up the flower symbols of the rooms. Monsieur, a talented *ébéniste*, has made all the furniture. There is a small salon for guests, and a pretty terraced garden behind the house. Madame speaks good English and welcomes her guests warmly.

Off-load outside the door and park a few yards away in a private car park.

For evening meals a choice of five local restaurants are all within easy walking distance.

Lorraine

LORRAINE

- Town
- ◉ Chambres d'Hôtes

0   20km

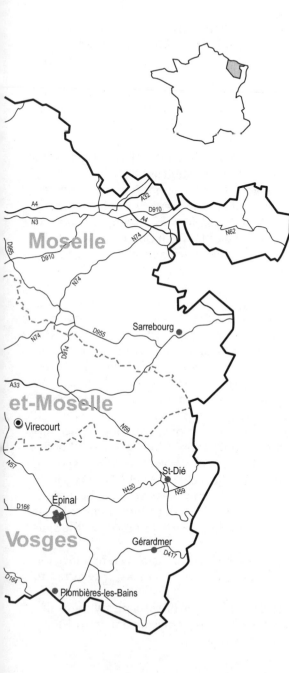

Lorraine

In the north-east of France, Alsace and Lorraine are often amalgamated by name, and it is sometimes difficult to visit one without passing through the other. The area round Metz was part of Alsace after the Franco-Prussian war.

Geographically and culturally they are very different. The natural border of the wooded Vosges mountains stretches from north to south between the two regions. A thousand small glacial lakes are hidden in the folds of these mountain; the highest of the peaks is 1,424 metres. Rounded and treeless they are aptly called *Ballons*. Skiable in winter, they are grazed in summer by sheep producing milk for the Munster cheese.

Lying on the western side of the Vosges, Lorraine has four departments. Mountainous VOSGES is in the south, where the *préfecture* of Epinal spans both banks of the river Moselle. Roman remains of an amphitheatre at Grand, in the west, are being excavated, not far from Domrémy-la-Pucelle.

MOSELLE in the north borders Bas-Rhin, Germany and Luxembourg. Metz, with its beautiful gothic cathedral is the county town, a more industrial area. Further south:- MEURTHE-ET-MOSELLE, stretches a finger north to the Belgian border. Nancy, the capital of all Lorraine, is its *préfecture*. Never miss an opportunity to visit the beautiful Place Stanislas in the centre of the old town (see Maizières, p32). Lastly (or perhaps first if arriving from the UK) MEUSE, the most westerly department, borders on the Ardennes and Belgium. Unremarkable Bar-le-Duc is the main town, but further north is much fought-over Verdun, and close by the magnificent *Ossuaire* overlooking the surrounding countryside where many bloody battles took place in the 1914-1918 war.

The cultural difference between the two regions is striking. Alsace has the affluent busy attitude of a Germanic society, but Lorraine is totally French, resolutely laid-back, and only in the north-east is German spoken.

Small farms with livestock and fruit fields, cover the land. The tasty little mirabelle plum is a great favourite, made into pies, jams, liqueurs etc. – almost a rival to the famous Quiche Lorraine. Some light industry near towns supplies work, as do towns like Vittel, where you can visit the spas and taste the water.

The region was a duchy until the death of Stanislas when, under the marriage agreement between his daughter and Louis XV, it reverted to France.

Louis XVI and Marie Antoinette were caught in Lorraine trying to flee the guillotine, Joan of Arc was born at Domrémy not far from Nancy. History is kept well alive in the various villages.

MEURTHE-ET-MOSELLE

CHARENCY-VÉZIN. 54260.
16 km E of Stenay. 50km SW of Luxembourg.

M. & Mme. Jakircevic
4, rue Coquibut.
category: (S)
tel/fax: 03.82.26.66.26.
B&B: 40€ for two.
Evening meals 12.5€ each.

Near the Belgian frontier, useful for a first or last night stop in the north of France. A rather dreary village.

Situated at the crossroads as you enter the village on the D142 the chambres d'hôtes is a 19th-century bourgeois mansion at No. 1 route de Velosnes. Gravel parking, behind white spiked railings, is locked at night. The double address is confusing until you realise the family live in a house round the corner which actually adjoins the chambres d'hôtes. Madame Jakircevic, who hails from Belgium, will welcome you with a cup of tea and offer you a simple evening meal, shared with the family, all drinks included, and a chance to polish up your French, but excellent kitchen facilities are provided if you prefer to self-cater. There are two family suites, one with bunks, the other with single beds, and a third room for two. All have TV, a choice of baths or showers and are well furnished. There should be traffic noise but it isn't a busy village and I didn't notice any. Only the TGV crossing the bridge up the road occasionally makes its presence felt.

There is a pleasant garden-room to sit in, overlooking their *potager*; a simple friendly place to stay, where the kindness of your hosts more than makes up for the rather dull outlook. It was raining the day I visited so perhaps I am being unkind. Madame is learning English, and went out of her way to draw us a map of the route to Brussels.

LANEUVEVILLE-DERRIÈRE-FOUG. 54570
8 km W of Toul.

Such a small village, beleaguered with such a long name; translated it makes sense. Unlike many northern Lorraine villages, which consist of one long wide street of terraced houses with the church at the end, this sleepy village is centred around the church in a dip between wooded hillsides ablaze with colour in the autumn. There is an ancient *lavoir* of some note and a pretty *fontaine des soeurs*. Strolling round one evening, I found friendly elderly inhabitants only too ready to chat while basking in the late sunshine

From the N4 15 km W of Toul, take a turning north to Foug, then the D 192 north off the D400.

M. & Mme. Antoine
4, rue des Pâquis.
category: (S)
tel: 03.83.63.87.74.
B&B: 35€ for two.
Evening meals 11.5€ each.

Arriving unexpectedly we found Madame Antoine digging her garden. Over the last twelve years she and her husband have completely restored their little village house. Madame, who is an accomplished *ébéniste* has laid parquet floors and made most of their furniture, while her husband, who combines teaching with his Mayoral duties, has dealt with other chores.

One small and simple guest room, tastefully decorated, overlooks their *potager*, with the church tower in the background. The low double bed, table and bedside tables have all been made by Madame, pretty green and peach wallpaper is reflected in the adjoining shower-room and loo, with matching thick towels. An extra double-bedded room across the landing, could be used for children, sharing the facilities. Downstairs, an open-plan kitchen/*salon* enables Madame to talk to her guests while she prepares the evening meal, which includes apéritif (wine extra), and often includes her delicious *tarte-aux-mirabelles*, something for which you should book ahead, as there are no restaurants nearer then Foug. Fresh grapes picked from the front porch arrived on the breakfast table.

MAIZIÈRES 54550.
13km SSW of Nancy.

Still my favourite place to stay for visiting Nancy, the capital of Lorraine and *préfecture* of Meurthe-et-Moselle. Though 1000 years old, the city prospered under the rule of Stanislas Leszczynski, the ex-king of Poland who was given the Dukedom of Lorraine by Louis XV when the king married his daughter, Maria.

Stanislas succeeded in making Nancy one of the loveliest cities in France. To this day the Place Stanislas is superb. Beautiful wrought-iron gates, railings, balconies and fountains surround the square, painted in maroon and gold. Floodlit at night it is like fairyland. An *Arc de Triomphe* leads from the square to the Place de la Carrière and the Ducal Palace, now a museum. The rue Maréchaux close by, where Victor Hugo's father was born, has many small restaurants with reasonable prices, but on a first visit you won't be able to resist a table outside one of the larger restaurants facing the square. The Hôtel-de-Ville, the Théatre and the Grand Hotel all magnificently overlook the Stanislas statue in the centre. Round off the day with a visit to the Church of Notre-Dame-de-Bon-Sécours on the other side of the town where the duke and his wife are buried, The church is almost entirely of marble – floors, walls, statues and altars. Wisely, Louis XV insisted that the Dukedom went back to France at Stanislas' death.

A day in Nancy will be complemented by a stay in the lovely home at Maizières of:

☆ **M. & Mme. Cotel**
69, rue Carnot.
category: (S)
tel: 03.83.52.75.57.
B&B: 35€ for two.
Evening meals 11€ each.
Reservation only.

In the village, it is easy to find. Coming from Nancy, look on the right-hand side of the road for large gates leading to the tree-lined courtyard of this large, terraced house, once the bishop of Toul's palace.

Three rooms, furnished with a mixture of antiques and modern beds, overlook the quiet green garden behind, ensuring tranquillity. A family room has a charming extra alcove bed. Comfortable armchairs and thick carpets, modern little shower rooms, matching drapes and pretty flowered wallpaper complete the picture. Evening meals in front of a log fire are imaginative and expertly served, while an enormous portrait of M. Cotel's great-great-uncle in Napoleonic uniform watches your every mouthful.

'M. Cotel is not only a farmer but something of a philosopher too. He is very proud of his organic farm and the fact that his pigs (we had the tastiest pork chops ever) were free range and corn fed. His home-made goat's cheese was excellent, as were the free-range eggs at breakfast.' P. de la H.

Evening meals, are available if reserved, wine not *compris*, but not thrust upon you.

This really is a charming place; you will want to stay many nights. It maintains a well deserved ☆.

VIRECOURT. 54290.
30 km S of Nancy. 1km S of Bayon by the D 112,

Easily found on the left of the road from Bayon as you enter the village.

The town of Baccarat, east of Virecourt, a pleasant drive across the countryside, is famous for its crystal – a large shop sparkles in the centre of the town. Visit the museum.

M. & Mme. Beyel
14, rue de la République.
category: (S)
tel/fax: 03.83.72.54.20.
B&B: 36.5€ for two. No Dinner

The well-kept house looks new but was built 150 years ago by a wine merchant. It descended to the present owners in 1974 and they have spent much time and money on re-styling house and garden and opened as a chambres d'hôtes in 1994. Madame has a diploma for one of the most flowery gardens in Meurthe-et-Moselle.

There are three guest rooms with quality family furniture, two for two with double beds, both well-carpeted right into the adjoining showers and separate loos. The smaller room faces the road; but is double-glazed. The blue room is much larger and overlooks the rear garden. On the second floor a family suite has two single beds behind a curtain, sharing the bathroom between them. Rooms are extremely good value. Only 9.5€ for extra beds, and the added advantage of a smart kitchen just for guests.

Independent entry from a locked car park is included in the deal.

'No evening meals' enables you to test the two restaurants in Bayon (*Le Ranch* is very reasonable) or others further afield.

MEUSE

ANCEMONT. 55320
10 km S of Verdun.

Stay here and visit Verdun cathedral which was badly damaged in the First World War; but fared better in 1939-45. It has a canopied high altar, held up by four gigantic barley sugar marble pillars and some very good stained-glass windows, particularly the rose window above the organ.

North of Verdun is the largest beer museum in Europe, at Stenay on the river Meuse. The Meuse rises near Domrémy-la-Pucelle and flows north to Verdun and eventually over the border to Belgium, changing its name to the Marne, heading for the North Sea. It is a restful narrow river, sometimes flowing beside canals with small boats cruising peacefully and tying up at villages en route.

From Verdun follow the D34 south along the Meuse, turn right in the centre of Ancemont and the château is on the left.

M. & Mme. Eichenauer. 'Château-de-Labassière'
category: (M)
tel: 03.29.85.70.21.
fax: 03.29.87.61.60.
Demi-pension 60€ each.

A very impressive château, with plenty of space for parking in the forecourt, and a covered garage. The garden at the side has an inviting swimming pool. Over the years the village seems to have encroached on the lovely building, but inside the château has maintained its former glory and the large rooms are very pleasant; one on the ground floor is richly furnished with a luxury bathroom, others on the first floor include a suite for six. M. Eichenauer, who speaks perfect English, prefers guests on demi-pension basis, and does a special rate with all drinks and wine *compris*. Reduced rates for children. Good value for all the amenities. A very pleasant place to stay if you want that little extra atmosphere of days gone by

SAINT-MAURICE-LES-GUSSAINVILLE 55400
23km E of Verdun.

For visiting the battlefields of the First World War, this would be one of my first choices. The most interesting areas are round Douaumont which lies off the D913 east of Bras-sur-Meuse. The *Tranchée des Baïonnettes* is a reconstructed trench which forms the graveyard of the men of the French 137th Regiment who were killed here in June 1916. The *Ossuaire-de-Douaumont* is a magnificent memorial to the 130,000 French and German soldiers killed on the battlefields of Verdun in the Great War whose bodies were never identified. On the first floor is a chapel and two galleries, each 140 metres long, containing 36 sarcophagi. The walls are covered with memorial tablets dedicated to individuals and regiments. In the chapel there are two tombs, that of Monsignor Charles Ginisluy, Bishop of Verdun, and Ferdinand Noël, chaplain to the *Ossuaire* who ministered to the bereaved. Mass is celebrated daily at 9a.m. (10.30 on Sundays). The *Ossuaire* is dominated by the 46 metre high *Tour des Morts*, and in front is the National Cemetery with the graves of 15,000 French soldiers marked by simple wooden crosses and red rose bushes. On the ground floor is the usual shop and a cinema with an audio-visual presentation of the battles. Shows last about twenty minutes and are given in French, English and German.

At FORT-DE-VAUX (5 km north-east) are the remains of an outpost defended to the last by 250 French soldiers under the command of Commandant Reynal, against ferocious gas attacks by the Germans from June 1st 1916 until their surrender seven days later. It was from here that Reynal sent an appeal for help by carrier pigeon, his only method of communication. Despite the hazards of gas and smoke, the pigeon got through on the 4th of June, dying on arrival at French HQ The fort was retaken by the French in November 1916. To this day there exists a society which commemorates this brave pigeon.

The pleasant drive along the N3 to Etain gives you time to reflect on the horrors of World War I.

This chambres d'hôtes is signposted at Étain or can be reached by the autoroute A4 exit Frensne-en-Woëvre, then the D908 north to Étain. The house is 7 km on the right.

Ferme des Vales
St Maurice-les G.

☆ **M. & Mme. Valentin.**
'Le Ferme des Vales'
category: (S)
tel: 03.29.87.12.91.
fax: 03.29.87.18.59.
B&B: 40€ for two.
Evening meals 19€ each.
Closed February, holidays.

This modernised barn proved to be a charming house, with a vast *salon* where one can stretch out in comfortable armchairs beside a log fire, burning merrily in September. The rooms are at each corner of the first floor, reached by a galleried balcony, overlooking the salon. Sunny and light, with double glazed windows, they are simply furnished in different colours.

One could be a bridal suite, with white lace *ciel-au-lit*. Extra bed 8€.

Monsieur, an ex-Air Force pilot, now an *avocat*, has rebuilt the barn himself, keeping all the old character but installing modern conveniences. Reserve an evening meal with local produce including wine and coffee – Madame Valentin's cooking is way above average for a chambres d'hôtes. Plentiful parking at the back of the house and now a swimming pool in construction. Such good value here, a well deserved ☆.

THILLOMBOIS. 55260.
34 km NNE of Bar-le-Duc, the préfecture of Meuse, a modern commercial town in the valley of the Canal de Marne-au-Rhin.

Not very exciting, but drive up to the old town on the hill and look down at it from the *belvédère*. Park in the Place Saint-Pierre and visit the well-kept church where there is a sculpture by Lizier of Duc René-de-Chalon (Prince of Orange) as a skeleton. He was killed at the siege of Saint-Dizier in 1544 and his dying words were that he should be immortalised as he would look in three years time. They certainly took him seriously!

For a night stop try Thillombois, a peaceful little village in the Meuse valley between Bar-le-Duc and Verdun.

Take the N35 north from Bar-le-Duc, in 26 km turn right on to the D101 and follow signs to Neuville and Courouvre then the D121 to Thillombois. The chambres d'hôtes is next to the château in the centre of this rural village.

Le Clos de Pausa

☆ **Mme. Tanchon. 'Le Clos de Pausa'**
Rue du Château.
category: (M)
tel: 03.29.75.07.85.
fax: 03.29.75.00.72.
B&B: 56/80€ for two.
Evening meals 25.5€ each (incl wine).

A much more sophisticated chambres d'hôtes than you would expect in the depth of the country. Tea and coffee-making facilities, a mini-bar and satellite TV in most guest rooms. Situated in a very pleasant enclosed garden the house was once the stables of the château next door.

Two pretty ground floor rooms, *La rose* and *Le Bluet*. The suite on the first floor, *Le Lilas* has an extra small double room sharing facilities.

Booking an evening meal, all drinks included, would be a wise decision so deep in the country. A lovely upmarket chambres d'hôtes and very pleasant *accueil*.

Aquitaine

AQUITAINE

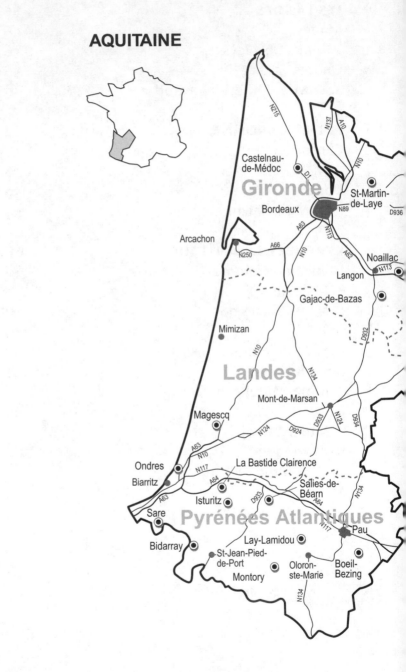

Town • Town
◉ Chambres d'Hôtes
0   20km

Aquitaine

From Bordeaux on the Atlantic coast to the Pyrénées on the Spanish border lies the region of Aquitaine, stretching inland to Gascony in the east and the Dordogne in the north. Occupied by Romans and Visigoths, in the 8th century it became part of the Frankish Empire and eventually a Duchy, owing allegiance to the Kings of France.

Eleanor of Aquitaine inherited the whole Duchy early in the 12th century; it then extended north to Périgord and Poitou-Charentes and east to the Limousin. Such an inheritance meant that she was courted by many. She married Louis VII of France, and had two daughters by him; but her light-hearted manner and conduct were not appreciated at court and Louis was persuaded to divorce her in 1152. Her dowry, the Duchy, was returned to her and she promptly married an old boy friend, Henry Plantagenet of Anjou, who became king Henry II of England two years later. The Duchy renounced its allegiance to the French and together Eleanor and Henry ruled the whole of England, Wales and all of Western France making their home at Poitiers. When Henry died in 1189 his son Richard (the Lionheart) succeeded, and he too spent only a few months of his reign in England.

The English control of Aquitaine was fairly weak, which led them to follow the example of their Languedoc neighbours in building fortified towns called *bastides*, whose inhabitants were granted several privileges to ensure their loyalty.

The French were not happy with this state of affairs, especially when Edward III claimed the French throne on the death of Charles IV in 1328. This led to the Hundred Years War and the English were finally defeated at Castillon-la-Bataille in 1453.

The five departments of Aquitaine are:-

To the north-east the **Dordogne** – so well beloved by the British tourist – is dominated by the river Dordogne running through its very pretty undulating countryside. Périgueux with its many domed cathedral and modern squares, is the administrative centre. There are still Roman remains around the old town.

The ancient name Périgord dominates the whole department, dividing it into four sections, *Périgord Vert, Blanc, Noir* and *Pourpre*. Besides the river the main attractions are the prehistoric caves and archaeological sites, near Montignac and Les Eyzies.

The Gironde in the west, with the large port of Bordeaux, is most famous for its production of wine. The vineyards are situated in many areas and produce different types of wine, determined by the soil and vines. Despite their differences they are all known as Bordeaux, whether red or white. The reds are often called 'claret' by the British.

Les Landes, once a long sandy coastal strip stretching from Arcachon to Bayonne, with a marshy hinterland, has now been rescued from the encroaching Atlantic sand by draining the land and planting huge forests of pine trees. The coast from Biscarrosse Plage to Bayonne is 200 km of sandy beach, backed by dunes and pines. The Dune de Pilat in the north is the most notable.

Lot et Garonne, south of the river Dordogne, is also a vine-growing area. Some of the best *bastides* can be found here. Agen in the south is the *préfecture*, a busy, uninspiring city. The western area is mostly flat, with pine forests – a continuation of Les Landes.

In the south the **Pyrénées Atlantiques** is sub-divided into Béarn and Pays Basque, bordering Spain. The Basque influence is strong here – all town names are in French and Basque. The old coastal resorts so loved by the Victorians grace the coast – Biarritz, St. Jean-de-Luz and Bayonne, which is on the estuary of the river Adour. The Pyrénées and the foothills to the north had been left very much to their own devices when France regained Aquitaine. Valleys run towards Spain, climbing abruptly up into the mountains. The weather is mild here, even in winter.

Pau, the high town in the Béarnais area, is the *préfecture* of the department, an area ruled over by the d'Albret family, ancestors of Henri IV.

DORDOGNE

Le BUISSON 24480.
29 km W of Sarlat. 10 km S of Le Bugue.

Often linked with Cadouin just up the road, where there are remnants of what some people believe to be the Holy Shroud in the abbey. For years this brought great wealth to the abbey, but modern science has cast doubts on its authenticity. Le Buisson lies along the Dordogne just before it is joined by the river Vézère.

Take the D25, direction Cadouin, turn left as you leave the town, where there is a double signpost to La Coste, go straight up the hill past a left turn to La Coste and La Feuillantine is on the left.

☆ **M. & Mme. Donval. 'La Feuillantine'**
La Coste.
category: (M)
tel: 05.53.23.95.37.
B&B: 44.5€ for two. No Dinner
Closed 15 Oct. to 15 Mar.

This very smart newly-built Périgord house, with views over the countryside, has proved a popular find. Three well-furnished ground-floor rooms have every comfort. Patio access is through double-glazed doors, extra bed 8.5€.

Many readers will be sad to learn that M. Donval has decided to discontinue evening meals, which were the *pièce de résistance* of this residence. However B&B is still available and the rooms and *accueil* are as good as ever. Restaurants nearby, or further afield outside Cadouin: the Auberge de Salvetat would be a pleasant place to eat on Summer evenings.

DOMME 24250.
8 km S of Sarlat.

Domme is an absolute must when visiting the Dordogne – a most attractive *bastide* built on a rocky crag during the Hundred Years War to keep the English out. They may have succeeded then, but not today. In summer there are more British cars here than French. Approach from Vitrac and enter by the Porte des Tours, the best preserved of the three old gates, where prisoners were once kept in the tower. Their graffiti are still on the interior walls. Follow the signs to large car parks on the Belvédère de la Barre *(payant)*. A new viewing platform on the terrace gives a panoramic view of the valley below, where the river Dordogne flows towards Beynac. Wander round the many little streets with pretty limestone houses bedecked with flowers. Finish up in the Place de la Halle, beside the covered market. Built in the 17th century, it has a wooden balcony and deep caves underneath where the people hid in times of trouble. Shops, restaurants and cafés to suit all tastes. Sit outside and watch the world go by; if possible avoid July and August when it does!

For a recommended chambres d'hôtes take the D50 east from Domme to Groléjac; at the lake, turn right, SP 'Liaubou-Bas' and in 3? kms Le Jaonnet Is In the hamlet on the left. Alternatively, from Sarlat in the north take the D704 to Groléjac and turn right at the lake, then first left, following signs to Le Jaonnet.

☆ **Mr. & Mrs. Holleis. 'Le Jaonnet'**
Liaubou-Bas. Nabirat.
category: (L)
tel/fax: 05.53.29.59.29.
email: keholleis@easynet.fr
Demi-pension 83/89.5€ for two.

Le Jaonnet, called after a Guernsey bay, is a 200-year-old converted farmhouse, an unexpected find hidden away in a well maintained hamlet of sandstone houses. The Holleis give a warm welcome to all their guests.

The galleried salon has a striking stone fireplace with carved figures. The piano is often played by guests and a musical evening develops. The dining table has hosted many a party. Konrad, an Austrian-trained chef, has worked and taught in Guernsey for many years, so you will be sure of a sumptuous meal. He and his wife Elizabeth speak French and English – no language problems here.

In a wing of the house two comfortable attractive double rooms, 'Saints' and 'Moulin Huet', no longer have to share a shower room, now having their own, as do all the other rooms. 'Icart' sleeps three people, as does 'Fermain', which has a private terrace and costs a little more. 'Portelet' is a suite for four, approached from the courtyard; 9.5€ for extra beds.

Demi-pension is now obligatory, all drinks included (with special rates for small children). I am certain you will find no better value meal in the area. In the high season a two nights' stay is no hardship and you will probably wish you had booked a week. Excellent value. Maintains a ☆.

MONBAZILLAC. 24240.
7 km S of Bergerac.

This small village on a hill has a large château surrounded by vineyards. It gives its name to the famous sweet white wine produced here.

From Bergerac follow signs to Monbazillac via the N21 south. In the village past the château bear right and the chambres d'hôtes is well signed,

M. & Mme. Gaubusseau. 'La Rouquette'
category: (M)
tel: 05.53.58.30.60.
fax: 05.53.73.20.36.
B&B: 56/104€ for two. No Dinner

A *belle chartreuse*, overlooking the château, with views towards Bergerac, this stately home is set in two acres of green lawns and flower beds. It has been a chambres d'hôtes for some time; but changed hands a few years ago, and the present owners have been lovingly redecorating and making some very comfortable rooms for guests, complemented with a warm welcome.

The dining room and the lounge/games room are vast rooms with natural stone walls and good views.

There are five guest rooms. On the first floor, *Roxanne* sleeps four, boasts a balcony with magnificent view, and is spacious and light. *Muscadelle* has double aspect windows, padded bed-heads and pretty curtains. On the second floor, *Belvédère* sleeping three, decorated in yellow, has an even better view of the Château de Monbazillac, while the aspect of *La Treille*, a pretty green room, is appropriately over the vineyard. The fifth room on the ground floor, entered from the garden, is tiled, which keeps it cool in summer. Behind its baldaquin are stairs to a mezzanine with a double bed suitable for children. Extra beds 9.5€.

Prices are determined by size of room. No evening meals but there are three restaurants close by, one at the château.

PROISSANS. 24200.
8 km N of Sarlat. 17 km SE of Montignac.

An ideal place to stay for – not to be missed – Sarlat. Lovely old buildings, the Boétie house by the tourist office, the cathedral, the *Lanterne des Morts* and many other sights will fill a whole day and more. The different squares and cafés are a delight (parking in the largest square, but not on Saturdays, market day). Just north of Sarlat is Ste. Nathalène where the Moulin de la Tour, built in the 16th century, is still making oil from walnuts and hazel nuts just as it did 400 years ago. You can watch the whole procedure – fascinating – and buy the finished product decanted into journey-proof tins. Also within easy range is the very famous *Grotte-de-Lascaux* at Montignac, where the prehistoric paintings of animals were discovered in a cave in 1940.

To find Proissans go north on the D 704 from Sarlat turn right in 4 km (signpost La Val d'Ussé); in 2 km turn right again (SP Les Chanets). L'Arche is 1.2 km on the right. If you book ahead you will receive a card with exact instructions from all directions.

☆ **Mme. Jeannette Deleplace.**
'L'Arche'
category: **(S)**
tel: 05.53.29.08.48.
B&B: 35€ for two.
Closed 15 Nov. to 1 Mar.

This old farmhouse, completely restored in 1992, overlooks rolling countryside, in a hamlet of only three houses. The six small rooms, with beamed ceilings, are most attractive, one is for a family, all have showers.

The Deleplaces will give you an excellent breakfast of fresh bread, croissants and home-made jams – no plastic butter here – but sadly, no longer, an evening meal. A restaurant is recommended 2 km away, where there are menus from 12.5€ and wine is *en pichet*.

A really charming home in which to stay. Some English spoken. Very good value for the Dordogne.

SAINT ANDRÉ d'ALLAS 24210
7 km W of Sarlat by the D25, past the village and on the left by the roadside.

M. & Mme. Lancauchez. 'Les Filolies'
category: **(N)**
tel/fax: 05 30 31 84
B&B: 42€

Right in the centre of the Dordogne, this was once an 18th century staging post, the original cobbles where the stage coaches pulled in are still in situ.

Only the cellars and one cool bedroom now front the road. Skilfully modernised and split-levelled the other rooms are above overlooking two acres of open grounds. In the guest rooms stone walls and beams have been maintained and smart new shower rooms installed. Three of the five rooms have an extra bed for families, opening on to a terrace they will be handy for the new swimming pool being built for 2002. Your young Anglo/French hosts provide a copious breakfast, which includes home-made cake, rather than *croissants*, eggs, and fresh fruit in season, fruit juice on request. Extra bed 14€. *Taxe de Sejour* 0.15 € per person per night.

SAINT MICHEL-de-RIVIÈRE. 24490 LA ROCHE CHALLAIS.
35 km NE of Libourne. 2 km SW of La Roche Challais.
Only just in the Dordogne – the river is the boundary line with Charente-Maritime. From the D674 south of La Roche Challais turn right on to the C260 and follow signs to the chambres d'hôtes. The small hamlet of St. Michel de Rivière is well off the main road.

Mme. Fare. 'La Moulinasse'
category: (M)
tel: 05.53.91.41.03
B&B: 44.5€ for two. No Dinner

I nearly missed this one, but spotted the ring round it on my map as we drove south from La Roche-Challais. Curious to know why I had ringed it, we went to investigate, and were not disappointed. Set in two hectares of garden bordering the river Dronne, the house appears to be newly-built but I was puzzled by the ancient beams and old floors until Madame explained that her father, a builder, had built it from bricks and wooden beams he had collected over years from pulling down old properties. There is a delightful lounge spanning the house which guests are welcome to use and where breakfast and evening meals are taken in inclement weather.

Up the rich elm staircase a suite of two rooms, both with double beds, shares a large bathroom. Along the balconied landing is a room for a couple with shower and loo. All rooms are thickly carpeted, well furnished and have good garden views.

The nice thing about this place is the peaceful setting – it would be a joy to laze under the trees beside the river on a hot summer day. There is a little boat and soon canoes will be available. I liked Madame Fare, who lives here with her elderly mother. There are plans to extend the property for her son. A caring family who will welcome you warmly. All very good value.

TOURTOIRAC. 24390 HAUTEFORT.
18 km N of Montignac.

The small village of Tourtoirac is 6 km W of Hautefort, where a very large château dominates the horizon. The château was burnt down at the beginning of the century and a replica rebuilt. Plenty of places to visit in the area, not least the caves at Montignac, due south, and a must for anyone visiting the Dordogne.

From Hautefort on the D704 take the D62 to Tourtoirac. In the village, just after the church turn left opposite the Restaurant des Voyageurs (small sign 'Boucle de Goursal 9 km') up a very narrow hill, follow this road (SP Thoirac) for 1km and the chambres d'hôtes is signed on the left.

M. & Mme. Mougin. 'Le Bas Portail'
category: (M)
tel: 05.53.51.14.35.
B&B: 52.5/57.5€ for two. No Dinner
Closed Christmas and January.

Situated in a perfect south-facing position with not a house in sight, this is a very well-kept residence backed by outhouses and a new *gîte*, all built of the lovely yellow Dordogne stone. The house is long and narrow, part being built before the Revolution and the rest added in the same style just afterwards.

Rooms lead off from a central salon, elegantly furnished with a variety of antique chairs, (Louis XV and Louis Philippe) all surprisingly comfortable. Doors open on to an old cobbled terrace above an herbaceous border and lawns extend to six hectares kept well cropped by four hardy Pyrénées pet sheep. A delightful *pigeonnier* is in one corner of the garden.

Two guest rooms are carpeted and centrally heated; one has a shower and loo disguised by cupboard doors, with plenty of space to move around the brass bed and large polished table and an excellent view of the garden. A very pleasant room. A second room is off the dining room at the other end of the house and has larger ablutionary facilities with bath, and also an adjoining room for one, sharing the bathroom. This room has a second entrance from the terrace. A hearty breakfast is served in the dining room, when Madame Mougin, who speaks good English, (learnt working in a hospital in England), is only too happy to correct your French if you keep her English up to scratch!

Altogether a pleasant genteel place to stay where you will be welcomed by both Monsieur and Madame Mougin, and I am sure you will want to stay many days.

GIRONDE

CASTELNAU-DE-MEDOC 33480.
21 km N of Bordeaux.

The Médoc area is renowned for its vineyards north of Bordeaux; Château Lafite, Margaux and many other well known names flash by as you drive along the flat roads; *dégustations* galore are available in these most prosperous properties. The Médoc can be reached by a ferry from Blaye to Port Lamorgue or take the dual carriageway N10 round the north of Bordeaux. Exit 7 on to the N215 north SP 'St. Médard' then right on to the D1 to Castelnau.

From here it is easy to visit the Dune de Pilat, the highest In Europe, overlooking Pyla-sur-Mer, a holiday resort with sandy beaches. The road suddenly turns inland and heads for the dune, 117m high, stretching for 2.7 km along the coast and 500 metres wide. It has been forming since the 18th century with a little help from man to prevent the sand slipping down into the forests. Well worth a visit, though now capitalised as a tourist attraction with large car park, little shops and cafés lining the route to the wooden *escalier* which takes you nearly to the top. It is worth the climb of 187 steps, in sections of twelve, with a small platform between each. Even the *Troisième Age* were making it to the top. Once on the last step it is wise to take off shoes and trudge up the remaining bank of sand to enjoy the aerial view of the surrounding wooded countryside, Arcachon with the Atlantic on one side and the whole width and breadth of the sandbank around one.

The *escalier pour descendre*, as it is euphemistically called, is non-existent, just a quick easy run down the bank, sinking in up to the ankles.

The chambres d'hôtes at Castelnau is on the Sainte-Hélène road (N215) just outside the town on the right.

M. & Mme. Pery. 'Domaine de Carrat'
Route Ste-Hélène.
category: (M)
tel: 05.56.58.24.80.
B&B: 48/56€ for two.

A warm welcome from Madame after you drive up the tree-lined drive to a large house with enormous integrated stables. A previous owner collected carriages.

Rooms are furnished tastefully with pretty flowery wallpaper. Two rooms can be let separately or combined with two smaller rooms for a family. Another very pretty room on the ground floor opens on to the extensive garden. Breakfast is taken in a large comfortable salon.

No evening meals, but a kitchen for guests has access to a pleasant sunny terrace.

A most attractive old house, full of character. I think a winner for the area.

Your hostess is charming and the price is right.

GAJAC-de-BAZAS. 33430
45km SE of Bordeaux.

The beautiful 13th-century Gothic cathedral of Bazas dominates the arcaded town square. The Bishop, Cardinal Pierre Eyt, is also Archbishop of Bordeaux. The very large sanctuary has beautiful arrangements of fresh flowers renewed daily. There is an annual parade of local beef cattle on the town's Carnival Day (St. John the Baptist – 24 June)

The chambres d'hôtes is easy to find on the D9 (direction A62) 4 km from Bazas.

M. & Mme. Dionis-de-Séjour.
'Cabirol'
category: (M)
tel/fax: 05.56.25.15.29.
B&B: 46.5€ for two. No Dinner
Reservation only 15 Nov. to 15 Feb.

Difficult to believe this is a working farm where beef cattle and baby geese are bred. The square golden stone farmhouse is surrounded by well-trimmed lawns and flower beds and the adjoining stables is now converted into a very large games room for wet weather.

The Dionis-de-Séjour are a lovely family whose children come home to roost at weekends.

We arrived early one September evening and with other guests were welcomed into the family circle with cool drinks served in the garden. Four cosy carpeted rooms on the first floor are charmingly decorated; two form a suite for a family sharing the bathroom. Extremely good bedside lamps and extensive views from the windows. Others have a choice of double or single beds, adjoined by gleaming white bathrooms with pretty flower friezes and nearly all have baths and separate showers. Another room on the ground floor has direct access to the car park. There is a small kitchen, off the salon, for guests, and a sunny terrace overlooking the garden.

A hearty breakfast included freshly picked raspberries from the garden served with lashings of *crème fraîche*. No evening meals, but an easy drive straight down the road leads to Bazas where you will find plenty of restaurants in the lovely old square. Little English is spoken, so guests who speak some French are preferred here.

NOAILLAC. 33190.
50km SE of Bordeaux. 9 km S of La Réole.
A handy place to stay so close to the Autoroute des Deux-Mers

Exit 4 (La Réole) from the autoroute A62 then turn left on to the D9 towards Bazas, over the autoroute bridge and take the first left in 250 metres, then follow the 'Chambres d'Hôtes' signs for 3 km.

La Tuilerie
Noaillac

M. & Mme. Laborde. 'La Tuilerie'
category: (M)
tel/fax: 05.56.71.05.51. or
06.03.03.16.76.
B&B: 52€ for two.
Evening meals 20€ each.

On a hillside this 19th-century Bazadoise farmhouse is as rustic as they come, but has been renovated with great taste, keeping all the old stone, wood and tiles, creating a delightful relaxed atmosphere. The dining room with an enormous round table in front of the patio doors adjoins a most comfortable lounge, once the cow-shed, where the wooden partition through which the cows were fed is still in place.

Five attractive rooms in different colours and design have their share of beams and stone walls, cosily carpeted upstairs, a choice of bath or shower adjoining them. Downstairs one room, especially designed for a wheel chair with wide doors, has two single beds and a spacious adjoining shower and raised loo. All rooms can accommodate children.

The garden is suitably enclosed for small children The Labordes have three of their own, so toys and bikes abound.

This really is a most attractive place, with the advantage of Madame being English and Monsieur French, so language problems are solved.

An evening meal, wine *compris*, prepared by Monsieur, a professional chef, is an added bonus. A reader writes *"The accommodation is superb and our meal matched that of any we could have had in a top class French restaurant. Since your visit they have added a swimming pool, so as you have asked for confirmation for an arrow, I would not only give them one, but add the bow and Robin Hood!"* Derek Pape. Praise indeed, I am not surprised.

SAINT-MARTIN-DE-LAYE 33910.
12 km NE of Libourne. 46 km NE of Bordeaux.

Up a track from the D22 between St.Martin-de-Laye and Bonzac.

Mme. Garret. 'Gaudart'
category: (S)
tel: 05.57.49.41.37.
B&B: 35€ for two
Closed. 15 Oct. to 15 April.

On the northern fringe of the wine-growing area of Bordeaux is this very comfortable home, not far from Pomerol and St. Emilion. I have been reprimanded by a reader for not doing justice to the kindliness and friendliness of the Garrets. I must admit I have had only glowing reports from guests who have stayed here. Certainly my drawing doesn't portray the quality of this chambre d'hôtes. Mea culpa!

Situated in large, grassy lands with a perimeter of trees, this restored farmhouse of honey-coloured bricks looks very plain from the outside, but don't be misled. The large high ceilinged-rooms have beams and independent entry through French windows. One room for three decorated in *toile de Jouy* faces south and has a palatial bathroom. A second room in a detached building is tiled and spacious and also has a bath and separate shower. There is a smaller room facing north, extra beds 14€., 10% reduction after 4 days, except in July and August.

The salon, where breakfast is served, has many lovely pieces of antique furniture, collected over the years. Sadly no longer evening meals, but suggestions for restaurants will be given. Good shady parking.

ST. SÈVE 33190
56 km SE of Bordeaux

From the A62 (Autoroute des Deux Mers) exit 4 take the D9 to La Réole, then the D2 north to St. Séve.

M. & Mme. Chaverou. 'Domaine de la Charmaie'
category: (M)
tel: 05.56.61.10.72.
fax: 05.56.61.27.21.
B&B: 35/41/48€ for two.
No Dinner

'We stayed at the home of Mme. Chaverou, whom we would recommend wholeheartedly for an entry in your book. An exceptionally tranquil place with beautifully furnished bedrooms, a large garden with swimming pool and wonderful meals. She has two double and one twin room, each with en suite facilities. Well worth a visit'. J & R Gay.

Thank you Mr and Mrs Gay you have done my work for me! I did call on Mme. Chaverou, but because all the rooms were occupied I couldn't see them. The twin room is on the ground floor and the comfortable salon has a striking blue couch and billiard table. I envied the people staying there, the swimming pool looked most inviting.

LES LANDES

MAGESCQ. 40140.
14 km NW of Dax.

A nice little town within easy reach of all the Basque towns like Biarritz and Saint-Jean-de-Luz which are just over the *département* border. Leave the village by the D150 to Herm, which crosses over the N10 and in about 300 metres Le Cassouat is on the right.

Mme. Desbieys. 'Le Cassouat'
category: (M)
tel: 05.58.47.71.55
B&B: 46.5€. for two. No Dinner

An ultra-modern house, situated in a large park of pine trees, complete with lake. I have often seen pictures of this place, but nothing I have read about it really does it justice. A very warm welcome awaits one.

Two rooms upstairs share a luxurious bathroom, good for four friends or a family as they are up a private staircase. One has pleasant views from the enormous ceiling-to-floor window looking towards the lake. Two ground floor rooms have their own small balcony with tables and chairs. A fifth room has been added since my last visit.

An excellent breakfast started with the 'house' speciality, a mixture of fruit juices and honey, all beautifully served at one table but every couple having their own special tray of butter, jam, coffee etc. The village, with a choice of four restaurants, is under a kilometre away, so no problem about an evening meal. Prices reduced for long stays.

ONDRES. 40440.
6 km N of Bayonne.

Ondres Plage is an extension of Ondres, a town practically on the coast within easy reach of Biarritz and all tourist spots on the route to Spain. The vast sandy beach has excellent parking bays. There is no promenade, just one café and restaurant. All along this coast the Atlantic waves can be dangerous.

☆ **M. & Mme. Puyravaud. 'Le Bout-des-Landes'**
Avenue de la Plage.
category: (M)
tel: 05.59.45.21.87
B&B: 48€ for two. No Dinner

I can't tell you how glad I was to hear this chambres d'hôtes is open again. It had closed owing to illness, but all is well now and Mme. Puyravaud is once more welcoming guests. An ideal place for a holiday by Les Landes coast. Though a modern villa in a residential avenue leading to the beach, what it loses in style it gains in comfort. There are two lofty rooms in an independent building, beside the swimming pool. Furnished in pine, decorated in peach and blue, a choice of double (with *ciel de lit*) or single beds and TV. Each has a secluded private terrace overlooking the forest behind, and a spacious well equipped shower room. No smoking allowed in rooms.

Your hosts are friendly and helpful; their daughter lives in England, so English is well understood. Breakfast here would put many a large hotel to shame. Orange juice, cereal, eggs, cheese, yoghurts, fruit, croissants, home-made jams etc. – it begins to read like Mole and Ratty's picnic in *The Wind in the Willows*.

No evening meal but an excellent fish restaurant, 'La Plancha' is on the beach, within walking distance for the fit, or there are restaurants in Ondres. Book well in advance in summer to avoid disappointment. It maintains a well deserved ☆.

LOT-ET-GARONNE

CANCON. 47290.
40 km S of Bergerac. 19 km NW of Villeneuve-sur-Lot.

This area of Lot-et-Garonne is most interesting historically. There are some lovely *bastide* hill villages to mull round, many built by the English in the hundred Years War. It is within easy reach of all the Dordogne attractions and close to the last stretches of the river Lot, before it flows into the Garonne.

From Cancon take the N21 towards Villeneuve-sur-Lot for 3 km and the sign to the chambres d'hôtes is on the left; the turning up a long narrow lane is on the right.

M. & Mme. Vrech. 'Manoir de Roquegautier' Beaugas
category: (M)
tel: 05.53.01.60.75.
fax: 05.53.40.27.75
B&B: 35€ for two.
Evening meals 18€ each.
Closed 1 Oct. to 1 Apr.

A lovely surprise awaits you here. The manor house, originally built in the 13th century, rebuilt in the 18th, has been completely restored by the young owners over the last ten years. The lawned terrace and the swimming pool below have a superb view of the surrounding valleys. Climb the wood and stone steps in one of the four towers to find four enchanting guest rooms. Suitable for year-round occupation with carpets and central heating and well modernised shower or bathrooms. One with a charming *ciel de lit* for two has a bathroom in a tower. Another, a small suite with a double and two single beds in an adjoining tower room is most attractive. Climb higher to two more rooms, a small double with adjoining room for three with single beds, through a low archway in the tower again. The use of tower rooms and the mixture of ancient and newer beams gives much character to all the rooms and windows of varying shapes and sizes keep them light and airy.

There is a small TV room downstairs for guests and meals are taken in the high-ceilinged dining room or out on the terrace in warm weather.

Evening meals, (on reservation) all drinks *compris*.

Annexe rooms, which I didn't like, are offered in July and August for 49€. Picnic snacks available by the pool if you fancy a lazy day in. Room prices seem to have risen sharply.

DOUZAINS. 47330.
3 km SW of Castillonnès. 30 km S of Bergerac.
From Castillonnès take the D254 to Douzains. Le Capy is on the right just before the village.

☆ **Mme. Jacquot. 'Le Capy'**
category: (S)
tel: 05.53.36.83.68.
B&B: 35€ for two
Evening meals 10.5€ each.
Closed 1 Nov. to 1 Apr.

The small village of Douzains is very quiet – just a church and a few houses. Close to the N 21 at Castillonnès, it is an easy runs to Bergerac and Monbazillac.

The large old farmhouse has seen better days; it must have been a very palatial house when it was built. Repairs are steadily taking place to counteract the wear and tear, and rooms have been considerably modernised since my first visit. Mme. Jacquot's son runs the farm and he and his sister occupy one end of the house.

Mme. Jacquot has been unwell recently, but her daughter and son more than adequately welcome guests and show them to one of the three guest rooms, well-furnished in keeping with the age of the house, off the 27-metre long corridor. French windows lead out to the garden and there are fresh flowers by the bed. A new shower room in one of the rooms has left space for a sitting area beside the window. Towels are in generous supply. There is another room for two on the other side of the house, and two rooms for a family share a bathroom on the corridor, extra beds 9.5€. Wide terraces run the length of the house on both sides. A homely place. Children will love exploring the garden. Guests may also use a washing machine and fridge, free!

'Mme. Jacquot provided us with an amazingly value-for-money stay in a peaceful setting with wonderful meals. We would certainly be glad to return for a longer stay.' J & R Gay

Don't miss an evening meal here, Mme. Jacquot's daughter cooks as well as her mother, and produces real farmhouse fare, enough to satisfy the hungriest hiker, all with plentiful wine. The dining room where breakfast and evening meals are served looks over fields to Castillonnès on a distant hill. The peaceful atmosphere of the rural garden and warm welcome from the family combined with comfortable rooms make this the best budget stop in the department. ☆ accordingly.

PYRÉNÉES-ATLANTIQUES

LA BASTIDE CLAIRENCE. 64240.
25 km E of Bayonne.

A most attractive well kept Basque village, where the main street on a hill is lined by typical timbered white houses with red roofs tiering above each other.

Mauon Marchand
La Bastide de Clairence
64

M. & Mme. Foix. 'Maison Marchand'
category: (M)
tel: 05.59.29.18.27.
fax: 05.59.29.14.97
email: Valerie.et.Gilbert.Foix@wanadoo.fr
B&B: 46/56€ for two.
Evening meals 20€.

The 'Maison Marchand' is no exception; the front door step is on the roadside. A reader found this one for me. *'An old Basque farmhouse that has been sensitively renovated to retain much of its original character. Rooms are all beautifully appointed. With temperatures in the low 60s when we were there, the underfloor heating in the tiled bedroom and bathroom was greatly appreciated! The host and hostess are delightful people, very friendly and sociable. In the real tradition of chambres d'hôtes they join their guests for an excellent evening meal (vin compris)'. P de la H.*

This narrow house is surprisingly large with four guest rooms on the first floor and a fifth one on the ground floor, which has a small terrace with access from the garden.

A large covered terrace overlooks a small rear garden leading to a garage for two cars (others park outside on the small road behind). The terrace is very pleasant and meals can be taken there on most days in this mild climate of the South-West.

Rooms have their original wooden doors and walls all are quite different. *La Mer* and *Le Moreaux* overlook the garden. *Les Fleurs* is a cosy room with terracotta brick and wood walls. *Le Pigeonnier*, the largest room was the *grenier* and has a king-sized bed, and is heavily beamed. All have excellent shower rooms; some, for three, have practical mezzanines for double or single beds with a washbasin and loo, and the shower room complementing the single bed below, an unusual luxury, as is the mineral water in each room. Prices 6€ higher from 1 July to 15 September.

Evening meals offered on Tuesday, Thursday and Sunday and, if booked ahead on the day of arrival, small children can have an earlier meal.

A balcony from the first floor runs along the back of the house with steps down to the garden. You certainly forget the house is on the main street when inside.

M. Foix is French and his wife is Irish, both bilingual, so no problems linguistically. Extra beds 15€.

Another address 3 km S of the town by the D123. Look for the signs on the left

Mme. Darritchon. 'La Croisade'
category: (M)
tel: 05.59.29.68.22
B&B: 52.5€. for two.

A very gracious family farmhouse dating from 1643, more of a '*maison-de-maître*', situated in the country in a well established garden. It has a great warmth of welcome, especially when vivacious Mme. Darritchon receives you. There is a salon with comfortable armchairs before a large fire for winter days; a pleasant dining room adjoins it.

Stairs lead to a wide landing where there are four bedrooms, all very different, Madame has had great fun decorating all the rooms in various bright colours, orange checks with a bright green carpet, wood floors in the blue room with red curtains. Halfway upstairs an attractive family room has a blue carpet and yellow double bed, beams divide the room from two singles with pretty gingham covers. Extra beds 13.5€, cots 8€. All well worth it.

Rooms are so originally decorated it would be difficult making a choice. Sadly evening meals are no longer offered.

BIDARRAY. 64780.
17 km NNW of Saint-Jean-Pied-de-Port. Closed 15 Nov. to 1 Feb.

This small village is not far from St. Jean-Pied-de-Port, the celebrated Basque town teeming with *commerces*, it is the border town where pilgrims to Saint-Jacques-de-Compostelle have their passports stamped. A must when visiting the Pays Basque.

Coming from the north on the D918 turn right over the river Nive to Bidarray. The tiny village is on the left. Ignore this, turn right and in about 200 yards the spotless little chambres d'hôtes with the unpronounceable name is easily found by the roadside on the left.

☆ **Mme. Haran. 'Gaztanchoania'**
category: (S)
tel: 05.59.37.70.37
B&B: 38.5€ for two.
Evening meals 12€ each.

The rising sun catches tips of the surrounding peaks of the Pyrénées before it bursts on this well-kept farmstead where Languedoc cattle graze peacefully beneath your windows. Monsieur and Madame Haran have converted four large rooms into comfortable guest rooms, a choice of baths or showers. Two have balconies, all are warmly carpeted, 8€ for an extra bed.

This was a peaceful oasis late one evening after a heavy day of visiting chambres d'hôtes. Madame was quite happy to give us a meal and a very pleasant room with a view of the Pic d'Iparla. We joined other guests relaxing in comfortable armchairs in the dining room for an aperitif before a meal of local specialities such as leek tart, *poulet Basque*, Pyrénées cheeses and *gâteaux maison*, all wines included. Children half price. Lively young Mme. Haran presided over the meal, while her husband was out supporting the local team, playing *pelote*, a very serious game in this part of France.

Open all year, with central heating. Spacious parking in the garden.

"Here we were late owing to brake problems descending the Pyrénées. Mme. Haran and her guests waited until 9 p.m. to have dinner with us. The food and the welcome was marvellous, the room large, comfortable and spotlessly clean. Quiet and restful. Terrific value. close to the sea too." Min Lee. A well earned ☆.

BOEIL-BEZING. 64150.
15 km S of Pau.

The Pyrénées Atlantiques has two distinct areas, the Pays Basque and Béarn. At one time, when the Basque area was independent, there was a strict borderline between the two, with customs posts. In Béarn, Pau, the chief town, was the seat of the d'Albret family. Henri d'Albret married Marguerite d'Angoulême, sister of François I, king of France, and their grandson later succeeded to the French throne as Henri IV. The Béarnais are still proud of their history and royal connections.

Coming from Pau on the D938, in about 15km at roundabout take exit SP 'Boeil-Bezing' to centre of the village, turn right and in 1km just past the Medical Centre turn right again. Well-signed.

Mme. Minot. 'La Lanne de Bezing'
category: (S)
tel: 05.59.53.15.31.
fax: 05.59.53.15.21
email: pminot@wanadoo.fr
B&B: 39€ for two. No Dinner

Quite the best chambres d'hôtes I have found for families with young children. This old building has been beautifully restored in the garden of the original house where the Minots live. The large salon on the ground floor where meals are taken has a log fire, and there is a kitchen which guests may use. Outside there are plentiful toys for small children. The house is on the fringe of a thriving village, well off the main Pau road.

Sunny rooms which were originally named after flowers have now become fruity – 'Blackberries', 'Blueberries', 'Strawberries', 'Grapes' and 'Cherries', and all have TV, showers and loos. Every amenity available for babies – baths, changing mats, cots etc. – and best of all, at the end of the corridor, is a delightful nursery with comfortable chairs for Mum and Dad while they watch the little ones play with the numerous toys supplied; even a cot here for the youngest. Madame has young children of her own and has thought of everything. Extra beds 8/13€.

ISTURITZ. 64240.
30 km SE of Bayonne. 9 km S of La Bastide Clairance.

The village is noted for its prehistoric *grottes* a couple of miles away.

5 km from La Bastide Clairance on the D10 turn left on to the D251, just before the village on the left.

Mme. Airoldi. 'Maison Urruti Zaharria'
category: (M)
tel: 05.59.29.45.98.
fax: 05.59.29.14.53.
email: urruti.zaharia@wanadoo.fr
website: www.urruti-zaharriah.fr
B&B: 44.5/49.5€for two.
Evening meals 17.5€ each
(reservation only)

Isabelle is a friendly, charming hostess who speaks very good English. A new challenge for her after working in Paris, she has moved down to this lovely corner of France with her teenage daughter and bought this ancient farmhouse converting it into a delightful place to stay.

A medieval farm building, it is now carefully restored, keeping all the original features of ventilation holes and small windows. The entrance hall, once the *grange* where animals lived, has comfortable armchairs where you enjoy an *apéritif*. Penetrate through to the old cowshed, now a very pleasant dining room extending into a modern kitchen.

A sloping grass entrance from the car park leads to a comfortable sitting area and access to all five guest rooms. A lot of thought has gone into the design of the rooms to make them attractive yet simple and comfortable. Adjoining shower rooms are very modern, with temperature-controlled power showers, vanitory units and excellent lights. Tasteful matching curtains and duvet covers, king-size beds, some with delicate *ciels des lits*, all reflecting the names of the rooms – *Salade de Fruits* is a family room with a sloping beamed ceiling, double and *bateau* bed. *Amaryllis* and *Herbier* catch the morning sun, while *Clafoutis* basks in the afternoon glow with a lovely view of the hills beyond. *Clelia* facing south, necessitates a step up to see out of the window, but a velux window keeps the room light. All rooms have wood floors and comfortable convertible couches suitable for children. Practical use is made of sloping corners, making them into hanging areas with ample room for suitcases.

Isabelle joins her guests for breakfast, when freshly squeezed orange juice, crisp baguettes, cereal and delicious jams are all laid out on elegant china to tempt you. Evening meals, wine and apéritif *compris*, are offered EXCEPT on Monday and Wednesday. In July/August and school holidays this changes to Sunday and Wednesday. However this gives you a chance to sample Mme. Margarèthe's cooking at the 'Auberge Goxoki' in St. Martin-D'Arberoue, a village 4km away, where you will be made most welcome.

Prices according to season; high season from 1 July to 15 August approximately.

LAY-LAMIDOU. 64190.
4km S of Navarenx. 26 km S of Orthez.
Take the D2 out of Navarenx and the house is well signed in Lay, more a farming hamlet than a village with distant views of the Pyrénées.

M. & Mme. Desbonnet
category: (M)
tel: 05.59.66.00.44.
B&B: 48€. for two.
Evening meals 16€ each.

This house is one of many well-established dwellings which have been in the village since the 16th century. The large flat, walled garden with green lawns, bushes and island flower beds, has open fields beyond. We were given a warm welcome on arrival, gathered into the garden for a cool drink on a hot evening, introduced to family and other guests before being taken to a charming room, elegantly furnished in Louis XV style, with pretty floral pink curtains and bed cover. The attached shower room and separate loo in marble tile had everything for comfort. Dual aspect windows overlooked the road and courtyard, making it very light and airy. Madame Desbonnet's acquisitions from antique sales decorate the room with great taste.

Another room with a garden view has a quaint corner wardrobe. Room three comes complete with a very large bathroom, all on a private corridor. Evening meals (now only on Monday, Wednesday and Friday) and elegantly served breakfasts, make this a must for a visit to the Béarn. You really do feel you are a private guest of the family here.

M. Desbonnet is a retired general and Madame an accomplished book-binder. How she finds the time for such an exacting occupation I don't know.

MONTORY. 64470.
20 km SW of Oloron-Sainte-Marie.
Deep in the country, this is just the spot for keen fly-fishermen or anyone wanting perfect peace.

From Montory take the D749 to Haux and follow the signs for 3 km.

M. & Mme. Ruata. 'Maison
Sallenave'
category: (S)
tel: 05.59.28.59.69.
B&B: 40€ for two.
Evening meals 13.5€ each.
Closed 15 Nov. to 31 Mar.

Built in 1806, this rustic little chambres d'hôtes was once the Customs House between Béarn and the Pyrénées Atlantiques, and was recommended to me by a French lady who stayed there. Madame Ruata was as charming as predicted. The simple beamed rooms with polished wood floors have modern showers, and views over the Pyrénées. There were fresh flowers in all the rooms, even though Madame Ruata was not expecting us. A pleasant salon opens on to a rural garden, and there is a courtyard for *al fresco* meals. Dinner with wine *compris* is also recommended.

There was a rustic freshness about this place which I thought most attractive.

M. Ruata will instruct you in fly-fishing.

SALIES-de-BÉARN 64270
From Autoroute A 64 exit 7. Take 1st road right SP Salies, in 1.5 km at roundabout take 1st right to Guilhat, in 1.8 km the house is on the left, adjacent to the 'Pépinières'.

Mme. Potiron. 'La Closerie du
Guilhat'
category: (M)
tel: 05.59.38.08.80
email: guilhat@club-internet.fr
B&B: 46/52 € for two.
Evening meal 15.25 €. each.

Until recently three generations of horticulturists from the Pépinière next door owned this house, now the new owner, Madame Potiron, has inherited an intriguing selection of plants. The comfortable salon opens on to a terrace and little hidden gardens descending the hillside where white loungers dot the small lawns. There are four rooms on the first floor for guests. 'Iris' for two has double aspect windows and a shower.

'Tournesol' has twin beds also with shower. If you prefer a bath choose 'Papyrus', it has it all – luxury bathroom with bath and a separate shower plus dual aspect windows. For a family 'Bruyère' contains two rooms sharing facilities. Extra bed 11€. Two gîtes share the gardens.

Madame gives much time to her guests, joining them for evening meals she has produced from regional recipes. Carafe of wine 3€. Guests here are treated as private friends, and keen gardens would find much to interest them.

SARE. 64310.
9 km SE of Saint-Jean-de-Luz

Situated on a hill, this is a less pretentious village than nearby Ascain but with a natural charm of its own, dominated by a huge *pelote* wall. Close to the Col Ignace where the Petit Train de la Rhune chugs up to the top of the mountain on the Spanish border. Rather like going up Snowdon in Wales, but the Spanish shop at the top does a roaring trade on cut price alcohol.

From the A63 exit 3 or the N10 take the D918 to Ascain, then the D4 over the Col Saint-Ignace. Look carefully for a chambres d'hôtes sign on the left about 1 km before the village. It's a typical red-painted Basque house, easy to miss from the roadside.

Ibar-Gaina
Sare

Mme. Garbisco. 'Ibar-Gaina'
category: (S)
tel: 05.59.54.21.89
B&B: 43€. for two. No Dinner

I couldn't believe my luck when I discovered this charming house. A south-facing terrace for breakfast has a fabulous view over the Pyrénées, as does the delightful room above, which has a large balcony, plenty of room for three and its own shower and loo. Another room at the back has a bath and a pleasant view of the countryside, but no balcony. Cosily furnished, both have carpets and attractive decor. Madame was charming, even when we disturbed her at the unforgivable time of 12:45 p.m. No evening meal; but there are restaurants in Sare and at the Col Ignace. Parking in the front garden. No English spoken. I first found this place too early for a night stop, and regretted it so much I returned a year later and was able to confirm my first impressions and enjoy the room with a balcony, in spite of inclement weather. Such a useful place to stay for a shopping expedition into Spain.

Auvergne

AUVERGNE

Town
Chambres d'Hôtes
0   20km

Auvergne

The Auvergne, an area often referred to as the Massif Central, lies south-east of the Loire valley and is dotted with extinct volcanoes. It derives its name from the 'Averni', a Gallic tribe who under the leadership of Vercingetorix strongly resisted Roman control. Julius Caesar finally conquered the area and executed the valiant Gallic chief in 46 BC. Local place names ending in -ac, like Aurillac and Mauriac, still exist, originally Roman settlements dating from this period.

After the collapse of the Roman Empire the Auvergne passed through a troubled time politically, being fought over by many rulers, from Merovingians and Carolingians to Henry II, in the 12th century, when it was part of England. A line of defences, 11th and 12th century châteaux, on the eastern edge of the Puy-de-Dôme, marks the old border between Aquitaine and Burgundy. The Bourbon family, which ruled France from 1589 until the Revolution, originated from Allier, and this part is still known as *le Bourbonnais*.

There are four departments, mainly agricultural with mixed farming – *Bleu d'Auvergne* cheese hails from here. There is a local vintage; not a lot of Auvergne wine sells outside the region, but the mineral waters of the Auvergne such as 'Volvic' and 'Vichy' need no introduction. Some industry is concentrated round the central capital of Clermont-Ferrand.

Allier in the north is fairly flat farming land, cold in winter but often dry and hot in summer. It is dotted with small châteaux and villages, and fields of Limousin cows. There are three major towns, Moulin, the *préfecture* to the east; Vichy, which was the seat of the French government after the fall of France in the Second World War, and Montluçon in the south-west, a fast-growing town. Driving south one enters the real volcanic area of the **Puy-de-Dôme** department. High rounded peaks, with a typical dip in the middle, and plateaux with many good roads span out from the *préfecture*, Clermont-Ferrand, which is overlooked by the Puy-de-Dôme peak, 1465 metres high. For up-market chambres d'hôtes in old family houses you are spoilt for choice in this area.

The Mont Doré and Bourboule area further west is totally geared to the tourist trade, with many lakes, hotels, camp sites and purpose-built flats, etc. Orcival is a delightful little village nesting in the hills west of the Puy-de-Dôme. It has a fine Romanesque church, a real picture floodlit at night. Saint-Nectaire also boasts a lovely Romanesque church as well as producing the famous cheese. At Ambert an old paper mill is still producing paper by the same method used at the end of the 16th century.

Haute-Loire to the south-east is a gentle undulating *département*, frequented by *randonneurs*, where in spring, fields of wild narcissus border the banks of the young Loire as it bubbles through valleys on its way north

Some small farm chambres d'hôtes are hidden here, excellent value for a holiday, or en route to the south.

The church of Saint-Paulien in Le Puy-en-Velay was built in the fifth century and is one of the official starting points for the annual pilgrimage to Santiago-de-Compostella in Spain; but the largest Romanesque church in the Auvergne is the Basilica of Saint-Julien in Brioude, dating from the fourth century; it was completely rebuilt with many different stones in the eleventh and twelfth centuries.

The Cantal to the south-west of the region does feel less populated, with its sweeping hills and less wooded countryside. It has its own extinct volcanoes. The Puy-Mary (1787 metres) and the Plomb-de-Cantal (1858 metres) can be visited during most months of the year when there is no snow. Some lovely old houses with the lauzes tiled roofs make the villages most attractive, notably Salers.

ALLIER

COULANDON. 03000.
8 km W of Moulin by the D945 to Sauvigny, signed on the left. Follow signs for 1km up winding lanes and the house is on the right, hidden by neighbours.

M. Pompon. 'La Grande Poterie'
category: (M)
tel: 04.70.44.30.39. or
06.68.22.20.73 (Mobile)
B&B: 54€ for two.
Evening meals 19€
Closed Nov. to Mar. except on
reservation.

It is always a joy to stumble unexpectedly on a nice place like this. Now flying the flag of four stars from *Gîtes-de-France,* it really is a delightful little chambres d'hôtes.

M. Pompon has created a holiday retreat in central France. What was once an old grange is now a charming house just for guests. His own home is across the garden, the other side of a blue swimming pool.

Enjoy breakfast on a covered terrace and dine at night in a tasteful small dining room as the sun goes down. Monsieur, a single host, serves and cooks meals from a little kitchen most people would kill for, so prettily tiled and designed.

Three fairly small first-floor rooms overlook the garden and pool, accommodating two or three persons, all tastefully decorated in different colours. One is virtually a suite, with a single bed by the shower room and a double on a mezzanine, 62.5€. Two single beds in another and a third, I loved, with iron bedstead, a couch and a charming green shower room. Evening meals, wine not included.

POUZY-MÉSANGY. 03320.
60 km SE of Bourges. 34 km NW of Moulins. 17 km N of Bourbon-l'Archambault.

The ancient little town of Bourbon-l'Archambault is delightful, with much history to pursue. It was the birthplace of the Bourbon dynasty of French kings.

Take the N76 SE from Bourges to Sancoins, then for about 1km the D951, branch on to the D40, SP 'Lurcy-Lévis', which becomes the D1 as you cross the border into Allier, continue on the D1 to Pouzy-Mesangy. Take the D234 out of the small village in the direction of Le Veudre and in one km the farm is signed on your left.

Mme. Raucaz. Manoir 'Le Plaix'
category: (S)
tel: 04.70.66.24.06.
fax: 04.70.66.25.82.
B&B: 41€ for two.
Evening meals 16€ each.

Early pictures I received of this manor house failed to express its charm. A treat awaits you here – it really is most interesting.

The farmhouse dates from the 13th century when it was a fortified defence post. It has been carefully modernised, losing none of its old and interesting appeal, and is now a working farm for dairy cows and sheep. M. Raucaz has retired but his son carries on, living across the farmyard.

The salon opens into the garden. The immense fireplace extends from the dining room into the bedroom above.

There are five guest rooms, approached by the original stone spiral staircase in the tower. Just a few steps up is a double room with one extra bed for a child. You must stay for a week in this room to qualify to use the small adjoining kitchenette. Up another turn are two more rooms, beautifully furnished, with a choice of double or single beds, one with the giant fireplace, both with shower rooms. On the second floor at the top of the tower are two larger rooms, each with a bath. These are particularly nice, but all are so interesting that a choice is difficult.

Evening meals with farm produce.

This makes a very handy night stop on the way south, not far from the Bourges-Moulins *nationale*, but I am sure you will regret not staying longer. There are many places to visit from here and four hectares of land to roam around.

Wise to book ahead, and discuss your preferences with Madame.

SAINT-AUBIN-le-MONIAL 03160.
30 km W of Moulins.

Turn off the D11 at Ste. Hilaire Gare on to the D1 to Bourbon l'Archambault. The farm is on the right just before the left turn to St. Aubin-le Monial.

M. & Mme. Mercier. 'La Gare'
category: (S)
tel: 04.70.67.00.20
B&B: 36.5€ for two.
Evening meals 13.5€ each.

A charming welcome from M. and Mme. Mercier, who have a sheep farm, run by Madame. Monsieur, a retired butcher, helps her entertain the guests, often initiating them into a game of *boules* before dinner.

The ivy-covered old farmhouse has a large front garden with a huge shed for garaging cars, well back from the road.

Three rooms, one on the ground floor and two adjoining family rooms upstairs plus a very pretty rear room for three, all have shower rooms.

Charming, friendly *accueil* makes this a recommended budget stop. Their daughter steps efficiently into the breach if Madame is away.

Evening meals are exceptionally good with regional dishes cooked by Madame and shared by all at a long table in the dining room.

SAINT-BONNET-TRONCAIS. 03360.
56 km SE of Bourges.

Right in the middle of one of the largest oak forests (Forêt-de-Tronçais) in Europe.

From the A71 south of Bourges leave at exit 8 SP 'St.Amand-Montrond', take the D951 SP Charenton-du-Cher, to junction with the D953 SP Cérilly; in 9 km take the D39 to St. Bonnet.

M. & Mme. De Pomyers. 'La Beaume'
category: (S)
tel: 04.70.06.83.76.
fax: 04.70.06.13.46
B&B: 35€ for two.
Evening meals 12.5€ each.

This house was built just after the Revolution as a dwelling for families who worked at the Forge, which supplied some of the cables for the Eiffel Tower in Paris until 1920. It is now a small homestead, with sheep, chickens and a large vegetable garden. Don't let first impressions, with the house, hidden behind another building, put you off. The three rooms on the first floor are very comfortable, spacious and warm. One, for three, has a single bed round the corner en route to the shower and separate loo. A sunny west window awaits afternoon arrivals, and a tray of tea and biscuits on arrival, brought up to your room, if desired, is the ideal welcome. Other rooms have a bath or single beds.

Evening meals with the family wine *compris*, are very satisfying, using all their own produce, and honey for breakfast comes from their own hives. Monsieur is happy to give you directions for tours of the forest, or will even accompany you.

CANTAL

ALLY 15700

11 km S of Mauriac.

The Cantal, in the south west of the Auvergne is one of the quietest areas of the Massif Central, not on a busy tourist route it is often neglected by the British tourist. The rolling countryside is dotted with volcanic peaks. Salers is a charming historical village. From Mauriac take the D681 to Ally the château is signed just before the village at the junction with the D29.

M. et Mme. Fayet de la Tour.
'Château de la Vigne'
category: (L)
tel: 04 71 69 00 20
email: la vigne@wanadoo.fr
B&B: 110€. for two
EM 31€ each.
Closed 1 Nov. to 16 Apr.

A 15th century Château with 18th century additions on the edge of the village. A truly lovely site with views over to the Cantal peaks.

From the tree-lined drive this many towered edifice resembles more a fortress than a château, but rounding the corner to the entrance, the warm welcome from your hosts, dispels any doubts. Though an historical monument, furnished throughout with genuine antiques, open to the public on occasions, it has the rare distinction of being first and foremost a comfortable lived in family home.

Even in the 18th century this château belonged to thoughtful caring owners, the spiral steps, built of lava, in the tower leading to the guest rooms, are wide with easy treads and a built-in stone handrail must be a first for any château. All rooms are in connecting suites; but can be let to two people. Polished wood floors, carved wood panelling, *baldaquins, ciels de lits* and genuine antique furniture in keeping with their period are found in all. Well modernised adjoining bathrooms have been added by cleverly using the many *échauguettes* (turrets) attached to the outside walls. One family suite has three adjoining rooms, but the end room can be separated to accommodate two guests who then have access by a private staircase, this room contains the largest bed I've ever seen and the comfort of a log fire for chilly nights.

A dining room wall supports a tall cupboard for wine glasses, towering to the ceiling, other walls are hung with 16th/17th century Flanders tapestries giving the room a cosy feeling. Breakfast and evening meals are served here, the latter cooked by Madame and your hosts will join you for aperitifs.

The salon has vast Aubusson tapestries covering much of the delicately painted paneled walls and is furnished in Louis XVI style.

Many a family baptism has taken place in the chapel at the foot of the southern round tower where the vaulted gothic roof has 15th century paintings of angels carrying tools of the passion. A tour of the château includes Monsieur's comprehensive collection of dinky toys

This is a really lovely place to stay where English is spoken. If you want to stay a week, there is a gîte in the garden.

BASSIGNAC. 15240.
16 km N of Mauriac on the D922.

This delightful château, which the Grand Condé once visited incognito, is well signed on the main road between Bort-les-Orgues and Mauriac, just a slip road up a hill on the left 14 km S of Bort-les-Orgues.

M. & Mme. Besson. 'Château de Bassignac'
category: (L)
tel/fax: 04.71.40.82.82.
B&B: 56/89.5/105.5€ for two.
Evening meals 44.5€ each (wine incl).

The tree-lined drive gives a promise of something exciting and suddenly this neat little château leaps into view. It is a real family home – Madame Besson was born here. Her family bought the château in 1886 and it has been well-maintained and lived in ever since. You are invited to share all the rooms and are treated as private guests.

The dining room, where you sink into comfortable armchairs by the enormous fireplace, overlooks the hillside speckled with trees, as do all the other rooms which have southern aspects. The huge kitchen leads on to a long terrace where breakfast is served in the summer. There is a more formal lounge with a tower corner where Monsieur exhibits his paintings.

Up the stone stairway it is difficult to choose a room, all are so different. A suite of two rooms shares a bathroom off a private corridor. Marble fireplace, old family furniture, brass beds, wooden beds *ciel de lit*, you name it. The rooms are comfortable and homely with furnishings little changed since the restoration of the château last century. Bathrooms have been added in nooks and crannies. Now all are prettily decorated in yellow, green or rose, some with flowery wall paper but never losing the original style. A fourth room for a single person is also en suite.

Optional dinner with your hosts includes all drinks, *charcuterie* and *gâteaux* made by Madame from favourite family recipes.

Young M. Besson, their son, runs a *ferme-auberge* just outside the gates, useful for alternative evening meals.

A wonderful peaceful ambience, yet so easy to reach from the main road.

MARMANHAC 15250
12 km N of Aurillac

Aurillac, the *prefecture* of the Cantal is a very pleasant town with some interesting churches and good car parking near the tourist office. 12 km north at Marmanhac is the residence of

Château Sédaiges
Marmanhac

Comte & Comtesse de Varax.
'Château de Sédaiges'
category: (L)
tel: 04 71 47 30 01
email: bdeverax@netcourier.com
www.chateaudesedaiges.com
B&B: 100/107€. for two.
Closed 1 Oct. to 30 May

In the village in a sheltered valley surrounded by six hectares of wooded grounds this four-towered ivy-covered château has been in the family since the 12th century. Rebuilt in the 15th and finally in the 19th century. It is an historical monument, open to the public every afternoon in the Summer, but now offers a few guest rooms.

Well worth a visit. The entrance hall was originally a courtyard open to the sky, with a balcony round it, now closed in, it has a splendid oak spiral staircase to the surrounding gallery, and is hung with an impressive 18th century Flanders tapestry, given by Louis XVI to an ancestor of Patrice de Varax. A high-lighted commentary of this is given in the tour. Two 14th/15th century furnished salons lead through from the dining room, all firmly roped off. The dining room has rare identical sideboards and plates from all regions of France decorate the walls.

The old chapel is on the ground floor and in a nearby room is a splendid glassed-in collection of Mattel's Barbie dolls robed in *haute couture*. It is a fascinating collection, changed each year, so it never ceases to be interesting. Maybe not for all, my husband took one look and retreated to the chapel. Resident guests have the advantage of being able to roam the château and re-visit all exhibitions and rooms. It is impossible to take in everything in an afternoon guided tour

A small salon with Louis XV furniture is reserved for guests where they enjoy an aperitif with their hosts on arrival.

Two suites of guest rooms are on the first floor corridor pleasantly furnished with a variety of antiques and have adjoining bathrooms, a third room has a shower room but shares the loo with one of the suites, a long trek down the corridor. The pretty blue flowered suite is the nicest with a private bathroom dividing the two rooms.

Breakfast, a highlight of your stay, is served in front of a log fire in the original kitchen hung with copper pans, sitting on forms at a long table, it is virtually a brunch, the bacon and egg brigade would be happy here!

So much to take in with an afternoon visit to the château, better by far if you can afford to stay the night, enjoy the swimming pool and copious breakfast and Madame will give you a private tour of all rooms and a detailed show of the beautiful Flanders tapestries. No evening meals. Restaurants in the village or Aurillac.

SALERS. 15410.

47 km N of Aurillac.

Salers is a most attractive little village well worth a visit, but try not to visit on public holidays when it is packed solid. The medieval village, built on a layer of basalt, was founded by the Baron de Salers in 1069 and in 1428 Charles VII authorised its fortification against the English and the *Routiers* (roving bands of highwaymen, not today's lorry drivers). Under Henry II in 1550 the town became the seat of government of the Royal Bailiwick of the High Mountains of the Auvergne *(Bailliage Royale des Hautes Montagnes de l'Auvergne)*. The Knights Templar had close connections with Salers and the museum in the Maison des Templiers is worth a visit. Little remains of the really old town apart from the church door, parts of the walls and some street staircases but there are lots of cottages and artisan shops in the village. 1km outside the village on the Route de Puy Mary you will find:

☆ **Mme. Vantal.**
category: (M)
tel: 04.71.40.74.02
B&B: 38.5€ for two. No Dinner

The Vantals are dairy farmers, who always make you feel welcome, they have adapted one end of their house for guests. There is a private entry to five first floor rooms. A choice of baths or excellent showers, single or double beds, one family room for four, all prettily papered and painted, with good central heating, plentiful hot water and country views. Nothing fancy about them, which could come as a relief after an overdose of bric-a-brac. Lovely white cotton sheets and at least four fluffy white towels. Breakfasts with orange juice, fresh bread and croissants and a selection of jams and honey are all individually served in the new salon for guests. This is one of those chambres d'hôtes which goes from strength to strength, arm chairs in the rooms bedrooms are next on the list. The ☆ still stands.

No evening meals. There is a good choice of restaurants in Salers. Try the La Poterne for local specialities.

HAUTE-LOIRE

LISSAC 43350.
20 km NW of Le Puy-en-Velay.

This is high, flat farming country, surrounded by distant hills, through which the river Loire descends on its way north. From the N102, 47 km S of Brioude take the D27 SP 'Darsac' and the farm is on the corner of the road to Lissac.

M. & Mme. Sigaud. 'Freycinet'
Route de Darsac.
category: (S)
tel: 04.71.57.02.97.
B&B: 32€ for two.
Evening meals 9.5€ each.

This must be the budget stop of the book. Dairy farmers, the Sigaud family welcome their guests warmly and even arriving unexpectedly at six o'clock will offer you a drink and count you in for a meal with the family. The house is newly-built with a ground floor wing designed for guests. Four simple spotless pine-clad rooms have beds for two or for a family of four with sturdy bunks. Tiled floors, adjoining shower rooms, only 41€ for four.

All inclusive evening meals (to satisfy the hungriest walker) are convivial occasions with the family and other guests. The youngest daughter speaks some English. A lovely, friendly family where children are welcome.

SENEUJOLS. 43510.
18 km SW of Le Puy. Closed 15 Nov. to 1 Mar.

Old houses in Haute-Loire are often built with the rather dull dark-grey volcanic stone and this is typical of many in the area.

From the autoroute south of Clermont Ferrand exit 20 take the N102 to the junction with the D906 at Coubladour, follow the D906 for 17 km to St. Christophe and turn right on to the D31 to Seneujols. The farm is on the right as you enter the village.

M. & Mme. Boyer
category: (S)
tel: 04.71.03.19.69.
B&B: 33.5€ for two.
Evening meals 11€ each.
Closed 1 Nov. to 31 Mar.

'*The Boyers live in a converted farmhouse and have refurbished an adjacent building to provide spacious and comfortable accommodation on the first floor. The energy and enthusiasm they bring to their business is an example of how an ideal chambres d'hôtes should be run. Nothing was too much trouble here, all meals over-supplied, using their own fresh vegetables and meat from relatives' farms and all prepared to a high standard. Highly recommended*'. – H. Coe.

Certainly the welcome is friendly here. There are three rooms, simply furnished, one for a family with one double and bunk beds, 43€. Another leading directly on to a new terrace over the garages which are used as a games room in summer. In the guests' salon is a kitchen area for preparing picnics and drinks. If you are staying for a few days Madame will even pop your washing in the machine for 2.5€. Another welcome budget stop on the way to the Cévennes.

PUY-de-DÔME

COMBRONDE 63460
10 km N of Riom.

Leave the A71 at Riom (Exit 13) and drive north on the N144. Turn right, SP 'Chaptes', just before Combronde and follow signs to the chambres d'hôtes at Beauregard-Vendon

Mme. Beaujeard. 'Chaptes'
category: (M)
tel: 04.73.63.35.62.
B&B: 52.5/56€ for two. No Dinner.
Open all year, by reservation only
1/11 to 1/4

Madame is a kindly hostess, who welcomes you to her lovely old house which was built at the time of the Revolution and has been in the same family ever since.

Original floors, fireplaces and stairs of volcanic lava are still in place. Most rooms face south with views to the Puy-de-Dôme, overlooking the sunny lawned garden. Amenities here include a covered terrace with a fridge, for picnics, and enclosed parking, and a pleasant salon/dining room for breakfast. Three guest rooms on the first floor are large and elegantly decorated, with matching bed linen, some with *ciel de lit*. Just one room faces north, but has a country view. Extra beds 16€, but free for a baby.

No evening meals but Madame tells me there are many excellent restaurants in Riom.

COURPIÈRE 63120.
14 km SE of Thiers.

I am inclined to agree with Georges Sand that Thiers is a black town. Sprawling up a hill, it is divided by the narrow, relentless N89 with shopping precincts on either side and certainly as you leave the town on the east side the tall houses look ill-kept and pretty miserable. But park in the covered car park (*payant*) near the *mairie* and descend down narrow streets to the *vieille-ville* and you will find much more of interest. There is a free car park by St-Génis church but it's a bit difficult to find in the maze of narrow streets. Almost every other shop is a *couterie*. At nearby Monnerie knives in all shapes and sizes are produced in profusion. The Sabatier factory is here. There is also a museum of knives in the old town. So don't dismiss Thiers with first impressions. It has more to offer.

Don't try to find this château from Courpière – easier to head for Thiers, leave by N89 in an easterly direction, in 9 km turn right on the D7 to Celles-sur-Durolles, past the village, still on the D7 towards Sainte-Agathe you will pick up a discreet sign to the château on your right.

☆ **M. and Mme. Dumas de Vaulx.**
'Château de Vaulx'
Ste-Agathe.
category: (M)
tel: 04.73.51.50.55.
fax: 04.73.51.54.47.
B&B: 48/56€ for two.
Evening meals 16€ each.
Closed: 15 Nov. to 1 Apr.

Such a gem of a château, set in extensive parkland, with four towers and a moat, looking like a fairy-tale castle yet still a real family home, with every room in use. Originally built in the 13th century, it has had its ups and downs but remained in the same family. Such sensible use has been made of all the tower rooms, kitchen, butler's pantry, bathroom but best surprise of all, through the library, is a charming circular chapel licensed by Pope Leo XIII for mass and all other sacraments, with a really ornate altar and even a child's prie-dieu.

An extract from a letter.: *'We found the château from your book, and were so impressed by the welcome and the homely service provided on our journey south, that we phoned French friends in Paris to ask whether they would like to spend a weekend there with us on our return journey. They were as captivated as we were. But the icing on the cake must be the warmth of M. & Mme. Dumas themselves. One could not wish for nicer hosts.'* H & I Glasby.

Three rooms are in the château. One, enormous, has a double bed with *ciel de lit*, the monogrammed white sheets once belonged to Madame's grandmother. The bathroom attached to this room is in a tower and the bath stands regally on clawed feet. Excellent lighting and hot water.

The circular room in one of the front towers, now has a dainty *baldaquin* over the bed. Entered by a dressing room with wash basin, the private shower and loo is adjacent, curtained off for privacy. Now a ground floor room has been made into a bedroom. Furnished with family heirlooms, it has an adjoining shower and loo, and large windows overlook the grounds.

Before you complain about lack of luxury carpets, remember that you are going to bed up the same stone stairs the family have used for hundreds of years and looking out at the same view down the valley from a château where the English defended Aquitaine from the Duke of Burgundy.

Sometimes an evening meal is available, taken in the dining room where the Dumas family crest adorns the fireplace. Before dinner you may be invited to inspect the cellars, where the family hid a priest during the Revolution. Down here Monsieur has made an intriguing bar where aperitifs are often offered.

☆ for good value and kindly hosts. Do book ahead to avoid disappointment – it is very popular.

ROYAT 63130
5 km W of Clermont-Ferrand.

A town only a few kilometres from the Puy de Dôme which has a toll road almost to the top. On a clear day one can see for miles in all directions. A great tourist attraction – parking, restaurants, *'table d' orientation'* – it's all at the top.

From Royat follow signs to the golf club at Charade, via the D5f, and the château is next door.

Mme. Gaba. 'Château de Charade'
category: (L)
tel: 04.73.35.91.67.
fax: 04.73.29.92.09.
B&B: 67/76.5€ for two. No Dinner
Closed 1 Dec. to 1 Apr.

Our closest chambres d'hôtes to the capital of the Massif Central.

You will have a very friendly welcome from the young owners who bought this 19th-century château a few years ago and have been steadily restoring it. It now has six guest rooms, a salon with a large billiard table and an adjoining dining room.

The grounds, with many rose bushes and bowers, and pleasantly shady, are bordered by the lane leading to the local golf club (9 holes). Keen golfers can slip that extra round in while the rest of the family relax at the château.

Three large rooms on the first floor are furnished in keeping with the age of the château – polished wood floors, flowery wallpaper and velvet Victorian chairs, but there is modern plumbing in all bathrooms. Some rooms have a small adjoining tower room, others duel aspect windows. *Chambre bleue* has a vestibule with separate bath and loo, *chambre verte* comprises two adjoining rooms for a family sharing facilities. On the second floor beamed high ceilings make the rooms very light. I liked the yellow room facing south. Every sort of accommodation catered for here, with breakfast in the garden or in the dining room in inclement weather. Extra bed 20.8€.

No evening meals; but a small restaurant close by produces light meals, or *gastronomique* if reserved, plenty of choice further afield in Royat.

VERNEUGHEOL. 63470.
40 km E of Aubusson. 60 km W of Clermont-Ferrand.

Take the D941 from Aubusson towards Clermont-Ferrand, in 35 km turn right on to the D82 towards Herment. Before the village turn right on to the D240 to Verneugheol and the chambres d'hôtes is signed in the village.

M. & Mme. Thomas. 'La Glufareix'
category: (S)
tel: 04.73.22.11.40.
B&B: 32/39€ for two
Evening meals 11€ each.

A quiet country farm near the hill-top village of Herment, between Aubusson and Clermont-Ferrand.

We arrived about 6 p.m. to be welcomed by Madame with a big smile and a large jug of orange juice. After the preliminary greeting, etc. we were shown to our accommodation, a large first-floor bedroom containing two large double beds, a huge wardrobe, bedside tables and a writing desk. Ample lighting, wooden beamed and carpeted. The adjoining shower room was light, modern and very inviting. All spotless. The farm is 18th century, recently renovated but maintaining its original character. Huge dining room with a massive fireplace in stone, wooden beams, etc. The sitting room with TV is similar. Madame is a great cook. Plenty of good solid regional home cooking, five course dinners with a different menu each evening beautifully presented and wine included. M. Bernard is a busy man, 100 cows to be milked morning and evening, he is also the Mayor for the region and a host without equal – J. C. Thomas.

After such a glowing account I just had to visit, and agree entirely. There are five rooms, including a suite for six. Extra beds, 11€, include breakfast. In the salon there is an interesting display case of tools for making sabots. Prices reduced September to May.

Brittany

BRITTANY

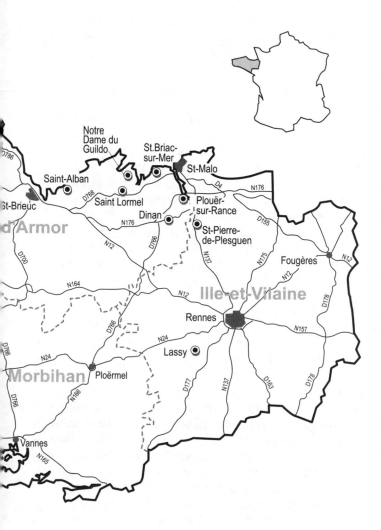

Brittany

One third of France's coastline is to be found in Brittany, and that's a lot of sand, rocks, surf, headlands, fishing villages, bays and beach resorts. The snag here is that, unlike its more sophisticated Paris-fed neighbours – Normandy and the Loire – Brittany tourism dies for the whole winter. *Toussaint* (1 November) to *Pâques* (Easter) is the normal closure, but October to May is a distinct possibility, too. This, after all, is the cold windswept north, and the heating bills make landladies think twice before incurring them. When you reckon that there's rarely an unoccupied bed to be found in this No 1. bucket and spade region in the school holidays, that doesn't leave much of the year to take pot-luck.

It's worth the effort to plan ahead. Brittany, land of myths, ghosts, will-o'-the-wisps, legends, is pure magic. You sense it most powerfully in the central Forest of Brocéliande, the home (so say the Bretons) of the Arthurian legend, and in the far north-west in wild Finistère, where the miracles worked by local saints, many of them monks from Britain, are still revered, and pagan spells are accepted side by side with colourful Christian traditions. This is Brittany at its most Breton – home of the unique *clos paroissiaux*, astonishing church enclosures crowded with amazingly elaborate carvings of triumphal arches, calvaries and ossuaries, parish vying with parish over several centuries to produce the most glorious combined effect, working with the rough, local granite. At the most famous in Guimiliau are 200 figures depicting Passion stories.

It is in the south, in Morbihan, that you are most likely to catch another Breton phenomenon – the *Pardon*, an impressive local religious procession, where the *coiffes*, collars and costumes handed down through the generations are brought out and proudly paraded. The principal *Pardons* are listed in the companion guide, French Entrée to Brittany, along with another treat – the markets. In this land of superb fish and vegetables, they are exceptionally attractive to supermarket-weary eyes

I can never decide which is my favourite area – Côtes d'Armor with its fantastic coastline, marvellous beaches, pink granite rocks, the beguiling river Rance, and two of Brittany's most attractive towns, St Malo and Dinan, or the south, with the astonishingly Mediterranean-like Gulf of Morbihan with an island for every day of the year. I love the twists and turns of the river Bélon and picturesque Pont Aven, I love the seaside resorts of Finistère, like Benodet, and the fishing villages of the west, like Douarnenez and Concarneau; I would not neglect exploring the interior, particularly the canals and towns like Josselin and Dinan. Nowhere is very far from the feature that dominates the landscape and the character of the Bretons – the sea. Nowhere is sophisticated – forget your night-clubs and smart clothes – everywhere is very, very beautiful.

Because this is a region where tourism is a top industry, Brittany has one of the largest crops of chambres d'hôtes to choose from. They range from severe, granite châteaux, whose owners are exceptionally friendly – to simple farm accommodation. Many a Breton farmer has blessed this supplement to his income in agricultural hard times.

There is so much to see, so many things to do, so many new experiences to savour that I wager the first visit won't be the last.

CÔTES-d'ARMOR

DINAN. 22100.
30 km S of St. Malo. 20 km S of Dinard.

A gem of a town, situated high on a hill above the river Rance, probably the most interesting and attractive in the whole region and not to be rushed through on any account. Penetrate into the heart of the old town with cameras well loaded, to record the photogenic crooked gables, pillars and beams of the houses built for 15th-century merchants whose trades are echoed in the street names:- *Cordeliers, Merciers, Lainerie, Poissonerie.* The rue d'Horloge is one of the most picturesque, with its strange 15th-century clock-tower enclosing four bells, one of them a gift from the ubiquitous Duchesse Anne.

Stallholders used to sell their wares in the shelter of the arcades formed by the stubby granite pillars supporting overhanging upper stories – as practical today for keeping off the Breton rain as ever was. Visit the fish market, open every day in the narrow rue de la Chaux, part of a tangle of little streets around the old market. The main market takes place on Thursday on what used to be a medieval fairground, the Places du Champ and du Guesclin, full of cars on other days.

When the delightful meandering round the old town is complete, take a closer look at the port, where the pleasure boats take off for a fascinating trip down the Rance to St. Malo in summer, by walking down one of the most beguiling lanes in Brittany. It leads from the English Garden, via the rues du Rampart and Michel, into the rue du Jerzual and its extension, the rue du Petit Port, winding through the 500-year-old Jerzual Gate, between the elegant houses now owned and restored by craftsmen, right down to the water.

Arriving by car via the bridge over the R. Rance climb the hill to Dinan bear left at the Porte St. Louis.

Mrs. Lockwood.
55 rue de Coetquen.
category: (S)
tel: 02.96.85.23.49.
B&B: 56€ for two.

This bijou little town house right on the road side, has doubled in size, parking outside is permissible, as it is such a quiet little street; a larger free car park is close by. Since spreading into next door house Mrs Lockwood, has a second room to offer guests. You will be assured of a warm welcome as a very private guest from your English hostess who has lived in France for over thirty years. With two well-furnished double rooms, each having an attached bathroom, you will want to avail yourself of her offer of staying a week and getting one night free.

There is a patio and garden on the cliff-side behind the house. Altogether a charming little house, almost in the centre of Dinan.

No evening meals, but all the restaurants of Dinan are within walking distance, give or take a few hills. Reserve well ahead for winter visits as Mrs L is sometimes away.

NOTRE-DAME-DU-GUILDO (St. CAST). 22380.

36 km NW of Dinan. St Cast is situated on a narrow peninsular with small sandy beaches looking across the bay to St Briac-sur -Mer,

M. & Mme. de la Blanchardière.
'Château du Val d'Arguenon'
category: (L)
tel: 02 96 41 07 03.
fax: 02 96 41 02 67.
B&B: 77/99 €.
Closed 30 Sept. to 1 Apr.

A stunning 16th cent. château by the sea. The grounds slope gently down to the water's edge and a private beach. It has been in this family for over 200 years. The present owners who are charming, have opened their home to guests. There are high ceilings in rooms furnished with antiques. Each of the five guest room is different, the *toile de Jouy* room has a sea view, another is named after Châteaubriand, who is reputed to have stayed here. There is a tennis court in the grounds and many paths lead to the coast. No Evening meal. English spoken.

PLOUBEZRE 22300.

8 km S of Lannion by the D11 then the D30 to Ploumilliau, first left after the railway crossing.

M. Mme. de Bellefon. 'Manoir de Kerguéron'.
category: (L)
tel: 02 96 38 91 46.
B&B: 80€ for two.

The lady of the manor is the sister of the Comte de Kermel. (Château de Kermezen) This delightful Breton manor house in large grounds surrounded by fields is every bit as elegant inside as out. Nothing has been spoilt in its reconstruction after the revolution. The two guest rooms are furnished with antiques, in one bathroom, the site of the original latrine is incorporated in the modernised design. The manor, on restoration, won the coveted *Vieilles Maisons Françaises* first prize. Your host's son runs a thoroughbred stud farm on the premises and lives in part of the house. No evening meals, but aperitifs are offered to guests before they go out to dinner. A delightful home and most charming hosts who speak English. By reservation only.

PLOUCRESCANT. 22820
7 km N of Treguier. The little village on the rocky Pink Granite Coast has a church with a crooked tower, turn left here to find the château.

Vicomte & Vicomtesse de Roquefeuil. 'Manoir de Kergre'ch'.
category: (L)
tel: 02 96 92 56 06 &
02 96 92 59 13.
fax: 02 96 92 51 27.
B&B: 92€ for two

In summer old-fashioned climbing roses rampage over the lovely granite facade of this 17th century manor house so close to the sea. The delightful young chatelaine is a superb hostess, who welcomes you into her lovely home. All the four guest rooms are quite irresistible, from the large suite on the ground floor with door to the garden, to the first floor rooms up the spiral stone stairway, where one has duel aspect windows, they are furnished exquisitely with usable antiques but comfortable modern beds, some with *ciels de lits*, luxury bathrooms have gleaming white baths, dual washbasins large towels and bathrobes. The oldest room, has a bed in the rafters for a child and in the bathroom a modern loo where the medieval latrine once took pride of place. Breakfast is a sumptuous affair, with Breton specialities like *crêpes, far breton, and chausson de pomme* as well the usual fresh bread and home-made jams. Your hosts join you for breakfast and offer advice on the day's outings. Very good English spoken.

PLOUËR-sur-RANCE. 22490.
20 km S of Saint-Malo. 9 km N of Dinan.

A favourite area, blissfully little-known. There are fabulous views over the wide and wonderful Rance and good walks on both sides of the river. Plouër boasts a marina, so there is usually plenty of colourful activity and at La Hisse you can hire boats for river explorations. Handy for the St. Malo ferry.

Take the N176 from le Mont-Saint-Michel to Saint-Brieuc. After you cross the river Rance, take the first exit, marked 'Plouër' then take the 'Plouër' exit from the roundabout. You are now on the D12 (SP 'La Hisse'). Drive past the village, and the house is on the right in 1 km.

☆ **Mr. & Mrs. Robinson. 'La Renardais'**
Le Repos.
category: (M)
tel: 02.96.86.89.81.
fax: 02.96.86.99.22
email: Suzanne.Robinson@ wanadoo.fr
B&B: 56/61€ for two.
Evening meals 16/20 g each.
Closed 1 Nov. to 1 Mar.

This fine sturdy house was once a *café/bar/épicerie*. British owners have completely renovated it, effectively keeping the old granite fireplace in the large lounge, interspersing local stones with smooth white walls, and incorporating the stable to create a dining room which opens on to a sheltered patio and rear garden.

Up the original chestnut staircase are five guest rooms, warmly carpeted. Those on the top floor are beamed. Choose between singles, doubles with king-sized beds, and a family room, bath or shower, all with many extras like hair-dryers. Four have adjoining bathrooms, the other has a basin with a private loo/shower on the corridor. So book well ahead and ask for your preference.

The evening meal is cooked by Susanne, served with quality wines from 8/24 € a bottle, or by the glass. The clientele is a good mix of French and

English. *'The evening meal was a succession of courses served with precision by John and the table for six was set as if for a banquet, which indeed it was. The six of us retired well after midnight'.* Breakfast includes fresh O.J. and an excellent selection of croissants and bread.

Parking in the gravelled front garden. Altogether an excellent place to stay, well worth a ☆.

POMMERIT JAUDY. 22450.
9 km S of Tréguier by D8 and D6.

The valley of the river Jaudy is a particularly green and pleasant area of northern Brittany. The rugged coast is not far away, but the scenery here bears no relation to its harshness. All is lush and gentle.

☆ **Comte & Comtesse de Kermel.**
'Château de Kermézen'
category: (L)
tel: 02.96.91.35.75.
B&B: 76.5/92.5€ for two

Comte de Kermel was a coffee planter in Africa before he returned to claim his inheritance of the 15th-century château that had been in his family 550 years. The colonial tradition of hospitality is still evident. If you ever felt intimidated at the thought of being entertained by a count and countess, forget it. This hostess patently enjoys sharing her gorgeous home with guests, many of whom have become friends. It's hard not to be friends with the ebullient Comtesse de Kermel, who is the unstuffiest Comtesse imaginable. She claims that she was pushed (by the energetic François de Valbray at Briottières) into B&B business but, given no option but to get out the paint brush and start decorating the rooms that had been empty for the past forty years, she typically buckled to and made the best of what has proved to be a very good job.

The bedrooms are all lovely. On the first floor is chambre *Coq*, newly decorated, with a bathroom overlooking the rear garden. Next door is smaller with *directoire* beds, rose-covered fabric on the walls and a tall window looking directly down the drive, which is flanked by two solid *pigeonniers*. Reaching the second floor involves a steeper climb up the stone tower staircase, crooked enough to necessitate hanging on to a rope with unengaged hand. But here is probably the nicest room of all. Freshly decorated in yellow, carpeted luxuriously, it has a large twinned-basined bathroom. Another two rooms on this floor have mezzanines for a third person.

Leave time for a walk here. Comtesse de Kermel, who loves nothing better than organising, will distribute maps. In early spring the banks of the lane that follows the rushing river are covered in bluebells, ragged robin, wild garlic, primroses, buttercups, violets, star of Bethlehem, and wild cherry blossom.

This is a lovely place to stay, with the kindest of hosts. You'll want to go back and back. No evening meals but a superb restaurant nearby at la Ville Blanche. A ☆ of course.

ROSPEZ. 22300
60 km E of Roscoff, 41 km NE of Morlaix. 6 km E of Lannion

Legend has it that in the 6th century the Welsh monk Dogmael came over from Pembrokeshire and worked in this area, the tiny church in the field next to the chambres d'hôtes is dedicated to him. A choice of many lovely sandy beaches in the area. Looking for somewhere to stay close to the renowned Ville Blanche restaurant I was pleasantly surprised to find this chambres d'hôtes.

Take the D 65 (heading SE) out of Lannion for 6 km, the house is on the left.

M. & Mme. Berezai. 'St Dogmael'
category: (S)
tel: 02.96.37.68.33.
fax: 02.96.637.68.33.
B&B: 40€ for two.

Sheep and pigs were venturing to greet us in the front garden when we arrived, hastily marshalled away by Monsieur who then came to welcome us. We had arrived unexpectedly when Madame was out. Sideways on to the road in a well kept front garden, the old stone farm house, extended over the years, is in pristine condition.

A ground floor room entered from the garden has a private adjoining shower room, but was out of function having a new shower fitted, so we were offered one of the two first floor rooms in the house. Comfortable, simple rooms with double glazing to combat any passing traffic, have a choice of bathroom or cheerful red shower room opposite, a separate loo is shared. These rooms may not be truly en suite, but everything is provided for comfort, towelling gowns, hair drier, numerous toiletries, changing mats for babies, 'Pampers', and even plastic boats for bath-time entertainment. This must be a first!. Both your hosts take great delight in entertaining their guests. A generous breakfast at the large table in the dining room, will set you up for the day. Swings for children in the rear garden where you can relax among the herbaceous borders. There is also a very well equipped *gîte*. No evening meals. So the chance to dine at 'La Ville Blanche' restaurant, the best in the region, should never be missed, less than two miles away, but book well ahead in the season.

SAINT ALBAN. 22400.
9 km N of Lamballe by the D791.
At St. Alban take the St. Brieuc road for 2 km. Signed on the left. Farming country not far from the coast.

M. & Mme. Legrand. 'La Ferme de Malido'
category: (S)
tel: 02.96.32.94.74.
fax: 02.96.32.92.67.
B&B: 38.5€ for two. No Dinner

Situated along a farm lane, a large field for parking has swings and ample space for children to play. Comfortable rooms – three in a wing of the house, one, a suite, in a separate barn with high raftered ceiling – have a rustic prettiness about them with sunny ceiling to floor windows. All have showers.

Friendly young Mme. Legrand serves a very good breakfast in the long salon, which has an enormous stone fireplace at one end, and there is a summer kitchen in the barn as well as wet weather games. I liked this one and thought it was extremely good value, with the option of eating out for dinner at nearby restaurants or self-catering, with a mini market down the road open all hours.

SAINT-LORMEL. 22130 PLANCOËT.
3 km N of Plancoët via the D19.
From Plancoët take the D768 towards Créhen, in about 1km turn left SP 'St. Lormel', at T junction left again and immediately right and follow signs to 'La Pastourelle', deep into the countryside.

Mme. Ledé. 'La Pastourelle'
category: (S)
tel: 02.96.84.03.77.
B&B: 42.5€ for two.
Evening meals 15€ each (drinks incl).
Closed 15 Nov. to Easter.

This typical old Breton farmhouse on the banks of the river Arguenon has been in the family for four generations. Family heirlooms, like those lovely polished *armoires* that are given to young couples on their wedding day, furnish many of the rooms, flowery country wallpapers lighten up the walls, and chintzy canopies hang over the beds. The vast stone-walled salon had a cheerful fire burning on a cool spring day and a giant leather halter on the staircase was put to good use as a key-holder for the guest rooms. Of the five rooms one has a bath, the rest have shower and loo. There is now a family suite of two rooms, one with bunks. Reduced rates for stays of longer than four days, extra beds 12.5€.

Madame Ledé is a very professional hostess, recommended in many guidebooks; she serves excellent breakfasts, and dinners (by reservation) at separate tables, and cooks delicious meals on a wood-fired range, using local farm produce. Book early here. I've never been able to get a room on spec.

TRÉGROM. 22420 PLOUARET.
25 km NW of Guingamp by N12.
Take the Louargat exit, then the D33 to the village, a pretty, sleepy hamlet of grey stone houses covered in roses. In the centre opposite the church is:-

☆ **Mme. Nicole de Morchoven.**
'L'Ancien Presbytère'
category: (M)
tel: 02.96.47.94.15.
B&B: 48€ for two.
Evening meals 20€ each.

A great favourite with readers. Open the blue door on the village street and discover a magical secret garden. A flowery courtyard fronts the 17th-century presbytery, a lovely grey stone building with blue shutters. The walled rear garden exudes an extraordinary atmosphere of serenity, now lawns and flower beds where the monks once tended their vegetables. Parking is behind locked gates.

I like everything about le Presbytère – the warm kitchen with an old porcelain stove, dried flowers hanging from the ceiling, and fresh ones in great bunches on the table. Up the stone staircase, are the bedrooms – the peach one with a big bathroom and tub; up again, the twin-bedded one with beams and blue *toile de Jouy* fabric, with shower, the red *toile de Jouy* (ditto). Most of all I like the atmosphere of a comfortable family house presided over by nice Mme. de Morchoven. If reserved, she prepares dinner for your first night and occasionally afterwards.

FINISTÈRE

LANDUDEC 29710.
11 km S of Douarnenez. In the wild wild west of Finistère

M. Davy. 'Château du Guilguiffin'.
category: (L)
tel: 02.98.91.52.11.
Fax: 02 98 91 52 52.
email: chateau@guilguiffin.com
B&B: 70/115€ .
Closed 15 Nov. to 15 Dec. and 10 Jan.
to 1 Mar.

From a German reader:- *"What most impressed me was the Château-du-Guilguiffin which is, out of question, the best kept, the most interesting and extraordinary castle in Brittany, with a beautiful vast parkland, charming and 'mysterious'. The rooms are big, comfortable with the special charm of authentic furniture, carpets and fabric. I was astonished not to find the Château Guilguiffin in your very good guide."* Marget Körner. It is now, thanks to you pointing me in the right direction.

It is a magnificent château but still a real family home. It is a classified historical site, in a particularly enchanting part of Brittany, the grounds extend over 1,000 acres. In the same family for 900 years, it was rebuilt in the 18th century in the neo-classic style with a simple proportioned facade and a magnificent colonnade of stone pillars that encircle the front lawn. The bedrooms are resplendent with rich fabrics and antiques. Breakfast is served at one long table in a sunny yellow and blue kitchen. Dinners are more formally presented in the beautiful panelled dining room. The gardens are famous, not least for the Spring-time display of daffodils numbering into the hundreds of thousands. In spite of all the grandeur, M. Davy is down to earth and delights in his guests rapport with the wonderful surroundings of his home. The prices vary according to season. Excellent English spoken.

NEVEZ. 29920.
12 km SE of Concarneau

South-west of Pont Aven at Nevez take the D77 to Port Manech. Turn right to Raguenès before you go down to the port and almost immediately turn left down a small lane to Kérambris which will be signposted on the main road.

☆ **Mme. Gourlaouen. 'Kérambris'**
Port Manech.
category: (S)
tel: 02.98.06.83.82.
B&B: 41€ for two.
Closed. 15 Nov. to 15 Mar.

This farm house is in an excellent position away from the main road down a private lane, a short walk to the cliff paths across Kérambris' fields. One mile away there is a lovely sandy beach for children at Port Manech. There are garden chairs and tables in a large orchard. Mme. Gourlaouen is a charming hostess, always on hand to help you. The six rooms, with independent entry from an outside staircase, are very compact with efficient shower rooms adjoining. They look out over farm buildings and fields. Breakfast is a real treat here, not only fresh bread and buttery croissants, but also a local speciality such as *far breton*, all served at a long table in the dining room. This is a wonderfully central place to stay for visiting the coast from Concarneau to Pont-Aven. Good restaurants and a *crêperie* are only a mile away. There are also three large *gîtes* at one end of the farmhouse.

On a recent visit I was glad to see nothing had changed; even better; velux windows in some rooms are soon to be replaced with full length mansarded ones. – just awaiting planning permission. Spacious parking. Some English spoken. Only good reports come in from this old favourite, so the ☆ firmly stays.

PLOUGONVEN 29640.
16 km SE of Morlaix on the D109 between Plougonven and Plourin-les-Morlaix.

M. & Mme. de Ternay. 'La Grange de Coatélan'.
category: (M)
tel: 02 98 72 60 16.
B&B: 40/54 € for two

Once a farm house, now tastefully converted into a delightful Crêperie/Auberge where a huge chimney dominates the long dining room and a log fire is a welcome sight on a wet June night. Patio doors to a terrace have views to the Mont d'Arrée. Menus are kept simple – delicious soups, salads, *crêpes* and a dish of the day, followed by desserts. Yolande de Ternay cooks while Charlick, her artist husband, attends to the guests. Book ahead, the locals have found it and come out regularly from Morlaix. Two guest rooms are in the rafters above the restaurant, the third in the converted bull's stable a few steps away has a mezzanine for children. Bathrooms, all with baths, are particularly attractive. Two more rooms in the pipeline hopefully for 2002. Breakfast is the best ever, a wonderful selection of fresh bread, and much more, really copious. Highly recommended. English spoken.

ST-MARTIN-DES-CHAMPS. 29600.
25 km SE of Roscoff.

St-Martin is a suburb of Morlaix which is in a steep-sided valley, where the rivers Jarlot and Queffleut join, and dominated by a giant viaduct. It's a pleasant colourful town, with many yachts tied up at its entrance. Traces of antiquity remain in steep cobbled streets and 16th-century mansions like Duchesse Anne's house, one of the town's showpieces.

Coming from Roscoff on the D58, at the first roundabout at Morlaix before going under the N12 motorway take the first exit (the Renault garage should be on your left) and at the next roundabout take the third exit following small blue signs to the chambres d'hôtes Kéréliza. Easier to find in daylight.

Mme. Abiven. 'Kéréliza'
category: (S)
tel: 02.98.88.27.18.
B&B: 38.5€ for two. No Dinner

Situated in large grounds, where strawberries are grown, not far from the Morlaix by-pass. A frequently used budget stop by travellers to and from the Roscoff ferry. Dual steps sweep up to this tall house which has been carefully renovated by the young owners in keeping with its age. It now has five guest rooms on two floors, all with modernised shower rooms. There is a pleasant dining room where a good breakfast is served. Some English spoken. No evening meals, but a recently-added kitchen for guests next to a splendid table tennis room, now make self-catering an option. Restaurants in Morlaix, or a café at the hypermarket *'GÉANT''* nearby.

ST. THÉGONNEC 29410
32 km S of Roscoff, 8 km SW of Morlaix. From the N12 exit at St. Thégonnec and follow signs to the village past the large car park turn right SP Guican, left at the next crossroads D231 and left again, the mill is well signed just 1km from the village.

M. & Mme. Conilly. 'Moulin de Kerlaviou'
category: (S)
tel: 0 2.98.79.60.57.
B&B: 40€ for two.

Tucked down by the river Penzé this little farmhouse is in an idyllic position, built 150 years ago it is positively modern compared with the original farmhouse, which is 500 years old and still standing, now inhabited by chickens. The river flows gently past the garden under a bridge, joined by smaller streams. It is all incredibly beautiful and peaceful.. In the evening cows descend from the surrounding fields over the little bridge past the house on their way to the milking sheds. Monsieur has retired and his son now farms the 60 hectares. The Cornilys are a charming couple who have two cottage guest rooms on the first floor. Large mats keep feet warm on the wood floors, double beds, each has a spacious adjoining bathroom. One in the main house has a carved oak suite and a good view of the garden, the other with a velux window has private access through the guest lounge.

M. Cornily delights in conducting people round his garden, pointing out the terrace where the old mill stood, now long gone, the 15th century grave stone he retrieved from in the river, chunks of meteorite and other treasures dug up in the fields, finishing with a stroll through his 'Promenade des Anglais', a small pine forest he planted twenty five years ago leading to a little sheltered arbour. All their water comes from a spring, continuously flowing into an enormous tank. Madame Cornily is less loquacious, but produces an excellent breakfast with homemade jams, milk from their cows and multiple breads from the local boulangerie. You will want to return and return. Restaurants for evening meals in St. Thégonnec. Little English spoken.

ILLE-ET VILAINE

LASSY. 35580
20 km SW of Rennes.

Handy for visiting Rennes the capital of Brittany, which is now a booming city.

Take the D177 heading south west of Rennes and in about 16 km turn right on to the D776 (SP: Guer) in 1.5 km ignore the sign to Lassy (D38) and keep on the D776. In 5 km turn left on to the D62 (SP Guignen) and the mill is on the left, just before the 'Pont de Bignon'.

M. & Mme. Krust. 'Moulin de Bignon'
category: (S)
tel: 02.99.42.10.04.
B&B: 40€ for two.
Evening meals 16€ each.

Your hosts hail from Alsace and moved here, attracted by the sound of running water which reminded Madame of her childhood near Munster.

A farmhouse for the family and a tiny mill house for guests with two equally small rooms. The gardens are most refreshing on a hot day, tiny bridged wooded islands of lawn dotted among the flowing river. Although close to the road the small amount of traffic is muted by the mill wheel which is up and running now. You could hide away in the summer to picnic, snooze or read with water in every direction. A bijou little place with parking under the windows.

The mill house contains a *petit* salon/kitchenette on the ground floor with a fireplace, wooden stairs lead to two small bedrooms above. A choice of double or two single beds, both with dual aspect windows, and tiny shower rooms, which have lots of little luxuries – tissues, soap and hair drier and plentiful large towels. I liked the double room with the wheel turning right under the window, facing south and west. The bed fitted into an alcove has just room for wall lights over it. A large wardrobe and armchair fill the room. Floors are carpeted and there is central heating for all-year-round occupation.

A copious breakfast and evening meals are served in the farmhouse. Madame is an excellent cook and produces dishes from Alsace, such as *tarte flambée*. Four courses with wine *compris*.

The welcome and your hosts' good English make this a pleasant budget stop – and not another house in sight.

SAINT BRIAC-sur-MER. 35800. DINARD.
16 km W of St. Malo by the D168 across the barrage, then the D603.
This popular seaside resort happens to have a chambres d'hôtes worthy of it. St. Briac is blessed with a variety of beaches, some just coves, some sizeable stretches of sand, facing in virtually all directions, so that there is always one sheltered. Whichever way you look there are vistas of rocks, islands, bays, boats, begging to be painted. Lovely walks, lovely picnicking, either on the beach or on one of the benches along the St. Brieuc road, with super views over the water.

Some 3 km from the village, from the D168 between Plouabalay and Dinard take the D3 to St. Briac, well signed from here down country lanes.

☆ **Jean François Stenou. 'Manoir de la Duchée'**
category: (M)
tel: 02.99.88.00.02.
B&B: 56/76€ for two.

The little 16th-century manor has been converted by M. Stenou and his sister into a picture postcard home, covered in roses. A spacious lawned garden with inviting white loungers under the trees exudes rural calm. Rooms named after flowers, have been tastefully decorated in country style, beams to duck under, colourful *ciel de lits* hang over the beds, each has a well equipped bath or shower room, even two for 'Rose'!. 'Lilac', a climb up winding stairs to the second floor has a small balcony for summer basking, but would be cosy and warm in winter. 'Camellia' has a salon and hidden alcove bed. All are fascinatingly different. Breakfast served in the *jardin d'hiver* is copious. Don't be put off by Mme. Stenou's seriousness, she is concentrating on keeping everywhere perfect and is rather shy.

No evening meal. Plenty of restaurants in St. Briac, but I found the Créperie L'Hermione a few streets away in a residential area, was unusually elegant and served dishes other than crêpes.

SAINT-PIERRE-de-PLESGUEN. 35720.
13 km E of Dinan by D794 and N137.

Take the St. Pierre-de-Plesguen exit, turn right towards the village, turn left on to D10 for 2 km. Do not get confused by two other chambres d'hôtes signs on the same road. It's a very pretty drive at the edge of the forest.

☆ **Mme. Michel. 'Le Petit Moulin du Rouvre'**
category: (M)
tel: 02. 99.73.85.84.
B&B: 60.5€ for two. Evening meal 24€ (wine incl).

Without doubt there's something very romantic about old watermills. The setting for this converted 17th-century mill is highly photogenic, fronted by a huge lake, with vast mill wheel still intact.

The file has been unanimously enthusiastic about the Petit Moulin and Mme. Québriac's welcome. She has been doing B&B for over twenty years now so she should be pretty good at it. The rooms are cosy and extremely comfortable, each with a private bathroom. The furniture is mostly antiques, with colourful plates on the stone walls, and a big salon for the guests' use. Visiting recently I was sitting by the lake when Ratty swam past with a mouthful of iris leaves, I expected to see Mole at any minute – sheer WITW.

Mme. Michel is completely charming. Sadly, she has given up serving evening meals, but a dear little restaurant has opened up in the village, just by the church, within easy driving distance, so all those wives whose husbands make them drive home after a meal need have no fear!

With a strong track record, Le Petit Moulin comes highly recommended, but make sure you book – it's now in plenty of other guide books.

MORBIHAN

MELRAND 56310.
17 km SW of Pontivy.
This is a blissfully quiet countrified area of Brittany far removed from the bustling coast. The little church at Kernascléden would be well worth a visit, one of the prettiest little churches in France, built by the Rohan family in the 15th century, it is famous for the delightful frescoes on the ceiling, visit in September and you may have it all to yourself. 4km from the village on the D2 to Pontivy. Signed at a bend in the road.

M. & Mme. Chauvel. 'Quenetevec'.
tel: 02 97 27 72 82. or
06 83 75 08 52.
category: (M)
B&B: 42/46 € for two
Closed 1 Nov. to 1 Mar.

Originally a tiny hamlet of four granite houses, boarded by a trout stream, this is now an extended lovely granite faced family home in a large lawned garden with a swimming pool.

Guest rooms are spread over two wings, one on the first floor, luxuriously carpeted is very large, a smaller one on the ground floor is pleasantly cosy and a family suite in another wing has a private entrance. Swimming pools in chambres d' hôtes are never crowded and the extensive view from this one is particularly nice and peaceful. No longer evening meals.

PLUVIGNER 56330.
11 km from Auray by D768.
A hilltop village with 12th-century church dedicated to 'Our Lady of the Nettles' (must be a history there). **But the chambres d'hôtes is not in Pluvigner.**
From the *'Voie-express'* (N165) Lorient to Auray in about 15 km take the Landevant exit then the D24 out of Landevant (direction Baud). In 6 km pass through the hamlet of Malachappe and take the second turning left following signs.

☆ **M. & Mme. Grèves. 'Chaumière de Kerreo'**
category: (M)
tel: 02.97.50.90.48.
fax: 02.97.50.90.69.
B&B: 46.5/51€ for two.
Evening meal 16€ each.

Found by accident, this has proved to be one of our most popular chambres d'hôtes in Brittany. It really is a treasure. Apart from the fact that it is an extremely pretty thatched 16th-century cottage, with decorative old beams, big log fire and pleasant garden, the big bonus is that Gérard is a professional cook. He used to be chef at the prestigious Moulin-des-Ducs and was also an instructor at the hotel school, so you can rely on eating well here, not only at breakfast (nothing plastic – *crêpes*, eggs, real butter and home-made jams) but also at dinner, when he offers a *repas du marché*, on reservation, wine included (six days a week not on Fridays.). Gérard also keeps up the twice yearly tradition when locals arrive to share a meal cooked in the old *four* in the garden. One of the dates is 15 August.

He and Nelly have been in the B&B business for quite a few years now. They started with three bedrooms with showers, well fitted and country-pretty. There is now a fourth room – *Niniane* – a spacious double, with a bathroom. A terrace and lawned garden for lazing; for the more active there are several good golf courses nearby.

Nothing but praise rolls in for this one, the ☆ firmly stays.

ROCHEFORT-EN-TERRE 56220.
30 km E of Vannes. Signed on the D774 from Malestroit to Rochefort.

M. Soulaine. 'Château Talhouët'.
category: (L)
tel: 02 97 43 34 72.
fax: 02 97 43 35 04
B&B: 110/155€ Evening Meal 39€

On the edge of the Lanvaux moors, the Château Talhouët commands a view of the peaceful Azé Valley and the grey spires of the fortress at

Rochefort-en-Terre. The owner has had the rare privilege of seeing a childhood dream come true. Since he was a young boy of eight growing up nearby he dreamt of living in the château and restoring it to its former glory. This he has done with great feeling for this ancient residence. In spite of the grandness of the salon, the astonishing sculptured ceiling of the billiard room, and the imposing 15th-century carved wood panelling, the château retains a lived in feeling. The eight bedrooms are vast. The Louis XIII room encompasses the entire breadth of the château with dual windows overlooking park and woodland. A monumental carved granite fireplace with *fleur de lys* dominates the *Chambre d' Honneur*, once reserved for the aristocracy. The orangerie is now the dining room, decorated in multiple blues. M. Solaine loves to cook and will prepare exceptional family meals for guests. In high summer he works closely with a hired chef. Terraced gardens and formal pools overlook the pastoral landscape. An *allée* of hydrangeas lead to the weathered grey stones of the château chapel. Guests at Talhouët imbibe the history and ambience of Brittany just by being there. English spoken

ST. NICHOLAS-DES EAUX 56310.
16 km SW Pontivy. From the bridge in the village take the road up river on the right bank to the end.

Mme. Maignan. 'Lezarhy'.
tel: 02.97.27.74.59.
category: (S)
B&B: 36 € for two

The road ends on the banks of the river Blavet and peace reigns. This is the 'other' Brittany, the inland landscape beloved by the locals and far less trammelled by tourists than the coast. Once a dairy farm, the long low buildings now contain the Maignans' home, Philippe's pottery studio and a little guest cottage which has a kitchen for self-catering. Two rooms above are spacious and light and both are en suite. Delightful walks from the door, peace and quiet ensured. No Evening meals. Boat trips are available on the river from St. Nicholas. A restful budget stop.

Burgundy

BURGUNDY

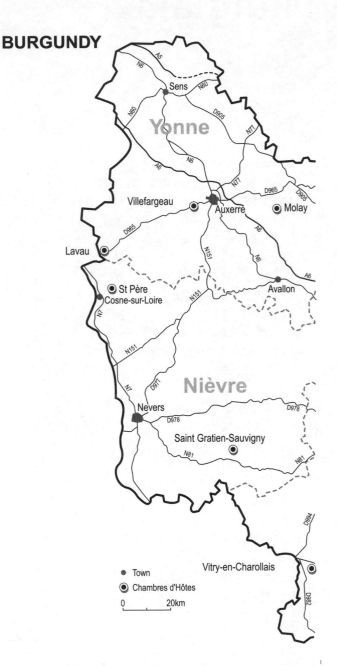

Burgundy

The name suggests good living, good wine, richness, generosity and mellow fruitfulness. Like the Burgundian hills, a rounded dignified quality is implicit – nothing hurried – sleepy villages, slow-flowing water, time-honoured traditions, centuries of history sun-baked in the old roofs and placid squares, and everywhere the cult of the grape.

Viticulture now may be highly scientific – has to be – but the views over those vine-covered hills can't have changed much since Roman times. The Romans knew a thing or two about wine and lost no time in planting the south-facing gravelly slopes with the vines that would keep them well supplied. Names like Vosne-Romanée commemorate their dedication. They found the result greatly to their liking.

As did the monks in the middle ages, who continued the tradition. They created vineyards like Le Clos-de-Vougeot eight centuries ago. Pope Gregory XI accepted thirty barrels from this vineyard and was so impressed that he made the Abbot a Cardinal in recognition of his talents, temporal if not spiritual.

The kings of France preferred Burgundy wine to any in their realm. Madame de Pompadour's favourite tipple was Romanée Conti, while Napoleon preferred Chambertin. By the 18th century the superiority of the wine was recognised throughout the civilised world, new markets opened up abroad, and Beaune became the first trading centre for Burgundy wine, followed by Nuits St. Georges and Dijon.

Today, mercifully recovered from the 19th century ravages of phylloxera, thanks to the clean American vines grafted on to French stock, benefiting from the latest oeneological research, the wines have never been finer, and the opportunity to taste the (often) superb results and to buy some to take home should not be resisted. To drive through unassuming villages with names like Nuits-St.-Georges, Pouilly, Mercurey, Vosne-Romanée is like opening a wine catalogue.

Even without the vines it would be attractive countryside, rolling, wooded, expansive, and dotted with the distinctive white Charolais cattle that for me are as good a sign saying 'You have arrived in Burgundy'. It is threaded with rivers – the Saône, the Seille the Yonne, the Loire – and canals, particularly the Burgundy and the Nivernais, providing plenty of variety for cruising. The tempo of a barge holiday seems exactly right to view this region.

Burgundy's appeal as a tourist area does not stop with its wine. As a medieval and Renaissance art and architecture centre it is unrivalled in France. Since Roman times the duchy has been a crossroads for travellers, who brought their skills and knowledge to Burgundy, and the enlightened dukes of the 15th century encouraged artists and sculptors from Paris and Flanders to live and work here, leaving behind unique examples of their talent. The Romanesque buildings of the 11th and 12th centuries alone would merit a journey – Tournus, Cluny, Paray-le-Monial, La Charité-sur-Loire, and Autun are prime examples, but hundreds of small villages have stunning Romanesque churches as their hearts. Don't miss any opportunity to dive inside and marvel at the length of time that has passed since their builders laboured to affirm their faith.

A century later Vézélay was the beginning of a new look, known as the Burgundy Romanesque school, more elaborate, leading to the Gothic, like Notre Dame in Dijon, and subsequently to the Renaissance classical revival – look at St Michel in the same city.

Burgundy was a bit slow to recognise the potential of the B&B market but it is fast catching up and there is no shortage of choice now. As the two major autoroutes used by holidaying Brits pass through the area, and as it is a comfortable drive back to the ports to catch an afternoon ferry, a lodging here makes good sense. It may only be one night the first time, but it would certainly be a shame not to spend longer and taste more of the delights of the region on the next occasion.

CÔTES D'OR

COUCHEY 21160
14 km N of Nuits-Saint-Georges.
From the A31 (Sortie Dijon Sud) take the D122 A to the N74 south for 3 km. Turn right on to the D122 B to Couchey.
In the heart of the vine-growing valley south of Dijon. Your hosts' vineyards surround the village.

M. & Mme. Brugère
7 rue Jean Jaurès.
category: (M)
tel: 03.80.52.13.05.
fax: 03.80.52.93.20.
B&B: 46.5/54.5€ for two. No Dinner

Drive through the village and you will find No 7 well signed beside the *dégustation Marsannay* of *Domaine des Courtes Charrières*. The 300-year-old house is sideways on to the road in a small courtyard-garden full of roses. Once a *cuverie* where barrels were made, it was bought by the Brugère family thirty years ago. They have maintained all the lovely old features of stone arches, heavy beams, huge fireplaces and meandering rooms. One suite has an independent entry from the road with bedroom and separate luxury bathroom (sunken bath, two wash basins, etc.). There are regency-striped green walls in another room. All have private shower or bath and loo, though not all are adjoining. These sunny rooms all face south-west over the garden and are quite delightful, as is the welcome from a charming hostess. Monsieur, who speaks English and German, will conduct you round his cellars for generous *dégustations* on the spot. Recommended highly. Book well ahead, especially at weekends.

ÉPERNAY-SOUS-GEVREY. 21220 GEVREY CHAMBERTIN.
12 km from A31, exit Nuits St George, 22 km S of Dijon.
From Dijon take the D996, turn right on to the D25 at Corcelles-les-Cîteaux and Epernay is through Savouges in 4km, near the Route du Grand Cru, or from the A31 take *sortie* No. 1 (Nuits St George), then northwards on the N74 to Clos de Vougeot then right on to the D25 and you will find Epernay in 6 km. Ideally situated in fact for visits to all the great wine villages, and Dijon and Beaune. It's a quiet little village, in whose tree-lined square is to be found:

Jules and Jane Plimmer. 'La Vieille Auberge'
4 place des Tilleuls.
category: (M)
tel: 03.80.36.61.76
fax: 03.80.36.64.68.
email: jules@planetb.fr
B&B: 57/93€ for two.

It may have been *vieille* once, but the Plimmers have completely restored the old farmhouse, re-surfaced the crumbling walls, installed new brown shutters, put on a new roof and generally spruced the place up inside and out, so you might be forgiven for thinking it was brand new. Jules hails from Dartmoor and Jane from Folkestone, so those nervous of airing their school French should feel quite at home here, I admire their courage and enterprise – Jane with a young family still manages to look after five rooms, functional, clean, all with bathrooms, one for three has a balcony, two family rooms, in fact you would rarely be turned away out of season as they also have a *gîte* which can be brought into use as guest rooms on occasions.

There are swings, a paddling pool and Plimmer children to play with, so this would make an ideal family holiday. The Plimmers now have a shop of imported quality pine furniture where you can view at leisure. Evening meals no longer available.

VANDENESSE-en-AUXOIS. 21320
19 km NW of Beaune.
A pretty village alongside the Canal de Bourgogne at the foot of the hill village of Châteauneuf-en-Auxois. Only 7 km from the Autoroute du Soleil (A6), *sortie* Pouilly-en-Auxois.

M. & Mme. Jansen-Bourne.
Péniche 'Lady A' Port du Canal
category: (M)
tel: 03.80.49.26.96.
fax: 03.80.49.27.00.
B&B: 48€ for two.
Evening meals 20.8€ each.
Closed 1 Dec. to 31 Jan.

Yes, this is a chambres d'hôtes on a real barge anchored beside the canal. Very popular it is all year round, so you have to be quick off the mark here if you want to book a room. Skiers heading for the Alps use it as a halfway stop even in January.

Trip up the gangplank and you are on a deck of green plastic grass where white tables and chairs among bright flower boxes, invite one to stop at once and enjoy an *apéritif*. The salon/dining room is very comfortable, windows overlook the 'going-on' on the canal and dinner is served here for eight each night. Everyone wants to eat on board, though there are restaurants a few steps away in the village.

Three neat cabins are carpeted, have double or single beds and each an adjoining shower and loo, cupboard space and good sized windows.

Dutch hosts speak all major languages. An intriguing place to stay, but book ahead. Parking on the quayside beside the barge.

NIÈVRE

SAINT-GRATIEN-SAUVIGNY 58340.

44 km SE of Nevers.

Undulating countryside around here, rather like Dorset.

From Nevers take the N81 through Décize, 14 km after Décize fork left on to the D37 to Cercy-la-Tour then the D10 northwards and the farm is signed in 4km.

M. & Mme. Perreau. 'Domaine de la Marquise'
category: (M)
tel: 03.86.50.01.02.
fax: 03.86.50.07.14
B&B: 48€ for two.
Evening meals 16€. each.

Well away from main roads, this is more of a manor house than a farm house, though the small windows on the first floor do perhaps remind one of a converted granary. Guest accommodation takes up all of the first floor, a staircase erupts into the middle of an extensive salon spanning the width of the house. This is a most practical and charming room; settees and arm chairs are grouped around leaving ample space in the middle for tables etc. Hidden behind a wall is a kitchen bar for guests, which even has an electric kettle.

On either side of the salon is an identical suite of two very nicely decorated bedrooms, warmly carpeted, light and airy with dual aspect windows, one with a double bed the other with single beds. A large modern bathroom lies between them, ideal for a family, or friends sharing. The only snag is that the loo is on the landing between the two rooms, in each case. This should have put me off, but somehow the whole set up was so charming, it didn't. Two rooms for a family 73€.

Madame will give you an evening meal if reserved, wine *compris*. The swimming pool in the garden is a bonus.

SAINT PÈRE 58200

2 km from Cosne-sur-Loire by the D14 SP Alligny-Cosne, then signed.

In the *Sancerre, Pouilly-Fumée* and *Côteaux du Giennois* wine districts of the Loire.

M. & Mme. Kandin. 'L'Orée des Vignes'
Croquant.
category: (M)
tel/fax: 03 86 28 12 50.
email: loreedesvignes@
wanadoo.fr
website: www.france-bonjour.
com/Orée-des-vignes
B&B: 45€ for two.
Evening meals 20€ each.

Only 2 km from a busy town, yet perfectly quiet in a country lane. Grandma lived to be 100 in this old farmhouse, now her granddaughter and her husband have given it a new look. Completely renovating five rooms for guests (one on the ground floor), keeping their beamed ceilings and natural stone walls, everywhere pristine clean with luxury new shower rooms and many thoughtful touches like stands for suit cases, the water colours on the walls are painted by Madame. One room has three singles beds.

Step down from the dining room to a sitting area where patio doors open on to a terrace overlooking the garden and fields beyond. Madame is so well organised she both cooks and joins you for evening meals, when meat from a neighbouring farmer, vegetables from the garden are on the menu and local wine is complementary. Children under 12 yrs. 12€

Open all year with central heating. Stay a week and have the seventh night free. Extra bed 17€ . English spoken

SAÔNE-et-LOIRE

POISSON. 71600 Paray-le Monial.
8 km S of Paray-le-Monial by the D34. In the village follow signs to Charolles (D458).

Mme. Edith Dor. 'Château de Martigny'
category: (L)
tel: 03.85.81 53 21.
fax: 03.85.81.59.40.
B&B: 80€ for two.
Evening Meal 32€ each, 128€ (demi-pension for two).
Closed from Nov. to Easter.

Perhaps this one should come with a warning – 'For lovers of amateur theatricals only'. Martigny is more house than château; the situation of the house and pool is superb, with views in all directions. Mme. Dor has filled it with lovely possessions, decorated the bedrooms with perfect taste, and welcomes her friends to share her treasure. She is the kind of lady that naturally assembles friends around her – the sort of gathering that used to be called a salon. Artists, musicians, actors arrive and practise their arts in her theatre, a converted barn. Others guests with varying degrees of expertise are prevailed upon to perform in the lounge after dinner. If it doesn't appeal to you – run a mile!

The choice of room is difficult. All five rooms are spacious and very comfortable, and have extra beds, fresh flowers on arrival, changed at once if Mme. Dor catches them wilting.

The pretty Laura Ashley blue room has a shower, but you might prefer a bath. The *chambre d'honneure* the largest and most impressive, has a bathroom with two! One reader felt this was ridiculous. It wouldn't worry me, provided I don't have to clean them; though I should have thought one would be more fun. *Rubins*, named after the enchanting green and pink ribboned wall paper – the green picked out in the paint-work – has double and single beds. Dinner optional, eaten at one big table, includes wine, but hasn't always come up to expectations, I hear, so for the time being the arrow is withdrawn.

SAINT-MARTIN-du-TARTRE. 71460.
30 km SW of Chalon-sur-Saône. 20 km NW of Taize.

Taizé is a tiny hill village north of Cluny now world-renowned since Brother Roger Schutz started a small ecumenical religious community here in 1940. The community is self-supporting and concentrates its spiritual work on young people. The movement has grown every year and is now known in about twenty countries world-wide. An ultra-modern church has been built and there is hutted accommodation for all who come to join in the worship and companionship. The original tiny village church is still there.

To find Maizeray travel north from Cluny on the D980 for 21 km then right on the D983 for 12 km then right on to the tiny D80.

Mme. Bergeret
Maizeray.
category: (S)
tel: 03.85.49.24.61.
B&B: Rooms 48€ for two.
Evening meals 20.8€
Closed 15 Oct. to 1 Apr.

You would never find this lovely little chambres d'hôtes accidentally, tucked away in the tiny hamlet of Maizeray. The restored farmhouse has a flowery balcony overlooking the small pretty garden. Utterly peaceful, well away from the main roads.

The salon on two levels is just for guests, and up a few steps are two charming countrified guest rooms. Pretty pink flowers or dainty forget-me-nots adorn the walls. Both have baths and separate loos, little baskets of necessities beside the wash basin. Double/single beds with duvets. One room is large enough to take an extra bed for a child, 13.5€. Nothing has been forgotten.

You will love Mme. Bergeret, an artist in her spare time. She does everything to make her guests feel welcome and will cook you an evening meal if you reserve ahead.

A copious breakfast can include eggs, cheese, home-made cakes and jam.

Well worth a detour. Write and tell me if you like it.

VERZÉ 71960
Some of the loveliest Burgundian countryside is to be found in this area, vines in the foreground, views of distant mountains, and a series of old villages with pink stone houses covered in roses.

From the N79 take the 'La Roche Vineuse' exit just west of Macon, leave La Roche Vineuse by the D85 north, signposted Verzé and the château is on the left after Berzé-la-Ville and before Verzé.

Château d'Escolles
Verze

M. & Mme. de Potter. 'Château d'Escolles'.
category: **(M)**
tel: 03.85.33.44.52 or 06.83.36.52.50
fax: 03 85 33 34 80
email: info@gite-escolles.com
website: www.gite-escolles.com
B&B: 60 €. for two.

Carry on past château gates to find an entrance further on the left. The château dates back to the 10th Century, when there were four towers, only one remains. It was completely destroyed and rebuilt in the 16th Century and then left to the mercy of the state until the present owners bought it and are completely restoring it.

The detached stables, with attractive circular windows, have been cleverly reconstructed to incorporate five smart guest rooms on the first floor, luxuriously carpeted and decorated in different colours which are picked up by the towels in bath or shower rooms.

A breakfast room is below, where Madame will serve a copious French breakfast, and will advise on places to visit. There is no other salon, but the grounds with large lawns, well-tended flower beds and a lake, would be a relaxing place to stroll round after a long day in the car. No evening meal. Good restaurants in Berzé-la-Ville.

A further four even larger rooms are being constructed in the adjacent granary. *Accueil* is pleasant and correct. The château is your hosts' private home, but they will be there to meet and greet and at breakfast time. Good English spoken.

LA VINEUSE 71250
9 km north of Cluny and within easy reach of Taizé.

An excellent place to stay for visiting Cluny, just down the main road. The famous old abbey, which was built in the 11th and 12th centuries, was a thriving community until the Revolution when it was systematically destroyed, taking nearly as long to dismantle as it did to build. Now in the ruins is a college for engineers. In 1806 Napoléon decided to revive the National Haras (stud farms) and one was built here of stones recovered from the abbey. The huge stables are a joy to visit. Most of the horses are in loose boxes. There are beautifully groomed riding horses, small Connemara ponies and Arab steeds all looking wonderfully healthy. The riding horses are particularly friendly and seem to enjoy fresh faces.

From Cluny take the D980 SP Montceau-les-Mines, in 5 km left on to the D7 SP St. Bonnet and in 4km right to La Vineuse.

La Vineuse   La Maitresse

Mme. Serres. 'La Maîtresse'.
Le Bourg.
category: (M)
tel: 03 85 59 60 98.
email: serres.chris@wanadoo.fr
B&B: 61€; 76€ for suites for two.
Evening meal 23€
Closed 1 Oct. to Easter.

An establishment which was once the Auberge of this tiny hill village is now a splendid Chambre d'Hôtes with fabulous views of the countryside. The Serres have catered for all tastes when renovating. Guest rooms now occupy one end of the building. All have courtesy fridges and TV, and well equipped bath or shower rooms, tea making facilities, and hair dryers etc. One on the ground floor has a private kitchenette and patio. Two on the first floor 'Vineuse I and II' are suites for three or four with a mezzanine salon. Two smaller rooms for two, are just as comfortable. There is a fully functional kitchen downstairs for all guests so you have the option of self-catering during the week; or trying local restaurants. At the weekend Madame offers evening meals in her large dining/salon where there are comfortable chairs in front of a log fire for winter guests. The terraced garden has a swimming pool surrounded by plentiful white loungers, a suntrap where you can enjoy the view between swims. Games and swings to share with the family children. Usefully, there is a public carte-telephone just outside the gates. All rooms are 'no smoking'. Weekend evening meals if reserved. Some English spoken.

A warm welcome, a relaxed friendly atmosphere and so many amenities here, I longed to stay on and on. I did break my rule and stayed two nights!

VITRY-en-CHAROLLAIS. 71600.
3 km W of Paray-la-Mondial.

Paray-le-Monial has become one of the great centres of Christianity, the home of the communities of many religious orders. In 1873, 30,000 people made the first pilgrimage to the town and dedicated France to the Sacred Heart, a policy advocated by sister Margaret-Mary, a 17th-century nun, who received many visitations here. A vow was made in 1870 to build a church dedicated to the Sacred Heart – the realisation can now be seen by visitors to Paris on the hill in Montmartre. In Paray the lofty Basilique du Sacré-Coeur stands on the right bank of the river Bourbince, approached by a promenade lined with weeping willows. Pope John Paul made a pilgrimage to the Basilique in 1986.

From the N79 just west of Paray-le-Monial take the D479 to Vitry-en-

Charollais and the chambres d'hôtes is well signed from the village For comfortable rooms in a farm house look no further than:

☆ **M. & Mme. Merle. 'Les Bruyères'**
category: (S)
tel: 03.85.81.10.79.
B&B: 38.5€ for two.
Evening meals 14.5€ each.

On a farm breeding cattle for beef the little farmhouse is hemmed in by barns. Two hundred years old, the dining room was once the granary, well beamed with natural stone walls. Breakfast and evening meals are taken at the long scrubbed table looking out through the French windows. Two lightly beamed and prettily decorated rooms for four, with double bed and bunks, have access to small lawned gardens. Carpets stretched into the shower rooms. I liked our green room best, with the appropriate spray of flowers painted on the door. There is a small sitting room for guests just off the dining room. Flights of stairs lead to other rooms, all differently decorated, including a salmon-coloured family room for four, single beds not bunks in this one, and it even has its own sitting area on the landing, at 52.5€. for four it is excellent value. A fifth room downstairs is smaller and has a tiled floor.

Simple evening meals of their organic farm produce with wine *compris* are served by Madame who with Monsieur join their guests for the cheese course. Monsieur Merle enjoys a good chat after a heavy day on the farm. You will be made most welcome here. An ☆ for all round value.

YONNE

LAVAU 89170
8 km SW of St. Fargeau by D965. 52 km SW of Auxerre by the D 965.
Wooded countryside, flattish, peppered with lakes, un-touristy.

☆ **Mme. Marty. 'La Chasseuserie'**
category: (S)
tel: 03.86.74.16.09.
B&B: 44.5€ for two (first night),
38.5€ (second night). No Dinner
Closed Christmas and New Year.

Take the Bléneu road, D74 for 3 km out of the village. Then well signed.
   One of those cottages one dreams about, tucked away in the countryside. I liked this one immediately. Perhaps it is the welcome of nice Mme. Marty (who speaks English) or the sight of the sparkling new swimming pool on a very hot day after a long car drive, or the peace of the garden, or the well-furnished rooms, each with bath. Or perhaps the knowledge that we were getting a bargain in an upmarket room, reduced if we stayed a second night. It would be tempting to do so, either to enjoy the pool or to appreciate the log fire in winter.
   ☆ on all counts. Patricia found this one first and I loved it too.

MOLAY 89310
Close to Noyers, a lovely old town, 18 km SE of Chablis.

From the A6. SE of Auxerre take the Nitry. exit then the D944 north SP Tonnerre, turn right in 5.5 km on to the D956 and first left SP Molay, you will arrive in Arton on the way.

☆ **M. & Mme. Collin, 'La Calounier',**
5 rue de la Fontaine, Arton.
category: (M)
tel/fax: 03 86 82 67 81. or 06 85 84
21 67:
email: info@lecalounier.fr
website: www.lecalounier.fr
B&B: 51 € for two.
Evening meal 19€ each.

Pictures of this old farmhouse, hidden in the hamlet of Arton outside Molay, give no indication of how well it has been restored. The entrance from the courtyard is through huge patio doors to a dining area where pictures from local artists liven up the natural stone walls. Above is a cheerful salon with plentiful books and games for inclement weather.

All rooms are tastefully furnished and have very well-equipped showers or bathrooms. '*Hortensia*', a fresh green and yellow ground floor room with twin beds, is suitable for the less able. Above '*Soleil*' is a double in golden yellow. '*Potiron*', for four' has a double bed on the mezzanine and stacker beds below by the bathroom. A small room on the second floor with velux windows has its own bath and loo behind a screen. Cross the courtyard to '*Abeilles*', a family suite of two rooms in an older wing of the house where there is a private salon on the ground floor and it is possible to accommodate five people; but offered to just two for a long stay.

Evening meals cooked by Madame, a dedicated cook, should not be missed, drinks are not included in the price, the local wine is Chablis.

An attractive circular stone seat surrounds the patio and soon, a swimming pool is a distinct possibility. Bicycles are included in the price; but absolutely NO smoking. Extra bed 17€ Good English spoken.

VILLEFARGEAU. 89240.
6 km W of Auxerre. From the A6 exit Auxerre (Nord), take the N6 (SP Auxerre) and in about 1 km turn right on to the D158 (SP Perigny & St.Georges-sur-Boulche). At a major crossroads turn right on to the D89 and in 2 km fork left on to the D22 (SP Les Bruyères). The chambres d'hôtes is on the right as you enter the hamlet.

M. & Mme. Jouillié. 'Le Petit Manoir des Bruyères'
Allée de Charbuy.
category: (L)
tel: 03.86.41.32.82.
fax: 03.86.41.28.57.
email: infos@petit-manoir-bruyeres.com
B&B: 96/128/160/192€ for two.
Evening meals 40€ each.

This house in one hectare of fragrant garden was once a factory but over the last 35 years it has been completely restored. The ivy-covered exterior, with Burgundian tiled roof, doesn't really prepare one for the luxurious interior. Friezes of dark wood carvings of grapes adorn the stair wells. The Italian-style loo on the landing with ornate pillars and painting on the walls is only a taste of things to come.

Tread the thick pile carpet into bedroom number 1, a replica of one slept in by Madame de la Vallière in the 17th century; it has fabric-padded walls matching the *baldaquin*. The ceiling is studded with tiny sunflowers set in squares, with larger ones at every corner in memory of the Sun King. Step into the luxury blue bathroom where fleecy towels and robes await you, gold-tapped bath and basin, all complemented by pillared corners. It is almost a relief to cross the thickly carpeted corridor to Madame Maintenant's room, the smallest room, with dark green *ciel de lit* and a small bathroom where the shower rains down on one between the basin and the loo. Does it really work in practice? The *pièce-de-résistance* is room three, *Montespan*, which stretches across the house, comprising a sleeping area decorated in deep salmon pink with a gold and white circular inset carved ceiling and a salon of pure Versailles. Portraits of Molière, Boileau, La Fontaine and Racine look down from the architraves while pillars of angels playing various musical instruments support the corners, a centre round table with 18th century chairs and a mantelpiece adorned with a collection of 80-odd china cats, and from all this a door leads to a bathroom where panels of cloudy blue sky beam down on you in the bath. 160€ buys this one!

A fourth room, *Sevigné*, has been added since my last visit, equally luxurious, with king-sized bed, a Louis XIV fireplace and a Chinese style bathroom with gold and ivory taps.

If you are wondering about your hosts by now, they are not a bit ostentatious, absolutely charming. Monsieur speaks English well and Madame is a cookery writer who will produce a *gastronomique* evening meal, if reserved, wine not *compris* but of excellent quality, produced from their vast cellars, partaken with your hosts at the very long dining room table, or in solitude if preferred. Breakfast is also copious – English, French, everything offered – I doubt you will need an evening meal, certainly not lunch.

Monsieur will take you mushroom-gathering in their woods where there are many varieties. For rainy days there is a vast salon under the eaves without windows where on long couches you can relax watching television or videos in all languages, browse through their library or play chess. On fine days wander round the garden and indulge yourself eating delicious red cherries straight from the tree in season.

Though the decoration of the rooms was very much over the top, the comfort was, too, and I enjoyed the company of the Jouilliés the longer I stayed with them. Prices are high; but not compared with hotel prices in the UK when you include the luxuries and the exceptionally friendly *accueil* which, after all, is 90% of a good chambres d'hôtes.

Champagne-Ardennes

CHAMPAGNE / ARDENNE

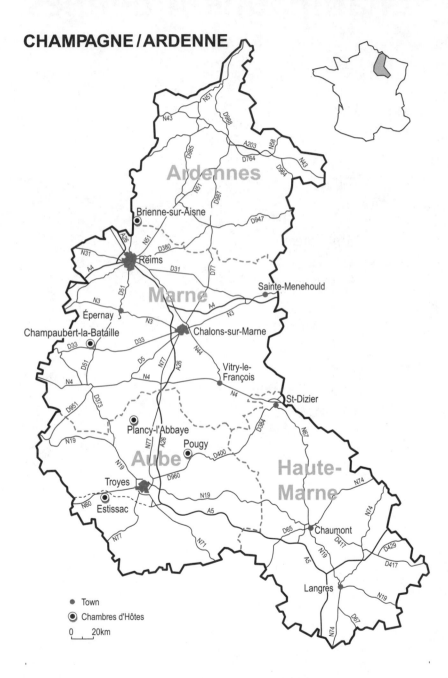

Ardennes

Brienne-sur-Aisne

Reims

Marne

Sainte-Menehould

Épernay

Champaubert-la-Bataille

Chalons-sur-Marne

Vitry-le-François

St-Dizier

Plancy-l'Abbaye

Pougy

Aube

Troyes

Estissac

Haute-Marne

Chaumont

Langres

- Town
- Chambres d'Hôtes

0   20km

Champagne-Ardennes

Companion French Entrée *guide to:* Champagne-Ardennes.

Champagne is a unique area, visited by thousands of tourists every year, principally to sample its famous eponymous product. Although grapes are grown throughout the area, the champagne industry centres on Epernay in the **Marne** *département*. A visit to the world-renowned cellars here is a must for any itinerary in the area but I would not devote more than a couple of days to the town, which is otherwise without interest. Reims is much more rewarding, with its glorious cathedral, and some memorable restaurants, thanks to the patronage of the wealthy champagne-growers. Accessible both by Autoroute or Nationale, there has been a settlement in Reims for over two thousand years. In 496 St. Remi, the Gallic evangelist, converted and baptised King Clovis the Frank, along with 3000 of his warriors.

Building commenced on the twin-towered Gothic cathedral Notre Dame, in the centre of the town, in 1211. All but two of the kings of France were crowned here. Stand back from the western door and gaze up at the delicately sculptured facade; so many figures, but try to pick out the smiling angel. Stroll round to the east side to get a good view of the magnificent flying buttresses. Badly damaged in the First World War, it has been sympathetically restored.

Surprisingly, inside the cathedral seems almost plain until you turn round and your eyes light on the two beautiful rose windows above the west doors, separated by the nine windows of the Triforium. With blue predominating, the great rose window is dedicated to Our Lady, the smaller one, to her Litanies. The rich blue of these windows is picked up again in some more modern stained glass windows in the transept where the champagne window depicts the art of wine making. In 1429 Joan of Arc persuaded the Dauphin to 'receive a worthy crown' here, becoming Charles VII. In the side chapel of the Virgin Mary, Pope John Paul knelt at prayer when he visited in 1996.

Spare time to visit the Basilica of St. Remi in the oldest part of the town, well signed all the way. Small gardens of common herbs surround the outside of the building. St. Remi, born in 438 AD became Bishop of Reims in 460 and died in 533, aged 96. His magnificent tomb lies behind the high altar. An enormous candelabra with 96 candles (signifying his age) hangs from the new rafters in the nave, placed there after a fire destroyed the roof several years ago. Quietly contrasting with the cathedral, this basilica has more of the feel of a parish church, in spite of the long echoing aisles and high vaulted ceiling. A tablet on the north wall, close to the west door records the nobility buried nearby.

There are many caves under the city, where the champagne is stored, so much part of this city's every day life. But I didn't notice a single jackdaw!

The Marne is a mighty river, which ought to be more picturesque than it turns out to be. Little capitalisation, other than that of industry, has been made of its green and pleasant banks.

Much the most appealing *département* scenically is the **Ardennes**, with a capital, Charleville-Mézières, that deserves to be better known. A truly delightful town, with vast central market square bordered by delightful old buildings. This territory has been fought over and on for many generations and has affiliations way beyond its borders. The Ardennes spills over into Belgium and so do the principal rivers, the Meuse and the Semoy, carrying picturesque barges throughout the watery Northern European network. If you are looking for an inexpensive, away-from-it-all, scenically attractive holiday you should certainly consider the Ardennes, but I fear that chambres d'hôtes are few and far between. Any discoveries would be particular good to know about.

ARDENNES

BRIENNE-sur-AISNE 08190.
20 km N of Reims.

Follow the river Aisne along the N925 from Soissons through quiet little villages to Neufchâtel where the D366 from Reims joins the D925 and round a bend is the small village of Brienne-sur-Aisne.

M. & Mme. Leriche.
category: (S)
tel/Fax: 03.24.72.94.25.
B&B: 36.5/40€ for two. No Dinner

A warm welcome at this restful farmhouse on the far fringe of the village. Three rooms full of character are on the first floor of the adjoining building; two have sitting rooms and beds on the mezzanine above, accommodating a family of five. So many amenities: indoor games for children, bikes for hire, a washing machine for 1.6€, a pleasant garden and country views from the windows. No evening meals but a shared well-equipped kitchen with microwave (2.4€ extra per day). Very useful if you don't want the expense of eating out; but there is an excellent restaurant 'A la Bonne Volonté' at the other end of the village (1 km away). We ate well there; menus from 14.5€ and wine *en carafe*. Most attentive service.

The Leriche's young son has made an interesting museum of fragments of shells, cooking utensils, etc, remnants of the First World War found in the surrounding battlefields.

AUBE

ESTISSAC. 10190.
22 km W of Troyes.

An excellent stop for visiting Troyes or even Chaource where the cheese is made and the church has a remarkably life-like *'Mis en Tombeau'*. Look for it down a few dark steps left of the high altar, well worth seeing.

Exit 19 on the A5 from Paris. From Calais on the A26 to Troyes then the A5 towards Paris, exit 20. The chambres d'hôtes is 10 km from the autoroute. Take the N60 to the town then the D23, past the Credit Agricole then first right for 1km.

M. & Mme. Mesley. 'Moulin d'Eguebaude'
category: (M)
tel: 03.25.40.42.18.
fax: 03.25.40.40.92.
B&B: 57.5€ for two.
Evening meal 18.5€ each.

Forty years ago this mill was a complete ruin on the river Vanne. The Mesley's have built it up into a thriving trout and salmon farm. They now have a fine display of goodies in a large shop on the ground floor, where a glass panel in the floor allows one to observe the fish swimming past.

On the first floor is a very large salon used for groups but guests in the chambres d'hôtes rooms dine at one table with their hosts. Monsieur is the chef and is a master at cooking fish. *Menus-Auboise*s are recommended. Comfortable couches form a sitting area for guests, overlooking the river and the grounds.

Five warm rooms on the second floor with dormer windows have private baths and bidets. Even a sauna on the corridor. An interesting place with refined *accueil*.

Plenty of room for children to play, swings etc in the park. Parking for guests is by the house. The larger car park is for shoppers and anglers.

PLANCY l'ABBAYE 10380.
37 km N of Troyes. Exit from autoroute A26 at Arcis-sur-Aube, then N for 1.5 km on the N77, turn left on to the D56 for 13 km, then left into the village.

Plancy is a pleasant, sleepy village grown up around a large, open square, centring on an old, iron bandstand. Tourists rarely venture in this direction, as prices indicate. On one side of the square is the long apricot-painted facade of an old presbytery. Looks good but not half as good as from the garden side.

☆ **Mme. Patricia Misswald**
1. Place du Maréchal Foch.
category: (M)
tel: 03.25.37.44.71.
B&B: 56€ for two (first night), 48€ (thereafter). No Dinner

A secret garden, squares of shady lawns interspersed with paths and flower beds run down to the bank of the river Aube. There are tables dotted about the lawns and on a little terrace at the water's edge. Willows dip into the river, fast-flowing here because of the defunct lock gates which funnel the stream. A shady public walk on the opposite bank. The house, facing south, presents a sunny honey-coloured aspect, grey shutters enclosing deep windows, mellow old roof tiles. All quite serene. At present there are three guest rooms, each with bath or shower and loo. Two, approached by an outside staircase, face the village square – one of these comprises a suite for a family – but my favourite room is at the other end of the house. It has two large windows overlooking the garden and river, a rich red carpet complemented by a white bedspread and *toile de Jouy* headboard, an original fire place and lovely Louis XVI furniture, TV thrown in and a very large shower/dressing room. A room you could stay in for ever. Outstanding value. There is a full kitchen available for guest's use as is the elegant salon. Mme. Misswald is utterly charming but has now handed over the running of the chambres d'hôtes to her delightful daughter, who is waiting to open the huge gates to the spacious parking as soon as you arrive.

A ☆ for lovely house, kind hostesses, superb position, good value.

POUGY. 10240.
120 km S of Reims. 25 km NE of Troyes. 15 km from the A26 exit Arcis-sur-Aube, then the D 441 east for 20 km.
This small village is close to Longsols where there is the oldest wooden church in France. Water sports on the Lake Aube and the Reservoire Seine-et-Marne are nearby. Brienne-le-Château, where Napoleon went to school is just down the road. A good halfway stop between Calais and the Mediterranean.

M. Antoine Morlet. 'Château de Pougy'
Grand Rue
category: (M)
tel: 03.25.37.09.41.
fax: 03.25.37.87.29.
B&B: 40€ for two
Evening meals 14.5€ each.

This is a well-maintained 18th-century château. As you enter the gates there are neat parking bays on either side of the circular lawn. A shady hectare of lawns and trees surrounds the property.

In the same family since the Revolution, it has now been handed down to young M. Morlet, but his parents help out on occasions. His mother still cooks the evening meals, with specialities of the region. The rooms, with modernised facilities, are furnished in their original style, using good quality family furniture.

When I visited it was full of wedding guests. Large rooms have high ceilings, fireplaces, and oak floors. A pretty green room has a vestibule and a large shower room, a blue one has a bath and double bed. A family suite with bunks in a side room, shares a bathroom. Two smaller rooms in another wing of the château, can be a private suite, one very pink, both have showers. Quickly opening doors to showers and bathrooms I was brought up short by finding in one room not an expected cupboard but a minute chapel with a lovely statue of the Virgin Mary backed by a blue window with a small prie-dieu in front.

A pleasant salon is on the first floor with semi-circular windows overlooking the garden. The dining room is downstairs, where at separate tables breakfast and evening meals are served by Monsieur, who speaks some English. All excellent value.

MARNE
CHAMPAUBERT-la-BATAILLE. 51270
46km W of Châlons-sur-Marne.

This area was in the thick of the German retreat during World War II. The D51 is known as the *'Route des Quatre Victoires'*
   Signed at the crossroads of the D51 and the D33, on the right towards Paris opposite a silo.

M. & Mme. Legret.
category: (S)
tel: 03.26.52.80.22.
fax: 03.26.52.06.26.
B&B: 33.5€. for two
Evening meals 11/13.5€ each.

You won't be tearing round country lanes looking for this farm, it is so easy to find on the main road. The house is modern on this 100 hectares farm. Situated on the plain, just outside the village. If you want to arrive with full camping gear you have the advantage of being able to park in one of the large locked barns.

   Pristine rooms on the first floor have all modern amenities, including mini-baths. All are simply, but adequately furnished, one with natural wood floor, one with carpet with a double bed and another with two small single beds. The salon/dining room has good views over the plain and a fine terrace for sunny days.

   An evening meal is offered using products of the farm. Wine is not *compris* as champagne is the only wine produced in the area.

   Rooms are extremely good value, and I strongly recommend a stay here with pleasant farming hosts.

Franche-Comté

FRANCHE-COMTE

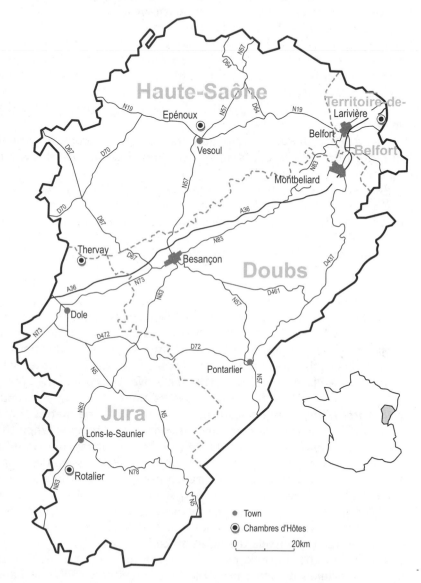

Haute-Saône

Epénoux

Vesoul

Territoire-de-

Larivière

Belfort

Belfort

Montbeliard

Thervay

Besançon

Doubs

Dole

Pontarlier

Jura

Lons-le-Saunier

Rotalier

● Town
◉ Chambres d'Hôtes
0   20km

Franche-Comté

A region lying east of Burgundy, nestling against the Swiss border. There are four départements, Haute-Saône and Territoire-de-Belfort to the north, Doubs in the east and Jura in the south-west.

Haute-Saône is low agricultural land and not quite so interesting as the other *départements* though it is trying to promote itself as a holiday area and many lakes and holiday sites have been constructed. Vesoul, the *préfecture*, lies at the foot of La Motte, a hill dominating the valley of the Durgeon. So damp was this valley that it was only in 1854 that the church of Notre-Dame was built on top of the hill in thanks to God for ridding the town of cholera.

A very small part of Haute-Saône, bordering Burgundy, produces wine at Champlitte from mostly Chardonnay and Pinot Noir grapes, the white being the most renowned.

In the north at Fougerolles is the centre of the wild cherry growing, the source of *Les Griottines*, cherries soaked in kirsch and eau-de-vie.

Territoire-de-Belfort is one of the smallest *départements* of France. It lies in the north-east of the region, bordering on Alsace. Fairly flat farming land surrounds the industrial *préfecture* of Belfort, famous for railway engineering.

Doubs is altogether a different, more sophisticated *département*, having the old Roman town of Besançon as its *préfecture*, well worth visiting with large bridges spanning the surrounding river Doubs. Park in the large shady car park by the Pont de Brégille and you will be within walking distance of the fascinating old town. In the square Castan are the remains of an old Roman theatre among trees. Victor Hugo was born close by in what is now the Place Victor Hugo, a plaque is over the door of the house. Going up to the cathedral the road passes under the lovely second-century *Porte-Noire;* and then leads up to the Citadelle, 118 metres above the town of Besançon. In Roman times it contained a temple. When the Spaniards conquered this part of France they built a fortress here in 1688 and the French went on building when they regained possession. It has been a state prison, a barracks for officers and cadets in the time of Louis XIV, and a place of execution for many patriots shot during the Second World War. Now it is owned by the city of Besançon and is a leisure and cultural centre, with zoo and aquarium. Good parking and a large restaurant at the top outside the ticket office.

Jura, by far the best known by name of all Franche-Comté *départements*, takes its name from the mountains between France and Switzerland. The wine produced along the Burgundy border is well known in France, but not a lot is exported.

The countryside varies from vineyards on the western slopes to high plains and thickly wooded mountains in the east. Some of the tallest trees in Europe are on the slopes of the Jura mountains.

Lons-le-Saunier in the south of the *département* is the *préfecture*, a pleasant town with a dominant railway station. A quiet drive through this region makes a pleasant change when heading for the Rhône Valley.

JURA

ROTALIER 39190.
12 km S of Lons-le-Saunier.
Follow the N83 and in 11 km turn left to Rotalier. The château is well signed.

M. & Mme. De Boissieu. 'Château Grea'
category: (M-L)
tel: 03.84.25.05.07.
B&B: 76.5€ for two.
Evening meals 15/18.5€.

In the same family since 1758, more a family house than a château, it is situated on a hill surrounded by vineyards. A large sheltered courtyard leads to the front door where you will have a very warm welcome from Mme. De Boissieu. This is a homely 'L' shaped château with the comfortable salon leading to a terrace.

On the first floor is a large comfortable bedroom with good views; it has a correspondingly large bathroom with bath to wallow in, adjoining a room with bunks for children, all so light and airy. The second bedroom on a floor above is smaller but very prettily decorated in pink, a double bed and shower goes with this one. Madame will provide a light meal on your first night, but afterwards you have the use of a complete kitchen leading to a terrace. Breakfast is in the adjacent dining room. A really comfortable family home here.

THERVAY. 39290.

48 km SE of Dijon

Only a few kilometres below the old hill village of Pesmes, perched on a hill overlooking the valley of the River Ognon.

Take the D 475 north from Dole. In 16 km turn right at the cross-roads to Thervay. The chambres d'hôtes is the first house on the left before the village.

M. & Mme. Poncelin. 'La Raye'
category: (S)
tel: 03.84.70.20.04.
B&B: 35€ for two. No Dinner
Closed 1 Oct. to Easter.

All-weather accommodation here, inside the extensively railed garden reposes a house basking in sunshine, with central heating in all rooms.

Mme. Poncelin will welcome you with tea in the guest salon in front of a log fire. You can see I visited in winter! Her two rooms decorated in blue or red, with the obligatory antique wardrobe, have polished wood floors and are complemented by smart new shower rooms with excellent lighting and large fluffy white towels.

M. Poncelin works for the post office, but maintains a large *potager*. There is ample parking behind the house.

The peaceful country outlook is little disturbed by passing traffic. With a copious breakfast of cereal, fruit, yoghurt, a variety of breads and the attention of your hostess you will want to stay many days.

No evening meals but there are restaurants in Pesmes. The Logis is probably the best.

HAUTE-SAÔNE

ÉPENOUX-PUSY. 70000.
4km N of Vesoul.
As you enter the village of Épenoux from Vesoul, the château is on the left.

☆ **Mme. Gautier. 'Château d'Épenoux'**
Route de Saint-Loup.
category: (L)
tel: 03.84.75.19.60.
fax: 03.84.76.45.05.
B&B: 72€ for two. No Dinner

'Mme. Gautier's small château was another charming surprise. Madame served us an elegant dinner and breakfast with artistry and charm. A winner.' E. Metters. This more than compensates for the lack of other chambres d'hôtes in the department. The compact little château is situated in 3 hectares of parkland where the oldest weeping beech tree in Europe makes a tent on the lawn. The four guest rooms are charming, with polished wood floors, central heating, marble fireplaces, pretty drapes, some *ciel des lits,* and huge, carpeted, modernised bathrooms. On the second floor is a suite of two rooms for a family. On the way up you will pass a very old etching of Paris in the 19th century, spanning the wall.

A lounge, furnished with antiques but with comfortable modern armchairs, is a delightful place to meet your fellow guests before dining together. Madame does all the cooking.

A tiny chapel stands in the front garden; it even has a small balcony (perhaps for the servants?) and an old dalmatic hanging by the altar. The château was once used as a leave centre for army officers serving abroad.

☆ for good value.

TERRITOIRE-de-BELFORT

LARIVIÈRE. 90150.
12 km from Belfort

Not a lot of chambres d'hôtes within easy access of Colmar and the Vosges mountains. So I was particularly pleased to find this one. Easy to spot in the village right beside the church.

M. & Mme. Ligier.
4, rue du Margrabant.
category: (M)
tel: 03.84.23.80.46.
B&B: 41€ for two. No Dinner

A truly charming flower-bedecked house immaculately kept, in a neat garden, with parking. M. Ligier teaches German and speaks a little English.

The two guest rooms, for two or three, are both thickly carpeted, as are their private bathrooms. It is well worth a detour to stay here. No evening meals but restaurants in the vicinity and rooms are very reasonably priced, with extra beds 8€. Book well ahead, to avoid disappointment. Even a swimming pool now, I hear.

Languedoc-Roussillon

LANGUEDOC-ROUSSILON

- Town
 Chambres d'Hôtes
0 _____ 20km

Languedoc-Roussillon

The Mediterranean coastline of this region extends along roughly 175 km of seashore stretching from the Spanish border almost to the Camargue at the mouth of the Rhône. The name of the region signifies the north/south division of France in earlier times, when 'Yes' in the north was 'Oui' but in the South-West the word 'Oc' was used, hence 'langue d'Oc,' a language still understood today by about ten million people in the region.

In the **Pyrénées Orientales**, the most southerly *département*, the Catalan influence is very noticeable. Sovereignty passed from France to Spain and back again regularly for centuries, and although the southern part of the region is now firmly in France, most of the native inhabitants think of themselves as Catalan first and French second. Here at the eastern end of the chain of mountains which separates France and Spain was the escape route for many Allied servicemen during the Second World War. The *Pic du Canigou* (2784 metres) dominates this area. The first bonfires to celebrate the feast of St. John the Baptist (Midsummer's Day, 24 June) are lit at the top, attended by notabilities from both sides of the frontier. Although the peak is covered in snow for most of the year, the flora and fauna are still magnificent in the gorges and pine forests on the lower slopes, and as early as March the hillsides are yellow with mimosa.

Perpignan is the county town of this mainly agricultural *département*. The earliest cherries come from this area, and it is a great centre for tourism, with sandy beaches and camp sites by the coast stretching to the Spanish border.

Boulou is now bypassed by the autoroute to Spain. The N116 runs along the R Tet to Prades, and climbs to Font-Romeu. Close by, at Odeillo, the sunniest place in France, is the world's most powerful solar furnace, with concave mirrors collecting the sun's rays. Just south of Font-Romeu is the tiny Spanish enclave of Llivia, about a kilometre from the Spanish border and totally surrounded by France. Close by is the border town of Bourg-Madame where the road begins the long climb up into Andorra.

Aude, a *département* further north, contains the hot dry lands of the *Corbières*, whose wine, once despised as supermarket plonk, is vastly improved thanks to American and Australian technology and investment. This was the heart of the Cathar region.

Carcassonne, the *préfecture,* in the north of Aude is two separate towns really, with the *Cité* a fairy-tale fort (albeit a clever 19th century reconstruction) on top of a hill, overlooking the newer town which itself dates from the Middle ages. West of Carcassonne is Castelnaudary, famous for its *cassoulet*, a pork and bean casserole.

l'Hérault, to the north-east of the region, is pure wine country; there are few ordinary farmsteads, just vineyards. Names such as *Minervois* spring to mind. The *Canal du Midi* is a feature of this *département*. Starting at Toulouse, it runs for 240 km to the *Bassin-de-Thau* at Sète. Montpellier, the *préfecture*, is a large and prosperous town, which has spread considerably in the last few years, a mixture of old and smart modern buildings. The town of Agde, founded by the Greeks and given the name of 'Agatha' is an impressive town, but the beaches near Cap d'Agde have become a boring conglomeration of characterless holiday flats and complexes, crowded in summer and deserted out of season.

Yet further north is the department of **Gard**, rich in Roman history; the arena at Nîmes, the *préfecture*, is one of the best-preserved in Europe. Nîmes was colonised in about 40 BC as it lay on the *Via Domitia* – the main route from Rome to Spain – 1480 km of road used by merchants and the Roman legions, so of course it was fortified along its length. The name derives from the Roman god 'Nemesus' (the god of rivers and fountains). In the 16th century Nîmes was a Protestant stronghold, having come under the influence of the Huguenots who came down from the Cévennes. It was consequently right in the centre of the religious wars which followed the revocation of the Edict of Nantes by Louis XIV in 1685. The word 'denim' originated here, as the material comes from the fabric *Serge-de-Nîmes*.

There are interesting geographical phenomena to visit in the north-west, such as the *Grotte-des-Demoiselles*, where a funicular train takes you into the mountain, and the curious *Cirque-de-Navacelles*, where the river winds so much that it leaves one bank high and dry, best seen from the hill top.

Further north in the region is the **Lozère**, a very different terrain, with the sweeping, massive hills better known as the Cévennes. Wave after wave of these chestnut-covered hills fade away into the sunset. It is the poorest department of France, but not in scenery. Robert Louis Stevenson tramped its hills and valleys with his donkey. In the south the *Corniche des Cévennes* runs from St. Jean du Gard to Florac, and the entrance of the famous Gorges-du-Tarn. Further north the N 106 winds its way between the *causses*, eventually reaching Mende, the *préfecture*, a compact little town encircled by a charming boulevard, sheltered by the *causse* (high plain) on one side, and skirted by the river Lot on the other; the cathedral and shopping area are tucked firmly in the middle. Even the industrial area, now an inevitable addition to all French towns, lies discreetly on the other side of the river.

AUDE

CONHILAC-de-la-MONTAGNE. 11190.

35 km S of Carcassonne. 12 km S of Limoux.

Here you will find hilly open countryside with scattered hamlets on the approach to the Pyrénées.

Leave Limoux by the D118 southwards, in about 2 km turn right on to the D121 towards Magrie, follow the signs to Roquetaillade on the D421 and continue through this village, forking right to Conhilac. The house is on the right at the far end of the hamlet.

Mr. & Mrs. Williams. 'Les Genêts'
Chemin du Pla de la Lano.
category: (S)
tel/fax: 04.68.31.45.82.
B&B: 40/46.5€ for two.
Evening meal 16€ each (incl. wine, reservation only)

The Williams's moved here from Manchester some five years ago and found this modern bungalow high up in the mountains with a fabulous view of the Pyrénées from the *Pic du Canigou* to the peaks of Andorra. The tiny hamlet has no shops and few houses, but is only 15 minutes from Limoux and very central for all the Cathar châteaux. Gwyn is Welsh, a retired PE teacher and Martine is French. Their three guest rooms have white furniture with flower transfers to match the names of the rooms. 'Rose' has a double bed and French windows to a private terrace behind the house but shares a bathroom with your hosts – (guests have priority).

'Sweet Pea' with two singles and 'Glycine' with a double bed have wash basins and showers but share a loo on the landing.

The terrace, where you can indulge in al fresco meals early in the year overlooks the vineyards. Evening meals, if reserved, will be well above average and they include all drinks. Picnics provided too. A reduction after three days.

Your hosts will often join you for walks or excursions. You will be entertained as part of the family sharing their salon. The advantage of English and French spoken here. An ideal place for a lone traveller.

CUCUGNAN 11350.

Closed 1 Jan. to 15 Feb. and 1 Jul. to 28 Jul. and 1 Oct. to 28 Oct. 60 km SE of Carcassonne, 38 km NW of Perpignan

An attractive hill village between two famous Cathar châteaux, Quéribus and Peyrepertuse. An ideal spot to stay if you want to explore both these châteaux.

M. & Mme. Verheven 'L'Amandière'
3, Chemin de la Chapelle.
category: (M)
tel: 04.68.45.43.42.
B&B: 43€ for two.
Closed Jan. and 13 Jun. to 12 Jul. and
20 Sept. to 24 Oct.

Your genteel Belgian hosts, now retired, have lived in this hill village for many years. They have a small vineyard in the garden of their modern hillside villa. Two rooms on the ground floor have their own terraces and private shower rooms. There is fresh green-painted furniture in the one for three. An upstairs room in the main house has a bath but the private loo is downstairs. No need for evening meals to be offered, you have a choice of two restaurants in the village up a few steps through alleyways to either the Logis or the 'Auberge-de-Cucugnan' both serving regional dishes at correct prices and local wine in *pichets*. Note closing dates.

MONTMAUR. 11320.
42 km SE of Toulouse. 50 km NW of Carcassonne.

A small village, with a château and interesting local history, within easy distance of the village of Montlieu, north-west of Carcassonne. now an interesting centre for old books; specialist book shops have cropped up in every street.

From Montmaur drive down towards the D43 and La Castagne is signed on your left.

Le Castagne

Gerda & Willy Vanderzeypen. 'La Castagne'
category: (M)
tel: 04.68.60.00.40.
B&B: 44.5€ for two.
Gîtes 320/480€ per week.
Evening meals 19€ each.

A change of ownership here – the Martins retired in November 1998. You will be welcomed into this beautifully restored farmhouse, part of which was once a guard-house for the château, by the new Belgian owners. Not a lot of changes have been made. Guest rooms are much the same, one in the main house and one in the ground floor annexe, both with shower rooms, Little niceties like wine and chocolate have appeared in the rooms.

The galleried landing looks down on a very comfortable salon with a large fireplace, where now, instead of regular cooking classes, you can improve your bridge under the tuition of Willy, an international player, or just relax with an *apéritif* before dinner, prepared by your hosts, which I am sure will be a feast. Breakfast is so copious, you will need no lunch. The blue swimming pool is still enticing and the fields around where horses graze offer plenty of space for children. Bikes supplied, riding lessons and countless outings can be arranged.

Fluent French, English, German and Dutch spoken. Sometimes with change of ownership chambres d'hôtes deteriorate, but this one being less specialised, has gone from strength to strength. Great value for money. Two gîtes beside the pool, are let by the week.

PALAJA. 11570.
5 km S of Carcassonne, close to the entrancing Vieille Cité, which is a clever reconstruction of the original.

There is a delightful legend that Carcassonne owes its name to a foreign princess, Dame Carcas, who held the fortified city against the armies of Charlemagne. When the people had nothing left to eat but one solitary pig, she ordered the body of the pig to be thrown over the walls to show how well-off for food they were. Charlemagne fell for the bluff, lifted the siege and retreated. However, history does not support this charming story as the *Cité*, one of the largest fortresses of Europe, was fortified by the Romans in the first century BC and given the name *Carcasso*. Situated as it is at a strategic cross-roads, it was taken by the Visigoths, then the Saracens, who were chased out by the Trencavel family in the eighth century. This family also ruled over Albi, Nîmes and Béziers.

The Vieille Cité is well worth a full day's visit. There is adequate parking outside the walls. A good way to start is to take a trip round the outer walls in a horse-drawn coach, complete with commentary from the driver. Then wander around the fascinating old streets, visit the cathedral, sit in one of the many little shady squares, enjoy a cool drink and watch the world go by – and there's a lot of world in Carcassonne in the summer! After this, a visit to the main town hardly seems worthwhile.

From the Autoroute-des-Deux-Mers exit 'Carcassonne West' turn right (SP Limoux) and at the T junction in 1km turn left (SP La Cité) then first right on to a new wide road (SP St.-Hilaire) carry straight on, NOT taking the turning to Saint-Hilaire; but at the Charlemagne roundabout take the first right (SP Cazilhac-Palaja), bearing right to Cazhilac. Opposite the *mairie* turn left where the sign to the chambres d'hôtes is hidden in bushes behind the fountain. At the cemetery bear left and the *Ferme* is on your left in 1km.

Chris Gibson & Dianne Warren. 'La Ferme de la Sauzette'
Route de Villefloure.
category: (M)
tel: 04.68.79.81.32.
fax: 04.68.79.65.99.
B&B: 64€ for two.
Evening meals 24€ each.

English Dianne and Chris will give you a very warm welcome in their newly restored farmhouse in the woods. They have five rooms on the ground floor, one especially designed for the handicapped. All have tiled floors, double or single beds, beamed sloping ceilings and modern bathrooms, one with a bath. The well-lit corridor has many thoughtful baskets of goodies for guests – hair drier, hot water bottles, shoe cleaning materials, shampoos and a first aid kit.

The lounge and dining room open on to a terrace where meals are served in the summer, and there is an open-sided summer kitchen for guests, but people with babies are welcome to use the main kitchen for feeds, etc. Dianne and Chris have tried to think of everything for your comfort in this quiet hideaway. Dianne loves cooking and you will be sure of a tasty and copious meal. A reader's letter was full of praise wishing they had booked for longer.

PÉPIEUX. 11700.
33 km NE of Carcassonne. 28 km NW of Narbonne.

A little town right in the middle of the Minervois vineyards, north of the ruins of the Cathar châteaux and close to Carcassonne. An ideal place to visit out of season, when the weather is mild and few people are about.

From the D610 at Hompes take the D910 to Olonzac, then the D52 to Pépieux. Easy to find in the middle of the town, where parking is beside the church opposite the front door.

Mrs. Worthington.
1, rue de l'Étang.
category: (M)
tel/fax: 04.68.91.69.29.
B&B: 64€ for two.
Evening meals 32€ each.

On a corner of the road this attractive 17th-century posting house has been superbly redecorated and furnished by Sally Worthington, a retired English interior decorator and designer. There is a choice of two lounges with really comfortable armchairs.

Double doors open into a large light guest room on the ground floor overlooking a small garden, luxuriously carpeted through to the bathroom, every comfort supplied, including towelling gowns.

Two rooms up a wide stairway have *terre cuite* floors, original fireplaces and carpeted bathrooms, equally light and airy. One faces the road with thick double-glazing, the other has a bathroom up a few steps, shared by an adjoining room, for 48€ with two single beds – suitable as a family suite. Central heating, thick duvets, pretty dressing tables and deep armchairs make these rooms far better than most luxury hotels. Such an elegant house is not really suitable for children under 12 years, and smoking is strictly prohibited indoors.

Mrs. Worthington, a professionally trained cook (Prue Leith's) offers three-course evening meals using local products including wine. Hasten to book; you won't find such luxury at these prices for miles around.

PEYREFITTE-du-RAZÈS. 11230.
20 km W of Limoux. 30 km SW of Carcassonne. 15km E of Mirepoix.
On the D626 from Mirepoix to Limoux turn left in the village on to the D62 for 1 km, well signed.

M. & Mme. Ropers. 'Domaine de Couchet'
category: (M)
tel/fax: 04.68.69.55.06
B&B: 56€ for two.
Evening meal 20.8€ each.
Closed 1 Nov. to Easter except for reservations of at least three nights.

Isolated on a hillside, this is an idyllic spot for country lovers. The 18th-century ivy-covered house has an adorable pebbled and lawned terrace above sloping fields cropped by the family donkeys.

As you pass through the main gates a sensor alerts your hosts of your arrival and you will be greeted at once, shown to your room, and if you time your arrival right 'le five o'clock' with delicious cake awaits you on the terrace. Not a house in sight, trees and hills in every direction, yet only a mile from the main road and within easy reach of all the Cathar châteaux, and the Pyrénées and Andorra making this a restful spot for a holiday. The possibility of a swimming pool being built makes it even more enticing.

Rooms are named after Cathar châteaux; *Montségur* with a delightful view has quality furniture and a de luxe shower room just outside the door which can be shared by two children in *Quéribus*, the little room with bunks across the corridor. *Puilaurens*, with shower room adjoining, has a *velux* window with a view of the cliff-side. *Puivert*, reached by a private staircase has a very large shower room almost adjoining. Extra beds 12.5€.

A buffet breakfast includes multiple *biscottes*, home-made and local brioches, and a dozen jams made by your busy hostess. A toaster is provided.

A galleried library looks down on a very comfortable lounge where in winter a large log fire burns.

In summer, dinner on the terrace is a real treat. Madame Ropers is an imaginative cook who still manages to join you for meals, making it a family party. All drinks from *apéritif* to coffee included. A lovely place to stay. English spoken.

GARD

ARAMON. 30390.
11 km SW of Avignon.

Though the postal address is in the Gard, this one is close to Avignon in Provence. From the D2 Avignon to Aramon road turn right on to the D126 to Saze. In about 2 km fork left at sign to 'Le Rocher Pointu'. Coming from Avignon the D126 is just before the Pont de Barbentane over the Rhône. Aramon is a quaint old town almost on the banks of the Rhône, partly walled, with tiny passageways and a rampart on one side.

☆ **M. & Mme. Malek. 'Le Rocher Pointu'**
Plan de Deve.
category: (M)
tel: 04.66.57.41.87.
fax: 04.66.57.01.77.
website: www.rocherpointu.com
email: amk@rocherpointu.com
B&B: 64/74€ for two. No Dinner
Closed 1 Oct. to 30 Apr.

Only good reports come in from this one.

If you are looking for a true old Provençale atmosphere the rooms in this large meandering house nestling under the Rocher Pointu are just the thing. Four cosy rooms, every one different, one with a mezzanine for one or two children. Rocky paths round the house, leading to the swimming pool, are not for the handicapped. A high terrace extends past the pool with magnificent views to Mont Ventoux and all around. No picture does it justice. No shortage of plastic loungers beside the pool and a covered sitting area (with fridge) traps the sun.

Evening meals are not available, but there is a nice little kitchen and barbecue for guests, in the corner of a terrace, leading from a large comfortable sitting room.

Restaurants in Aramon are recommended, only 3 km away.

Beside the house there are a few studios for 2-4 which are equally well furnished.

CASTILLON-DU-GARD. 30120.
2 km from the Pont du Gard. 25 km W of Avignon.

A tiny hill village noted for its restaurants but also close to the spectacular Pont du Gard, part of an aqueduct built to carry water to Nîmes from Uzès. Although it was built some 2000 years ago, the Pont has suffered little damage, and a thorough restoration programme is now in process. There is a Pay and Display car park on both sides of the bridge, but entry is free, even though this is the third most popular tourist spot in France.

From the autoroute A9 *sortie* 23 'Remoulins' take the N100 to Remoulins; after Remoulins take the D19 *direction* Pont du Gard – Rive Gauche, and shortly turn right on to the D228 to Castillon du Gard up the hill. Turn right in the village and follow signs downhill on the left.

M. & Mme. Vic. 'Domaine du Mas Raffin'
category: (M-L)
tel: 04.66.37.13.28.
B&B: 62.5/88€ for two. No Dinner

I have searched for a suitable chambres d'hôtes near this village for some years, so was very pleased when I heard this one had opened.

A large bleak-looking old farmhouse which improves when you see the blue shutters overlooking the courtyard where parking is excellent behind heavy locked gates.

Rooms are all named after the *cépages* of local wines. Two rooms on the ground floor have tiled floors, natural stone-vaulted ceilings; one for three is vast, with a bath and separate shower, telephone, TV courtesy fridge (payable) in the room. *Syrah*, for two, is smaller with shower and a separate loo. A room across the courtyard for three overlooks the swimming pool and is slightly more expensive but handy, with the car alongside. Upstairs there are two suites of beamed rooms, each with a double bed and a mezzanine also with double bed; these rooms have a small kitchen corner. Prices vary according to size. Breakfast in a large vaulted salon with a log fire augured well, but proved disappointing, just fruit juice and toasted bread and jam. Madame was away, perhaps that was why. I suppose you can't win 'em all.

No evening meals but the advantage of three very good restaurants in the village. I particularly like 'Le Clos des Vignes', closed out of season on Monday and Tuesday. .

GÉNÉRARGUES. 30140.
11 km SW of Alès. 3.5k. N of Anduze.

This small village is situated at the foothills of the Cévennes. There is a steam train from Anduze to Saint-Jean-du-Gard, the gateway to the

Cévennes and the start of the Corniche-des-Cévennes, leading to Florac and the Gorges-du-Tarn.

From Anduze take the D910 east over the river and turn immediately left on to the D129, SP 'Générargues'. In the village turn left on to the D50, SP 'Mialet'. In 2 km you will pass *'le Roucan'* on your right and the Hôtel les Trois Barbus on your left. In 150 metres on the right is the entrance to the chambres d'hôtes between two low pink walls.

The Hon. Mr. & Mrs. Vivian. 'Le Gamaos'
Vallée-de-Mialet.
category: (M)
tel: 04.66.61.93.79.
B&B: 48€ for two.
Evening meals 19€ each.

Nestling on a hillside of acacia and wild cherry, this attractive house has views across the valley through the trees. Guest rooms are at one end of the house on the ground floor. Two compact rooms with showers and loos open on to a terrace by the pool, with a choice of double or single beds. Another room with shower and loo has a sofa bed and a pretty blue kitchen corner, and can be let with either of the others as a family suite. The Vivians provide an excellent evening meal on reservation, or alternatively there are restaurants within easy walking distance. A good place to stay where you can relax with English hosts, and put away that French dictionary.

LARNAC. 30700 UZÈS.
30 km N of Nîmes. 15km from Pont-du-Gard. 6 km N of Uzès.

This *auberge* is easy to find 6 km north of Uzès on a bend of the D979 to Lussan, yet only one hour from the Mediterranean or the Cévennes.

Mme. Thérèse Delbos & M. Paul Stengel 'Ferme-Auberge des Cruviers'
Montée de Larnac, Route de Saint Ambroix.
category: (M)
tel: 04.66.22.10.89.
fax: 04.66.22.06.76.
B&B: 51€ for two,
Evening meals 17.5€ each

For those who prefer the anonymity of hotels this golden stone *ferme auberge* would fit the bill. Tucked into the hillside, it has been rebuilt from an old farmhouse, and now has four identical neat guest rooms for two, or four with mezzanines, facing south absorbing the sunshine and extensive views towards Nîmes. Floors are tiled but carpeted above in the mezzanine; and rooms are heated for year-round occupation.

Meals are served in the *auberge* dining room, at separate tables, with pretty blue and yellow Provençale table cloths and walls covered with photographs of the many bell towers of the Gard Department. Meals consist of four copious courses.

Demi-pension is an option after two nights. Lunches and dinner are served daily to non-residents, so you will never be eating alone here. Wine is included in the price of the meal for resident guests, and Mme. Delbos chats to her guests as in a chambres d'hôtes. Ample parking and garden furniture, though not a cultivated garden.

L'HÉRAULT

BÉDARIEUX. 34600.
66 km W of Montpellier. 35 km N of Béziers.

Right in the middle of the Hérault vineyards this busy town could do with a by-pass. Just outside, northwards on the Lodève road (D35), is a large 300-year-old house the other side of the river Orb. Try not to knock the fishermen into the water as you drive across the *passerelle*, which can be impassable in full flood. Luckily this rarely happens.

M. & Mme. Bonnal. 'Domaine de Pelissols'
category: (S)
tel: 04.67.95.42.12.
fax: 04.67.95.04.64.
B&B: 40€ for two.
Evening meals 14.5€ each.
Closed 1 Nov. to 31 Jan.

Don't be put off by the dilapidated exterior of this massive house surrounded by vineyards, once the home of a *vigneron* now handed down to the daughter and son. The daughter runs her half as a chambres d'hôtes, helped by her competent husband while her brother continues to tend the vines. The ancient cobbled courtyard enclosed by high walls makes a safe parking place. A twelfth-century fountain on one wall faces the arched entrances to the *caves* where the wine is stored. The living quarters on the first floor are reached by well-worn steps to a crumbling terrace. Inside, all is modernised. There is a long salon/dining room where well-presented meals, including house wine, are cooked and served by young Madame Bonnal.

Two neat family guest rooms, one with bunks, open on to the terrace; upstairs are three rooms for two or three. Rooms are simple, newly decorated and spotlessly clean; all have new showers and loos, and quality wooden doors to fitted wardrobes; central heating is a great comfort in chilly weather. South-facing they look out over the vineyards. A good budget stop. There is even a swimming pool for the summer months. All very French, not a word of English spoken.

LOZÈRE

CHEYLARD l'EVÊQUE. 48300.
13km S of Langogne.

Turn off the N88 3 km south of Langogne on to the D71, SP St. Flour de Mercoire, and in 10 kms of winding lanes you will drop down into this tiny hamlet nestling in a valley of the *Forêt de Mercoire*. Robert Louis Stevenson found it with his donkey 120 years ago and it has changed so little it is positively time-warped – no shops and few houses, just utter peace in lovely walking country. Long may it stay like this.

Le Refuge du Mourt

M. & Mme. Simonet. 'Le Refuge du Mourt'
category: (L)
tel: 04.66.69.03.21.
Demi-pension 72/76€ for two, wine *compris*.

The small *auberge/gîte-d'étape/chambres d'hôtes* is situated opposite the small church, which peals the 'Angelus' dead on time. Finding this delightful spot one warm September day, we couldn't resist a stop for a drink on the sunny terrace. I was delighted to find that the auberge had a few guest rooms, basic though they are. One for three has adjoining shower/and loo. Three others, each with shower and wash basin, share two loos across the landing. A pleasant salon with comfortable couches beside a log fire augurs well for winter guests.

Downstairs, the dining room is open for all, with four-or five-course meals, using recipes of the region. Demi-pension is practical here, as there are no other restaurants for miles.

Monsieur Simonet speaks good English. This would suit anyone bent on following in the steps of Robert Louis Stevenson, whether walking or driving. Donkeys are still accommodated at 5€ each!

MARVEJOLS. 48100.
29 km W of Mende.

An old town with some picturesque stone archways, probably better known for its association with *La Bête du Gévaudan*, a wolf-like monster which terrorised the area in the 18th century. A modern sculpture of *La Bête* is in the centre of the town.

Take the D1 SP 'Montrodat' for about 1km, look for signs to the *'Clinique Gévaudan'* on the right and in 200 metres on the left, the château gateway is up a slope.

M. & Mme. Mialanes. 'Château de Carrière'
L'Empéry.
category: (L)
tel: 04.66.32.28.14.
or 04.66.32.02.27.
fax:04.66.32.17.87.
B&B: 50/56€ for two. No Dinner
Closed mid-September to mid-June.

Not far from the N9, this would make a very pleasant break on the route south. The château, once owned by descendants of the Lafayette family, is built into the cliff, high above the road. It has a pleasant garden and an old orangery. Up two sweeping flights of stone steps is a swimming pool. There are various salons, decorated in fitting style, one for TV.

A choice of five different bedrooms await you. Four on the first floor, the smallest having a shower and loo; others with marble fireplaces tall windows, mostly facing south have luxurious bathrooms with two washbasins. The fifth room, on the second floor is a large tower room with high beams and has a mezzanine bed for a child.

Breakfast in the dining room is buffet-style, but you may collect yours on a tray and take it out to the terrace or even up to your room.

Your hosts are very pleasant, and will do their best to make your stay enjoyable. Note the short opening times.

QUÉZAC. 48320.
10 km NW of Florac.

At the eastern end of the Gorges-du-Tarn, one of the loveliest *gorges* in France, 62 km long though rather too popular in August. At other times the winding road is a pleasure to drive, stopping at small villages, with canoeing for the more active; so it was with great delight that I found a true chambres d'hôtes here.

From Ispagnac on the D907 in 15km turn left over an old stone bridge, SP 'Quézac'. The house is in a narrow road just past the church.

Mme. Méjean & M. Parentini. 'La Maison de Marius'
8, rue de Pontet.
category: (M)
tel: 04.66.44.25.05.
B&B: 44.5/64€ for two.
Evening meals 16€.

Madame's mother ran a chambres d'hôtes in the village until recently. Now her daughter is continuing the family tradition in her own home. Murals of the village surround the stairs to the first floor, where a huge mirror accosts you. There are five rooms: three on this floor and a couple for a family above. *La Rivière* is cosy, with a reproduction Louis XV bed and prettily decorated, *Le Pontet*, larger, has dual aspect windows, a double bed and a couch for children. *Le Moulin* for two has an 'Angel' bed head, picked up in the bed covers to lull you to sleep; each has smart adjoining shower rooms. Extra beds 16€.

On the second floor the main bedroom is very large and light. It has a sitting area and a bathroom luxurious enough for the grandest château, with separate bath, shower, bidet and loo. A second room across the landing has two large beds for children sharing these facilities. Suite 64€ for four.

Madame keeps the rooms supplied with fresh flowers from the garden, meals are taken on the terrace in fine weather overlooking Monsieur's large *potager* with views to the hillside-château. The *accueil* is superb and evening meals wine and *apéritif compris* are shared with your hosts. Quite the best address in the area. I am sure heading for a ☆. Parking for four cars beside the house.

PYRÉNÉES-ORIENTALES

ARGELÈS-sur-MER 66700.

20 km SE of Perpignan

Argelès-sur-Mer, is a pleasant flat town with an interesting port and good beaches south of the more purpose-built holiday resorts that make this Mediterranean coast so busy in the season.

From the N10 take the Route d'Elne. After the post office turn right at the Tricolores traffic lights, then under the railway bridge, then straight on, with the cemetery on the left. Follow the sign 'Maison de Retraite Les Capucines,' pass under the bridge of the RN 114 and turn left; in 200 metres turn right in the direction 'La Montagne', and in 2 km take the right lane to the chambres d'hôtes.

☆ **M. & Mme. Romero. 'Mas Senyarich'**
category: (M)
tel: 04.68.95.93.63.
fax: 04.68.81.17.27.
B&B: 57.5€ for two.
Evening meals 19€. each.

So near the coast, but away from the noise and bustle.

'WONDERFUL! The entire experience was brilliant. Our room was warm, comfortable and we had a lovely view. Nothing seemed to be too much trouble for our hosts. The food was excellent (Catalan), eaten en famille which was fun. The most enjoyable holiday accommodation we have ever stayed in! THIS DEFINITELY DESERVES A ☆'. M. Hough

Just the recommendation for which I have been hoping, so happily now an arrow.

The typical rambling Catalan *mas* is approached up a narrow tarred track, 4km from the sea but having sea views from all the rooms. Five rooms, all differently furnished in country styles, patchwork quilts, tiled and wood floors, heating for early visits, bathrooms and a definite Spanish touch.

A spacious comfortable lounge has a large fireplace of stone carvings depicting the various occupations of the area; the attached dining room has an enormous window looking over the swimming pool. Evening meals, all drinks included, are available.

There is shady parking and a garage for two cars. Use of a washing machine for a small payment adds to one's comfort. Meals are not obligatory, so you have the option of trying the many restaurants in Argelès. There is a small *taxe de séjour* payable here. Book well ahead and you will receive full directions.

CAIXAS. 66300.
26 Km SW of Perpignan, 17 Km SW of Thuir.

From Perpignan take the N9 towards Spain as far as Villemolaque then the D2 west to Caixas.

High in the Pyrénées Orientales, overlooked by the Pic-du-Canigou, this little village consists of scattered farmsteads and modern houses chequered over the hillside. The chambres d'hôtes is in an intriguing position, down a tiny lane leading to the Mairie which is situated on a spur of land with a circular lookout. Next door is a church (open once a year on feast day); but it is to the old house beside the church that you should head.

☆ **Jane Richards & Ian Mayes.** '**Mas Saint-Jacques'**
category: **(M)**
tel/fax: 04.68.38.87.83.
B&B: 52€ for two. No Dinner

First impressions are not very exciting but you will soon change your mind. Three storeys tower up from the little patio outside this tall dwelling; further inspection will take you along the terraced garden to two summer rooms with expansive views, for two or three people. Hidden behind a wall is a sheltered swimming pool. In the main house the open-plan kitchen and dining room leads to a new covered conservatory, facing west, for breakfast on cooler days. Up the stone and wood spiral stairs, rooms are named after the ancient regions of Cerdanya. On the first floor there is a family suite of two rooms, a double and two singles, sharing a bathroom. The top floor is taken up with a lounge and two more bedrooms, a treble with a balcony and one with two single beds, overlooking the pool and countryside, *Capcir* and *Rosello*. All rooms are light and airy, with good quality pine furniture, duvets and pristine white linen on the beds, luxury towels, and even hot water bottles for out-of-season travellers.

There is plenty to do in this hidden mountain retreat where the air is so pure. Climb Mt. Hélèna for a breathtaking view of the mountains and coast, perhaps visit Céret where Picasso once lived, take a day trip on the Little Yellow Train round the mountains, or just relax by the pool. End the day with a convivial meal with your charming English hosts, Jane and Ian, who will have prepared you a feast of fresh local produce, all drinks included.

Special courses in wine tasting can be arranged on a weekly basis.

Proving a popular haunt. The ☆ remains.

Limousin

LIMOUSIN

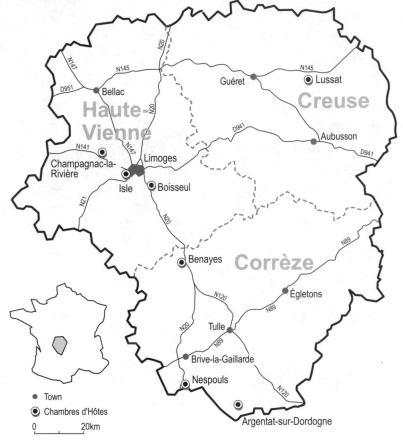

Guéret

Lussat

Creuse

Bellac

Haute-Vienne

Aubusson

Champagnac-la-Rivière

Limoges

Isle

Boisseul

Benayes

Corrèze

Égletons

Tulle

Brive-la-Gaillarde

Nespouls

Argentat-sur-Dordogne

• Town

◉ Chambres d'Hôtes

0   20km

Limousin

An agricultural region, west of the Auvergne, perhaps best known for its beef cattle. Limoges, the *préfecture* of **Haute Vienne,** is famous for the manufacture of porcelain. North-west of Limoges is the martyred village of Oradour-sur-Glane, well worth visiting, but be prepared for the sombre reminder of the horrors of Nazi occupation. The whole village was wiped out by fire on 10 June 1944. To this day they are not sure why. A completely new village has been built nearby and the original Oradour left in ruins, as a memorial to the 642 people who lost their lives. Sadly, I hear rumours that this memorial village may have to close, as souvenir hunters are stripping it bare. A memorial will be built in its place. Such a pity – it is the most heart-rending memorial I have ever seen.

In the east the **Creuse** *département* is purely agricultural, with the *préfecture* Guéret hugging the hillside, overlooking orchards of apples and pears. On the whole the region is undulating farmland, especially in the north-east. In the south-east you will discover Aubusson, the Axminster of France, with a very fine Museum of Carpets and Tapestries.

The southerly *département* of the Limousin is **Corrèze**, still mostly agricultural. To the east is the plateau of Millevaches where the river Vienne rises. As the name suggests it is the grazing land of handsome brown cows. Bordering on the Dordogne, it has many notable medieval villages such as Martel, Turenne, and Collonges-la-Rouge. The upper reaches of the river Dordogne cut through the high land, entrapped by a large *barrage* north of Argentat before flowing gently on.

CORRÈZE

ARGENTAT-sur-DORDOGNE. 19400.
25 km SE of Tulle. 45km W of Aurillac.

A small town on the upper reaches of the river Dordogne, well away from the normal tourist scene. It is famous for its oak trees. Before modern means of transport arrived, the inhabitants of the town sent their wood to Bordeaux to make the casks (*tonneaux*) in which wine was shipped to England. They made flat-bottomed barges out of their felled oak trees, filled the barges with wood then waited for the flood to whisk their craft down the Dordogne to the Garonne and Bordeaux. There they sold their cargo, broke up the barges and walked home. This way of trading has now ceased, but the oak is still used by the Bordeaux *viticulteurs*.

Take the N120 Tulle to Aurillac in 25 km at Argentat turn right on to the D116.

Mr. & Mrs. Mallows. 'Au Pont de l'Hospital'
category: (M)
tel: 05.55.28.90.35.
fax: 05.5.28.20.70.
B&B: 48€ for two. No Dinner
Closed 15 Nov. to 1 Mar.

A haven for *pêcheurs*. The Mallows are English and have been quietly running this charming little guest house for some years now. Not really a hotel, as it has no bar, not really a chambres d'hôtes, as there are 10 rooms. Situated a mile from Argentat beside the bridge over the river Maronne, a tributary of the Dordogne, it is in an idyllic position. A reader suggested I visited and it certainly has an old-fashioned French charm, not spoilt by modernisation. Only three guest rooms have bathrooms; the others all have the statutory washbasin and bidet, but share a shower and loo on the landings. On the other hand the rooms are spacious, well-furnished, warmly carpeted and all have large windows overlooking the river or garden. Breakfast (English 2.4€ extra) in summer, is enjoyed out on the datura-shaded terrace. Evening meals served off-season if reserved, (there are plenty of restaurants in Argentat); but in July and August barbecues are sometimes offered in the garden beside the river Shady parking is across the lane beside the river.

BENAYES 19510.
40 km SSE of Limoges
Just off the N20 between Limoges and Brive turn at Masserat on to the D20 to Benayes; you will find Château Forsac signposted on your left in 4km.

Mme. de Montbron. 'Château Forsac'
category: (S)
tel: 05.55.73.47.78.
B&B: 35€ for two.
Evening meal 9.5€ each.

If you feel like a night in a real château which has been in the family for over a hundred years and is steeped in history, then come to Forsac. Four plane trees in front of the house were brought from Marie Antoinette's garden at Le Petit Trianon by a captain of the king's guard, who was a regular visitor. When the château was first built in feudal times it had four towers; one of the originals is still standing and is part of the house; the only other one has been rebuilt to preserve it. Situated in 200 hectares of wooded land it is a paradise for early morning walkers and children. In spring drifts of scillas and daffodils light up the lawn opposite the arched door, which has the family motto *'Moins Dire Que Faire'* (Actions speak louder than words) above it.

This château has proved popular with readers of earlier editions. Madame is a charming young countess (de Cherade de Montbron) who speaks perfect English. They are in the process of restoring the château internally and still have much to do, so don't expect perfection. The wide staircase leads to three large bedrooms, one with a crested bed-head! Two rooms can be inter-communicating for a family. Electric heating is not really suitable for cold winter weather, but the château is open all the year if you want to brave it. There is a sunny sitting room for guests adjoining the three rooms. *"You correctly point out the still-unrestored aspect of most of the interior decoration. But our room was newly-decorated, huge ,and very comfortable. It was enjoyable to talk with Mme. Demontbron about the château at breakfast, surrounded by the wall panels depicting it a hundred years ago. It was an interesting place to stay, and very conveniently placed for a stop on the drive north".* Min Lee

No evening meals on a regular basis, but should you arrive tired and late Madame will take pity on you and knock up a light meal of omelette, salad.

So ignore the peeling walls and settle for the charming *accueil*, the tranquillity and improving your history. It is a bargain. Feel you are contributing to the château's restoration!

NESPOULS. 19600.
16 km S of Brive-la-Gaillarde.

A useful stop, just off the N20, close to Turenne, a small hill village with narrow, flower-bedecked streets winding up to the old castle. The counts of Turenne often took their family holidays at the neighbouring village of Collonges-la-Rouge, so called because all the houses have been built in red brick. A very pretty little place to visit but unfortunately a popular stop for all the tour coaches. It becomes packed in the high season, but is well worth a detour at other times.

From the N20, travelling south, at Nespouls take the D19 SP 'Larche' and then immediately right SP 'Belveyre' to the small hamlet where two chambres d'hôtes are signed.

M. & Mme. Lalle. 'Aux Sabots du Causse'
Belveyre.
category: (S)
tel: 05.55.85.84.47.
B&B: 32€ for two.
Closed 1 Oct. to 1 May

A typical towered Périgord house, this one has four rooms. One on the ground floor off the salon has garden access, and there is a similar room above. Entry to the two others is from an external staircase; one has a terrace, the other a family room for five (one double, one single bed and two beds in the mezzanine up a ladder), sharing a large shower room with two washbasins.

These compact rooms are carpeted, have natural stone walls and beds for three, dainty white *ciel de lit* or pretty flowered *tête de lits* and matching sheets etc. There is a fridge in every room, with cold drinks for 80 centimes each. Shower rooms have numerous extras such as hairdryers, razors – nothing forgotten here. All very good value

A copious breakfast. Evening meals served at a long table in the large salon, wine *compris*.

Regretfully, Madame says she cannot speak English – just the place to brush up on your French.

CREUSE

LUSSAT 23170
37 km E of Guéret, the county town of the Creuse department. Do visit the little Abbey church at Moutier d'Ahun, renowned for its 15 to 17th Century carvings, SW of Lussat.

M. & Mme. Ribbé. 'Château de Puy-Haut'.
category: (M)
tel: 05 55 82 13 07.
website: www.admtc.com
Evening meals 17.77€ each.
Rooms 53.36€
Closed: 1 Nov. to 1 Apr.

Not in Lussat at all, look for signs on the D915 km E of Gouzan.

At the end of a long lane in a small hamlet this 17/18th century little château, resembles more a *maison de maître*, surrounded by farm buildings and fields. The Ribbé family are lovely, a warm welcome is given to all especially to children who will find space to play, often joined by the Ribbé children. The rear garden has a large swimming pool surrounded by sun loungers. Wide well-worn old oak stairs lead to four guest rooms which have changed little since the château was built, there are polished wood floors, marble fireplaces and high built-in cupboards, furnished with all necessary requirements but nothing fancy; large modernised bathrooms have been contrived out of adjoining rooms giving a feeling of spaciousness. There is one ground floor room for those averse to stairs.

A rather austere salon with table and Louis XV chairs has television. The dining room with its large fireplace and kitchen corner, which guests may use at lunch time, is where all meals are served and enjoyed in a relaxed atmosphere, with your sociable hosts who strive hard to speak English.

Very quiet and excellent parking.

Evening meals cooked by Madame are well worth booking.

HAUTE-VIENNE

BOISSEUIL. 87220.
8 km SE of Limoges.

Limoges, the *préfecture* of Haute-Vienne, has been renowned for hundreds of years for its production of porcelain. The city has large attractive open squares. The cathedral of St. Étienne is mostly gothic; it has some colourful blue windows and an interesting balcony with two spiral staircases under the organ. Occasionally on Sundays *brocante* fairs are held in the forecourt. Walk behind the cathedral to find the Botanical Gardens tiered down to the river Vienne, where every plant has a name tag. However, the most striking building in Limoges is the railway station, built in 1829, on a hill overlooking the city, with its green domed roof and clock tower in which the Stationmaster dwells. The wide approach-roads are lined with flower beds. The spacious entrance hall is where you can always find your English newspapers.

Porcelain exhibitions are held in the city during the summer, but there is no need to brave the traffic looking for your purchases. As you approach the city the roads have many small wayside shops with a choice of china, and the owners can direct you to the factories, now mostly outside the town, if you wish to place larger orders.

Take the A20 south from Limoges direction Toulouse then exit 37 'Boisseuil Zone Commerciale', then follow signs to chambres d'hôtes, past the school in Boisseuil.

Mme. Brigitte Ziegler. 'Moulinard' category: (S)
tel./fax: 05.55.06.91.22.
B&B: 36.5€. for two. No Dinner

This has proved very popular with readers, only ten minutes from the centre of Limoges, but a world away from all the noise and traffic. The farm is on a promontory between two valleys and guest rooms are in an old *maison-de-maître* across the courtyard. Picnic or sit in the walled garden under the trees.

You enter the house through the kitchen which has an interesting old floor tiled with moulds from the porcelain factories in Limoges.

Four large rooms, have polished wood floors and antique furniture. Good radiators for cold weather in the bedrooms.

Breakfast in Mme. Ziegler's own farmhouse is beautifully served in her kitchen overlooking the garden. Fresh *baguettes*, home-made jams and the usual plentiful coffee, tea or chocolate with fresh flowers on the table make this a really enjoyable start to the day. There is no evening meal, but there are two Logis quite near at Solignac. Madame speaks a little English.

CHAMPAGNAC-la-RIVIÈRE 87150
This tiny hill village is easily missed, which is a pity because it is within easy reach of both Limoges and the martyred village of Oradour sur Glane. It is also on the route of Richard Coeur de Lyon, and who better to fill you in with all the history than your host in this lovely Gothic Château, who is president of the Society.

M. le Comte et Madame la Comtesse de Manoir de Juaye. 'Château de Brie'.
category: (L)
tel: 05 55 78 17 52.
fax: 05 55 78 14 02.
email: chateaudebrie@wanadoo.fr
B&B: 92€ for two
Evening meals 38€ each.
Closed 1 Dec. to 31 Mar.

The château was built in 1484 to celebrate the marriage of Jean de Brie with a daughter of the Hautefort château in the Dordogne. It descended, often by the female line, to the Mirebeau family in the 18th century. It was built in the grounds of an ancient turreted grange which had been used to defend the area and shelter the villagers. The grange with its original *schiste* stone walls with rifle holes still in place, is now used for weddings and other receptions,

Situated on high ground with compelling country views, it is a charming family home, which the family are happy to share with guests. Four large and light bedrooms are reached by the granite spiral staircase in one of the towers. All have adjoining beautifully modernised bathrooms, most cunningly fitted into the shape of the original latrines in the *Échaugettes* (small watch towers built in medieval times). 'Mirabeau', in a tower has a double bed, the washbasin lurks behind a cupboard door; but the bathroom is off the vestibule. Up the tower to the second floor a wide T-shaped corridor leads to the 'Empire' room, where turquoise and yellow *ciels de lits* adorn three beds. 'Béatrice' is a more floral room with marble fireplace and a larger prettily tiled bathroom which luxuriates in bath and separate shower. Along the corridor is 'Céline' with fabricated walls of blue and gold and a double bed in the Napoleon III style.

The salon has a delicate fresco ceiling which was painted by Italian workers only 100 years ago and is furnished in Louis XV and Louis XVI style, a light pleasant room in which hangs a painting of Charles II and his family, a copy made in the Vandyke studios, the original is owned by Queen Elizabeth II.

The dining room, is used occasionally when a full complement of guests reserve dinner, otherwise meals including breakfast are taken in the cosier library where a coat of arms stands by the window.

In the 1000 acres of land surrounding the château is a lake for fishing, a swimming pool and a tennis court. Excellent English spoken.

An alternative location for evening meals is a little cottage restaurant 'La Grille' just outside the château gates, at present run by an English lady.

ISLE. 87170.
8 km W of Limoges.

Leave Limoges on the N21 south and in about 8 km, just after the turn to L'Aiguille there will be a chambres d'hôtes sign on the right and a right fork will take you up a country lane to the Brunier's house, also on the right.

☆ **Mme. Brunier. 'Pic de L'Aiguille'.**
Verthamont.
category: (S)
tel: 05.55.36.12.89.
B&B: 36.5€. for two. No Dinner

A modern dormer-type bungalow on a hillside outside Limoges, with extensive views and a swimming pool. Two carpeted rooms, with modern shower rooms, are extremely pretty, large wardrobes to stow your gear and patio doors to private terraces with tables and chairs. A third room for a family is on the first floor under the eaves.

The Bruniers receive one as a real friend of the family. Drinks offered on arrival. Unfortunately evening meals are no longer offered, but the Bruniers will direct you to restaurants in the area. Some English spoken. Very good value.

Loire Valley

LOIRE (VALLEY)

Loire Valley

Companion guide, French Entrée to Loire

One of the most popular of French tourist destinations. For many good reasons. With autoroutes and TGV linking the main cities, Parisians can, and do, nip down for the weekend. This means sophisticated hotels and restaurants and sophisticated prices. It's handy for the Brits too – a halfway stop on their way to the Med. and accessible after a fast three/four-hour drive, making it ideal for the first or last night from and to the ferry.

The area offers great variety – wine production, university cities, cathedrals, abbeys and river attractions. But, of course, its unique attraction is the châteaux. There are legions of them, strategically sited to defend, enhance and profit by the mighty river which used to be the main highway through the land. To come to this area and not visit some of them would be unthinkable. But do resist the temptation to tackle too many too quickly. Ration the daily allowance. One or two will do nicely, and be selective. Some, like gargantuan Chambord, lovely Chenonceau and verdant Villandry, should be on every list. Others like Loches and Valençay are for connoisseurs. The Loire is the big name but some of its many tributaries are even more attractive than this shallow, sandbanked, often silted giant. Follow their courses, picnic by their willow-fringed banks and take a boat ride upon them, getting acquainted with areas other than the tourist-ridden Loire banks.

All this potential is good news for bed providers. There are hundreds of chambres d'hôtes to choose from here and elimination is particularly hard. There are more in the 'L' bracket than in any other area for obvious reasons – the super abundance of châteaux begging to be converted being one. Some are just too good to leave out, their standards being just as high as luxury hotels and, price for price, far superior. I did manage to find a few under 48€ away from the main tourist areas. Those on a really tight budget should look elsewhere. In whatever category the availability of chambres d'hôtes' hosts for discussions scores highly here – they will advise on how best to allocate the time between so many fascinating diversions.

Here is a brief run along the river, from east to west:

Sancerre-Orléans: some of the finest scenery of the whole route. Sancerre is unique, with sizeable hills covered with vines contrasting with the general flatness of the region. The river here is fast-running and island-dotted. The first important château is at Gien, famous for its porcelain, then Sully, where the river banks are sandy and the countryside somewhat dull. Châteauneuf is a pleasant, underestimated town and the river here is impressive. Further north the forest of Orléans, peppered with lakes, is delightfully unspoiled.

Orléans-Blois: Orléans is the administrative capital of the region, mostly new but well laid out, with good shops.

South of Orléans lies the little known region of the Sologne, wooded hunting country, spilling over into three departments, mostly Loir-et-Cher, Loiret in the north and the rest in Cher. Very pretty villages. Chambord and Cheverney are the principal châteaux.

Along the river the châteaux now come thick and fast and the roads along the banks can become busy at weekends. Meung and Beaugency are both worth a visit.

Blois-Tours: Blois is the first big château-town actually on the river and consequently congested. Amboise is best out of season; then it has much to offer. A diversion from Tours following the river Cher leads to the jewel in the crown, Chenonceau. Montrichard is a narrow strip of a town between river and escarpment. St Aignan is infinitely more attractive.

Tours-Saumur: Tours is a lively university town, with some attractive restoration in its old quarters, good restaurants, outdoor cafés and markets. Cross to the southern bank and don't miss Villandry, Azay-le-Rideau and the fairy tale Ussé. Chinon on the river Vienne has probably the most historically important château of them all.

CHER

BERRY-BOUY. 18500.
8 km W of Bourges.

What a pleasant drive it is down the N76 beside the Canal du Berry close to the river Cher, passing small villages overlooking the canal between Villefranche and Vierzon. The nearby A71 has exits at Vierzon (6) and Bourges (7), so this is a handy stop whichever way you are going. From Mehun-sur-Yèvre south of Vierzon on the N76 take the D60 to Berry-Bouy. The farm is 1 km on the right on the other side of the village.

Mme. de la Farge. 'L'Ermitage'
category: (M)
tel: 02.48.26.87.46.
fax: 02.48.26.03.28.
B&B: 44.5/48€ for two. No Dinner

An old manor house on a working farm. The spiral wood staircase in the tower leads to two very old rooms, modernised with every comfort. One, for a family, has a double and two single beds, with attached shower room, and is really large. *Attention les pieds* here, a beam runs right across the room at floor level to trip the unwary. The other room, for a couple, has twin beds, and has a bath. A third room just off the dining room would avoid climbing stairs. Three well-modernised rooms in a separate building are exceptionally nice. In the dining room in the old house Madame serves a good breakfast with fresh bread and *croissants*.

There are two restaurants within 3 km. One, upmarket, is in the village with menus from 22€. The other is at Marmagne only 2 km further on, where, opposite the church at *Les Trois Amis,* Madame dispenses no-choice evening meals of five courses, each left on the table to help yourself and a litre bottle of red wine, all of which will cost you 12.5€, including Madame's friendly chat between courses. Full of locals playing cards and supping.

MONTIGNY. 18250 HENRICHMONT.

15km SW of Sancerre by D955 and D44 through Montigny. Signed after 5 km. Still wine country, though now mixed with cereals; so near to Sancerre, yet so rural.

☆ **Madame Elisabeth Gressin. 'La Reculée'**
category: (M)
tel: 02.48.69.59.18.
fax: 0.48.69.52.51.
B&B: 39/46€ for two.
Evening meals 18€
Closed 15 Nov. to 15 Mar.

An absolute favourite, starred on all counts – welcome, comfort, position, good value and good food.

Since the death of her husband Elisabeth still gallantly runs the farm (with help) and the chambres d'hôtes which are in converted farm buildings decorated with great style and imagination. The rooms are named after flowers and coloured accordingly – I liked *Bleuet* (Forget-me-Not) best, with twin beds, fresh blue and white covers and curtains and a blue bath. *Liseron* (bindweed) is pink and green, *Primevère* is naturally enough primrose and *Bouton d'Or* (buttercup) is a deeper yellow. *Cocquelicot* (poppy) is the most striking, all red and white with high ceiling and a shower. Lots of blond wood has been used to give a Scandinavian feel and dispel the gloom that sometimes attaches to old buildings. The salon and kitchen (guests may use) follow the theme. Elisabeth cooks light refreshing meals, using her own farm produce. A gem.

INDRE-et-LOIRE

AMBOISE 37400
25 km E of Tours. Situated on the Loire noted for its castle and the home and museum of Leonardo da Vinci.

M. & Mme. Belknap. 'Le Vieux Manoir', 13 rue Rabelais.
category: (L)
tel./fax: 02.47.30.41.27.
email: info@le-vieux-manor.com
B&B: 122/138€. each.

Right in the middle of town is not where you would expect to find a small manor house with an enclosed garden and parking. Originally an 18th Century convent, the Belknaps, your American hosts (making a dream come true), have restored the house, furnishing it with well chosen antiques, collected over many years, and have converted first and second floor rooms into six cosy guest rooms, reflecting the period and life style of the famous French ladies after whom they are named. Bathrooms are luxurious and vary in size and shape. A large conservatory overlooks a small rear garden where breakfast is served.

The entrance gates now open on to a formal French garden where a central fountain plays, surrounded by lawns and flowers beds. At the side of the house is a small two-bedroomed gîte available for longer stays.

No evening meals The whole town of Amboise with its many restaurants is within walking distance. A trifle expensive, but being able to park and tour on foot might make it worth while.

ATHÉE-sur-CHER. 37270
20 km SE of Tours towards Bléré and 6 km west of Bléré turn north on to the D45 to Le Vallet. Signed from the N76 down a quiet lane.

M. & Mme. Chaudière. 'Le Pavillon'
Le Vallet
category: (M)
tel: 02.47.50.67.83.
fax: 02.47.50.68.31.
B&B: 48/56/64€ for two.

Close to the banks of the Cher, and once a dependency of the abbey at Cormery, the 18th-century building had just been bought by the Chaudières when I visited. It had been a chambres d'hôtes, but previous owners had ignored the over-run garden and done little to enhance the rooms. It is situated in a quiet lane, wisteria covers the walls, the rustic front garden contains a bread oven, behind the house lawns slope down to a tributary of the Cher. Two sparsely furnished rooms on the first floor with airy bathrooms are for three, a four-poster sinks into a green carpet in one, single beds in the other rest on tiled floors. Comparatively small windows look on the garden. An interesting third room for two has independent entry from the garden. Very rustic with old tiles, natural stone walls and a huge fireplace, it has a double bed and bedside lamps, a fairly modern bathroom and benefits from a private enclosed terrace. You will either hate it or love it. In summer I would love it. Extra bed 16€. A spacious lounge/dining room spans the house, where copious breakfasts and evening meals are served. A pleasing situation detached but not isolated. The new owners have worked hard to restore both house and garden, combining its historic past with modern comfort.

AZAY-SUR-INDRE. 37310.
20 km E of Tours by the N143, D17 and D58.

The river Indre is probably the most attractive of the Loire's tributaries – more attractive, I believe, than the mother river itself. Follow its banks for as long as you need to absorb the atmosphere of green tranquillity. Good picnicking here.

The chambres d'hôtes is not in the village of Azay, but up on the tip of the plain. From Azay take the V 01 up the hill, signed 'Dolus-le-Sec', turn right and follow the chambres d'hôtes sign on the left. Ignore all others.

M. & Mme. Bouin. 'La Bihouderie'
category: (S-M)
tel: 02.47.92.58.58.
fax: 02.47.92.22.19.
B&B: 40/43€ for two. No Dinner

An isolated farm surrounded by acres of sunflowers, a little oasis on a very exposed plain.

Young Mme. Bouin was strimming her lawns when we arrived late one hot May afternoon, and we tentatively asked if she had a room, and was it too late for a meal? No problem and would we like a beer or cold drink. We would. Two others guests were expected, but before dinner four extra cyclists arrived hungry and tired. They were shown rooms and joined us for dinner. What energy Mme. Bouin has! For those who have stayed here before, she has since remarried and now has a five year-old son to add to her teen-aged family; Chris, her husband arrives late for dinner from the farm and introduces himself to all the guests. A comfortable family atmosphere.

This is a typical long low Loire farmhouse; the large gravelled courtyard accommodates all the cars, leaving plenty of room for dotted shaded white tables. Lawns behind the house where dinner is served in summer overlooking the dazzling *tournesols*.

Guests are accommodated in four ground-floor rooms at one end of the farmhouse, approached from a comfortable sitting room, where there is now a drinks machine. Doubles, singles all with baths or showers – take your pick if you come early enough. Many thoughtful extras are supplied in the shower rooms.

You can even buy tee-shirts to commemorate your stay

BEAUMONT-en-VÉRON. 37420
5 km NW of Chinon.

This village is situated on the little peaceful peninsula which juts out into the confluence of the Loire and the Vienne rivers. Every second Sunday in the month there is a large *brocante* market on the quay at nearby Montsoreau. This makes an excellent place to stay for visiting the charming little town of Chinon, strung out along the river Vienne, backed by the crumbling ruins of the many towered château, historically more interesting than many in the Loire. It was here that Joan of Arc started to persuade the reluctant Charles VII to regain his throne as king of France and be crowned eventually in Reims. Joan's tower is one of the many roofless ones to explore. Many happy hours can be spent wandering round the ruins and gazing over the town from the ramparts.

Mme. Degremont. 'La Balastière'
Hameau de Grezille.
category: (S-M)
tel: 02.47.58.87.93.
fax: 02.47.58.82.41.
B&B: 38.5/51€ for two. No Dinner

Hidden in the countryside, yet so close to Chinon and other Loire châteaux, this extended farmhouse dates from the 15th century, with additions in the 17th and 18th.

Madame Degremont speaks excellent English and will give you a very warm welcome. There are large grass surroundings and outbuildings as rustic as the house itself.

A choice of two rooms with adjoining kitchens and bathroom. One for a family consists of a suite of two singles and a double, and is on the tiled ground floor. One above, which I liked best, is carpeted, has a double bed and a large sitting area with kitchen corner, very light and sunny, extra beds for small children possible, well worth staying many nights.

A tiny third room in the oldest part of the house is heavily beamed but has a double bed and a dear little window at floor level so you can lie in bed and look at the garden. Though small, the amenities are just as good – chairs, table, bedside lamps, a sensible painted wardrobe, cosily carpeted and centrally heated, shower room, everything you could wish for at a budget price.

Breakfast is served in Mme. Degremont's salon at the other end of the house or outside in summer. If you ask Madame nicely and give her a few days' warning she will prepare you an evening meal on arrival, but there is a good Logis restaurant about 500 metres away, or the option of self-catering if you choose the right room.

BOURGUEIL 37140
Worth a few days here, so central for the Loire west of Tours and only 5 kms north of Bourgueil, with its notable wine.

From the D10 bypass north of Bourgueil take the D749 SP Gizeux for 4km and turn right beside the Auberge de Touvois, the house is on the left in a few metres.

M. & Mme. Marchand. 'Le Moulin de Touvois'.
category: (M)
tel/fax: 02 47 97 87 70
B&B: 53.35€ for two,
Evening meal 12.20€ each.

Such a handy place to stay a few steps from a charming restaurant.

The cottage, though by the roadside, is in a quiet lane. A small stream flows past the rear patio, step over the bridge to find a much larger garden with a swimming pool surrounded by lawns and shady trees. Bliss when you have it all to yourself on a hot summer's day

Four rooms, one on the ground floor is next to the parking, a large, airy room refreshingly redecorated in yellow, peach and green shades. Bathroom and separate loo. Tiled floors would make me wary of this one in cold weather. Three smaller rooms on the first floor, with mansarded windows have carpets, one with steps up to the shower room.

M. Marchand is an architect, and he and his wife share an evening meal with you, all drinks included. A pleasant way to spend an evening, especially eating on the terrace by the stream. Should you want to ring the changes, the popular Auberge Touvois is on your doorstep.

Breakfast is served on a rather special Moroccan table tiled in blue and yellow.

GENILLÉ 37460.
22 km SE of Tours. 22 km SW of Montrichard

The *Auberge* in the village is named after Charles VII's lady friend Agnes Sorel. Less than 1km from the village, a left turn off the D764 from Genillé to Montrichard, at the junction with the D 10, is this charming mill house.

M. & Mme. Miéville. 'Le Moulin de la Roche'
category: **(M)**
tel: 02.47.59.56.58.
fax: 02.47.59.59.62.
B&B: 56€ for two. No Dinner

The mill is situated beside the little river Indrois. There is a lawned garden with inviting white loungers beside the old *four* which is used as a barbecue on summer evenings. The house is delightfully rustic; the dining room, incorporating the old mill wheel as an office-cum-bar, adjoins a very comfortable lounge with log fire, which guests are welcome to share.

One double room in the main house, prettily decorated in green, has its own bathroom. Other rooms in an adjoining wing have a separate entrance. One on the ground floor with fresh blue and white tiled floor, has a shower and washbasin, but the private loo is a few steps across the corridor. Above are three other rooms all warmly carpeted. 'Terracotta' for three has single beds, and *velux* windows are low enough to enjoy the view. Another, twin-bedded for two, is yellow, and the fourth, with steps down to the bathroom, is for three. All are individually furnished and absolutely charming. Extra beds 14.5€.

All drinks included in Madame's evening meals, on reservation, or a short walk across fields to the village will take you to the *auberge* for sustenance. You will love Madame Miéville who is French, her husband English.

MONTRÉSOR. 37460.
20 km. E of Loches.

Lying in the valley of the river Indrois, it is the only village in France bearing this name. As early as the 10th century the land belonged to the treasurer of the Diocese of Tours, hence its name. A fortress was built here in 1005, two towers were added in the 12th century. It came into the hands of the Bastarnay family in the 15th century and a château was built within the fortress. Imbert de Bastarnay was the confidant of four French kings. Many famous lords followed him until the château was almost destroyed in the Revolution. Now only one wing remains.

What is now the parish church was built as a mausoleum for the family in the 16th century, and has many fine paintings once owned by Cardinal Fesch, uncle of Napoleon I. In 1849 the château was bought by a Polish count, Xavier Branicki, a friend of Napoleon III, restored to a beautiful home, and to this day descendants of the family live there. The castle is open to the public for guided tours from 1 April to 1 Nov.

The village is a strange mixture of medieval and new, having many facilities.

The chambres d'hôtes is signed from the village on the D10 to Genillé.

Le Moulin

☆ **M. & Mme. Willems de Laddersous. 'Le Moulin'**
category: (M)
tel: 02.47.92.68.20.
fax: 02.47.92.74.61.
email: alain.willems@wanadoo.fr
B&B: 46.5/54.5€ for two. No Dinner

Dairy farmers Alain and Sophie have most tastefully restored the mill house, a typical stark high building. The spacious lounge with t*erre-cuite* tiles has a large fireplace and comfortable armchairs, a door leads to the dining room for breakfast where glass panels in the floor light up, surprising one with a delightful view of rushing water under the mill.

There are four very pleasant light airy rooms on the first floor offering every comfort, doubles and singles, green, yellow, and two blue; all are carpeted and have neat little bedside tables covered to match the decor of the room. Each has excellent large modern bathrooms, country views from all the windows.

As yet the surrounding garden is mostly gravel; but lawns are fast appearing and trees will doubtless follow. A nice surprise on a more recent visit was a pristine new swimming pool.

No evening meal, which is a good excuse to head for the *Le Moulin de Chaudée* 2 km along the road to Genille, where M. Bouclet will welcome you warmly as he turns the steaks on his large log fire. A ☆ for comfort and accueil.

ST JEAN-ST GERMAIN. 37600
7 km S of Loches by the N143. The village is signed on the left of the nationale. Follow the D492 across the first bridge over the R Indre, and prepare to swing immediately left, continuing over the second narrow bridge.

St. Jean- St. Germain 37

Mme. Sue Hutton & M. Andrew Page. 'Le Moulin'
category: **(M)**
tel: 02.47.94.70.12.
fax: 02.47.94.77.98.
email: millstjean@aol.com
B&B: 58/61 € for two.
Evening meals 25€ each.
Closed December and January

The Indre is a lovely river – far prettier than its parent Loire – the mill stands astride a boat-shaped island. A flowery garden leads to a little sandy beach where dinghies are provided to explore the waterways. New this year is a small swimming pool. In the mill house it's a real home from home where guests are pampered by kindly Sue, ably aided by her partner, Andrew. who is a superb chef, producing dinner no matter how late you arrive.

Bedrooms on different floors, vary in size and shape but are so comfortably furnished you feel you really are staying in a friend's private house, most overlook the mill stream and the river beyond. Doubles, twins and a triple, all with baths or showers, and prettified with Sue's delicate stencils.

The evening meal is the high spot of the day, either in the cosy rough-walled, peach-curtained dining room, or on the terrace. Guests are offered a choice of *apéritif*, in typically generous style. Conversation is flowing by the time Andrew brings in the first course. Guests love it here, and return and return, but perhaps not for young children or the less able.

SAVONNIÈRES. 37510.
14 km W of Tours by the D7, direction Villandry. Signed on the left at the entrance to the village.

M. & Mme. Salmon. 'Le Prieuré des Granges' (L)
category: (L)
tel: 02.47.50.09.67.
fax: 02.47 50.06.43.
email: Salmon.eric@wanadoo.fr
B&B: 94.5€ for two. No Dinner

New owners since this mansion last appeared in FE 15. but the Salmons have changed little. This lovely 17th-19th-century residence is unusual, long and low, elegant, local stone, Renaissance in character, furnished with antiques, set in seven hectares of grounds with swimming pool. The dining room (for breakfasts in winter) is particularly attractive, dramatically decorated with professional skill in blue and white *toile de Jouy*.

Hard to say which of the five bedrooms in an adjoining wing is the nicest – those on the ground floor have independent terraces with little gardens for sunbathing, but some of those on the first floor have spacious balconies for the same purpose. 160€ buys you a suite for four.

Breakfasts are excellent, but there are no evening meals. A very comfortable stay in elegant surrounding in a strategic position, with an English-speaking, friendly host.

SEPMES. 37800.
27 km S of Tours. 22 km WSW of Loches. Take the D59 through Sepmes SP 'Loches'.

☆ Mme. Vergnaud. 'La Ferme des Berthiers'
category: (M)
tel: 02.47.65.50.61.
B&B: 43/48€ for two.
Evening meals 19€ each (incl. wine and coffee).

A firm favourite with all readers who stay here. The large gates of the Ferme des Berthiers stand well back from the main road just outside the village of Sepmes on the road to Loches. Inside is a square courtyard surrounded by the tall farmhouse and other farm buildings. Our room was one of three on the first floor, very large and artistically decorated, using natural stone walls and warm floor tiles, with a yellow pristine shower room to match. Two comfortable armchairs by the sunny window, fresh flowers on a low table and still plenty of room to move about. The other rooms are blue and red, with even loo seats coordinating. A new room is available on the ground floor, gold and blue with superb bathroom fittings. Mme. Vergnaud, who speaks some English, is a perfectionist, and a stay in this lovely house, very handy for visiting the Loire châteaux, is not to be missed. An evening meal on reservation only, including all beverages, is still excellent. The ☆ firmly remains.

LOIR ET CHER

CHAUMONT-sur-LOIRE 41150
30 km east of Tours.

Chaumont château was given to Diane de Poitiers, when she was ousted out of Chenonceau by Catherine de Médicis, it passed through many owners until finally the state bought it in 1938. Not a lot to see in the château itself, but an interesting international garden festival is held in the grounds from June until October each year, depicting especially mosaic garden designs.

From Tours by the N152 to Onzain then right over the Loire bridge, and right again past the *Office de Tourisme* in Chaumont and take the first left up the hill beside the château entrance and the house is on the right corner at the T junction.

M. Gombert. 2, rue des Argillons
Les Hauts de Chaumont.
category: (M)
tel: 02 54 33 91 45.
fax: 02 54 33 91 45.
email: gombart@free.fr
website: www.com.france-bonjour.com/hauts-de-chaumont/
B&B: 47€. for two.

High above the Loire, easy to find. This chambres d'hôtes was once a dependency of the château, now beautifully restored the house in a large garden, behind locked gates, has a salon for guests over which are three bedrooms, comfortably furnished, each with a modern shower room, hair driers etc., everything thought of. Forget *minuteries*, corridor lights come on as you step out of the rooms. Relax by the pool in a very pleasant garden after a long journey or a days châteaux visiting. Swimming towels supplied by the pool. A copious breakfast at separate tables is elegantly presented. For a house situated on the corner of a road traffic noise was surprisingly little and dies at night; but double glazing takes care of any noise light sleepers may hear. No evening meals, La Chancelière restaurant is down the hill beside the Loire, or you are welcome to use the little kitchen corner in the salon and picnic in the garden. The Gombarts are the best of hosts and make one really welcome. Reductions after three nights. Extra beds 12€. Highly recommended.

DANZÉ. 41160.

15 km N of Vendôme by D36 to Danzé, then the D24 towards La Ville-aux-Clercs.

Lovely unspoiled rolling countryside. Vendôme itself is an enchanting little town, built over several branches of the river Loire.

La Borde
Danzé 41

☆ **M. & Mme. Kamette. 'La Borde'**
category: **(M)**
tel: 02.54.80.68.42.
fax: 02.54.80.63.68.
B&B: 38.5/51€ for two. No Dinner

From Danzé take the second chambres d'hôtes sign, down a made-up road, rather than the first which leads very bumpily through the forest. It's a 1930s house set in ten hectares of green and pleasant land in pleasingly hilly countryside. The rooms are all large and well-furnished with modern bathrooms (shower or bath). One has its own terrace, two others (forming a suite) have floor length windows looking over the garden; all are miles away from traffic fret. All good news.

Even better and more unusual is that there is a covered swimming pool in the garden. And there's nice Mme. Kamette, who learnt her English teaching French at Sherborne, so conversation will flow. But best of all are the prices; Madame knows that she cannot compete with accommodation along the Loire as far as site is concerned, but she certainly beats them hollow in value-for-money terms.

MER. 41500.

16 km N of Blois on the RN 152.

Mer is one of those forgotten towns on the Loire that no-one has ever heard of. No châteaux, no great river views. It came as a pleasant surprise to find this chambres d'hôtes in a quiet pedestrian precinct.

The easiest way to arrive by car is by the N152 from Blois, turn left to the church where there is a small car park. The private garden entrance is left at the church along the tiny rue des Idrets and the green gates of Le Clos are on the right, next to No 12.

☆ **M. & Mme. Mormiche. 'Le Clos'**
9, rue Dutems.
category: (M)
tel: 02.54.81.17.36.
fax: 02.54.81.70.19. Credit cards are
accepted.
B&B: 46.5/56€ for two. No Dinner

The house, bang on the road, in the pedestrian precinct is grey and undistinguished with Claude's framing shop fronting it. It is not until you penetrate to the rear that all its 16th-century charms can be appreciated, especially the unexpected garden.

There are more pleasant surprises in store; the rooms are all light and airy, with good, white bathrooms. One is delicate pale blue and white, overlooking the garden, another with grey paint has two white-covered beds, with the possibility of two more being squeezed in, and there is a choice of baths or showers. The rooms overlooking the road have double glazing. Extra beds 9.5€.

Breakfast, taken in a nice beamed room, or outside in the garden, is almost the best I have ever had in a chambres d'hôtes. It is a real bonus to find a place like this in the heart of a town, yet with parking in a shady garden. No evening meals, but you can step out to restaurants or have a picnic upstairs in the little salon, which also has a kitchenette. Both Claude and her farmer husband Joelle, are exceptionally friendly and pleasant, but speak no English. I really like this one – atmosphere, situation, rooms and hosts, so a firm ☆.

MUIDES SUR LOIRE. 41500

15km NE of Blois on the south bank of the Loire. The château is set back from the main road, the D951, just before the town of Muides.

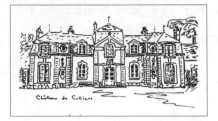

Château des Colliers

☆ **M. & Mme. de Gélis. 'Château des Colliers'**
category: (L)
tel: 02.54.87.50.75.
fax: 02.54.87.03.64.
B&B: 120€ for two.
Closed 1 Dec. to 1 Mar.

Most of the châteaux of the Loire lack any view of the wide shallow river that was their *raison d'être*. Many of the others, especially on the north bank, have offensive *'nationales'* and main railway lines running between them and the water, ruining both the view and the night's repose. The Château des Colliers suffers from neither disadvantage and is probably the best-situated of any entry in this book. The floor-to-ceiling windows of every room look directly out over a grassy terrace to the fast-flowing water and reedy islands, unimpeded on this quiet stretch by man-made views. There is a lovely walk along the river bank, which I thoroughly recommend after a day's car cramp, heading west directly into the evening sun, duplicating its effect on the water.

The 1750 château, bought in 1779 from the Chevalier de Beba, has been in Christian's family for eight generations. He was born and raised here. Portraits of his dignified ancestors look down from their gilt frames in reading room, salon, and dining room, where they have to compete with Sistine Chapel-esque murals and ceiling paintings. Over the main door is the family crest and motto in Basque, which, translated, reads. 'If you are happy here stay a while.' advice which I am sure you would wish to follow.

In spite of the elegance of the building, with gravel courtyard raked every morning, lovely panelling, antique furniture, the atmosphere is far from intimidating. How could it be – this is, after all, a family home in which modest Marie-France has raised a family. Now they have fled their enviable nest, she cooks for even larger numbers – twelve guests often sit round her dining table and eat her delectable dinners.

The rooms, of course, are all different. A ground floor one, has blue *toile* walls, flowery curtains and spread, magnificent *directoire* beds, walnut chest and armoire and, best of all, a fire in the marble grate. The bathroom is unrepentantly luxurious. The room next door is the oldest, with gorgeous ceiling mouldings and double bed, another upstairs with brass bedstead has a secret winding staircase leading to an unexpected large terrace where sun-worshipers can tan privately while taking in the view.

A lovely place to stay, stunning building, charming hosts, comfort and style. And very well situated.

NEUNG-SUR-BEVRON. 41210.
40 km SSE of Orléans.
A pleasant little town close to Chambord château.
From the A71 take *sortie* 03 'Lamotte-Beuvron' then the D923 through la Ferté-Beauharnais to Neung (17 km). or leave the N20 south of la Ferté-St. Aubin by the D922 to la Ferté-Beauharnais then take the D923. Go through the town towards Blois on the D923 and you will find 'Breffni' on the right just after the Crédit Agricole on the left and the turn to la Marolle (D925) on the right.

Mrs. Mary Ellen Crehan. 'Breffni'
16, rue du 11 November.
category: (M)
tel/fax. 02.54.83.66.56.
B&B: 44.5/56€ for two.

A typical Loire house, with dormer windows, on the roadside at the edge of the village. Not a house I would have picked out if the Mayor hadn't written to suggest I was missing something.

The warm welcome by Irish hosts who speak French fluently (Madame lectures at Orléans university) made me sure people would appreciate a visit here. The garden behind the house has adequate parking

Carefully chosen *brocante* furniture makes this little house a very homely place. Steepish stairs lead to the first floor where there are three rooms all with bathrooms. 'Innisfree' has a double bed and shower. 'Innismann' two singles, 'Innismar' a double with a bath. One room on the roadside is perhaps best for early risers.

A guests' salon with TV is also on the first floor, but breakfast is in the yellow dining room which has the original marble fireplace and a charming set of Henri II chairs with the St. Jacques crest.

In term-time if Mary Ellen is working, Patrick steps into the breach and all flows smoothly.

An alternative proposition is the ground-floor *gîte* in the garden, for five, 48€ a day for a family WITHOUT breakfast is good value, or 44.5€ for two with breakfast.

Evening meals, only exceptionally, on arrival. There are two good restaurants in the village. You will wish you had booked a longer stay in the friendly atmosphere of this home.

ONZAIN 41150.

15km SW of Blois on N152, direction Tours. In Onzain take the first left immediately after coming out of the underpass, then the first right then left at a T junction and the house is on the left opposite a Citroen garage.

☆ **Mme. Martine Langlais**
46 rue de Meuves.
category: (M)
tel/fax: 02.54.20.78.82.
B&B: 57.5€ for two. No Dinner
Closed December to April.

Probably more letters of commendation have come in on this one than any other chambres d'hôtes in the Loire. Truth to tell, after all this praise, first impressions of the little house on the main road are somewhat disappointing, in spite of the lovely wisteria-covered walls in May, and it is not until you push open the big iron gate that you begin to see what all the fuss is about. The rear aspect is entirely different, cottagey, with multiple flower beds in the long garden which does indeed extend to the river (but not the Loire, just a very minor tributary). M. Langlais proudly showed us his garden and pointed out the small private parking slot in the front, off the main road. Madame Langlais was out when we arrived but Monsieur efficiently entertained us to tea, elegantly served in the delightful salon, with yellow painted beams and matching chairs and curtains. His good English made conversation easy. Breakfast is taken in the garden or in the pleasant sitting-room with French windows to the garden, exclusively for the guest's use. The five rooms are all extremely pretty with attractive country fabrics, a green flowery version with twin beds and a pink *toile de Jouy* fabric on the walls of another. All have excellent bathrooms, just one is not adjoining.

A really copious breakfast set us up for the day. No evening meals, but the recommendation that we should eat at *'La Chancelière'* overlooking the river at Chaumont-sur-Loire, only a short drive away, was indeed a good one – excellent menus at reasonable prices. Another good reason for staying at Onzain.

A charming place which maintains its a ☆, though prices are creeping up a bit.

LOIRET

JOUY-LE-POTIER. 45370.
20 km S of Orléans. 10 km from Bellefontaine.

Exit 2 from the A71 continue south on the D15 for 11 km and follow signs off the La Ferté-St. Aubin road.

M. & Mme. Becchi.
778 rue de Chevenelle.
category: (M)
tel: 02.38.45.83.07.
B&B: 41€ for two.
Evening meals 15€ each.

Just outside the neat village of Jouy-le-Potier in a residential area of modern houses with spacious gardens, this immaculate chambres d'hôtes, is well signed. A very restful stop after a fast drive from the Channel ports, and easy to find, but book ahead as there is virtually only one room .

You will receive a warm welcome and be entertained to an excellent meal as real guests of the Becchis. The well-furnished main guest room is on the first floor and has two single beds, thick carpets and huge built-in wardrobe. and a very spacious shower room. It overlooks the back garden and fields beyond. There is another room on the ground floor which has an adjacent loo, but no washing facilities, suitable for an extra member of the family, sharing the upstairs shower room. Since my last visit there is another room upstairs, but only for the same family, as bathroom facilities must be shared. Also on the landing a cosy sitting area with TV and plenty of books on the Loire provided.

Mme. Becchi speaks good English, and has decorated her house with some striking dried flower arrangements. An elegant stop in the Loire valley where your hosts will be delighted to give you any information about the area.

'I used your guide this year for the first time and booked B and B with M. and Mme. Becchi at Jouy le Potier. It lived up very much to expectations as described in your book. I look forward to using your book again next year'. Chris Cusson.

MÉNESTREAU-en-VILLETTE. 45240.

25 km S of Orléans. 15km E of La Ferté-St.-Aubin.

In the Sologne region of the Loire near to the more northern reaches of the river. From Marcilly-en-Villette take the D64 (SP Sennely) and in 6 km look carefully for a sign to Les Foucault down a forest track on the right, easy to miss.

☆ **Mme. Rosemary Beau. 'Ferme des Foucault'**
category: (M)
tel: 02.38.76.94.41.
B&B: 57.6/67€ for two. No Dinner

Driving down this track penetrating into the forest you will think you are getting nowhere, but in one kilometremail boxes come into view. After this take a sharp right, and you have arrived

This red brick farmstead, typical of the area, doesn't look particularly exciting and the rural grounds have outhouses yet to be converted. However, once through the front door the whole place is amazingly attractive.

American Rosemary Beau and her French husband have converted this woodland dwelling from a complete ruin, into a spacious home, offering chambres d'hôtes for the last few years.

The lounge, with interesting picture windows overlooking the forest, is light and airy; a mixture of modern and ancient furniture extends to a dining area.

One guest room on the ground floor has thick pile carpets, a private sitting room with a convertible for children and a separate bathroom. Nothing stinted here.

Upstairs is even better. An extensive white-walled bedroom, lushly carpeted, stretches across the house past countless windows of all shapes and sizes. The mixture of old beams, modern king-size bed, duvet and pretty fabrics, is perfection. I wished I could be like their black cat who just strayed in from the forest, knew a good thing when he saw it and stayed firmly put! A third room, even more luxurious, is now ready, and it will soon have its own balcony. Again stretching across the house, it has many windows, luxury bathroom with dual washbasins, bath and separate shower. Extra bed 12.5€. No evening meals, but Rosemary, whose easy American welcome is charming, will direct you to local restaurants 10 mins. drive away.

I just loved everything about this place, particularly the relaxed atmosphere and utter quiet. The price depends on the luxury of the room. Minimum stay is now two nights. With 70% of her guests returning you will need to book well ahead to avoid disappointment.

Well worth a ☆ for the superb accommodation and welcome.

Western Loire

LOIRE (WESTERN)

Town
Chambres d'Hôtes
0   20km

Western Loire

It is a highly confusing piece of administrative bureaucracy that half the Loire valley should be in the region of 'Centre Val de Loire' and the other half 'Western Loire'. Just to make matters worse the latter is sometimes referred to as 'Pays de la Loire'.

The tourist office in Chinon cannot help you with information on neighbouring Saumur, and vice versa, The 'Centre' gets most tourists because of proximity to Paris and because of the abundance of famous châteaux, but in many ways I prefer Western Loire. The river here is more interesting. As if sensing that the end of its journey is near, it hurries along, rather than dawdling among sand banks. There are islands, some inhabited, like charming Béhuard, and small fishing villages right up to the Nantes agglomeration. The pace is slower here, the crowds thin out, beds and meals cost significantly less. The roads following the river are quieter, with more space, better views, fewer lorries. Particularly attractive is the stretch between Saumur and Les Rosiers on the south bank, and so is the Corniche Angevin, high above the water, with lovely views down to the river and the vineyards.

If I had to pick just one base along the whole Loire it would be Saumur; if I had to pick just one city it would be Nantes – both in this region. The former has multiple interests – a fine château overlooking the river, famous sparkling wine, the prestigious *Cadre Noir* riding establishment and the mushroom caves, to name but a few. pedestrianisation and the restoration of the medieval section has been a great success, and Saumur is now a good town, of manageable size, to cover on foot. Nantes, again with a fine château and fascinating history, is elegant and underestimated.

The *département* of the **Loire-Atlantique** is still considered by many (myself included) as part of Brittany. Historically and culturally yes, administratively no. Nantes certainly leans towards the Loire, but the rest is distinctly Breton in character.

The northernmost *département*, **Mayenne**, deserves to be better known. It suffers from an identity problem – associated neither with Normandy nor the Loire Valley, so that many people have difficulty in placing it geographically. I was surprised to find how few guide books even bother to mention it. However, it is a pity to consider it purely as a transit area since it encompasses some lovely green, unspoilt countryside and the river from which it takes its name flows swiftly through lush meadows. The two main towns, Laval and Château-Gontier, both on the Mayenne, are well worth a visit. The old part of Laval has some picturesque 16th-century houses clustered round a rather grim 12th-century château and Château-Gontier offers a fine Romanesque church and a pleasant walk through the old priory gardens *(le Bout du Monde)* to the narrow streets around the riverside.

Maine-et-Loire is the *département* most closely associated with the Loire, with most of the tourist attractions (and chambres d'hôtes) within its confines. The *préfecture*, Angers, is actually 8 kms north of the Loire, on the banks of a very short river indeed, the Maine, formed by the confluence of the rivers Sarthe and Mayenne. From the château, one of the most interesting in the entire region thanks not only to its position and antiquity but to the miraculous Tapestry of the Apocalypse it houses, is a magnificent view of all the watery configuration below. There are good shops and restaurants to visit on gloomy days and as this is a university town, plenty of café activity. Angers prides itself on being the cultural centre of the region, so you can also bank on a variety of concerts and exhibitions for further interest. Saumur comes within this *département* and the final resting place of the Plantagenets – Fontevraud – both of them top priorities on any tourist's list. North of Angers the tourists fade away and the prices tumble, but there is plenty of attraction still in the rivers that flow towards the Loire – this is the best area for a boating holiday.

Sarthe too has its share of tributaries; notably in the pleasant bustling country town of Sablé-sur-Sarthe, famous for its buttery biscuits – *'sablés'* – where streams of the Sarthe, the Erve and the Vaige crop up all over the place. Neighbouring Solesmes is famous for the Gregorian chant heard in its elephantine abbey, where many recordings of the newly-popular plainsong have been made. The main city of the *département*, Le Mans, is of course famous for the 24-hour motor race which brings hordes of enthusiasts into the area for one brief frenzy, filling the hotel beds for miles around. I wonder how many bother to explore the medieval city, let alone the cathedral where Geoffrey Plantagenet married Matilda of England, the grand-daughter of William the Conqueror. Their son, Henry, later to become king, was born here.

The **Vendée** is an area that often surprises those who believe they know all there is to know about France. Inland lies a unique watery network where the residents go about their business by flat-bottomed boat and the light filters eerily green through the overhanging leaves. The coast is one long sweeping sandbank, ideal for family holidays. It is a region more appreciated by the French than the British and tends to die outside their holiday periods. Consequently few chambres d'hôtes.

LOIRE-ATLANTIQUE

GUÉNOUVRY 44290.

64 km S of Rennes. 50km N of Nantes. 25 km E of Redon.

On the edge of the Forêt du Gâvre on the borders of Western Loire and Brittany. This would make a good stop for walkers as the 'GR' paths along the River Don run just behind it.

Mr &. Mrs. Skelton. 'Le Tournesol'
Les Rivières.
category: (S)
tel: 02.40.51.14.32.
email: chrisylvskelton@ wanadoo.fr
B&B: 32/40€ for two, 56€ for family room.
Evening meal 15€ each

The Skeltons have retired to France after many years in Africa and the Middle East, and in this rustic hamlet have converted a 150-year-old farmhouse, into a very pleasant family home. Many souvenirs of their years abroad give the house a comfortable lived-in feeling. Sideways on to the road, particularly nice walled gardens are the ideal spot for lazing in summer and meals are often taken outside. All rooms are warmly carpeted, on the first floor the 'African' room, with pretty blue linen shares a bathroom with the Sunflower room; there is one en suite room suitable for a family of four.

When not entertaining guests, Chris Skelton, an artist, retreats to his top floor studio to paint.

Continental breakfast is included but 2.4€ extra buys you an English breakfast. Evening meals with a half-bottle of house wine are good value and you can even have a buffet lunch for 7.2€.

Somehow the vibes seemed right here and I felt lone travellers would find this a particularly friendly place to stay, where they would quickly become part of the family.

MONNIÈRES. 44690.

11 km SE of Nantes.

Close to the city of Nantes, in the centre of the wine-growing area of the Loire, famous for Muscadet and Gros Plant.

Take the N249 to Haie-Fouassière, then the N149 SP 'Clisson', then the D7 right to Monnières. The château is signed in the village. Take the D76 from the square, then left in about 1km.

☆ **M. & Mme. Calonne.** 'Château Plessis-Brézot'
category: (L)
tel: 02.40.54.63.24.
fax: 02.40.54.66.07.
B&B: 75/107€ for two. No Dinner
Closed 1 Nov. to 30 Mar.

The Calonnes have moved from Calais and bought a charming 17th-century château in two hectares of lawns and woodland surrounded by 30 hectares of their own vineyards.

The entrance to the château is through a gateway into a courtyard where there is a small chapel complete with bell tower opposite stable accommodation for horses and the all important *chai* where the Muscadet is made. *Dégustations* on the spot.

They have renovated much in the few years they have lived here. Monsieur has a great penchant for antique shops and never visits one without buying something to add to his collection. Attractive carved wooden friezes to put over the beds, tiny shelves and tables, choir stalls, panelling for the walls and antique wood doors all find their niche in the many rooms in the château.

In the entrance hall is a magnificent stone carved archway at the foot of the tower stairway. Uncovered by chance by Monsieur, it had been totally bricked up for years. The primrose panelling in the lounge is only a small part of the renovations.

There is something particularly magical about waking in the early morning sunshine in a château and looking out at surrounding vineyards and feeling you are part of it, if only for a short time.

There are five guest rooms in a wing of the château, incorporating two of the towers, which have independent access from a new-panelled salon.

One room on the ground floor, especially designed for the handicapped, has a large shower room overlooking the rear lawns.

Two rooms on the first floor have baths, heated towel rails, luxury white towels, soap, shampoo, etc. A twin-bedded room in front has a view over the vineyards, the swimming pool and the *chai*. The smaller double-bedded room overlooks the peaceful rear woodland. On the second floor are two similar rooms but the higher you go the better the view.

A charming natural welcome from both Monsieur and Madame and their daughter. You will treasure the memories of a stay here. No evening meals, but helpful advice offered on where to dine. ☆ for *accueil* and comfort.

PIERRIC. 44290.
50 km S of Rennes 4km S of Le Grand Fougeray. The tidy little village of Pierric is just over the border from Brittany.

From Rennes take the N137 to le Grand Fougeray then through the town take the D69 towards Pierric. In about 2 km cross the River Chère and take the next right (SP 'La Bignonnais'), then first left (SP 'La Couillais'). At the junction of three roads take the one to the right and the house is third on the right.

Mr. & Mrs. Hough. 'La Bignonnais'
category: (S)
tel/fax: 02.40.07.91.78.
email: donmonhough@
compuserve.com
By reservation only from October to Easter.
B&B: 36.5€ for two.
Evening meal 13.5€.

This pretty elongated cottage nestles in the countryside 2 km from the village. A short front garden leads you to the red-painted front doors. Your English hosts have tastefully restored the cottage, from a ruin keeping many old features. One guest bedroom has its own entrance from the front garden, large enough to include a sitting area by a wood burning stove and room for an extra bed, (8€) and an adjoining shower room and loo. Warmly carpeted, it would be comfortable at any time of the year. Another room upstairs is prettily decorated in blue and white; a small window looks over the garden, and a large skylight adds plentiful light. A private bathroom with a bath is opposite across the landing.

You can have an English breakfast for 3.2€ extra, and evening meals if reserved ahead, with a carafe of red or white wine. This establishment has recently been approved by the tourist board and awarded two Gîte de France stars.

A 10% deposit is required on booking

MAINE-et-LOIRE

CHAMPIGNÉ 49330

32 km N of Angers, by N162 and D768. Go through the village of Champigné and take the road for Sablé. The château is signed on the left after approx 3.5 km. This is unspoiled farming country between the rivers Mayenne and Sarthe, relatively undiscovered by tourists, with plenty of interest – boating, châteaux, Angers, Sablé, Solesmes – all within easy reach.

Champigné 49 — Château des Briottières

☆ François and Hedwige de Valbray. 'Château des Briottières' category: (L)
tel: 02.41.42.00.02.
fax: 02.41.42.01.55.
website: www.briottieres.com
email: briottières@wanadoo.fr
B&B: 120/336€ (rooms/suite) for two Evening Meals 48€ each, breakfast an additional 10.4€.

François is everybody's friend, especially his guests'. A pioneer of the stately-home chambres d'hôtes, he shares his acquired experience (some of it bitter, mostly lyrical) generously. He inherited the stunningly beautiful 17th-century Les Briottières and took on the daunting task of restoring its fading beauty. It's a never-ending mission. One year it is the stables (now used for wedding receptions) that get the treatment, then the lovely *orangerie*, now converted into a charming villa, then the doll-sized chapel where the increasing brood of the Valbrays (six at the most recent count) get baptised, then the swimming pool, much appreciated by his guests in the long hot summers. Welcome extra income accumulated from letting out the whole château to the film crew making *'Impromptu'*, the story of George Sand and Chopin, who made two most attractive innovations – they painted the lovely glassed-in promenade panelling in Chinese yellow and added a trellis to the verandah.

Grandma's room has been redecorated, *La chambre de mon Grandpère* is the most expensive room, at 176€. Another, with twin beds, decorated in pink *toile de Jouy*, with marble bathroom, costs 144€, as does *La Petite Chambre Rose*, where François has resurrected an old, green, claw-footed bath and lined the walls with old door panels, and there is another smaller but perfectly good version at 120€. Eight rooms altogether, all charming.

With family commitments, it is no longer possible for your hosts to dine with you, but Madame still does all the cooking and François ably helps with serving and entertaining. He is a natural host, whose gusts of laughter soon break down the shyest guests' inhibitions. There is now an honesty bar in one of the salons, enabling guests to help themselves to drinks at all times.

It is no use going to Les Briottières in search of bland luxury hotel perfection, even though rooms have multiplied over the last few years. Go rather for appreciation of a charming French family, living in a lovely building, good company and the *joie de vivre* of your host.

CHAZÉ-SUR-ARGOS. 49500.
13km W of Le Lion d'Angers.

This is fertile watery countryside, with several rivers speeding through to join the mighty Loire. Lots of opportunities to explore them by boats hired from Le Lion d'Angers and other pleasant bases.

Take the Candé road, the D770, and the turning is on the right 3 km after Vern d'Anjou, well signed up a long drive lined with young trees.

Susan and Peter Scarboro. 'La Chaufournaie'
category: (S)
tel/fax: 02.41.61.49.05.
B&B: 41€ for two.
Evening meals 18.4€ only in summer.

The Scarboros first visited the region when their home village was twinned with Vern d'Anjou, and liked it so much that they resolved to buy something suitable for B&Bs. Word of mouth from satisfied customers has ensured that without the assistance of any guide books, thank you very much, they welcomed many guests from England and elsewhere, and are enjoying their new lifestyle very much. The five rooms are well equipped with thoughtful extras like tea-making facilities, and although the windows are dormer, there is plenty of light and space. One family room has an additional bed for 14.5€. Easy access from the parking area is from an outside staircase.

A converted barn makes an excellent wet-weather retreat, with board games, books, a full-sized billiard table and an old English institution which must puzzle the natives – what is French for shove-h'apenny? The English fry-up breakfast costs 5.6€ supplement, and nice Susan Scarboro also provides a further taste of home cooking in the evenings. 'Nothing fancy', she modestly disclaims, at dinner-time – four courses including *apéritif*, wine is extra, but no wine costs more than 6.4€ a bottle. Sitting on the lawn imbibing *apéritifs* with your hosts in the evening sunshine is a very civilised ending to a busy day of golf or excursions. Great hosts and very reasonable prices.

ECUILLÉ 49460.
20 km N of Angers

Going north on the D768 from Angers to Champigné turn right at the signs to 'Château la Roche', just after the junction with the D74 to Ecuillé. The farmhouse is on the left a short distance along the drive.

Patrice & Régine de la Bastille.
'Malvoisine'
category: (M)
tel: 02.41.93.34.44.
B&B: 59€ for two.
Evening meal 24€ each.

The old farmhouse (of the Château la Roche, which still belongs to Patrice's father) has been renovated to make an interesting home, in which there are now three rustic and prettily furnished guest rooms. One on the ground floor has a double bed and bathroom and windows open on to a sunny terrace. A smaller room opening on to a different terrace is in pretty green check, with a shower in the corner but a private loo just outside. Upstairs a room for three, double and one single, is carpeted and decorated in red persuasion, again with a good bathroom.

Régine will prepare you an evening meal, wine *compris*, served in the old beamed dining room. Easy parking beside the house adjacent to farm buildings. A nice quiet stop with young, friendly hosts who have made their rooms most attractive.

Recommended by François de Valbray.

FONTEVRAUD l'ABBAYE. 49590.
16 km SE of Saumur, 21 km W of Chinon.

A few introductory lines is no way to describe even a small part of the treasures of Fontevraud. Buy a guide book (or even better *French Entrée* on the Loire!) and fill in the gaps on what should be an essential stop on every tourist's Loire itinerary. Particularly every British itinerary, since in the abbey here, dubbed the Westminster of the Plantagenets, lie four effigies that belong to our heritage – Henry II of England, his wife Eleanor of

Aquitaine, their son Richard Coeur de Lion, and Isabelle of Angoulème, second wife of their son John Lackland. All most moving, especially if you get there early or late and can view them without the distraction of other tourists. Painted in faded blue and red, all individuals, Isabelle carved in wood and the others in tufa stone.

Their resting place is the largest and virtually complete ensemble of medieval monastic building in France. In fact a whole village, within a village. Take a tour, but leave time to visit the Romanesque parish church of St. Michel. The pleasant little town has plenty of comfort stops – a well-known family hotel, a Michelin-starred restaurant, several bars and a good *salon de thé*, so a visit here can be rewarding gastronomically as well as spiritually.

More comfort is at hand if you turn off the D947 some 3 km before Fontevraud and follow the signs to:

☆ **M. et Mme. Dauge. 'Domaine de Mestré'**
category: (L)
tel: 02.41.51.75.87.
B&B: 65.5€ for two
Evening meals 23€ each.
Closed 20 Dec. to 1 Mar.

The monks of Fontevraud used the Domaine as an agricultural complex, and some of the weathered stone buildings round the courtyard date from the 12th century. Traces of Roman road indicate that there has been a settlement here since time immemorial. Good use has been put to the assorted outbuildings: one is now a shop selling tempting take-home souvenirs – fragrant soaps and toilet desiderata made from pure, natural ingredients, perfuming the whole room. In another building are four rooms, smaller than those in the main building and used in winter because they are easier to heat. A 12th-century chapel is now a lovely dining room, with dark, wormy beams straddling the lofty ceiling and a massive oak *armoire* presiding over all. This is where dinner is served, with lots of home-grown vegetables served as first course, along with meat or fowl then cheese and home-made deserts. Rosine Dauge does all the cooking, farmer husband Dominique serves and daughter Marie-Amélie helps out here and in the shop. It is very much a family affair and always has been – the Domaine has been in the same family since the 18th century.

The late Laura Ashley would have been delighted to see the good use that her fabrics have been put to here in the annex, but it is the main building that Rosine has had most fun, using different colour schemes in every room (with coordinating bathrooms) every one a winner, spacious and gracious, furnished with antiques.

There are extensive grounds attached to the Domaine and breakfast in summer is served on the terrace looking down to the green valley. All this is very good news indeed, at a reasonable price, with all the joys of Fontevraud thrown in; the bad news is that the word has got around and it is not easy to get a reservation in high season, even though there are twelve rooms. So be sure to book early and don't miss out on this one whatever you do. Dinner exclusive of wine.

GREZ-NEUVILLE. 49220.

16 km S of Château-Gontier by N162 D28. 20 km N of Angers.

One of those time-warped villages, utterly delightful, with grey, sun-bleached stone houses, that one sometimes stumbles upon in France. In this case the big attraction is the river Mayenne flowing flat and wide here, over a weir. There are boats for hire, trips up the river, walks along the bank, and the activity of a lock to contemplate. For evening meals a variety of restaurants and cafés are all of fifty paces from a most delightful chambres d'hôtes, next to the church.

La Croix d'Etain

GRE3- Neuville 49

☆ **Mme. Jacqueline Bahuaud. 'La Croix d'Etain'**
category: (M)
tel: 02.41.95.68.49.
fax: 02.41.18.02.72.
B&B: 60.5/76.5€ for two.

An immaculate *Directoire* period house, very French, all grey and white and proving to be much bigger than one might guess from first sight. The yellow salon, embellished with an amazingly ornate grandfather clock, is huge, and a very pleasant place to sit if the weather does not suggest a seat in the garden (where breakfast is served in the summer). The grounds, too, are surprisingly extensive – 1.5 hectares, much of it river frontage.

Four bedrooms, each with a luxurious bathroom, are all different; lovely, spacious, pleasantly furnished, even having tea-making facilities and like the rest of the house, look as if they have just been painted. Two have splendid river views.

I rate this one very highly as an agreeable, comfortable place to stay, in a particularly attractive village. Officially closed Nov-Easter, but Mme. Bahuaud is in residence throughout the year and welcomes guests in winter if they phone well ahead. Parking, not immediately apparent, is behind locked gates in the rear garden. I couldn't fault this one – the rooms are better than any five star hotel, and the hosts charming, the ☆ firmly remains.

LA JAILLE-YVON. 49220.

39 km N of Angers.

Turn off N162 to D189 and then D187 signed Chambellay. The château is well signed.

An excellent location, not only for an *en route* stopover, but as a base from which to explore this gentle watery territory, where a river is never far away. At Le Lion d'Angers, 9 km south, or at Cheneille-Changé, even nearer, you can take a soothing excursion on the meandering Mayenne. In total contrast, the urban attractions of Angers and many of the lesser-known châteaux are within easy reach.

Château le Plessis
La Jaille-Yvon

☆ **M. & Mme. Benoist. 'Château Le Plessis'**
category: (L)
tel: 02.41.95.12.75.
fax: 02.41.95.14.41.
email: plessis.anjou@wanadoo.fr
B&B: 131€ for two.
Evening meal 44.5€ each.
Closed 1 Nov. to 1 Mar.

M. Benoist is a pioneer in the aristocratic B&B business. The rule to join the illustrious 'Château Accueil' group to which he belongs is that the château must have been in the family for at least two generations. 16th-century Le Plessis certainly qualifies, since it has been in Mme. Benoist's family since well before the Revolution, when in 1793 all the furniture except one treasured table was burned by the rebels. However, to be able to say that the replacements date from the time of your great-great-grandfather is more than most of us can claim.

The continuity and the feeling that the furniture and house are there to serve the family, not to be regarded as 'antiques', permeates the atmosphere. This is a home that happens to be in a very beautiful and historic building; all is friendly and relaxed. Venerable trees and sweeping lawns, studded with primroses and daffodils in spring, surround the house and contribute to the calm. When I last visited, final preparations for their daughter's wedding next day were in progress, but they were still courteous enough to show me round. Eight guest rooms, all with bath.

M. Benoist used to work for Mobil Oil, so his English is fluent and Mme. Benoist is an unusually good cook, so that dinner round their large oval table, served with carefully-chosen Anjou wines is bound to be a rewarding experience. By reservation only, but not on Sundays.

LE LION d'ANGERS. 49220.
25 km NW of Angers.

5 km NW of Le Lion d'Angers, a left turn off the D863, signed on the left.

M. & Mme. Viviers. 'Domaine des Travaillières'
category: (S)
tel: 02.41.61.33.56.
B&B: 33/36.5€ for two. No Dinner

Recommended by a reader, this rustic farmhouse has been converted into a charming comfortable home. Well off the main road, quiet, with pretty gardens.

Two family suites have adjoining rooms for children, sharing the bathroom; one on the ground floor has access to the garden. Another, just for a couple, has a double bed. The interesting *outeaux* windows in the roof actually open into the rooms and give a pleasant through breeze on a hot summer night.

Evening meals are occasionally possible if reserved but there are many restaurants in the vicinity.

Vivacious Mme. Viviers is a superb cook and makes a tasty nut *gâteau* which often arrives on the breakfast table. Her daughter has painted many of the pictures decorating the walls. English understood more than Mme. Viviers professes. Really good value with budget prices. I think this one will prove very popular.

ST LAMBERT-DES-LEVÉES. 49400.
3 km W of Saumur on the north bank of the Loire.

From Saumur cross the river, but don't turn immediately left on to the river road. Take the next turning, past the railway station, the D229. 3 km further on look for the chambres d'hôtes sign on the right.

☆ **Helga and Jean-Pierre Minder.**
'La Croix de la Voulte'
category: (L)
tel: 02.41.38.46.66.
B&B: 67/83€ for two. No Dinner
Closed Nov. to Easter.

Look no further if you seek a chambres d'hôtes with enthusiastic English-speaking hosts, stylish comfortable rooms, within easy reach of the Loire and Saumur, with a swimming pool thrown in, and all for a reasonable price.

German Helga, and French Jean-Pierre, first opened these four rooms in the 15th-century wing of this mostly 17th-century house in 1990. Since then the Minders have continuously renovated and improved the property. Not only is the comfort exceptional but also the taste is irreproachable – the character of the old manor house is respected but with colourful touches to enliven the old stones. The rooms are all quite different and it is obvious that Helga has had great pleasure in choosing the decor for each one. The largest boasts a four-poster bed, massive stone fireplace and old *armoire*. Antique furniture throughout and low beamed fireplaces contribute to the atmosphere of times gone by (but with modern plumbing). The Minders like nothing better than to see their guests stretch out on smart recliners beside their pool. They also like to see them mellow. So in each room there is a *seau à champagne* – an ice-bucket so that guests can buy the local fizzy wine (who could resist?) and bring it chilled to drink by the pool side. Conviviality guaranteed. This is just one of the personal touches that make staying here such a pleasure. Jean-Pierre sees to it that the garden is full of flowers and a pleasant place to sit for breakfast. He is readily available to help plan the guests' day and advise on itineraries. Four rooms with a choice of shower or bath. No dinner offered because there are so many restaurants in nearby Saumur or Les Rosiers to choose from. Breakfast is optional, deduct 11€ from the price if you don't want it.

MAYENNE

CHAMMES. 53270 Ste-Suzanne.
35 km W of Laval towards Le Mans. Take the Vaiges exit from the autoroute A81. Chammes is 2 km from the village of Vaiges.

The medieval village of Sainte-Suzanne, besieged unsuccessfully by William the Conqueror in 1083 is only 5 km away and the whole of the Coëvrons area of the Western Loire is on your doorstep for horse trekking or rambling with a guide.

Le Chêne Vert

M. et Mme. Morize. 'Le Chêne Vert'
category: (M)
tel: 02.43.01.41.12. or 06 83 35 41 80.
fax: 02.43.01.47.18.
B&B: 41.16 € for two.
Evening meals 14.48 € each

A useful stop just off the A81. between Laval and Le Mans.

The Morizes are cereal farmers, who manage to combine hosting guests with farming and bringing up an ever increasing family. You will rarely be refused a room here (there are at least eight) or an evening meal. We were once offered the large family dormitory just for two of us, when all the others were occupied.

Rooms, both in the main house and in reconstructed outbuildings, are compact and very tastefully furnished, with all the best hotel amenities. In summer their swimming pool, is an added attraction for guests arriving early.

The evening meal of local produce, taken with the family at a long table includes cider, aperitifs and wine are charged, but always available.

English spoken, easy parking, swings for children, drinks from the bar on request, one of those welcome places where standards have been maintained for years, and prices haven't escalated.

LAVAL 53000.
146 kms S of Caen, 249 kms SE of Le Havre.

An under-appreciated town, generally conceived as merely a staging post on the way between port and the Loire valley. In fact, there is much to value, particularly in the old town which clusters round the castle on the sloping west bank of the picturesque River Mayenne. The modern town centres on the huge square, named after Marshal Foch, from which the main shopping streets radiate. Climb up to the courtyard of the *vieux château*, enclosed by ramparts from which there is a good view of the multi-coloured, multi-centred roofs of the old town. The bulk of the castle dates from the 13th and 15th centuries, but the windows, whose white tufa stone is carved with Italianiate scrolls, were added in the 16th century. The crypt and the keep are the oldest parts (12th and 13th centuries). The most interesting feature of the keep is the extraordinary timber roof built in 1100 in an ingenious circular design, incorporating great beams radiating from the centre and projecting beyond the 6 ft thick walls.

Take a walk along the quays on the east bank for the best overall views of Laval, across the now canalised waters of the river. The hump-backed *Pont Vieux* dating from the 13th century also offers good views of the slate roofs, the narrow streets of half-timbered houses and the castle keep. Lovely walks in La Perrine Gardens, with rose garden, ponds and waterfalls.

☆ M. & Mme. François Williot. 'Le Bas du Gast'
6, rue de la Halle aux Toiles.
category: (L)
tel: 02.43.49.22.79.
fax: 02.43.56.44.71.
B&B: 88/104€f for two. No Dinner
Closed December and January

This one is special on several counts. Although it is a rare city chambres d'hôtes, it is country-quiet by virtue of its setting in a sleepy square of dignified old grey houses and because of its surprising garden. The garden is typically 18th-century French, very formal and graced with no less than 85 box pyramids which the energetic M. Williot prunes himself every year. You can imagine yourself an elegantly dressed aristocrat as you play a gentle game of croquet, or settle for more plebeian boules.

Hard to choose between the four lovely bedrooms, each decorated with style and excellent taste. I liked the double-bedded *Chambre Jaune,* but the *toile de Jouy* version with twin beds, is pretty nice too. Then there is the very imposing *Chambre Napoléon* with three beds (supplement 40€ for third incumbent) or the suite of *Chambre Bleue* and *Verte* which can be opened up for one luxurious ensemble, 1150f, or booked separately. All have outstanding bathrooms with every conceivable freebie.

The dining room has two stoops for washing hands before a meal, one for the ladies and one for the gentlemen. Standing in the lounge, mirrors are so arranged that you can see through four in all directions. M. Williot is the friendliest, most accommodating, English-speaking host, who will go to endless trouble to point you in all kinds of right directions. A ☆ for all-round excellence.

LOIRON. 53220.
11 km W of Laval. 23km SE of Vitré.

In total contrast, a handy night stop on a farm just off the fast A81 which runs from Paris to South Brittany cutting through the northern part of the Loire region.

From exit 5 at La Gravelle take the N157 back towards Laval for 9 km. Don't take the right turn to Loiron but in 2 km look for the signs to the chambres d'hôtes on the right at La Chapelle du Chêne.

M. & Mme. Rabourg. 'La Charbonnerie'
category: (S-M)
tel/fax: 02.43.02.44.74.
B&B: 36.5/41.5€ for two.
Evening meals 12.5€ each.
Closed: 1 Nov. to 31 Mar. by reservation only.

A kilometre from the main road, surrounded by 40 hectares of fields where only the lowing of cattle is heard. The house was once a *maison bourgeoise* with a small chapel in the grounds, demolished in the Revolution. Only the chapel remains, where the statue on the epistle side is of Saint Denis, patron saint of Paris, with head tucked under one arm. Legend has it that when he was beheaded he picked up his head and walked away.

The present farmhouse, of typical stone and brick of the region, was built in the 19th century and has been in the same family ever since.

Two first-floor guest rooms are in a separate little cottage. The unadorned simplicity of the rooms is quite charming. A pretty pale blue room for three has a giant double bed (which can convert to two singles) with a delicate *ciel de lit*, spotless white sheets and a vast *broderie anglaise* duvet; there is plenty of room for the single bed under the eaves, little white pedestals support bedside lamps and the dual aspect low windows complement it all. The adjoining large bathroom has a bath with shower and a separate loo, good lights and hair drier. The second room for two is smaller and has a shower and, yes, both are fully carpeted! Extra bed 8€.

In the salon below is one of the largest bread ovens I have ever seen, now a feature fireplace. The dining room has a kitchen area. Mme. Rabourg joins her guests for evening meals., but Monsieur, busy on the farm, only occasionally makes it. Her generous *tarte-aux-pommes* was the best I have tasted. Guests may opt for use of the kitchen and self-catering, but I would advise eating here at least once. I think this chambres d'hôtes could prove very popular but there is not a lot of English spoken.

SAINT-JEAN-sur-ERVE. 53270.
46km W of Le Mans. 30 km E of Laval.
This tiny village has a *boulangerie, charcuterie* and a restaurant.

Follow the N157 from Laval to Le Mans and turn off to the village 7 km after Vaiges. The chambres d'hôtes is exactly opposite the Restaurant de l'Erve beside the bridge.

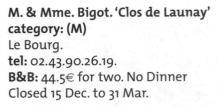

M. & Mme. Bigot. 'Clos de Launay'
category: (M)
Le Bourg.
tel: 02.43.90.26.19.
B&B: 44.5€ for two. No Dinner
Closed 15 Dec. to 31 Mar.

M. and Mme. Bigot have spent four years restoring their house. Now the garden with green lawns extends right along the small river bank. The house is in the centre of the village but double-glazing takes care of noise and there is little traffic. Mme. Bigot does not serve evening meals. She says it gives them more time to enjoy their guests, and there is a good restaurant on the doorstep.

Four immaculate rooms have been thoughtfully designed; double or twin beds, and showers with separate loos. A rear room, with a charming view of the lake and river, has three beds. Warmly heated, carpeted, this would be a welcome winter stop. In summer lazing beside the river, picnicking in the garden would be ideal. A large parking space behind the house keeps your car safe. Your hosts really enjoy their guests and have much information of the area.

SARTHE 72

GUÉCELARD 72230

The long village straddles the N23 9 km S of Le Mans. From A 11 exit 9 follow N 226 south of Le Mans to N23 SP La Flêche. In 10 km at traffic lights in Guécelard turn right direction La Suze, and in 1.2 km the château is on the right.

M. & Mme. Babault. Le Château de Mondan.
category: (M)
tel: 02 43 87 92 16.
fax: 02 43 77 13 85.
email: chateau.mondan@ wanadoo.fr.
website: perso.wanadoo.fr/ chateau.mondan
B&B: 55€/61€. for two
Evening meal 95€

Drive up to this little 18th century château surrounded by six hectares of parkland bordering the river Sarthe. Nothing fazes vivacious Mme. Baboult, our early arrival in the afternoon caught her doing the household chores, late, because she had spent the morning taking a children's catechism class. She still found time to show me her guest rooms before other guests arrived. Four in the château, two on the ground floor and two above, have private access. Colourful rooms, most with original polished wood floors and marble fire places and tall windows, king-size beds convert to singles when preferred, all have tea making facilities. 'La Vezanne' a very pretty green room on the ground floor is carpeted and has a bath, others enjoy large shower rooms with ample space for vanitory bags. In the original stables, one time caretaker's house, are two family suites, just as nicely furnished, one for six shares a bath, shower room and loo, the other is for four, each with direct access to the garden.

Pet horses graze in a paddock. Take a peaceful stroll along the river where cyclamen cascade down the banks, while the children indulge in more robust exercise in a large play area where there are swings, see-saws and climbing frames not to mention two tennis courts.

This is a real family home, with two comfortable salons and guests can join the family for an evening meal, all drinks included. Nothing stuffy about this château lady, as she says 'If there is anything you want, don't panic, just ask me!'. Monsieur is the local pharmacist, if you have forgotten your pills you might strike lucky here! Breakfast would put many a five star hotel to shame – cereal – yoghurts – fresh fruit – every variety of croissant, elegantly served in front of a log fire on cooler days. All way above expectations.

Stay a week or four nights mid-week, and one night is free. For a three night week-end 20% reduction.

ST LÉONARD-DES-BOIS. 72590.
19 km SW of Alençon by D315.

At Moulin-le-Charbonel turn left on to the D258 St. Léonard-des-Bois. At T-junction just before St. Léonard turn left away from the village, and the mill is signed on the right about 200 metres along the road.

If for nothing else (and in fact there is a lot) I would be grateful to this entry for the chance to discover the gorgeous countryside in the area. I had never visited Les Alpes Mancelles before, and now I find it a region of, if not Alps as we know them, sizeable hills, beech forests, deep valleys, rushing rivers, lush green vegetation. Yes, now I come to think of it, it is a bit like lowland Switzerland, without the cuckoo clocks. What is more, it is a perfect *en route* stop from the ferry ports on the way south.

☆ **Mme. Claude Rollini. 'Le Moulin de L'Inthe'**
category: **(M)**
tel: 02.43.33.79.22.
B&B: 56€ for two. No Dinner

Deep countryside, the river rushes by, around and through the property, whose gigantic old wooden mill wheel is cleverly incorporated into a glassed-in appendage to the lovely sitting room. Mesmerising hills slope down to water, picnic spots abound, there are walks galore, swimming in the river and riding nearby.

The old mill has been perfectly converted to retain its rusticity – rough brick walls, beams and tiles – while insisting on comfort – deep chintzy armchairs and a huge log fire burning (though it was morning and they didn't know I was coming).

Five first-floor bedrooms with river views, have cheerful colours, a mix of old and new furniture, and very modern bathrooms apiece. Everyone loves this one. A ☆, of course. Evening meals are no longer available at the Moulin, but M. Rollini has opened a new restaurant in a nearby village, (open Easter to October), so you can still enjoy his culinary expertise.

THOIRÉ-sur-DINAN. 72500.
40 Km SE of Le Mans.

Right in the middle of the flat agricultural and wooded valley of the Pays de la Loire. Take the D304 from SE of Le Mans to Saint-Pierre-du-Lorouër then the D63 towards Flée, turning right to Thoiré, the house is first on the right.

Mme. Claudine Cissé. 'Le Saut-du-Loup'
category: (M)
tel: 02.43.79.12.36.
B&B: 43€ for two.
Evening meals 14€.

Letters still come in assuring me *Le Saut-du-loup* is as good as ever. The Cissés spent three years planning their chambres d'hôtes, visiting many others to make sure they had thought of everything.

The farm is now run by their son, who lives close by and he offers cream teas in the summer; but for accommodation and an evening meal look no further than the long low farmhouse, sideways on to the road, where you will be given a splendid welcome and shown to one of their three rooms, one of which is for a family, with curtained-off adjoining room with two beds, sharing the shower room. Rooms are simply furnished but comfortably warm for all-year-round occupation.

The evening meal with Monsieur and Mme. is great fun. Mme. Cissé is an excellent cook and she and her husband really enjoy entertaining; conversation and wine flow freely. A cosy log fire at one end of the room heats the whole house. Large lawns and a *pétanque* court border the house. One of our most popular chambres d'hôtes.

Vendée

The Vendée is in the southern part of the Western Loire. Known as the Marais Poitevin, it stretches from Maillezais in the north to Mauzé in the south and from Bessines near Niort in the east to Marans in the west. In the 11th century the land was always being flooded in the winter from the rivers Sèvre-Niortaîse and Vendée. The monks got so fed up with their churches being under water they began to dig out canals to drain the land and the good work has been going on ever since. Now there are 12,000 kms of these linked canals. It really is a little-known area which the French keep to themselves.

A very pleasant way to spend a hot summer's day is lazing on a flat-bottomed boat with overhanging branches dipping into the water as you glide along. Cows and sheep marooned on islands step down to the banks to drink; no need for hedges to keep them on their grazing patch. Every house bordering a canal has its own boat tied to a pole. On a guided tour your guide will show you how pockets of methane gather under the canal bed by stirring up the mud and setting the canal alight. Luckily you are in a metal boat!

Motor boats are allowed only on the rivers, so peace and quiet are assured in the backwaters. The lesser used canals tend to be overgrown with green weeds and algae. At Arçais there is one part that sometimes looks like an emerald green lawn.

Fontenay-le-Comte, in the north, is the largest town in the Marais. Visit the Abbey Church of Notre-Dame, which has attractive royal-blue stained-glass windows and an ornate pulpit. The town was always Royalist and suffered badly in the Revolution. The ancient abbey at Maillezais is also worth a visit.

Le GUÉ-de-VELLUIRE. 85770.
15km S of Fontenay-le-Comte.
An interesting game called *'Palet'* is played in this part of the Vendée, throwing metal tags on to a board similar to *'Boules'.*
At the western end of the village, just before the river Vendée fork left.

M. & Mme. Bertin
5, rue de la Rivière.
category: (M)
tel: 02.51.52.59.10.
fax: 02.51.52.57.21.
B&B: 44.5€ for two.
Evening meals 16€ each.

A change of ownership here. I am told by a reader that M. Bertin is a jolly host, clearly anxious to make a success of his new venture; the house is most comfortable and the food excellent, but guests are discouraged from arriving before 6p.m., please note.

Though by the roadside, this is a gracious *maison-de-maître,* built before the Revolution, with the rear garden bordering the river Vendée. Five spacious rooms scattered across the first floor are furnished to complement their period but modernised with adjoining baths or shower rooms. Most have the original marble fireplaces and polished wood floors, and tall windows overlook the garden or roadside. Often two double beds make them suitable for a family. A pleasant breakfast room has doors to the garden. Evening meals are convivial affairs taken at a large oval table in the dining room.

See also ARÇAIS (Page 355) and COULON (Page 355) on the border of Deux-Sèvres in Poitou-Charentes

Midi-Pyrénées

MIDI-PYRÉNÉES

Sarrazac

Rocamadour

Gramat

La Croix-Barrez Mur-de-Barrez

Lot

N140

D13 N122

Figeac

Entraygues

Estaing

D911

Villefranche-
de-Rouergue

N140

D988

D911 Rodez

N88

D921

N9

D911

Aveyron

Campes

Cordes

Castenet

Albi

Rabastens

Loupiac

Tarn

N112

N126 Castres

Mazamet N112

N113

A61

Pamiers

D119

Foix

D117

N20

Millau

Le Truel

N9

- Town
- ⊙ Chambres d'Hôtes

0 20km

Midi-Pyrénées

The Midi-Pyrénées stretches from the Lot in the north to the Pyrénées in the south and is bounded by Aquitaine in the west and Languedoc-Roussillon in the east, incorporating eight *départements*, three of which lie along the Spanish border. In the middle are the Gers, Tarn, Tarn-et-Garonne and Aveyron and, most northerly, the Lot. Altogether a very large slice of South-West France.

Tarbes, the *préfecture* of the **Hautes-Pyrénées** is a rather ordinary industrial town with the main rail terminal from Paris and an airport with flights direct from Gatwick. The name most people associate with this *département* is Lourdes, a Mecca for the sick. There are hidden lakes high in the mountains, numerous *cols* to traverse for intrepid explorers and skiing in winter. The Cirque de Gavarnie forms a natural amphitheatre in the mountains near the Spanish border, south of Lourdes.

A small wedge of **Haute-Garonne** reaches down to the Spanish border, where the spa town of Bagnères-de-Luchon seems miles away from civilisation – a little Victorian-flavoured world of its own, and a great favourite with the British both then and now. Twinned with Harrogate says it all!

The river Garona rises in Spain to become the Garonne at Marignac; it then flows north to Toulouse, the fourth largest city in France, the *préfecture* of this *département* and capital of the whole region. The N117 runs from the Atlantic to the Mediterranean almost parallel with the Pyrénées but well away from them – with smaller roads cutting up the valleys into the mountains – and arrives at Foix, the *préfecture* of **Ariège**, the next *département*. The town, guarded by its old castle, with three distinctive towers high above the main streets, is squashed between high mountains, once a bottleneck for traffic, now considerably relieved by the N20 bypass leading to Andorra and Spain.

Gers, sometimes known as Gascony, lies north of the Hautes-Pyrénées. Armagnac, the local brandy, was already on sale in the 15th century, two hundred years before Cognac (not a word to use in this area). Armagnac is distilled once, as opposed to the double distillation of its rival, and must age for at least two years in oak casks to be *Appéllation*. The rich local *apéritif* often served in chambres d'hôtes is *Floc*, a mixture of Armagnac and grape juice, either white or red.

The Gers is a totally agricultural *département*, with rolling hills of sunflowers, corn and vineyards beside the quiet roads. Ducks and geese are everywhere, heading for the *foie-gras* market. Auch, the *préfecture*, sits regally on a hill in the middle, with all roads converging on it. On one side is the magnificent *Escalier Monumental*, a great stone staircase sweeping up to the cathedral above. A statue of d'Artagnan stands majestically near the top. The 370 steps have shallow risers – it isn't the stiff climb it looks. The Tourist Office is housed in the *Maison Fedel*, a 15th-century building. The Cathedral of Ste. Marie has eighteen beautiful windows painted by Arnaud de Moles at the beginning of the 16th century. As he was a Gascon, you will find other churches in the Gers with his handiwork. There is parking by the cathedral, but also in a large shady car park near the Place de la Libération.

The smallest *département* of the Midi-Pyrénées is **Tarn-et-Garonne**, but it certainly packs a lot into a small space. Montauban the *préfecture*, built in the red brick so typical of the Toulouse area, was originally built as a *bastide*. It suffered during the Albigensian crusade and is now strongly Protestant. Moissac, further west, is famous for the 11th-century cloisters at the Abbey. Close by, the Tarn joins the Garonne and at Boulou, on a hill a few kilometres west, there is a lookout which gives a wonderful view of the converging rivers. The rest of the *département* is mostly agricultural, with pleasant, small villages.

Tarn further east is north of Toulouse. Albi is the *préfecture*. Its red-brick cathedral, Ste. Cécile, is rather stark from outside, but inside the contrast is magical – one of the loveliest cathedrals in France. The red – blue – and gold-painted walls contrast with the white carved stonework, giving off such warmth that it affects all who enter. There are 29 side chapels flanking the nave, all different, but in the same colours. Beautiful oak choir stalls lead to the high altar. The vaulted ceiling is superb. So much to see, impossible to describe, far better to go and look for yourself.

Behind the cathedral beside the river Tarn is the museum of Toulouse-Lautrec, open every day 10-12 and 2-5 p.m. (closed on Tuesdays). Many of his paintings are here, among those of other artists. It is an old bishop's palace, so the rooms are interesting in themselves. It is also possible to visit the house where he was born, in a corner of the rue de Toulouse-Lautrec. Good pedestrian shopping precincts fill the centre of the town, where an antiques fair is held on occasional Saturdays. Nicer views of the cathedral are to be had from the bridges over the Tarn, which flows through the centre of the *département*.

There are many other places to visit, such as the hill villages of Cordes to the north of Albi and Lautrec to the south. West are the vineyards of Gaillac, both red and white wines can be sampled in the many *dégustations*. The *Appéllation Contrôlée* is one of the oldest in France, dating from the 12th century.

Aveyron. First impressions of this département are of high barren *causses* grazed by cattle and sheep, with the rather commercial *préfecture* of Rodez up on the plain, but the delights are hidden in the valleys of the major rivers which cut through it, notably the Tarn, the Lot and the Aveyron itself.

Millau in a valley of the Tarn, is an attractive town, famous for making gloves. But best by far in Aveyron is the valley of the river Lot, which runs along its northern border. Delightful, old villages like Entraygues, where the Lot is joined by the river Truyère, can be found on the banks of the river. The river flows north of Conques (which is almost a rival of Rocamadour in the popularity polls and not such an uphill walk from the car park), and wends its way to Cahors along the lush border valley of fruit trees, overlooked by the pretty hill village of Saint-Cirq-Lapopie.

The **Lot** to most people means the river and Cahors, an area producing dark red wine (this wine was once used by the Tsars as communion wine). Cahors is the *préfecture* and is situated on a bend of the river. The southernmost part of the *département* is known as the Quercy, where many old bastide towns were built in the Hundred Years War, all well worth visiting. North of Cahors is Rocamadour, probably the most impressive of all hill villages, which Henry 'Short Coat', the eldest son of Henry II, pillaged. He caught a fever and died later in Martel asking for his father's pardon. The whole area is full of history; you can spend many days visiting old fortified castles or take a more leisurely route along the river. Running alongside the rive are orchards and vineyards, interspersed with rocky outcrops (where the road has to leave the river or take to a tunnel).

ARIÈGE

GANAC 09000
8 km SW of Foix. D21 from Foix.

Mme. Piednoel. 'La Carcis'
category: (S)
tel: 05.61.02.96.54.
B&B: 32€ for two. No Dinner.
Closed January.

High up in the mountains above Foix is this little Hansel and Gretel cottage, quite enchanting, on the edge of the village of Ganac. The only sound you will hear at night will be that of a mountain stream trickling beside your room. Walks straight up into the mountains or fishing on the spot.

On the ground floor is just one room for three, warmly carpeted, comfortable armchairs beckon you after a bracing mountain walk. Entry either by steep stairs from the salon above where breakfast is served, or from a little private grassy terrace right beside the stream. Madame Piednoel no longer serves evening meals, but has provided a kitchen for her guests to self-cater. This is still a delightful and peaceful place to stay. Very little English spoken. Excellent value.

SERRES-sur-ARGET. 09000.
9 km W of Foix.
Take the D17 from Foix and follow the signs through the village.

Foix is about six miles away down winding roads and after a day out there seeing castle and museum, visiting the large market on Friday and fighting your way through heavy traffic, you will be glad to speed back to your mountain retreat.

M. & Mme. Brogneaux. 'Le Poulsieu'
category: (S)
tel/fax: 05.61.02.77.72.
B&B: 38/41.5€ for two (extra bed 8.5€).
Evening meals 12.5€ each.
Closed 15 Nov. to 15 Mar.

If you have always dreamt of a holiday tucked away in the mountains of the Pyrénées, but with lively company, this is just the place. You will think you are at the end of the world as you edge slowly up the last kilometre of the unmade track. Park your car out of sight and forget about it for a week.

Bob and Jenny Brogneaux (Belgian and Dutch, so there is no language problem) will give you a splendid welcome, they have five delightfully rustic, guest rooms, with a choice of double or single beds. There are four rooms in the main house and another family room for four in a small building across the courtyard, where young early risers can disturb only their own parents. This room has a double bed on the ground floor and a bathroom half-way up to a mezzanine area with two beds for children.

There are sunny tables for *apéritifs* in the courtyard but meals are taken at one long table on the large covered terrace adjoining the dining room, which has a splendid view of the wide valley and surrounding mountains. A refreshing swimming pool is on a raised terrace by the house.

A delightful house-party atmosphere prevails. You eat with your hosts and no-one bothers about taking dinner elsewhere. It is too far to drive back and nowhere else will you find such an international menu. Four courses, wine is offered as an *apéritif* and with the meal. Should you be desperate for something stronger you pay extra.

Demi-pension rates apply for a week. Prices have risen very little since I first stayed here, all extremely good value.

"'Le Poulsieu' was our third port of call, again a memorable one. Who could forget the enchantment of a leisurely breakfast out of doors, where nightingales sang and mist wreathed the mountainside. Again Jeni and Bob showed real, but never intrusive concern for the welfare of their guests, and the level of conversation at their table seemed straight from a classical French Salon. The food offered was of a very high quality. The generous quantities in no way daunted my stalwart husband. We shall return." Anne Bailey. A need to book well ahead.

AVEYRON

ESTAING. 12190.
60 km SE of Aurillac. 10 km NW of Espalion.
Situated on the river Lot, this old town has grown up round the château of the Estaing family, one of whose members was canonised. It is on the pilgrim route to Saint-Jacques-de-Compostelle. Even now true pilgrims can apply at an address in the village and will be given a room and meal for the night. It is well worth a stroll round the cobbled alleyways to see the ancient bridges. The town seems very quiet nowadays. As one elderly man said to me, 'All the young people have left'. The château towering above is open daily except Tuesday.

Take the D920 from Estaing towards Espalion and turn left on to the D655, signed Vinnac, and the farm is well signed.

M. & Mme. Alazard. 'Cervel' (M)
Route de Vinnac.
category: (M)
tel/fax: 05.65.44.09.89
B&B: and evening meal (all inclusive) 73.5€ each, 68.5€ if you stay longer than two days.
Closed: 10 Nov. to 1 Apr.

Raised above the road on a bend, this well-maintained house on a goat farm has four bedrooms, furnished with good quality family heirlooms and luxurious new shower rooms. Two family rooms, one has bunks for children, another a suite of two rooms shares facilities, extra bed 12€. Other rooms are for two people.

Evening meals include all drinks. Breakfast is taken in a room which doubles as a very pleasant sitting room for guests, complete with piano.

'Mme. Alazard is a very good cook, and uses farm and local produce with great ingenuity. Dinner is taken at one large table and when we were there M. Alazard was very generous with the local 'firewater' as well as wine'. M. A. Parsons.

Bikes for hire at 4.8€ a day. Some English spoken.

LA CROIX-BARREZ 12600.
45km SE of Aurillac. 22 km NE of Entraygues-sur-Truyère.
The small town of Lacroix-Barrez is high on the plain above the Truyère valley. Take the D904 north and in 3.5 km turn right to Vilherols, a small hamlet signed from here.

M. & Mme. Laurens. 'Vilherols'
category: (M)
tel: 05.65.66.08.24.
fax: 05.65.66.19.98.
Open July and August and school holidays.
B&B: 44.5€ for two. No Dinner

This exquisite cluster of buildings has belonged to the same family since the 12th century. Monsieur's parents live in the gracious manor house and he lives a few terraces below in a meandering old stone house. In between the two dwellings, charming guest rooms have been contrived out of unlikely material – one-time pig sties. Keeping the old stone walls and beautiful *lauzes* tiled roofs, two ground-floor rooms, identical in all but colours, have wide views over the fields around. Huge patio entrance doors lead to a sitting area with comfortable armchairs where, hidden behind doors, is a fully equipped kitchenette with a microwave. Up a raised step is a carpeted area with double bed and access to a luxurious shower room.

Approached by a paved slope, easily accessible, is a larger apartment with an extensive terrace, especially designed for the disabled This room has a double bed and a convertible couch for two people, shower room, washing machine, kitchenette and picture-windows.

A family suite, consisting of a double room and bathroom, with tower room above, up a ladder, is in Madame's own house, where a copious breakfast is served by English-speaking Mme. Laurens.

Exceptionally nice rooms, with a reduction out of season, if you stay three days.

There is a small restaurant/café in La Croix-Barrez or others at Mur-de-Barrez 3 km away. A renowned restaurant at Laguiole is 30 kms across country from here. No come-back from this one, perhaps because this part of Aveyron is a bit off the beaten track.

LE TRUEL. 12430.
57 km SE of Rodez, 70 km E of Albi, 47 km SW of Millau.

Chambres d'hôtes are scarce beside the river Tarn between Saint-Rome-du-Tarn and Brousse le Château. Driving beside the river on the tiny D200, with a husband anxious to know where he could lay his head that night, I was grateful to find that this small auberge, next to the mini-market, now has rooms. Truel is a delightful little village, just a handful of houses beside the river with others scattered on the hillside.

M. & Mme. Chambredon. 'Auberge de Truel'
category: (M)
tel: 05.65.46.42.98.
fax: 05.65.46.46.98.
Bed 35€ for two (without breakfast), 44.5€ (with breakfast). Evening meal 13.5€ each.

A restaurant during the day, this little auberge reverts more to a chambres d'hôtes at night. New owners offer five simple comfortable rooms, modernised only by en suite showers and loos. One tiny single room, a choice of double or single beds in the others. Windows overlook the hillside and family *potagers*. Breakfast is served on the terrace of the café/bar next door (when weather permits),belonging to the same owners.

In the *auberge* friendly hosts offer a set-menu evening meal with carafe wine on the table. All very good value. Stroll along the grassy river bank in the twilight and watch the locals fishing for their supper. It could be busy here in high season, but by September all is very peaceful.

HAUTE-GARONNE

CINTEGABELLE. 31550.
39 km S of Toulouse

This would make a pleasant change for visiting Toulouse. From close-by Auterive station, where parking is free, a train runs regularly into the centre of the city. A hassle-free way of enjoying a day out. Cintegabelle lies just off the N20. 17 km north of Pamiers, it is a small town with tiered streets, topped by the church, and there is a fair selection of shops and cafés.

From the town take the D25 towards Nailloux for 3.5 km and the chambres d'hôtes is well signed.

☆ **M. & Mme. Deschamps-Chevrel.**
'Serres-d'en-Bas' (S-M)
Route de Nailloux.
category: (S-M)
tel/fax: 05.61.08.41.11.
B&B: 44€ for two.
Evening meals 14.5€ each.
Closed 1 Oct. to Easter.

The old farmstead has been modernised. At one end is a completely new first floor with four simple, practical rooms offering modern amenities, doubles, singles, baths or showers, pretty matching decor. One room on the ground floor, and one a suite for a family.

The view from rooms is across the countryside or overlooking the swimming pool and tennis court in the front garden.

Excellent evening meals are very jolly, in winter beginning with an *apéritif* in front of a log fire, where a whole chicken may be turning on a spit, later to arrive on the table. Local specialities such as *cassoulet* are often on the menu. Wine is extra in July and August, at other times included in the price. Could there be a better reason for visiting off season? You dine with your hosts who take great delight in entertaining you.

Amenities for children include the usual swings, and a new games-room. A lot of 'chambres d'hôtes' for your money, adds up to real value and an a ☆. There is one *gîte* on the premises for four, but the chambres d'hôtes rooms are the best. I liked this home even more on a summer visit, lazing by the pool and eating outside in the setting sun. Horse riding can be arranged for the less idle. Book well ahead.

PALAMINY. 31220.
50km SW of Toulouse. 26 km E of Saint-Gaudens.
At the foot of the Pyrénées, Les Pesques lies on the opposite side of the River Garonne from the village of Palaminy.

Cross the Garonne, a wide, arrogant river, by the bridge at Cazères and take the D62 right for 1km. Look for signs to the farmhouse on your left along the D62.

M. & Mme. Le Bris. 'Les Pesques'
category: (S)
tel: 05.61.97.59.28.
fax: 05.61.90.20.41.
B&B: 32/40€ for two
Evening meals 12.5€ each.

Rustic and rather dishevelled, this square farmhouse is over 200 years old, situated in a pleasant high-walled garden just off the road. Lively young Madame Le Bris is absolutely sweet; she has capitalised on the rustic, keeping rooms simple with natural wood floors, furnishing with whatever came to hand, and originally it certainly wasn't modern bathrooms, relying on the happy carefree atmosphere of this home to do the rest. Up the wide stairs is a salon where you can relax in comfort, off which are two other rooms. One with double bed faces north and has no private ablutionary facilities but is only 28.5€ including breakfast. The other room is the one that I fell for: two windows, facing south, wood floor, iron bedstead, very simply furnished but it did sport a wash basin. The *pièce de résistance* was the little wooden wisteria-covered balcony, basket chair in position and rickety steps leading down to the garden. A family bathroom and separate loo is shared by all, a trek across the salon and landing. Downstairs there is a suite of two north-facing rooms furnished in pretty blue and yellow, having stone floors, which do have a private shower and washbasin with a loo just outside in the hallway. On a recent visit I found another room had materialised on the ground floor, two single beds on a painted stone floor, and this one is truly en suite with shower and loo. But I still love that room with the balcony, even though I hate obstacle races to the loo.

Interesting meals include wine and are served at one long table, taken with the family in the dining room or garden in summer. Breakfast with fresh bread, croissants, yoghurts and home-made jams is copious.

What you lose on the rooms you gain in the superb atmosphere and *accueil* here.

LE PIN MURELET. 31370.

45km SW of Toulouse

From Rieumes Take the D3 westwards (SP L'Isle-en-Dodon) for 5 km to the hamlet of Grande Carrière, then in 1km turn left beside a large house and follow the lane for 200 yds.

M. & Mme. Flous. 'En Jouanet'
category: (M)
tel/fax: 05.61.91.91.05.
B&B: 47€ for two, 16€ (children each).
Evening meals 13.5€ each.
Closed Nov. to Easter

Bordering on the Gers department, surrounded by fields, tastefully restored and modernised yet retaining all the old red brick and wood beams, it is difficult to imagine this was an old farmhouse. The salon, was once the stables and now has a sweeping chimney up to the lofty ceiling, where a huge Chinese sunshade breaks the height, suspended from a surrounding balcony.

On the first floor a suite of two rooms, where walls are of red bricks interspersed with wood beams, has an independent staircase from the entrance hall. It's a luxuriously large room, thickly carpeted, with shower and duplex wash basins; down a step the smaller room has two extra beds, but can be used as a salon opening on to a large private balcony partly shaded by trees, making this a very pleasant apartment for two or four. Pity the private loo is just outside on the landing. Downstairs a garden suite of two rooms, has a tiled floor and the advantage of a large fully operational kitchen for 6.4€. extra a day, which can be let with or without breakfast. Best to sort this out when booking.

There is the advantage of a cool blue swimming pool for guests, and bicycles for hire.

Evening meals, which include wine, sound especially delicious and will be elegantly served. An upmarket address with refined *accueil*. English spoken.

GERS

SARRAGACHIES. 32400.
8 km N of Riscle.

Close to the Termes d'Armagnac, where there is an historical Gascon museum. Up 149 steps of the dungeon tower there is a view over the valley of the river Adour.

☆ **M. & Mme. Abadie. 'La Buscasse'**
category: (M)
tel: 05.62.69.76.07.
email: buscasse@aol.com
B&B: 44.5€ for two.

Not a bit like a hotel. A *viticulteur*'s immaculately kept house, complete with tower.

'My wife and I stayed in two B&Bs for two nights each, taken from your guide, and wished we had stayed in more. At Sarragachies, a lovely house, set in sleepy relaxing countryside. Our bedroom was most comfortable and charmingly decorated, and the bathroom spacious and exceptionally well fitted. The breakfasts were generous and Madame Abadie a most interesting and charming hostess'. Ian McIntyre

I hardly need to add to this praise. Rooms are warmly carpeted, and there is a choice of showers or baths, double or single beds. Excellent parking behind the house with a private entrance to the rooms on the first floor. Extra bed possible only for a small child. Birds to serenade you in the morning and pleasant views across the garden, which now includes a well-positioned swimming pool. You may have laundry washed and dried for 7.2€.

Guests congregate in a comfortable lounge for *apéritifs* before joining the rest of the family for dinner around a long oval table, when specialities of the region are produced by Madame Abadie. Excellent meals, wine *compris*, but now served only on Tuesdays and Fridays. Good restaurants are recommended for other days. A very civilised place to stay, well worth a ☆ for all round excellence, a true chambres d'hôtes.

LOT

ALBAS. 46140.

27 km W of Cahors.

The river Lot west of Cahors twists like a snake between high cliffs and flat vineyards. The main road (D911) to Puy-l'Evêque is fairly straight but if you follow the river bank, crossing the few bridges from time to time, you will become quite disorientated, especially at Luzech where the loop of the river necessitates two bridges. It is a lovely drive past tiny villages. When you reach Albas follow signs to a chambres d'hôtes way up in the hills, climbing bends for 2 km, well signed.

M. & Mme. Vos. 'La Meline'
category: (M)
tel/fax: 05.65.36.97.25.
B&B: 44€ for two.
Evening meals 17.5€ each.
Closed 1 Oct. to 30 Mar.

Your Dutch hosts have lived in Lot for 20 years. The house stands on a hillside, so high you will be able to have breakfast on the sunny terrace looking down on morning mists in the valley below.

Though open all year, rooms are by reservation only from October to April. With a welcome cup of tea on arrival and a promise of a meal in the evening, you soon feel part of the family. There are three guest rooms, one on the ground floor for the disabled, with a bath and separate shower. Two above with bright white walls and dark beams are small, but well furnished, and have shower rooms.

Aperitifs are served in the compact lounge/dining room in front of a log fire before moving *à table* for a copious evening meal, all drinks included, and, of course, no language problems.

Their son is an estate agent working from home so this is just the place to stay if you are looking for property in this *département*!

GRAMAT 46500

34 kms NW of Figeac. 9 km SE of Rocamadour.

The busy small town of Gramat lies on the N140 south of Brive, close to Rocamadour, the Gouffre de Padirac, and the delights of the Lot and Dordogne valley.

Just 500 metres south of Gramat, turn off left down a small lane to the well-signed Moulin de Fresquet.

Moulin de Fresquet

☆ M. & Mme. Ramelot. 'Moulin de Fresquet'
category: (M)
tel/fax: 05.65.38.70.60.
B&B: 52/68.5€ for two.
Evening meal are 19€ each (incl drinks).
Closed 1 Nov. to 1 Apr.

In all the guide books, this well-known mill has lost none of its popularity, so book well ahead. The beautifully restored mill-house is surrounded by three hectares of wooded land through which a small stream flows, trickling under some of the rooms.

A delightful rustic dining room leads into an equally pleasant lounge where guests may relax among family portraits and many of Monsieur's charming etchings. The terrace for summer meals overlooks the mill stream, but the rooms are on a lower level, three having access to the garden. The smallest is *La Meunière* (the Miller's Wife). The *Bief* lies right over the stream and has an appealing view along it. Altogether there are four double rooms and a family room with two double beds, all with cool tiled floors, stone walls and beams, rusticity combined with modern furnishing.

Five-course evening meals feature traditional Quercy and Périgord cooking, with wine *compris*. Excellent parking; entrance gates are locked at night.

You will be made very welcome by the owners who have spent many years creating such perfection.

LAMOTHE-FÉNELON 46350
6 km north west of Peyrac.

The Fénelon family originated from this village. At Carennac along the Dordogne the tower still stands where François Fénelon wrote 'Télémaque' in 1699.

From Peyrac on the N20 take the D141 towards the village, turn left on to an unclassified road to Campanole, then right and the chambres d'hôtes is signed.

Gatignol

M. & Mme. Montarnal. 'Gatignol'
category: (S)
tel: 05.65.37.60.24.
B&B: 38.5€ for two.
Evening meals 13.5€ each.

Gatignol is a tiny hamlet of just three golden houses well away from main roads. The chambres d'hôtes are in a small semi-detached 18th-century farmhouse round which originally a small farm operated, including a few vines. Renovations include modern plumbing, but none of the old character has been lost.

The cellars where the wine was stored have now been converted into two rustic guest rooms where large mats keep the feet warm on natural stone floors, rough plastered walls are interspersed with the original beams; nooks and crannies, pretty matching curtains and bed linen complete the picture. A very modern shower room and loo have been installed. The blue room has prettily painted furniture and is slightly larger than next door; but each has white tables and chairs outside on the lawn. A third room is larger still, in a small stone house opposite the front door, and has a very pretty walled private terrace. Parking is adjacent to the small front garden; lawns and small fields behind belong to the property.

The salon, once the original kitchen, has lost none of its old charm. The ancient sink is still in place, a log fire burns merrily on cooler days in the massive fireplace. The table is set with pretty blue flowered-china and behind a bar in her kitchen corner Madame prepares tasty evening meals from Quercy recipes, aperitif, wine and coffee *compris*.

Monsieur, the local school teacher, is a knowledgeable host, and regales you with some interesting stories, but you need to speak some French as little English is understood.

SAINT-CHAMARAND. 46310.
32 km N of Cahors. 32 km south of Souillac
Coming south from Souillac on the N20 in 32 km turn right on the D704 SP Gourdon. The chambres d'hôtes is in a peaceful situation down a quiet lane just outside the hamlet.

Les Cèdres - Lescaille
St. Chamarand

M. & Mme. Champeau. 'Les Cèdres de Lescaille'
category: (S-M)
tel:05.65.24.50.02.
fax: 05.65.24.50.78.
B&B: 35/43€ for two.
Demi-pension 64/72€ for two.
Evening meals 15€ each.
Closed November to Easter except on reservation.

A large Perigordian house on three floors still undergoing restoration. Nevertheless, a very warm welcome from the owner, who appears to be successfully undertaking the refurbishment of this somewhat neglected old house with some style. We were offered tea on arrival and shown to our rooms on the top floor – beautifully appointed suites which retained all the original architectural features – exposed timbers and stone walls. A very enjoyable meal in the evening with M. & Mme. Champeau. While Mme. Champeau prepared the meal M. Champeau, whose English is excellent, provided the bonhomie'. H. Coe.

When I investigated I liked the rooms, especially the small round bedside windows with views, complemented by the velux ones which made the rooms so light. The communal tea-making facilities on the landing were a good idea and the swimming pool in front of the house was an added bonus in summer.

There is a choice of double or single beds and a family room, all with adjoining showers and loos, extra bed 9.5€. Evening meals include all drinks.

SALVIAC 46340
This bustling little town is typical of this area south west of Gourdon and north west of Cahors, rolling countryside dotted with small interesting little towns and villages far enough away from the hubbub of the Dordogne to miss the traffic, but near enough for day trips to the area. From the Tourist Office in Salviac take the small road opposite, whence the Chambres d'Hôtes is signed.

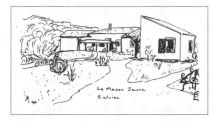

M. & Mme. Hauchecorne. 'La Maison Jaune', Bertrand-Joly Haut.
category: (M)
tel/fax: 05 65 41 48 52
B&B: 44€.
Evening meals 15€

High above the town with a huge vista, this newly built bungalow is immaculate. There are two family rooms, one with beds for children on the mezzanine up a spiral staircase, the other with two rooms. Bathrooms with showers each have the luxury of two wash basins. Madame Hauchecorne cooks excellent evening meals all drinks included. Their lounge/dining room is shared with guests. The new pool on the rear terrace will be greatly appreciated in summer. Extra beds 12€. All very good value for the quality of the rooms. A well-run true chambres d'hôtes.

SARRAZAC 46600.
26 km S of Brive.

Bordering the Limousin, hidden in the far north of the Lot department, the small village of Sarrazac has a Roman church where a hand, raised in a blessing, is carved in the stonework beside the door. The château was once a monastery and the village, now an unspoilt cluster of yellow houses with church, auberge and school, was the seat of the Turenne parliament. Close by are the well-known villages of Turenne, Collanges-les-Rouges, Martel, and the river Dordogne at Beaulieu. In the other direction the caves at Montignac are well worth a visit.

From the N20, 20 km S of Brive, turn off left at Cressensac on to the D87 to Hôpital-Saint-Jean. Continue on this road through the village until it meets the D100 and you will see the sign to the château on the right.

☆ **Mr. & Mrs. MacConchie.**
'Château Couzenac'
category: (M)
tel: 05.65.37.78.32. Open all year.
fax: 05.55.91.00.30
B&B: 48€ for two.
Evening meals 16€ each,
(reservation only).

A compact little château delightfully perched on the hillside overlooking the valley road to Sarrazac. The Scottish owners bought it many years ago as a bramble-ridden ruin abandoned for 50 years. In restoring it to its former glory, they uncovered a delightful flight of steps leading down to the front door. There is level parking by the old stables and a shady terrace under plane trees for summer breakfasts.

It is now a comfortable home, where you will be welcomed with a cup of tea. Lone travellers would love it here. Courses can be arranged for water-colour painting, French language and even dry-stone-walling.

Guest rooms in the four corners of the first floor all have bathrooms, dual aspect windows and natural golden stone walls. The stairs lead up to a large open library/sitting area, with windows overlooking the valley. A separate lounge and dining room downstairs is open to guests.

A large terrace room on a lower floor can be used for summer meals. Evening meals with all drinks *compris*, possible if reserved, but there is an excellent truly French *auberge* in Sarrazac, which is only ten minutes walk down the hill, one minute by car, where copious meals are served at excellent prices from 10/27€. So popular you won't be the only ones eating here even in winter.

This is a château I would love to return to. Reports are good, now a well earned ☆.

HAUTES-PYRÉNÉES

LOUBAJAC 65100.
6 km N of Lourdes on the D3.

Lourdes is an international pilgrimage centre for the sick. It owes its fame to the young peasant girl, Bernadette Soubirous, who, at the age of fourteen in 1858, claimed to have fourteen visions of the Virgin Mary at a grotto. She was told by Our Lady that the waters of the well flowing from this grotto had healing powers. Once these powers were proved to the satisfaction of the Roman Catholic authorities, the Church of the Rosary was built next to the grotto where the fountain runs and in whose waters the pilgrims are bathed. Bernadette became a nun at the age of twenty, died fifteen years later and was canonised in 1933. Over the central crypt is the Basilica of the Immaculate Conception with a bell tower, some 70 metres high. In front but on a lower level is the Basilica of the Rosary. Inside is a small chapel reserved for private prayer when no services are taking place. There is also a large Basilica underground, named after Pius X, which can hold 25,000 people (completed in 1958 to mark the centenary of the visions) and unadorned except for the central altar.

The Castle rises above the town and contains a Pyrénéen museum. Ste. Bernadette's birthplace can be seen at the foot of Castle Hill in the rue Bernadette Soubirous.

The town is crowded in July and August. Tourist souvenir shops abound and I wouldn't recommend a visit then. Parking is almost impossible and the queues to visit the grotto horrendous in the heat. September is calmer and the weather is usually pleasant and sunny.

Mme. Vives.
Route de Bartres.
category: (S)
tel: 05.62.94.44.17.
fax: 05.62.42.38.58.
Demi-pension 60.5€ for two

There is a good view of the Pyrénées from the Route de Bartres. Right beside the road is a small sheep farm where young Mme. Vives has now six guest rooms, four neatly beamed and warmly carpeted on the first floor, and two smart new rooms across the garden which share a large private terrace with a very pleasant view of the countryside. There is a small sitting area on the landing, and chairs in the garden for sunny days.

Evening meals with wine *compris*. Guests eat together in the dining room but not with the family.

A handy budget stop, close to Lourdes

OMEX. 65100.
4 km SW of Lourdes.
Even nearer to Lourdes. Take the D13 past the *'Basilique'* up a winding country lane.

Mme. Fanlou. 'Les Rocailles'
category: (M)
tel: 05.62.94.46.19.
fax: 05.62.94.33.35.
B&B: 52.5€ for two.
Evening meals 16€ each.

The little village of Omex seems quite cramped, with houses lining narrow lanes. One hardly dares to enter. 'Les Rocailles' is well signed and has enough parking for three cars as you turn in the gateway. A refreshing swimming pool and small garden separates Madame's own house from the little guest cottage.

Step into the salon/dining room where meals are prepared for guests, while they sit by the large fireplace in winter. One guest room downstairs, *La Costumière*, (reflects Madame's previous occupation in Paris), with twin beds, is delightfully decorated in red check cottage style, and has a private terrace. Two rooms upstairs are equally pretty. *Tourmalet*, with views of the mountains, has a large bed and a smaller one in an alcove for a child. *Bigorre* for three is larger, with two single beds under a *baldaquin* and a *bateau* bed. All three have luxurious bathrooms, equally pretty, with a feast of amenities, including thick towels. Tea-making facilities in all rooms as well as TV.

This little farm cottage is now an irresistible, companionable place to stay, summer or winter, for a visit to Lourdes, where evening meals await you, wine *compris*. Rooms are excellent value. Could well be worth a ☆ – reports please.

PINAS. 65300.

4.5 km E of Lannemézan on the N117.

20 km south east of the village the tiny independent city of St. Bertrand-de-Comminges sits on a hill. Originally founded by Pompey in 1 BC, it refused to amalgamate with the Ariège *département* in 1790, so the borders were stretched to include it in Haute-Garonne. St. Mary's Cathedral was built in 11th century enlarged in the 14th century in Gothic style and now is a close second to *Mont-Saint-Michel*. The choir is enclosed, with 66 canons' stalls all intricately carved, making it a church within a church, and the organ is similarly hidden away. It is now the centre of music festivals every summer. A few artisans' shops, good restaurants and cafés are beside the cathedral. Stay with :-

Mme. Colombier. 'Domaine de Jean-Pierre'
Route de Villeneuve.
category: (M)
tel/fax: 05.62.98.15.08. In winter by reservation only.
B&B: 44.5€ for two. No Dinner

A really gracious ivy-covered mansion, which has been in the family for many years and is well preserved. From the moment you enter the tiled hallway and climb the gently sloping stairs to the large airy rooms you will feel you could stay here for days. There are three large rooms with polished wood floors, well furnished bathrooms almost adjoining. Extra beds available for families. One room is warmly carpeted for winter use. A very comfortable lounge has one wall completely lined with books. Breakfast can be taken in summer on the extensive gravel terrace. Mme. Colombier (a keen golfer) is a very charming hostess who speaks some English and will look after you well. This is a true chambres d'hôtes, where you really are private guests.

No evening meals, but at the 18-hole golf course only 3 km away there are excellent restaurants, *Le Pré Vert* and *Le Swing*, also the *gastronomique* *L'Albatros*

SOMBRUN. 65700
.25 km N of Tarbes. 50 km NE of Pau.

Take the D935 from Tarbes, *direction* Bordeaux, in 23 km, in Maubourguet, take the road to Sombrun. In the village, on the D59 past the railway, just after the church and Mairie turn right.

Mme. Brunet. 'Château de Sombrun'
category: (M)
tel: 05.62.96.49.43.
fax: 05.62.96.01.89.
B&B: 64€ for two.
Evening meal 20.8€ each.
Closed 1 Dec. to 31 Jan.

Built in 1640, this château is still flourishing. There is a vast entrance hall, but it is in the old kitchen, the hub of the house, that you will find Mme. Brunet.

Polished wood floors along a wide landing lead to three large guest rooms in the main house, two of them family suites, and two other rooms in the rebuilt *chai* which now contains a long reception hall. Furnished with family heirlooms in excellent condition, all rooms have baths, one with claw feet, and tea-making facilities to add to your comfort.

There is a very comfortable lounge, a separate billiard room and a sunny yellow dining room with the original marble fireplace, where evening meals, inclusive of wine, are provided by Mme. Brunet, a lively hostess. The surrounding grounds have the advantage of a modern swimming pool. Good value for so many amenities.

TARN

CAMPES 81170
25 km NW of Albi.

1 km from the well known hill village of Cordes.
Take the D922 North, SP Languépie, and almost immediately turn right on to the D98 where the auberge/chambres d'hôtes is signed.

M. & Mme. Alunni-Fegatelli. 'La Bouriette'
category: (M)
tel: 05.63.56.07.32.
B&B: 44.5€ for two.
Evening meals 9.5/32€ each.

This is a gem of a *ferme-auberge*, in a delightful situation on raised ground surrounded by meadows and distant hills. Open to the public for meals, it has five very new rooms, tiled floors for which you will be grateful in summer, TV and smart shower rooms, towels changed and beds made every day, though space for clothes perhaps a little scanty. Rooms all overlook the swimming pool, where pool-side service is day-long. The best of all worlds here, combining the friendly *accueil* of charming jolly hosts, the easy-going freedom of chambres d'hôtes, washing lines etc., with the services of a smart hotel.

Meals are served at separate tables, wine *en carafe* or more expensive, not *compris*. Demi-pension possible. Breakfast: only one kind of jam and baguettes, orange juice, coffee – more the hotel variety.

Just the sort of place to convert people who are a little uneasy about using chambres d'hôtes. The higher price in July/August.

CASTENET. 81150.
11 km NW of Albi.

M. & Mme. Malbreil. 'Naussens'
category: (S)
tel: 05.63.55.22.56.
B&B: 32€ for two.
Evening meals 12.5€ each.

This *viticulteur's* farmhouse in the middle of the Gaillac vineyards is developing fast. Now three rooms in an adjoining building complement the two in the main house, for two, three or four. Mock wood floors, plainly furnished but all with respective shower and loo, and a price low enough to cheer many with dwindling francs. Simple evening meals are served on the large terrace in the setting sun, including Gaillac wine. Madame joins her guests when possible and is learning English.

A large *salon* below the rooms, is an added comfort for wet days, but in summer take advantage of the new pool with white loungers overlooking the countryside and you will realise what a budget stop this is. Many English have already discovered this one, and buy their Gaillac wine from Monsieur.

CORDES. 81170.
25 km NW of Albi.

One of the loveliest hill villages in France, sometimes known as Cordes-sur-Ciel. Often pictured floating in a mist above the valley, it was built as a *bastide* by Raymond, Comte de Toulouse, in the 13th century. It was involved in much fighting during the Cathar period. Now a peaceful Mecca for artisans, alive with tourists in summer, it has much to offer.

From the bottom of the village take the road left of the fountain (marked "Cité") up to the old village for 0.5 km then fork left down a track to "Le Bouysset". In 200 metres, round a hairpin bend left, the chambres d'hôtes is signed down a sharp bend to your right.

Mr & Mrs Wanklyn. 'Aurifat'
category: (M)
tel: 05.63.56.07.03.
B&B: 57.5€ for two. No Dinner
Closed November to Easter.

This old property has a beautiful location, our bedroom and bathroom had been skilfully modernised and were most comfortable. The breakfast were really excellent and Mr and Mrs Wanklin could not have been kinder and more hospitable. All in all, a delightful stay, and very convenient for the wonderful city of Albi.' Ian McIntyre. The property changed hands in 1999, so I was particularly happy to have this report. In the 13th century part of this house was a watch-tower guarding the village. A farmhouse was added in the 17th century and now an adjoining centrepiece in red Albi brick makes it into one complete home cunningly built into the hillside – so most bedrooms on the upper floor are level with the parking.

Light, airy, south-facing rooms are pleasantly furnished with modern beds, and have a sitting area as well as private balconies or terraces, where breakfast is usually served, taking advantage of the extensive views. Some rooms have carpets extending to the bathrooms – all can be heated for cooler days. The blue room is particularly nice, with a bath on legs but no shower. A family suite shares a bathroom with bath and shower. On the second floor the 'pigeonnier' room has a wood floor and beamed ceiling.

The Wanklyns' sitting and dining room are below, where breakfast is served if preferred. Below again is a very large pool and terrace entrapping the sun, and a summer kitchen with fridge and barbecue for picnics beside the pool. Alternatively there are plenty of local restaurants.

A place where you can be private or chat to your English hosts. Booking ahead ensures your room and full directions. Prices according to season.

LOUPIAC. 81800.
35 km W of Albi. 31 km NE of Toulouse.
Just the place to stay for visiting Toulouse or Albi, practically halfway between the two, with easy access from the *voie rapide*, exit 7, take D12 direction Rabastens then right to Loupiac for 3 km. Signed on the left.

M. & Mme. Crété. 'La Bonde'
category: (M)
tel: 05.63.33.82.83.
fax: 05.63.57.46.54.
B&B: 49.5€ for two.
Evening meal 15€ each.
Closed 15 Dec. to 15 Jan.

This long ivy-covered *maison-de-maître* surrounded by colourful gardens is elegantly furnished; a private sitting room with TV for guests is just one of the many comforts.

The two rooms are large and richly furnished. One, overlooking the back garden, has a luxurious bathroom, next door on the landing. The second room, with double bed, is most inviting, with two south-facing windows. This one has a small shower room adjoining, and private access from the floor below.

Madame Crété is a excellent cook and is noted in the area for her cuisine. You will dine in style. The price is excellent for such luxury, and an evening meal, which includes wine. Book well ahead.

MAZAMET. 81200
61 km E of Toulouse.

A large town at the foot of the *Montagne Noire.*

Tricky to find this one by car because of the one-way street. Coming from Carcassonne on the D118 turn left into the rue du Moulin (a one-way street) opposite Saint-Sauveur church, then left into the rue de la République by the Huguenot Temple and the chambres d'hôtes is on your right. Coming from the north (Albi and Castres) keep on the D118 through the town on the avenue Rouvière and the rue E. Barbay and turn right into the rue du Moulin opposite Saint-Sauveur church and carry on as above.

M. & Mme. Tricon
3 bis rue de la République.
category: (M)
tel/fax: 05.63.98.88.62.
B&B: 54.5€ for two.
Evening meal 16€ each.

The Tricon's home is a very gracious 19th-century *maison-de-maître* in the centre of the town in a large garden behind locked gates, within easy reach of restaurants and shops.

Recommended to me by a reader. *'The breakfast, which is taken in the main château, is the most comprehensive I have ever experienced and the welcome received from the proprietors, M. and Mme. Tricon, is faultless in its unobtrusive but cordial and thoughtful attention'.* J. C.

Three guest rooms, one for three, in an adjoining tower are on three different levels; each has a sitting area equipped with TV and all are furnished with great taste in sympathy with the style of the house. Impeccable white linen on the beds, and ample towels in the adjoining large shower rooms, one of which has a bath. For anyone seeking a restful visit to the area this would be ideal.

TARN-et-GARONNE

LA MADELEINE 82270 Montpezat-de-Quercy.
18 km S of Cahors. 5 km from Montpezat.
Easy to reach from the main road. Take the N20 south from Cahors and in 17 km at the 'Logis de la Madeleine' sign turn left and follow the signs for 1km.

M. et Mme. Toebak. 'Domaine de Cantecor'
category: (M)
tel: 05.65.21.87.44.
Mobile: 06.11.66.16.96.
B&B: 50/60€ (incl. gourmet Dutch breakfast), 15€ for extra bed.

As in many old Quercy houses, the living area is above the ground floor level, where the animals once lived. This typical golden farmhouse dates back at least three centuries, situated in a small farming hamlet where brown Limousin cows gaze at you on arrival. The house was recently renovated by an architect, keeping its rustic atmosphere, but the present Dutch owners are making their own impression on it, creating rooms for guests who can enjoy the many spacious facilities of the whole house, garden and swimming pool.

Three large guest rooms, high beamed, with yellow stone walls and prettily draped bedside tables are in the main house: 'Provençale' has a shower and loo and two single beds with a view; 'Quercyoise' sleeps three, has the original kitchen sink still in situ, two windows and a large bathroom with bath, bidet and loo; 'La Bonbonniere', a third room with all amenities, faces north. Three smaller rooms, reconstructed from the old cow sheds, are across the courtyard, all en suite, each with a private entry. Another larger room has been completed since my visit.

A salon at the end of a long the wide hall has an interesting oval-framed log fireplace, and comfortable armchairs and couches where guests enjoy their aperitifs in inclement weather. Tread carefully down the old wooden stairs to the ground floor where the cattle once fed, to find a rustic stone courtesy-bar, open all day for guests with drinks from 2€ each. Adjoining is the dining room, where the ancient bread oven is now used as a log fire to cheer guests at the table. Patio doors lead to the terrace and swimming pool.

Altogether a delightful home for a holiday at any time, where evening meals, all drinks included, are always on offer; even if Madame is away, as happened in my case. Book ahead and discuss rooms as they are all so different. Prices vary according to season.

MONTPEZAT-de-QUERCY. 82270.
24 km S of Cahors.

Take the N20 south from Cahors; in 22 km turn right on to the D20, signposted Montpézat-de-Quercy.

A delightful *bastide* village unspoilt by modernisation. Go through the village and turn left about 50m after the post office. Signed on the left.

☆ **MM. Bankes & Jarros. 'Le Barry'**
Faubourg Saint-Roch.
category: (M)
tel: 05.63.02.05.50.
fax: 05.63.02.03.07.
B&B: 325/56€ for two.
Evening meals 20€ each.

One of my favourites. On the ramparts of the village, this charming 17th-century terraced house is impeccably run, offering five spacious bedrooms, comfortably furnished but losing none of their old character. The sheltered garden, high above the road, with an inviting swimming pool, overlooks the Quercy countryside. Relax on the terrace and enjoy the green lawns and flower beds, a perfect setting for evening meals in fine weather, an alternative to the large lounge/dining room. Your English and German hosts really enjoy entertaining. Freshly squeezed orange juice for breakfast.

A great advantage here is being able to step right out into the old part of the town. The only snag is perhaps parking, which is under the wall of the garden on the roadside, but I have been assured that there has been no problem. Certainly worth a long stay here, to visit the lovely Quercy villages, or even Cahors and the Lot valley where the prehistoric grotto of Pech-Merle and the hillside village of St. Cirq-Lapopie are within easy reach. Evening meals include all drinks. Prices according to season. Stay a few days and qualify for demi-pension rates. In a delightful situation. A ☆ accordingly.

Nord/Pas-de-Calais

NORD / PAS-DE-CALAIS

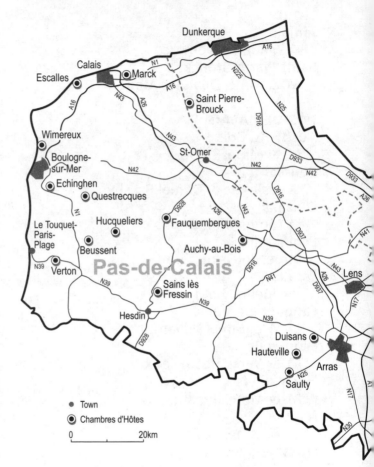

Nord/Pas-de-Calais

A much maligned area. Anyone who still believes that the North of France is featureless, flat, industrialised and boring should be dragged to the Boulonais hills, the time-warped villages a few miles inland, the fascinating towns of Arras, Montreuil and St. Omer, the sophistication of Le Touquet, the glorious beaches, the unique canal network and the *hortillonages* (market gardens), and made to repent. Of course there is industrialisation and whole tracts of mining territory that do not contribute to the holiday scene, but even here the biggest city, Lille, is underestimated. It is a prosperous city and destined to become even more important as the hub of a European multi-transport system. Its art galleries, restaurants and restored medieval heart rival those of many a better loved town.

The autoroute system through this area is superb – fast, efficient and uncrowded. Pick it up at Calais docks and Arras is just a short hop down the road. Don't always hurry on through. Devote a short break to the French region nearest to home, let the companion guide to the area, French Entrée to Calais point out the best bits, and I guarantee you'll be pleasantly surprised.

This is not a great area for chambres d'hôtes. Despised by French holiday-makers, who are even blinder to its merits than the Brits, it must rely largely on foreigners for trade. Things are looking up though and some welcome newcomers have opened up since the arrival of the tunnel.

NORD

JENLAIN. 59144.
8 km SE of Valenciennes by N49, direction Mauberge.

Industrialised suburbs, dominated by autoroutes, are not situations where one expects to come across a stunning château in lovely gardens. Don't despair when you turn off the *nationale*, following the signs to Jenlain (dreary). Before you turn right into the village you will see discreet gates straight ahead and a half-obscured chambres d'hôtes sign. This is it.

☆ **Madame Demarcq. 'Château d'En Haut'**
category: (M-L)
tel: 03.27.49.71.80.
fax: 03.27.35.90.17.
B&B: 46.5/57.5€ for two. No Dinner

Chambres d'hôtes don't come any more luxurious than this one. Your delighted eyes will alight, after a slow trip up an overgrown drive, on a large and lovely château, set in well kept and flowery grounds. It was bought by the Demarcqs some years ago to house the many antiques they had collected. Now guests can share their treasures.

Drive round to the back through the towered archway into the cobbled courtyard to find the *Accueil* door. Someone will be there to greet you, but not always the family. Float silently up the thickly carpeted stairs to your room, past the little alcove chapel, along Persian-carpeted corridors lined with gilt framed portraits and beautiful antiques. The corridor widens into a rather formal *salon*. Rooms are all elegantly furnished with very user-friendly antiques, nothing overdone, all quite lovely, with adjoining modernised bathrooms to match. All rooms are different; one has a family-single adjoining. I didn't see one I didn't long to stay in. Prices vary according to size.

A copious breakfast, is served by Monsieur in a sunny yellow dining room at long tables either side of a log fire in winter, bird song from the conservatory filters through, a good start to the day. You'll have to look elsewhere for evening meals. There is a restaurant in the village (not always open), and two others in Le Quesnoy 7 km south.

A perfect little château, well worth a luxury night stop at such affordable prices. Both Monsieur and Madame work, which accounts for the rather detached *accueil*. Madame is very pleasant when you can catch her, and there is always someone there to greet you if you book ahead

SAINT-PIERRE-BROUCK. 59630.
20 km E of Calais.

Exit 24 from the A16 (SP Saint-Omer) then via the D600, turn right to Capelle-Brouck, take the signs to St.-Pierre-Brouck and in the village, pass the Post Office, turn left and the house is on the left.

If you have never stayed in a chambres d'hôtes, arriving at Calais, this would be an excellent first choice.

M. & Mme. Duvivier-Alba. 'Le Château'
287, route de la Bistade.
category: (M)
tel/fax: 03.28.27.50.05.
B&B: 48/56€ for two.
Evening meals 16€ each, (incl wine).

On a wet and wintry day it was a real treat to find such a nice house. The red brick, turn-of-the-century *maison-de-maître* in this village stands in two acres of parkland. It has been diligently restored and decorated with great taste, keeping the original painted wall panels in the lounge; a comfortable modern couch intermingles with Louis XV chairs before a log fire. The adjoining dining room is painted a subtle pale green, harmonising perfectly with the polished table. Step into the sun lounge for summer breakfasts.

A first floor guest room decorated in blue has twin beds and a bathroom and looks over the rear garden to fields beyond where the family horses graze, On the second floor a suite of two adjoining rooms, yellow predominating, has a bed with a delicate white *baldaquin*, and large bay-windows, the shower room is shared with a charming single room which has its own loo and washbasin, – ideal for a family of three. The 'rose' room again with a large bay-window facing the front garden, has a shower. All have carpets and are centrally heated, a necessity in this northern clime.

Your hosts are delightful and Madame will cook you an evening meal joining you for *apéritifs* towards the end of the meal.

There is an excellent 18-hole golf course nearby with reasonable green fees. Monsieur, who speaks English, tells me that they often have British couples coming over for a weekend's golf.

Well worth a detour to stay here.

PAS-de-CALAIS

AUCHY-au-BOIS. 62190.

16 km W of Béthune.

Sortie 4 (Thérouanne) on the A26 from Calais then turn south in Thérouanne on to the D341. From Paris take exit 5 (Lillers) then the D916 through the outskirts of Burbure to Cauchy-à-la-Tour, then right on to the D341 northwards.

A quiet village, handy for the Calais-Paris autoroute.

Just outside the village past the church 500 metres on the right. Well signed. Be careful – there are two chambres d'hôtes in the village.

M. & Mme. Bulot.
28, rue de Pernes.
category: (S)
tel: 03.21.02.09.47.
fax: 03.21.02.81.68.
email: temp-libre-evasion@ wanadoo.fr
B&B: 43€ for two.
Evening meal 16€ each, (reservation only).

Drive up one of the entrances to this well-restored family complex high off the road. Colourful flower boxes of geraniums and petunias extend all round. The old farmhouse has been restored until it looks almost newly built. A firm handshake from Mme. Bulot senior who lives in the adjoining dwelling, once the stables, was our first welcome; but both the Bulots were soon out to greet us and we were immediately offered drinks.

This is a true chambres d'hôtes, where the family join their guests for all meals. How Madame manages to produce such a good meal and join in all the fun amazes me; but she is ably aided by Monsieur, a Rotarian, who speaks fluent English.

One family room on the ground floor is more like a gîte. Three others have independent entry up a flight of outside steps; a lot of thought has gone into these prettily furnished rooms in a variety of colours, which have a separate shower and loo apiece.

The night we were there we sat down with four other guests to a *quiche Lorraine*, followed by a whole fresh salmon with potatoes from the garden and a large cheese platter, *apéritif*, wine and *digestif* included.

BEUSSENT. 62170
10 km N of Montreuil.

In the village turn right by the church then left at a T-junction and the chambres d'hôtes is signed on the left.

☆ Josianne & Daniel Barsby. 'Le Menage'
124, Route de Hucqueliers.
category: (L)
tel: 03.21.90.91.92
fax: 03.21.86.38.24.
B&B: 72€ for two. No Dinner

The Barsby's 19th-century home, part manor, part farmhouse, is set deep in peaceful lanes. To find it drive past the Restaurant Lignier and climb a narrow leafy hill, with picnic tables thoughtfully set out to make the most of the surprisingly good view. After 2 km look for the house on the left – no sign, deliberately, but it's the only substantial property on the road.

They have hardly any need for signs – it is already well-booked by word of mouth.

Daniel is a sculptor in wood, as will be very evident immediately inside the front door. Examples of his talent – bold and distinctive, some begging to be bought (but not for sale) – are all over the house. His studio is stunning, rising to lofty rafters, with a gallery from which to look down on him working either at his sculpture or at the lace patterns which he designs for Calaisien lace manufacturers. He will happily show you the delicate painstaking designs of which he is a master.

The five bedrooms are all generous, in size, fittings and views. Bathrooms are definitely in the luxury class, with power showers and deep tubs. Colours, in keeping with the scale of the house are bold – lots of crimsons and forest greens, not pretty pastels. No skimping of the extras – bowls of fruit are provided in the bedrooms, bon-bons too, and bathroom perks, along with thick new towels.

The windows all look out on to unblemished countryside via extensive grounds. Outbuildings, where all manner of fowl – black swans, ornamental ducks, guinea fowl and doves – strut, chirp, screed and quack, are as immaculately preserved as the house. The new owners have obviously invested untold time as well as money in the restoration.

Breakfast, included in the price, is special again. Not only the usual French standard bread and croissants but also fresh farm eggs and of course freshly squeezed O.J. Or, I imagine, anything else that you fancied – Josianne is an extremely accommodating hostess.

An undoubted ☆ for unusually comfortable rooms and a good breakfast at a very reasonable price, charming hosts and the guarantee of a peaceful night's sleep, far away from the crowds but only 20 minutes from Boulogne

DUISANS. 62161.
5 km W of Arras.

If I had to pick one town in the North of France for a weekend break or for an autoroute stopover, it would be Arras. Big enough to offer good restaurants and shops, small enough to walk around, with easy parking. But that's far from it all; the place is packed with interest and history ancient and modern.

Its Grand' Place is the largest open square in Europe. The arcaded Flemish-style houses, with ornamental stepped gables, redbrick, old stone and heraldic signs, create an intensely satisfying total harmony; in fact few of them are the 17th-and 18th-century originals they would seem. The extent of the damage of four years' bombardment in the First World War can be seen in the photographs in the town hall (which forms one side of another glorious square, the Place des Héros). Almost incredibly, the rubble was used to create the Grand' Place exactly as it was. Tours are available to view the underground tunnels and cellars that run like warrens underneath the town centre and were used for shelter during both world wars.

Try and arrange your visit for Saturday and Wednesday, when the best market in the north fills the accommodating squares.

Take the N39 direction Le Touquet; after 5 km turn left on D56. The house is on the left.

☆ **Mme. Annie Senlis. 'Le Clos Grincourt'**
18, rue du Château.
category: (M)
tel/fax: 03.21.48.68.33
Open all year but by reservation only from Nov. to April.
B&B: 41€ for two. No Dinner

An elegant and spacious manor house, grey stone walls, white painted shutters, floor-to-ceiling windows. Built originally in the 17th century and added to over the intervening years, it was once an annexe to the next-door château.

Rooms are high-ceilinged, light and comfortable, furnished with family antiques and mementoes, so that the feeling is of a family home rather than intimidating grandeur. Readers have reported favourably of the welcome received from Mme. Senlis.

She can offer one suite of two rooms sharing a bathroom for 64€ and one other room, also with bath. The combination of elegant house, lovely garden, locked parking, proximity to Arras and readers' confirmation that there is good value here leads to a new ☆.

ECHINGHAM 62360

4km S of Boulogne sur Mer. 30 km S of Calais by the A16. exit 28 then the D 341 SP Baincthun, right on to the D234 to St. Léonard, a residential area of Echingham.

Chez Boussemaere
Echingham

Mme. Boussemaëre. 'Le Clos d'Esch'
rue de l'Église.
category: (M)
tel: 03 21 91 14 34.
fax: 03 21 31 06 41.
email: jp.boussemaere@ wanadoo.fr
B&B: 41€ for two. Gîte room 49€.

Past the church the long farmhouse is sideways on to the road, affording good parking and sunny south facing terraces for four guest rooms. Monsieur Boussemaëre is now the Maire. Madame has put a lot of thought into her rooms. One for a family is more a gîte, with a private terrace, kitchenette with fridge and micro-wave. Four others have en suite shower rooms and share a salon with tea making facilities and a tiny kitchenette also with fridge for picnic meals. The ground floor room is particularly light with patio doors to the terrace. If you are not into picnicking, Madame will direct you to local restaurants. Very good value here, stay more than two nights and the price is reduced.

ESCALLES. 62179.

14 km SW of Calais.

From the ferry follow the signs to 'Le Port', bump over the level crossing into the town, turn right over the swing bridge and follow the coast road – the D940 – all the way.

Once in Escalles turn left at the bottom of the hill and look for the signs a half km out of the village on the right.

The coast road will immediately give lie to the general theory that the Pas-de-Calais has to be flat and boring. The high chalk cliffs at Cap Blanc Nez are of considerable stature and the countryside is spectacularly rolling. There is a pebbly beach in Escalles and a very popular fish restaurant, Restaurant du Cap.

Jacqueline Boutroy. 'La Grand Maison'
category: (S-M)
tel/fax: 03.21.85.27.75.
B&B: 38.4/48€ for two.

This is one of the splendid old farm complexes that are such a pleasing feature of this part of France. Rustic buildings on three sides enclose a huge courtyard, big enough for small boys to be playing football when we visited, and an interesting square *pigeonnier* in the centre was soon pinpointed as the source of much contented cooing. The farm has been in Mme. Boutroy's family for generations and is now getting the facelift it deserves.

There was only one room left – the smallest – but it was pretty nice, all white with a blue frieze and garlanded curtains, bath and separate loo. The larger rooms, upstairs and termed 'studios', have less character but are good value for size and comfort, but cost a little more. One even has a kitchen for self-caterers. *Accueil* and breakfast are irreproachable. An excellent choice for port proximity, among many other considerations. No evening meals.

FAUQUEMBERGUES. 62560.
22 km SW of St. Omer. 40 km SE of Boulogne.

A26 from Calais, exit 4 to Thérouanne, then the D341 west to the D928.

A small town on the D928. Just off the town centre at traffic lights follow signs to *La Poste*. The chambres d'hôtes is exactly opposite across the square.

☆ **M. & Mme. Millamon. 'La Rêverie'**
19, rue Jonnart.
category: (M)
tel:03.21.12.12.38.
fax: 03.21.86.00.03
B&B: 48€ for two.

This 19th-century *maison-de-maître* right on the main road didn't have a lot to recommend it at first. When I had no answer from the front door I explored down a driveway beside the house and found it led to a pleasant garden, with parking. Young, vivacious Mme. Millamon happily showed us all the rooms. A twin-bedded room, a ground floor extension, in sunny yellow overlooks the garden. In the huge white bathroom, the gold claw feet of the large bath match the taps and shower fitting. The other two rooms, filled with light, are on the first floor, overlooking the road. Difficult to choose between them – dark green set off by dainty white curtains and bed covers, with a polished wood floor, or pink and beige with a *ciel de lit* and thick carpet, which I fell for. Both have modern showers. Fresh flowers in all the rooms. Central heating.

Comfy armchairs to sink into beside a log fire in the salon. Breakfast is served in the dining room on Limoges china with silver cutlery, or in the conservatory overlooking the garden. No evening meal but there are restaurants within walking distance.

Finding a chambres d'hôtes like this made my day, and I am delighted to say a reader felt the same. *'Another delightful place. We were in the ground floor room and I just had to try the bath – brilliant. The garden is not only lovely, but a bird watcher's paradise. This region tends to be driven through on the way south but I can see us using 'La Reverie' as a base to explore the Pas de Calais region for a few days at least. Another couple who turned up on spec could not believe their luck at the quality and value that they found here. A MUST FOR A ☆.'* Geoff Flood.

HAUTEVILLE. 62810.
15km SW of Arras. 60 km S of Lille. 50km N of Amiens.

In the Vallée-du-Gy, amidst farming land. Driving through this small village I spotted a *boulangerie* and a *boucherie*, always a good sign ensuring fresh bread for breakfast.

Chez Boussenaire
Echinchem

M. & Mme. Debaisieux. 'La Solette'
8, rue du Moulin.
category: (M)
tel: 03.21.58.73.58.
fax: 03.21.58.73.59.
email: lasollette@yahoo.fr
website: www.lasolette.com
B&B: 54.5€ for two.
Evening meals 16€ each.

Sideways on to the road, this long, low farmhouse catches all the sun, hence its name. It dates from 1825 and has been well renovated by your hosts who have a chicken farm. The stable and *pigeonnier* at one end of the house have been converted into three simple but charming guest rooms. One ground floor room *Le Bouton d'Or* is tastefully furnished with a pine double bed and very pretty blue and yellow wallpaper and curtains. It still has the stable door and a window overlooking the meadow where sheep safely graze. A convertible couch doubles as a children's bed. Excellent modern shower rooms, in all three. Upstairs, *Myosotis* has a velux window plus a peephole window by the bed and can also accommodate children *couchant*-style. A smaller third room, *Eglantine*, faces north but has a pretty, flowery washbasin in its shower room. Children under six years accommodated free.

In the entrance hall is a tiny kitchen corner for guests for dealing with drinks and picnic baskets.

There is a most attractive family dining room in Madame's favourite blue and gold colours, for breakfast and evening meals, when products of the farm are enjoyed by all. Occasionally Madame's duties as deputy Maire prevent the evening meal.

A comfortable salon with log fire looked most inviting. I had a job faulting this chambres d'hôtes, perhaps the tiled/lino bedroom floors might be bit chilly in winter, but rooms are electrically heated. The warm welcome and friendly family atmosphere makes this one rank very highly. The *Livre-d'Or* was full of compliments from satisfied British visitors. Go for it! you won't be disappointed – it is a true chambres d'hôtes.

HUCQUELIERS. 62650.

19 km NE of Montreuil. 28 km SE of Boulogne-sur-Mer. 29 km E of Le Touquet.

In the village drive up past the church and the chambres d'hôtes is on the left.

M. & Mme. Bertin. 'Le Clos' (M)
19, rue de l'Eglise
category: (M)
tel: 03.21.86.37.10.
fax: 03.21.86.37.18.
B&B: 51/62.5€ for two.

This *maison de maître* once belonged to a *Notaire*. Behind the tall railing and gates in a gravelled courtyard. The stable block has been converted into four studio type rooms with a sitting area and kitchen on the ground floor, plus loo. Up a spanking new pine staircase is a bedroom with a shower and washbasin. One of the rooms is extra large and can accommodate a family of five, using bunks and a single downstairs. Guests are welcome to use the large rear garden. Since I visited, two new more romantic rooms on the second floor have been created, both have a bath and a shower, *Le Clos Princesse* is in bridal white and *Le Clos Marquise*, with king-size bed in golden colours, has sofa beds for two more. Guests are welcome to use the rear garden.

A really copious breakfast including cereal and eggs is served in the dining room or sometimes in a bright blue salon where a corner is reserved for guests to watch TV.

Evening meals can occasionally be arranged and there is a taxi service to local restaurants, also possible baby sitting. Parking is up the lane beside the house in a private plot adjacent to the garden.

MARCK. 62730.
7 km NE of Calais.

From the A16 to Dunkerque take exit Marck or the D119. In the centre of the town take the D248 to Le Font Vert. The rear of this chambres d'hôtes overlooks the Calais aerodrome across fields.

M. & Mme. Houzet. 'Le Manoir du Heldick'
2528, Ave du Gal. de Gaulle, Le Font Vert.
category: (M)
tel./fax: 03.21 85.74.34.
B&B: 48€ for two.

This long red-brick manor house was once a farmhouse owned by M. Houzet's uncle. Occupied by German generals during the war, it was left empty on their retreat in 1944. Now it is a well-furnished manor house with prominent family antiques. Your caring hosts, who speak some English, offer three guest rooms, in a ground floor wing. *Bleuet*, with a double bed and cot has a large bathroom with bath and all facilities for a baby. *Les Roses*, with single beds in pretty green/pink, has a shower room. Both face the rear garden. *Coquelicot*, well-named with striking red wallpaper, has two single beds. Central heating tries to combat the tiled floors in winter. Two new rooms on the first floor include one for a family of four. All have welcoming trays of biscuits, tea and coffee-making facilities, extra beds 8€; baby cot free. Included in the deal is a copious breakfast.

An Empire-style salon for guests has stairs to another room above, with deep armchairs for watching TV. A well-furnished dining room, includes high chairs, and leads to a rear terrace. Confirmation of all bookings in writing please, preferably by fax. *"A very professionally run place, and Mme. Houzet was extremely helpful concerning where to eat in Calais (by the quiet back road), comfortably appointed, interestingly furnished. Excellent breakfast with freshly squeezed orange juice"*. Min Lee.

QUESTRECQUES 62830

15 km SE of Boulogne. The small village is deep in the country. From Samers on the N1 take the D 238 north and turn down a lane left at the crucifix just before the village.

M. & Mme. Halley des Fontaines.
'Aux Jardins d'Anais'
category: (L)
tel/fax: 03 21 87 06 56:
email: les-jardins-d-anais@ wanadoo.fr
B&B: 68/91€ for two
Closed 1 Jan. to 15 Mar.

Dating from the 16th Century this is probably the best preserved of all the Boulonnais fortified manor houses. Curious twin red-brick towers protect either end. It is still completely surrounded by fields. Recent inspired restoration as a private home includes four guest rooms, making it possible for you to share its ancient history in comfort. Three rooms on the first floor named after famous people are reached by one of the towers and are delightfully furnished with well chosen antiques, warmly carpeted through to modern bathrooms, two of which have jacussi baths, the smallest room just a shower. The fourth room, for a family perhaps, is in the long *bergerie* and has a salon with fireplace and a sunny south terrace overlooking the medieval *potager*, a double bed with adjoining bathroom which is shared by two beds on the mezzanine. All rooms have tea-making facilities.

The library, where breakfast is served still has the original red brick fireplace as has the adjoining salon. In summer you can indulge in breakfast on a covered terrace overlooking a small lake patrolled by black swans.

I visited on a beautiful autumn day, so could enjoy the small interesting gardens which Monsieur is making. Chickens freely roamed, family cats sunned themselves. The whole place has an unusual charm enhanced by kindly hosts who are thoroughly enjoying their new life style, and wish to share it with guests. Madame is the curator of the music museum in

Boulogne. Special week ends can be booked, rambling or riding in the Autumn, in Spring the theme is gardening. Evening meals occasionally by reservation. The Ferme Auberge Blaizel is recommended in the next village at Wirwignes.

SAINS-les-FRESSIN 62310
12 km NW of Hesdin, a small village on the D 155 from Fressin which is a turn off the D 925 from St. Omer to Hesdin. The house is well signed. One of the prettiest parts of the valley of the Canche from which seven valleys can be explored.

M. & Mme. Rieben. 'Chantelouve'
35 rue Principale.
category: (M)
tel/fax: 03 21 90 60 13.
email: chantelouve@
clubinternet.fr
B&B: 43€ for two
Evening meals 18€ each.
Closed December.

You will love the Riebens, who live in this ivy covered old farmhouse with dormer windows. It has a large modern sun lounge where guests enjoy breakfast overlooking an extensive garden and meadows where geese and chickens roam. A private suite for a family has a kitchen below and a suite of rooms above double and single beds for six sharing separate shower and loo on the private landing, towelling gowns provided. Two other rooms for three on the ground floor have private terraces, well furnished with a mixture of family heirlooms, the tiled floors would be appreciated in hot summer weather. One has a shower the other a bath, two basins and a separate shower.

Breakfast is *copieux* and your hosts go out of their way to ensure you have a happy stay.

Evening meals, all drinks *compris*: Tuesdays and Fridays on reservation only. Extra beds 12€. Suite 73€. for four.

SAULTY. 62158.
20 km SW of Arras. 17 km NE of Doullens by N25.

Conveniently placed for sorties into that most rewarding of northern towns, Arras.

Follow signs north from L'Arbret, on the N25 from Doullens to Arras.

M. & Mme. Dalle.
82, rue de la Gare.
category: (M)
tel: 03.21,48.24.76.
fax: 03.21.48.18.32.
B&B: 48€ for two. No Dinner
Closed January.

The impression given by the address belies the reality. Not many imposing neoclassical châteaux set in 15 hectares of grounds record their address as rue de la Gare. Montgomery chose it as a base in 1944, but had to be installed in an armoured van outside for security reasons. We can be more fortunate. Inside the handsome building the atmosphere is equally unpretentious. No heavy drapes and chandeliers – rather a casual modern decor, with each of the four rooms having its individual cheerful colour scheme and private facilities. Extra beds available. The dining room (breakfast especially recommended here) is particularly light and spacious.

Don't think either that château-grandeur is not compatible with children. They are warmly welcomed here, as indeed are all the guests. The large games room would particularly suit teenagers. No evening meals.

VERTON 62180
15 km S of Le Touquet,5 km E of Berck-sur-Mer a lively seaside resort where there is also a hospital for the cure of bone diseases, the strong iodine in the air is supposed to be especially beneficial.

From the A 16 exit 25 Verton follow signs into the village past the church and the chambres d'hôtes is signed on the right.

M. & Mme. Terrien. 'La Chaumière'
19 rue de Bihan.
category: (M)
tel: 03 21 84 27 10.
website: www.perso.worldonline.fr/
la chaumiere
B&B: 45€

Not all thatched cottages are old, this one was built just over 20 years ago with an extended wing for guests. Rooms are compact with delightfully different decor, bury yourself in roses by Sanderson or cool off with spring-like colours in the yellow room. The novelty of the *pigeonnier* would be enjoyed more by the young and agile as the blue and white bedroom is under the eaves, with shower room below. A fourth room is over the garage in the main house. Immaculate matching shower rooms have every extra for comfort. Time your arrival right and you might get a 'cuppa' in the adjoining smart black and white dining salon where elegant Madame Terrien presides over a really copious breakfast, the table now laid with chic black and white china. No shortage of restaurants for evening meals, the nearest being the rustic 'Auberge de Bahot' – 2 km away. Well worth a longer stay.

WIMEREUX. 62930.
4km N of Boulogne-sur-Mer by the D940.

☆ **Mme. Avot. 'La Goëlette'**
13, Digue de Mer.
category: (L)
tel: 03.21.32.62.44.
B&B: 48/80€ for two.

Turn right from l'Atlantic along the prom and dive behind the beach huts to find this 1930's cream and blue painted villa. How pleasing it is, incidentally, to see a building like this, constructed in the little resort's prime, put to good contemporary use and not pulled down to make way for apartment blocks, as in Le Touquet. Encouragingly, the signs are that Wimereux has learned that character is not a commodity that can be introduced instantaneously, and its older buildings are among its greatest assets.

The delightful owner, Mary Avot, describes herself a *celibataire* (single). Her parents helped her buy the tall narrow house a couple of years ago and her father has contributed to the conversion into a B&B, which opened a couple of years ago. Without any advertisement except word of mouth, the place is often fully booked for weekends and holidays.

Four charming rooms are furnished with chic restraint – bare polished wooden floors, antique pine furniture and lack of fussiness giving a Scandinavian look. The two front rooms are undoubtedly the ones to go for, with a fabulous view directly out to sea. The two rear rooms are pretty nice, too, but overlook roofs rather than waves. All four have luxurious bathrooms and smart bed-linen.

Breakfast lives up to the high standard, at present served in the front room. Mary was decorating the rear downstairs room to provide a bar and sitting area.

I owe the discovery of this gem to a kind reader, who sums up the situation *'We have discovered a fantastic place to stay. It has been opened recently by a charming young French lady, Mary Avot, who has supervised the decoration of this 1930s house to its original standard. The house faces the sea and is right on the esplanade. We were given a room facing Wimereux's beach on the first floor, with pine furniture, huge windows and we felt we were on a boat for a cruise'.* Patricia Marlborough.

Street parking is available at the back of the house.

Normandy

NORMANDY

Eu (Beaumont)

Dieppe

Ermenouville

N27

D915

Les Landes Aumale

A28

N28

N29

D925

Fécamp

Seine-Maritime

D926

N29

N29

D925

St-Sauveur-
d'Emalleville

N15

N15

N27

A28

D915

Caudebec-en-Caux

Le Havre

N15

R. Seine

Rouen

N31

N178

A131

Aizier

N151

A13

N15

N31

D180

A13

N178

Fourmetot

St-Denis-le-Ferment

Tricqueville

Pont-
Audemer

N138

D810

D840

N14

D181

D181

R. Seine

N13

La Croix-St-Leufroy

Fourges

D834

A13

N15

Bernay

N13

Eure

Évreux

N13

N138

N154

● Town

◉ Chambres d'Hôtes

0   20km

D840

N26

N12

N12

BASSE-NORMANDY

- Sainte-Geneviève
- Montfarville
- Cherbourg
- St Germain de Tournebut
- Négreville
- Géfose-Fontenay
- Crépon
- St Vigor-le-Grand
- Carentan
- Vouilly
- Bayeux
- **Manche**
- Saint-Lô
- Marigny
- Monts-en-Bessin
- Coutances
- Nicorps
- Meurdraquière
- Vire
- Flers
- Avranches
- Juilley

● Town
◉ Chambres d'Hôtes

0   20km

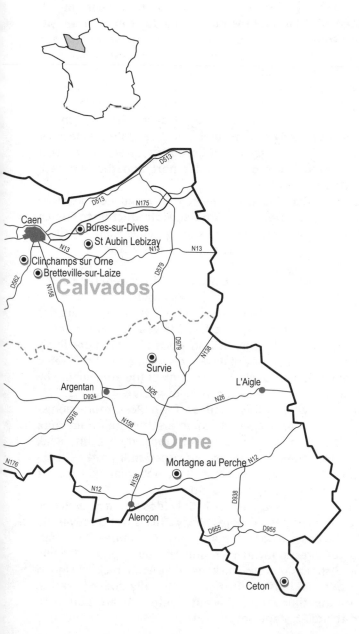

Normandy

Normandy has a special place in many Britons' affections as their first experience of a real holiday in France. The toe may have been dipped briefly into the waters of Calais and the north on a day trip or in transit, but it is frequently Normandy that proves to be the base for further exploration, leading to long-term addiction. Having no fewer than four ferry ports to choose from helps, of course.

Dieppe looks set to become a favourite, with a brand new ferry terminal, ever-decreasing crossing time and the short distance to Paris. Le Havre has excellent communications and frequent sailings. Ouistreham, right in the heart of the region, leads directly to some of its most appealing aspects of countryside and cultural heritage, and Cherbourg offers a shortish crossing, the calmer atmosphere of a smaller port and the laid-back atmosphere of the Manche.

The five *départements* that make up the region could not be more different: Between them they offer an unsurpassed introduction to French scenery, history, coastline, customs, food, drink and people. There are more chambres d'hôtes here than in any other region, from picturesque Auge farmhouses to impressive châteaux.

The most northern département, **Seine-Maritime**, is dominated by the capital of Upper Normandy, the lovely city of Rouen, set in a bend of the Seine, protected by encircling hills. Recovery from its wartime horrors has been skilfully achieved and the city now offers a rewarding amalgam of mostly old, partly new, urban delights. It's an open-air city, more light-hearted than its rival Caen, with plenty of incentives to linger at a café table in the historic and colourful market place or to drink in the atmosphere by the magnificent cathedral. There is an abundance of good restaurants.

Further north are the white cliffs familiar from Post-Impressionist paintings, fronting cobble beaches. Behind them are the chalky plateaux of the Caux area, dedicated mostly to cereal crops. It is a bit bleak sometimes, which makes the discovery of the occasional pretty village and rushing stream all the more pleasing. It is not generally tourist territory, which means more space to go round.

On the other side of the Seine we reach **Calvados** country, which is where the chambres d'hôtes cluster more thickly. This is Normandy at its most picture-book. The posters do not exaggerate. Guaranteed are half-timbered thatched cottages, hollyhocks round the door, gnarled apple trees, one dog, three sheep and six chickens. Take your pick of signed routes – *'fromage'*, *'cidre'* and just *'touristique'* – it really doesn't matter. Wherever you leave the thunder of the autoroute you are bound to stumble upon hard-to-credit, stage-set rusticity.

The coastline will be no less familiar. Honfleur, the favourite of artists for many a generation, is still as picturesque but perhaps threatened by too many tourists, thanks to the new Pont de Normandie (go out of season). Deauville, a mere hop and a skip away from the deepest countryside, is posh Normandy. Expensive, well-groomed, elegant, humming during the August races, a conference centre for the rest of the year, it adds yet another dimension to the department. Next door Trouville is earthier and cheaper, with beaches just as fine. Good for families who are looking for sea and sand for the kids alongside plenty of grown-up activity.

Three-quarters of Caen, the capital of Lower Normandy, was tragically destroyed in 1944, but it is still the home of two magnificent abbeys – built for William the Conqueror and his queen Matilda – an imposing castle in the city centre, some lovely churches and a thriving university. Linked by a canal to its port, Ouistreham, it makes a good winter base for shopping and eating. The Mémorial, a museum of peace, is one of the most moving and impressive museums I have ever visited. Don't miss it and do allocate half a day to its proper appreciation.

Bayeux is another must for any Calvados itinerary. Go early or late in the day to get the best value from the sensitively presented Tapestry, and enjoy its ancient narrow streets and massive Gothic cathedral. The nearby Bessin countryside is gentle and pretty, with some attractive fishing ports along the coast, which, after the landing beaches, bends north at the dairy centre of Isigny.

Most of the popular Normandy cheeses – Pont l'Evêque, Camembert, Livarot – come from Calvados, where the black-and-white eye-patch cows are most prominent. Acres of apple orchards provide the raw material for Calvados and cider.

The Cotentin peninsula forms most of the *département* of the **Manche**, which is, I suppose, my favourite. It is the least sophisticated, the friendliest, the easiest-to-handle. I recommend it for first-timers. Apart from Cherbourg there are no big towns and the pace is correspondingly slower. Inland some of the towns are boringly post-war, but a drive along the coast line is a good way to sample the scenic diversity that defied destruction.

West of Cherbourg one thinks of Cornwall – rugged cliffs, wild seas, granite cottages, fishing villages. The Nez de Joburg feels like the end of the world, not just France. Further south, and nature mellows considerably. Carteret is ideal for bucket-and-spade holidays, with lovely sands, rock pools, river estuary, trips to the Channel Islands and a Michelin-starred restaurant/hotel. Granville is a lively fishing port, looking across the bay to the fabled Mont St. Michel, rising like a floating mirage from the salt marshes.

Drive east of Cherbourg to Barfleur and St. Vaast to find colourful fishing harbours and marinas much favoured by British yachties. The seascape here is dotted with islands, the beaches sandy and undeveloped. Unless you are heading for the landing beaches, call it a day – the vast sandy Bessin bay is pretty featureless.

The **Orne** is an aristocratic *département*, rich in châteaux, manor houses and stud farms. Bagnoles-de-l'Orne, a dignified spa town, typifies the away-from-it-all, elegant relaxed atmosphere. The lovely river Orne flows through green, unspoiled countryside with attractive little towns like Mortagne, the cathedral at Sées and the stud farms in the Perche area to lend interest.

The mighty river Seine dominates the department of **Eure**. Exploring its looping course is a delightful exercise, revealing charming villages nestling in the escarpments, like Les Andelys. Giverny, the home of Monet, and its garden is a rewarding excursion. Approaching Paris, it all gets busier and more developed, so swing westwards to explore some of the tributaries, like the meandering river from which the département gets its name – the Eure.

CALVADOS

BRETTEVILLE-sur-LAIZE. 14680.

10 km S of Caen by the N158 towards Falaise, then right on to the D23 at La Jalousie. Just before Bretteville turn right on to the D125, where the château is signed.

M. & Mme. Cantel. 'Château des Riffets'
category: (L)
tel: 02.31. 23.53.21. fax.02.31.23.75.14.
B&B: 91€ for two.
Evening meal 40€ each.

The 15 hectares of immaculate park-land includes a heated swimming pool at this private château which has been restored by the present owners. Bedrooms, named after members of the family, on first and second floors are high, wide and handsome with luxury bathrooms. They accommodate two, three or a family in a suite. The public rooms have original period ceilings; 17th century chairs in the dining room and a large chest with a ghost which will reveal its secret, but only if you ask it nicely. During the last war the château was bombed by the RAF, losing its front facade and tower. The front is repaired and new sweeping steps lead to the entrance.

Dinner (optional) is served by a maid, but the family will join you if that is what you wish. All drinks included, even old Calvados, and vegetarians catered for.

BURES-SUR-DIVES. 14670.

15 km E of Caen. 15 km SE of Ouistreham.

A visit to Pegasus Bridge is an absolute must. It was here that the first British troops of the Sixth Airborne Division landed very early in the morning of 6 June 1944. They took the vital bridge over the Caen canal and liberated the café right by the bridge, the first house in France to be freed by the Allies. M. & Mme. Gondrée and their children were in the café at the time and for three nights no sleep was had by anyone. Sadly the original bridge was dismantled a few years ago and replaced by a new one, called Pegasus II. However the café is still open from April to October, run by Arlette Gondrée, one of the daughters. None of the decor has changed for fifty years, just enhanced by gifts from visiting servicemen. The original Pegasus bridge has now been installed in a Museum park at Ranville just across the river. Son et Lumière evenings are a feature in high summer.

Not far from the ferry at Ouistreham book a room at Bures-sur-Dives.

In the village of Troarn take the D95 to Bures, bear right to the church and the manor is down the lane alongside, well signed.

☆ **M. & Mme. Landon-Cassady.**
'Manoir des Tourpes'
rue de l'Eglise.
category: (M)
tel: 02.31.23.63.47.
fax: 02.31.23.86.10.
B&B: 48/64€ for two. No Dinner
Closed Nov. to Easter.

This elegant 17th-century manor house stands beside the village church, with sweeping lawns to the banks of the river Dives, where the water rises with the tide. Monsieur is American, but Madame is French. We were given a very warm welcome, Madame switching easily from French to English and back again as she showed us round, but generally the French atmosphere prevails throughout their home. Three bedrooms overlook the garden and river, all so different but each having a special allure, making a choice difficult. The largest almost a suite, is pure honeymoon material, with windows on three sides and the luxury of a real log fire. Thick carpets, fresh flowers by the bed, en suite bathroom in delicate peach and blue, thick towels and even a peach towelling gown. If the log fire isn't enough there's also an electric blanket. Next door, a smaller room with the most compelling view of all from the double bed, has a washbasin and a large private bathroom across the corridor with a deep old copper bath tub, but a shower too if you can't face the novelty. Not many do, Madame tells me. The third bedroom, with shower and toilet, boasts a balcony. Charming rooms and there is now a fourth bedroom to consider.

Breakfast in the lounge/dining room, where a cheerful log fire blazes away, is laid on an attractive round table and is not to be hurried over. A wide choice of cereals, fruit juice, yoghurt, fresh fruit, jams, bread, brioche and all the usual drinks. You won't find such luxury in any hotel at these prices. No evening meals, but there is a Logis in Troarn, or your hosts will advise for further afield.

You will need to book ahead. A ☆ for situation and good value.

There is also a new gîte in the grounds, especially equipped for small children, with a fenced-in garden.

CLINCHAMPS-SUR-ORNE 14320.

15 km S of Caen In the village turn left by the Mairie opposite the church and first left into rue Courtillage.

M. & Mme. Annick. 'Le Courtillage'.
category: (M)
tel: 02.31.23.87.63
B&B: 61€ for two.

In a hectare of garden with shady trees this 18th-century *Maison-de-Maître* feels deep in the country but is within walking distance of the village. General Rommel conducted his campaign, just before the invasion, from the salon in the house; but slept in an armoured car in the garden.

This is a home with great character, four sunny south facing guest rooms of which two are family suites, are charmingly furnished in different styles. Natural wood floors, pretty matching curtains and bed covers. *Écrivain* with dark red canopy accommodates four. The Swedish room is cosy for two. On the dullest day the golden Provençal room would cheer. Adjoining large bathrooms are successfully contrived out of rear north corners, toilets hide in cupboards, secret staircases lead to other parts of the house. Difficult to choose a room, such character in all. There is a library of rare books for adults only, but the salon is for all. A really charming place. No evening meals.

CRÉPON 14480

12 km NE of Bayeux. Near the coast between Arromanches and Courseulles, makes this a splendid place to stay for visiting all of the Landing Beaches, and within easy reach of the Memorial museum at Caen.

Mme. Poisson. 'Manoir de Crépon'
Route d'Arromanches.
category: (L)
tel: 02 31 22 21 27.
fax: 02 31 22 88 80.
website: www.gites-de-france-calvados.fr
B&B: 69€ for two. 99€ for four in the suite.

The slight wear and tear of the outer walls of this 17th/18th century manor house certainly doesn't extend to the elegant guest rooms. A drive round the circular lawn inside a walled garden passes the old stables where antiques for sale were being perused by Sunday afternoon visitors. Climb the wide stairs from the stone flagged entrance hall to an equally wide landing, where front corridors lead to four guest rooms. Surprisingly charming large rooms, luxuriously carpeted, furnished very comfortably with practical antiques. Most have marble fireplaces, and tall windows overlook the rear garden. All have tea making facilities, TV and large modernised bathrooms. Two rooms are family suites each with two rooms sharing the bathrooms. There wasn't one room I wouldn't have been happy to stay in, unfortunately nice Madame Poisson was fully booked.

There is a more formal salon and music room on the ground floor but breakfast is served in the comfort of the kitchen, sitting on forms at a long table guests get to know each other and plan the day's outings.

No evening meals. Plenty of restaurants in the area and along the coast.

GÉFOSSE-FONTENAY. 14230.
65 km SE of Cherbourg, 30 km NW of Bayeux by N13 west, just past St Germain-du-Pert, then D514 towards Grandcamp-Maisy. Turn left on to the D199 A to Géfosse-Fontenay.

Set in the vast bay of Le Grand Vey, looking north all the way past the landing beach of Utah to St. Vaast. The light around here is unique – enough to tempt you to pack some water-colours. Vast sandy beaches to walk along, and Bayeux within easy reach. More practically – halfway between the two ferry ports, Cherbourg and Caen.

On the road to the village, on the left before the church is:

M. & Mme. Leharivel. 'Ferme de la Rivière
category: (M)
tel: 02.31.22.64.45.
fax: 02.31.22.01.18.
B&B: 45.5€ for two.
Evening meals 16€ each.
Credit cards accepted.

Of all the fortified farmhouses near the landing beaches that I've visited this is probably the most compact. A reader's appreciation: *"This lovely old Norman farm remains very much a working farm in spite of modernisation. The bedrooms have been tastefully restored and equipped with all the amenities of a good hotel without destroying the 11th-century ambience.*

Furniture is mostly genuine antique, thus preserving a sense of history'.

Up the stone-flagged stairs, ceilings remain high in the three rooms for two or three on the second floor, where each has a shower and loo. A charming hostess provides evening meals (wine not *compris*) taken in a salon with the original stone fireplace complete with bread oven. High-backed red and green tapestry chairs pull up to the long oak table.

This is a dairy farm, and all their milk goes to Pont l'Évêque for the production of *Lanquetot* cheese.

Drive down the road past the church to the beach where among the seaweed at low tide tractors will be collecting mussels.

MONTS-en-BESSIN. 14310
18 km SW of Caen. 19 km S of Bayeux.

The Pré-Bocage area of Calvados is renowned for its cider and dairy products.

Take the D6 south-east of Bayeux direction Villers-Bocage and in about 18 km turn left on to the D92 (if you reach Fains on the D6 you have just missed the turn) and follow the signs for about 1km. The house is on your left.

☆ **Mr. & Mrs. Edney. 'La Varinière-la-Vallée'**
category: (M)
tel: 02.31.77.44.73.
fax: 02.31.77.11.72.
B&B: 59€ for two.
Closed 20 Dec. to 1 Feb.

A warm and friendly English welcome in one of the most lovely small manor houses I have had the pleasure to visit. It has been gracefully restored and decorated to a high standard. You'll love the entrance hall in Wedgwood blue with white friezes and a charming fireplace with plaster figures. The comfortable salon in deep rose and white is just a taste of the pleasures in store. Across the hall is the yellow dining room (shades of Monet at Giverny?).

Five carpeted bedrooms have views over the countryside from typical long French windows, and a choice of bath or shower; one features a bath on legs and a Victorian wash basin, others are totally modernised. A sunny family unit with double bed and adjoining white room for children with a single bed and cot share a shower-room. On the second floor two rooms share a bathroom on the landing for a family of five or friends travelling together, There is a small paddock where donkeys graze, and ample parking. No evening meals, but in Villers-Bocage, *Les Trois Rois* is one of the best restaurants in the department. Thank you to the reader who confirms that this one should have an a ☆. It is now very popular and prices are rising a little steeply.

SAINT-AUBIN-LEBIZAY 14340.
28 km E of Caen. From Dozulé on the N175 take the D85 for 5 km to Clermont-en-Auge, carry on for 1km then look for the 'Cour Épée' sign on the left, up a private drive.

M. & Mme. Tesnière. 'Cour l'Épée'
category: (M)
tel/fax. 02.31.65.13.45
email: ajtesniere@wanadoo.fr
B&B: 61€ for two.

Another warm welcome awaits you at this old *pressoir*, now converted to a long low *colombage* dwelling, typical of the Auge area. Situated in a well-kept garden, it has restful views over the countryside. There are 17 hectares, of wooded land to roam around and a barbecue in a *grotte* which guests are welcome to use. Two spacious beamed rooms in the main house are elegantly furnished, including thick carpets and tea-making facilities, (one has an extra bed) both have adjoining bathrooms. There is a most comfortable salon with a log fire for chilly days. The third room, in a small stone house in the garden, more suitable for Summer occupation, is a pleasant suite for three. No evening meals. Restaurants in Dozulé.

VOUILLY. 14230 ISIGNY-sur-MER.
7 km S of Isigny. 65 km SE of Cherbourg.

Isigny is not really *sur-mer* but near the mouth of the river Vire. There is a little quay, where colourful fishing boats unload their catch, and sheds of assorted crustaceans and molluscs. This is stomach-country, not only for the wonderfully fresh fish and oysters but also for all dairy produce – Isigny is the distribution centre – and for the flavoursome lamb that graze on the surrounding salt marshes.

From the N13 (Cherbourg to Caen) exit at Isigny and right on to the D5, in 4.5 km left to Vouilly, there are two villages Vouilly-la-Mairie and Vouilly-l'Église – you want the latter, round the church at Vouilly-l'Église then immediately left again, the château is on the right in about 200 yards, easy to miss the sign.

☆ **Mme. Hamel. 'Château de Vouilly' (M & L)**
category: (M-L)
tel: 02.31.22.08.59.
fax: 02.31.22.90.58.
email: chateau.vouilly@ wanadoo.fr
B&B: 54/62€ for two. No Dinner
Closed 1 Nov. to 1 Mar. *Carte bancaires* accepted.

Featured in all our guides and still going strong. A mellow old manor house rather than a château, full of character. It has many charms not least the five splendid bedrooms, all equipped with bathrooms. Built in the 15th and 16th centuries and enlarged in the 18th, it boasts a moat and a charming well-tended anglicised walled garden. Situated within easy reach of Bayeux. It must have been fascinating for the Hamel family, on the 50th anniversary of D-Day celebrations, to welcome back some of the 42 American war correspondents who were stationed at Vouilly, using the dining room as their press office. Now a delectable breakfast is served in this room, fresh roses adorning each table. A delightful place, with a friendly hostess. No evening meals. Restaurants in Isigny, Le Central Brasserie open on Sundays when everywhere else is closed. A ☆ as a very special château – book ahead, it would be a shame to miss it.

EURE

AIZIER. 27500.
45km E of Le Havre. 45km W of Rouen.

From the A131 take exit 27 to Bourneville, drive through the village, following the D139 to Aizier. In the village turn left on to the D2 and the chambres d'hôtes is on the right opposite the Mairie.

M. & Mme. Laurent. 'Les Sources Bleus'
category: (M)
tel: 02.32.57.26.68.
fax: 02.32.57.42.25.
B&B: 44.5€ for two.
Evening meal 13.5€ exceptionally.

This ivy-covered *maison-de-maître*, of the tall slim variety, makes an idyllic chambres d'hôtes, where every room from dining room and lounge to the topmost bedroom has a glorious view of the Seine flowing past the garden.

Ideal for families, as two first floor rooms each with bathrooms, have a tiny single room attached, where you can sit up in bed and see the river.

On the second floor are two heavily-beamed rooms under the eaves, each with double bed and two singles. A spare single room on the top landing can belong to either. A working chair lift for the disabled means they can enjoy the first floor rooms.

Nice Mme. Laurent, lives in a house across the garden and she serves breakfast in the dining room, where there is a kitchen bar, or in the garden under a canopy in summer.

No evening meals but there is a restaurant close by. Only an hour from Le Havre, this would make a good ferry stop.

LA CROIX-SAINT-LEUFROY. 27490.
100 km SE of Le Havre. 40 km S of Rouen

Much to see in the area. Les Andelys, Monet's garden and the Seine are all close by. Don't miss Les Andelys. Le Petit-Andelys is tucked in by the river under the hill on which the ruined Castle Gaillard stands, a fortress built by Richard the Lionheart to prevent the French king Phillipe-Auguste from reaching Rouen in 1196. For the energetic there is a lane up to it behind the Tourist Office; otherwise drive 3 km through Le Grand-Andelys and follow the signs. Once high on the car park, the view is fabulous. The Seine below like a silver ribbon winds in and out of view, protected by sharp white cliffs on the north-east bank. Barges steadily make their way to Rouen. A glorious place for a picnic. The farm is deep in the country on the plain above the small village of La Croix-Saint-Leufroy, just off the D10 but only 3 km from the A13.

☆ **M. & Mme. Senecal. 'Ferme de la Boissière'**
Hameau de La Boissaye.
category: (M)
tel: 02.32.67.70.85.
fax: 02.32.67.03.18.
B&B: 41€ for two.
Evening meal 15€ each.

Heating under the tiles really did keep our feet warm in the large ground-floor guest room. The equally large salon next door was just as comfortable. What a joy it was one cold November night to find such comfort. The old house dates back many hundreds of years when it was once used as a home for the monks at La Croix-Saint-Leufroy. Nothing has been spoilt in the reconstruction. The old beams and windows, now double-glazed, remain. The large light salon adjoins their own house.

Three other bedrooms, beautifully furnished and electrically heated, overlook the front garden where ducks and swans enjoy the large pond.

Madame is happy to give you an evening meal even if you arrive late. We had booked only half an hour before and were lucky to get a room and an excellent meal. We ate by a log fire, drinks *compris, Oeufs-en-cocotte au jambon, escalope de veau à la Normande* laced with cream, cheeses of the region and a delicious apple *crêpe*. The aperitif *Pommeau* (Calvados and apple juice) is to be taken cautiously. Madame joins you for an aperitif, but not always for the meal, there are often other guests to make up the numbers. Recommended as an all-weather stop. ☆ for excellent value.

FOURGES. 27630.
10 km E of Giverny. 50km SW of Beauvais. 65 km SE of Rouen.

From the A13 SE of Rouen take exit 16, the D181 to Vernon then the D5 past Giverny and through Gasny to Fourges.

☆ **M. & Mme. Stékélorum.**
24, rue du Moulin.
category: (S)
tel: 02.32.52.12.51.
fax: 02.32.52.13.12.
B&B: 40€ for two. No Dinner
Closed 1 Nov. to 1 Mar.

Praise rolls in regularly for this 17th-century farmhouse beside the road, the oldest in the village. It faces into a small garden hidden by high locked gates. Delphiniums blue, geraniums red and climbing roses grow rampantly. Lie beside the little pond and listen to the gentle trickle of water, where a lively frog hops among the lily leaves while the ducks stay firmly asleep.

The Stékélorums are charming people who love entertaining guests and offer a very warm welcome. The original inhabitable part of the old farmhouse, incorporating the old bread oven and many other rustic features, has been made into a salon for guests. Furnished with antique furniture which came with the house, it's a property which has long been in Madame's family. It is here round an oval table that a copious breakfast is served on pretty china, on cold days in front of a blazing log fire.

The granary is now the owner's private residence. Between the two is a charming double-bedded guest room with stable door opening on to a small terrace.

Across the courtyard on the first floor of the original stable are two rooms (one for three people) charmingly furnished with pretty fabric.

No evening meals but M. Stékélorum now recommends the restaurant, Le Prieuré Normand.

Down the road the owners also have a small gîte which is sometimes used for chambres d'hôtes guests staying for a few days. This has the advantage of a kitchen with washing machine. The ☆ firmly stays.

FOURMETOT. 27500
4km NE of Pont Audemer by the D139.

There is such a tangle of *autoroutes* and *nationales*, such a hurrying to be in Paris or Honfleur or Rouen, that this corner of Normandy, only a 40-minute drive from Le Havre, often gets neglected. Pont Audemer is an attractive little town, once you penetrate behind the railway sidings and dusty concrete outskirts and discover its ancient heart. Here rivulets from the river Risle thread their way beneath old bridges and beamy old houses overhang the water. The best market in the district takes place here on Mondays and Fridays, when the rue de la République is closed to traffic – priorities correct!

Follow the D139 to Fourmetot, turn right at the church past the turning on the right to La Croisée, and l'Aufragère is on the left.

☆ **Régis & Nicole Dussartre.**
'L'Aufragère'
La Croisée.
category: (M)
tel: 02.32.56.91.92.
fax: 02.32.57.75.34.
B&B: and Evening meal 112€ for two.

An 18th-century half-timbered house, restored by the Dussartres, provides five guest rooms, each with a different theme, and private bathrooms. The big attraction here, apart from the friendly welcome from the hosts, is English-born Nicole's culinary skill. She is a professional Cordon Bleu cook, making good use of the wonderful range of local produce in the market to produce a superb evening meal, all drinks included. If you want to cook like her, sign up for one of the long weekend or five-day gourmet cookery courses she organises at l'Aufragère. Régis too is involved in matters gastronomic. He is a cheese specialist and will share his expertise in advising which of the tempting display on his market stalls should be purchased to take home. He also makes his own cider in large wooden casks in one of the barns on the premises, so you can sample that, along with the local Calvados, of which he always has a good stock. With a minimum stay of two nights now, prices have escalated.

SAINT-DENIS-le-FERMENT. 27140.
8 km NW of Gisors. 26 km NE of Les Andelys.
Well away from main roads, one long narrow road runs through the village bordered by immaculately kept old and new houses, not an un-painted shutter in sight – an estate agents' dream village. In the centre of the village the rue des Gruchets climbs a small hill and the chambres d'hôtes is signed on the right.

Madame Rousseau. 'Le Four au Pain'
8, rue des Gruchets.
category: (M)
tel: 02.32.55.14.45.
B&B: 48€ for two. No Dinner

Behind locked gates this adorable rustic cottage is sideways on to the road, parking inside the gates. The garden is terraced down the hillside.

Madame Rousseau, a retired business lady, has one guest room for three under her own roof, with double and single bed, complemented by rustic beams and warm carpets and a quality en-suite shower and loo. A most comfortable room. There is the possibility of putting a fourth bed for a child on the landing. Breakfast in her dining room/salon, furnished surrounded by antiques and knick-knacks collected over the years, guests are welcome to use this room. The second room for two is in a small stone house in the garden, where the original four-au-pain takes pride of place, lit up inside, enhanced by an attractive display of fresh flowers. Here is a double bed, and a small kitchenette with all facilities for self-catering. The en-suite ultra-modern shower has temperature settings. The floor is tile, but this room has the advantage of a private lawned terrace.

No evening meals. There is an upmarket restaurant within walking distance in the village, but two more basic ones to choose from in Bézu St. Eloi, a short drive away.

TRICQUEVILLE. 27500.
32 km SE of Le Havre.

From the Pont de Normandie outside Honfleur take the D580, which becomes the D180 to St. Maclou; then the N175 SP Pont Audemer then almost immediately right SP Tricqueville through lanes for about 5 km. Turn right before the church in Tricqueville.

This chambres d'hôtes peacefully nestles in a large garden amid country lanes covered with primroses in the Spring.

M. & Mme. Le Pleux. 'La Clé des Champs'. Bucaille
category: (M)
tel: 02.32.41.37.99.
B&B: 44.5€ for two.
Evening meal 22.5€ each.

An excellent first or last night stop near Le Havre, this is a lovely old colombage house. Since their retirement Le Pleuxes have restored this old pressoir to make a delightful home, matching new beams to the original ones, so you can't tell the difference.

Hold the rope up a small winding staircase to two of the prettiest cottage bedrooms I have seen for a long time. 'Rose' with appropriate flowery wallpaper and wrought iron double bed, has two windows overlooking the garden, all delightfully rustic but with modern shower room and separate toilet. The second room is yellow, double bed also but a much larger shower room where tiny dried flower bouquets hang from the beams. Evening meals only occasionally on reservation when you may eat alone. I am sure you will enjoy the quiet surrounding. *Accueil* unobtrusive.

A gravel drive past lawns and trees in front of the house leads to easy parking.

MANCHE

JUILLEY 50200
The little village is close to Mont St. Michel and within easy distance of both Cherbourg and St. Malo.

M. & Mme. Tizon. 'Les Blotteries'.
category: **(M)**
tel/fax: 02 33 60 84 95.
email: bb @les-blotteries.com
website: www.les-blotteries.com
B&B: 55€. for two.

Standing in four hectares the main house was built after the Revolution; but the surrounding outhouses across the large courtyard date back further, probably to the time when this was a priory. A large *four* in one indicates that it was once a *boulangerie* which supplied the surrounding hamlet. The track of the original old road to the premises can still be seen, used before the main road to Saint-James was built.

M. Tizon has taken time off from his work as a fire officer, to convert his outbuildings, and one room in the main house into chambres d'hôtes. Three very pleasant rooms have modern bathrooms with every amenity, hairdryers plentiful towels etc,. Garden rooms have tiled floors, a family room for five faces north, another with south aspect for three has a private terrace shower room facilities adjoining and a bed on the mezzanine. Choose the large guest room in the main house for cooler days. Monsieur Tizon is planning a guests' kitchen in the old *boulangerie*, which would make self-catering feasible.

Discoveries of interesting old stones have come to light in the reconstruction. Numerous cosy corners, in the garden, sheltered from the sea breezes by stone walls, are being developed for guests to laze in. No Evening meals, restaurants in St. James or the Auberge de la Sélune at Ducey, if you are looking for gastronomic menus.

MARIGNY. 50750. QUIBOU
9 km W of St. Lô.

Take the D972 from St. Lô to Coutances and 3 km after passing through St. Gilles at St Leger immediately opposite the fork right to Marigny turn left into the driveway to the chambres d'hôtes, well signed.

Mme. Lepoittevin
Saint Leger. Route de Coutances.
category: (S)
tel: 02.33.57.18.41.
B&B: 33.5€ for two.

Madame Lepoittevin is a member of the *'Maisons Fleures'* club and they don't come much more *fleuri* than this one. Monsieur, once the local butcher, has now retired and will be happy to show you round his *potager*, but flowers are strictly Madame's *domaine*. This is a very smartly-kept old farmhouse. There are two well furnished rooms with modern beds and family wardrobes polished to the hilt, both with bathrooms. A family room on the first floor, has a convertible for the children. A spacious room for two is on the ground floor. No evening meals; but there is a restaurant in Marigny, or 5 km away at Cametours.

A good breakfast includes croissants and home-made jam in their modernised kitchen or outside in summer. A spotless budget stopover.

LA MEURDRAQUIÈRE. 50510.
12 km W of Villedieu-les-Poêles. 112 km S of Cherbourg.

From Gavray take the D7 south, in about 7 km turn right on to the D35e and the farm is on the right.

La Pouperie
Mesnil-Draguibre

M. & Mme. Vastel. 'La Pouperie'
category: (S)
tel: 02.33.61.31.44.
fax: 02.33.91.96.32.
B&B: 36.5€ for two. No Dinner

White railings surround the front garden of this typical 'Manche' farmhouse. Only one double room for guests, but a very comfortable one. After a welcome glass of home-made cider you will feel you are personal friends, the Vastels are so genuinely kind. The guest room contains grandmother's matrimonial Breton bed, beautifully carved. A thick carpet with added rugs and full central heating – it is really very cosy. Adjoining is a separate loo and a luxurious bathroom, vanity unit with two washbasins, cupboards galore, bath and a separate, highly efficient, shower where at least six jets baptise you from all angles! Freshly squeezed orange juice, appears with your toast and home-made jams for breakfast and sometimes a local speciality like *Riz-au-lait*.

Evening meals are now on offer with cider and wine *compris*. So you have a difficult choice – to take advantage of Madame's offer, or visit the *Auberge* at Le Mesnil-Rogues, 2 km down the lane where the portly Patron Joseph Cotentin cooks delicious meals on a wood fire, when not appearing on French TV. Try his *gourmand* dessert, a miniature selection of every dessert he makes., but don't blame me if you put on weight. Restaurant prices from 16€.

MONTFARVILLE. 50760.
27 km. E of Cherbourg. 2 km S of Barfleur.

Barfleur is a neat little port full of bobbing boats. The light from one of the tallest lighthouses in France at the Raz de Barfleur sweeps the port at night. This chambres d'hôtes is easy to find, just off the coast road from Barfleur to St Vaast. Leave Barfleur on the D9 and take the second turning right after the town exit sign, it is the next turn left. If you turn earlier you will be in the mess we were, circling the village of Montfarville. Matilda (wife of William the Conqueror) commissioned his ship here for the invasion of 1066 and all that!

M. & Mme. Gabroy. 'Le Manoir'
category: (M)
tel: 02.33.23.14.21.
B&B: 51€ for two. No Dinner

The tall granite manor house looks out on fields of thriving vegetables and sea views of the English Channel. There are two rooms in the manoir, large, warm and comfortable, one up a spiral staircase, the other, easy for off-loading, on the ground floor. No evening meal, but there is an excellent restaurant in Barfleur – the *Moderne* (see FE Normandy) Breakfast is served in a dining room/sitting room for guests, all attractively set on a flowery tablecloth.

'This year we were especially delighted with Madame Gabroy at the Manor at Montfarville. A lovely lady with a house and garden to match. We had the tower room enjoying the sea from one window and a perfumed breeze from the other – a wonderful find.' M. Lloyd.

NÉGREVILLE 50260.
21 km S of Cherbourg

Not in Négreville at all. South of Cherbourg on the N 13 take the St. Joseph exit, then the D 146 towards Rocheville, fork right at the first sign to 'Le Mesnil Grand' restaurant, on to the D 148 then opposite the next sign to the restaurant La Vignonnerie is signed first left up a winding lane.

M. & Mme. Rose. 'La Vignonnerie'.
category: (S)
tel: 02 33 40 02 58.
B&B: 31/32€ for two.
Open all year.

Deep in the country; but with the advantage of being 800 metres from a well-known restaurant. Your hosts are a delightful elderly couple who own this charming ivy-covered, south-facing farmhouse. Monsieur keeps busy on the land with a few cows, goats and sheep, happy chickens roam freely in the meadow below the terrace. A peaceful bucolic scene.

There is a private entrance to two guest rooms on the first floor, one for three with shower and loo has two windows, with an arresting view, double and single bed, carpeted, centrally heated, it has all the requisites of a good hotel. The second room for two has a shower but the private loo is on the landing.

What makes this place such a gem for last night accommodation before the ferry is the easy access to the car for reloading etc., the safe parking well away from main roads, the large kitchen giving guests a choice of self-catering or splashing out on a last French meal at the 'Mesnil Grand', within walking distance for the energetic.

NICORPS. 50200.
4km SE of Coutances. 40 km from Mont-Saint-Michel. 80 km S of Cherbourg.

A hamlet just outside the cathedral town of Coutances, amid narrow lanes with high hedges.

From Coutances take the D7 towards Gavray (Villedieu-les-Poêles), turn left to Nicorps on the D27, then it is well signed. Don't confuse it with another chambres d'hôtes further up the road in the same hamlet.

☆ **M. & Mme. Posloux.** '**La Ferme des Hauts Champs**'
La Moinerie-de-Haut.
category: (S)
tel: 02.33.45.30.56.
B&B: 32€ for two.
Evening meals 16€ each,
(reservation only).

The stone-built 17th-century farmhouse is flanked by a large old stone well.

Madame Posloux, who speaks a fair amount of English, told me that while the restoration was going on old papers were found hidden in the beams, dating the house.

There are two rooms on the first floor, both comfortably furnished, with a sunny south outlook. One with red moquette walls has a shower room adjoining, the other has a private bathroom along the carpeted corridor. There is a further attic room for children with climbing ability up a steep staircase, when they share facilities with the parents below. From a reader: *'Twice in the last three months I have stayed at one of your recommendations, at Mme. Posloux it is all as described in your book.-.Plus. If you wish Madame Posloux will make you an evening meal, when you join other guests in the house. My recommendation is, do not miss them, they are superb. The breakfasts too, all home made. After finishing an evening meal a fellow traveller, a first time visitor to France stated that he normally stayed in five star hotels, but this was far better.'* J. C. Thomas.

As this was the second time in one week that I received acclamations for this chambres d'hôtes, I feel Madame has earned a ☆. In addition, there is now a small gîte attached which is beautifully furnished; extras like wine, tea and coffee await you and you can still have an evening meal with Madame Posloux.

ST. GERMAIN-DE-TOURNEBUT 50700
27 km SE of Cherbourg, 8 km NE of Valognes signed on the D902 to Quettehou.

M. & Mme. Gentien de la Hautière.
'Château de la Brisette'.
category: (L)
tel: 02.33.41.11.78. fax. 02.33.41.22.32.
B&B: 75.22 €
Closed 1 Nov. to 31 Mar., in winter by reservation

Approached by a long wooded drive the château with private chapel is most impressive. Poised over a lake on one side. It has been in the same family since it was built in 1769, except for a few years when the German high command commandeered it between 1939 and 1944. Family ancestors gaze down on one from all the walls. Expect the five rooms to have polished wood floors, *bateau* beds and antique furniture, Empire or Louis XVI style rather than modern decor, though all have private bathrooms, TV and fridges, dragging them into the present century. Though furnished throughout with antiques, it is very much a family home and the young owners will welcome you warmly. Monsieur collects vintage cars and the stables now accommodate these, rather than horses.

SAINTE-GENEVIÈVE. 50760
3 km S of Barfleur. 24 km W of Cherbourg.

Close to the lovely north coast and quiet port of Barfleur.

From the D901 from Cherbourg 3 km before Barfleur turn right to Sainte Geneviève, then first left just before the village at signs to the Manoir which is in 300 metres.

☆ **M. & Mme. Caillet. 'Manoir de la Fevrière'**
category: (M)
tel: 02.33.54.33.53.
B&B: 61€ for two. No Dinner

The 17th-century manor house has been in the family since the 19th century and the large farm is now let for cultivation. The unusual rectangular tower at the rear gives easy access to the first floor rooms by a granite staircase whose walls and even roof are of the same stone – not at all like the spiral steps usually found in a Norman tower.

Charming hosts can offer you a choice of three rooms, two with showers and a larger with a bath. All are cosily carpeted right into the bathrooms. Double or twin beds. The larger pink and green room has a fireplace, grandma's wedding *armoire* and a fine bureau. The loo is in the entrance vestibule as it is in the pretty 'Poppy' room. A smaller room at the back is just as pleasant and comfortable, with steps down to the shower room. A small salon has a giant Normandy fireplace which Madame lights for breakfast every day for her guests, especially appreciated on a windy July day. Breakfast is a real treat, served on pretty Limoges or Villeroy et Boch china with enough French inscribed on it to give you your French lesson for the day, but should you stay in autumn you will have different china, appropriate to the season. I recommend you visit four times a year to get the full benefit. A wonderful ensemble of rusticity and comfort. The farm buildings surrounding give ample shelter for parking. No evening meals, but it's an easy drive into Barfleur where there is a choice of three restaurants for that first or last meal in France. Definitely a chambres d'hôtes I would make a detour to stay in and so sure am I that you will like it, I am giving it a ☆.

ORNE

CETON. 61260.
8 km NE of La Ferté-Bernard. 56 km SE of Alençon.
Just in Orne, a small town with a lake.

Approaching from the north, drive straight through the town on the D107. At the 'end of town' sign fork right, following the chambres d'hôtes sign. A long lane bearing right past a couple of houses will end in an attractive garden encircled by well-kept stone houses.

M. & Mme. Pinoche. 'L'Aitre'
category: (M)
tel: 02.37.29.78.02.
B&B: 44.5/51€ for two.
Evening meals 16€ each.

Not a lot of chambres d'hôtes cater purely for vegetarians, but kindly hosts in this one do. Even the wine is produced from organically grown grapes.

In a separate building is a large high-beamed salon/dining-room, with natural stone walls. Meals are normally served here but on occasions taken with the family. Central heating does its best in winter and Monsieur complements it with a log fire on chilly nights. Above is a family suite, and a room for two, both with private facilities, firm beds and many thoughtful extras. A further two rooms for a family, in the main house, share a bathroom. Extra bed, 8€.

Behind the house are lawns, a view of the lake and a parking area.

The evening meals are both interesting and nourishing with organic wine included. Prices reflect specialised amenities.

MORTAGNE au PERCHE 61400
38 km NE of Alençon. A delightful town in the Orne department, noted for its black sausage. From Mortagne take the D938 to Le Pin and then the D256 SP St. Jouin and look left for signs.

M. & Mme. le Motheux du Plesis.
'La Miottière'.
Le Pin la Garenne.
category: (L)
tel: 02 33 83 84 01
B&B: 69€ for two.
Evening meals 20€ each..

The lovely old 15th century manor house stands in one corner of an enormous courtyard, surrounded by fields. Outbuildings and stables have been converted into three individual units with bed/sitting rooms for two to four persons, bathrooms are well modernised. *Terre cuite* floors in all. In two there is a useful mini kitchenette so guests may picnic in the grounds by the lake. In some rooms the double bed is on the mezzanine with bathroom below. Ask for your preference.

Stroll over to the main house for breakfast in Madame's dining room, furnished with antiques in keeping with the age of the manor. Evening meals are also served here with wine, aperitif and coffee included, taking advantage opf this would give you a chance to get to know your hosts, who speak English. Alternatively there is a restaurant 'La Croix d'Or, at the bottom of the hill on the D256 in Le Pin.

SURVIE. 61310. EXMES.
120 km from Le Havre, 176 km from Cherbourg, 56 km from Caen.

In the Pays d'Auge just below the Falaise gap where the last battle in Normandy was fought. The small hamlet of Survie is on the D26 between Vimontiers and Exmes.

Mr. & Mrs. Wordsworth. 'Les Gains'
category: (M)
tel/fax: 02.33.36.05.56.
B&B: 52.5€ for two (one night), 48€ for two (longer stay).
Evening meals 20.8€ each.
Closed 1 Dec. to 28 Feb.

Having arrived here from the UK nearly a decade ago, complete with sheep and household goods, the Wordsworths have converted an old *fromagerie*, where Camembert was once made, into rustic guest rooms furnished with a mixture of modern beds and family heirlooms. There are three rooms for two or three. Two rooms overlooking the garden and pigeonnier, extra bed 11€, children especially welcome.

There is a salon/dining room for guests where breakfast and evening meals are served in winter, from which a door leads to the garden and terrace for summer meals beside the stream, inhabited by tame ducks. Alas, the fox had been around while I was there.

A friendly welcome from Diana, a true farmer's wife, busy with the lambing when we called but not too busy to cope with guests.

Not often are the English brave enough to take over a large farm as well as a chambres d'hôtes, but Kit Wordsworth, a descendant of William, was an established farmer before he came to France. Diana is a keen gardener and you will find many rare plants in her borders. If you are a lone guest you may well be invited to eat in the family kitchen, the real hub of the house. Interesting evening meals include *apéritif* and wine.

The Wordsworths also offer tours of Normandy, including sights such as: The Bayeux Tapestry, Normandy Landing Beaches, Monet's Garden. (One or five day tours.)

SEINE-MARITIME

ERMENOUVILLE. 76740.

7 km S of St.Valery-en-Caux. 70 km N of Le Havre. 30 km NE of Fécamp.

From the A13 direction 'Rouen' take exit 25 (Pont-de-Brotonne/Yvetot). At Yvetot take the D20 towards Saint-Valery-en-Caux. At Sainte Colombe 2 km after the village take direction Houdetot and the Château is about 2 km on the left.

Dr. & Mme. Kayali. 'Château du Mesnil Geoffroy'
category: (M)
tel: 02.35.57.12.77.
fax: 02.35.57.10.24. All year with reservation only.
B&B: 64/112€ for two
Evening meal 40€ each.

The ancient trees touch overhead in the drive up to this red-brick château, which has changed little since it was built in 1748 (look for the date scratched on to a pane of glass in the entrance salon). It is now a historical monument furnished entirely in 18th-century style. You will have a great welcome from charming hosts. The entrance salon with black and white chequered tiles spans the mansion and has a reproduction of a penny-farthing bicycle. People arrive for *réunions* with their own penny-farthings. There are marble fireplaces in all the rooms, where authentic Louis XV furniture is freshly upholstered to match the delicately-painted panelled walls. There are two other salons, one with TV for guests, and a pleasant dining room where brunch-type breakfasts are served. You may be invited to join your hosts for dinner, which is cooked by Mme. Kayali, using 18th-century recipes and her own foie gras.

The park and original garden, designed by Le Nôtre, has an aviary and a maze. Extensive well manicured lawns are dotted with cone-shaped bushes of *Buis* ('box', the shrub used on Palm Sunday in France, instead of palms). Red-brick walls were built round the main garden as protection from the salt winds. A statue of Neptune and one of Venus stand alone on the lawn.

Six surprisingly compact guest rooms of various shapes and sizes are named after previous owners. All have their original bathrooms, and oak floors. Although one still has the copper *chauffe-bain* in situ, modern plumbing has taken over and extra luxuries like hair dryers, towelling gowns and tea-making facilities now blend in with the original design.

One ground floor room has the bed slept in by Prince Montmorency, brother of Louis XVI, who was the original owner. Family portraits blend with scattered antiques like a *Directoire Poêle;* but nothing is overdone.

Five rooms up the oak staircase are all different. The *Marquis de Cany's* room (the most expensive at 104€) has a baldaquin and a bathroom hidden behind panelling down a few steps.

Most rooms face the rear garden but a very small room in a front tower (the *Ecuyer de Mainneville's* room), delightfully light with two windows and white ciel de lit, would be my choice. *Conseiller Belgard* has a double bed. *Chevalier d'Accainvillier* is yellow and blue.

Your hosts were born to château life, their original homes were either sold or destroyed by war, so they decided to buy Le Mesnil du Geoffroy ten years ago, furnish it in 18th-century style and offer guests a taste of château life. As it is an historic monument, it is open to the public on most days, but still remains a private home.

Rooms priced according to size. Breakfast 8€ extra. Evening meal *apéritif,* wine and champagne *compris.*

EU. 76260.
30 km NE of Dieppe. 19 km SW of St. Valery.
A small town in the valley of the river Bresle, 5 km inland from Le Tréport, rarely visited by tourists yet steeped in history. William the Conqueror

married Matilda in the château in 1050. The building was destroyed in 1475 on the orders of Louis XI, but re-building started in 1578. It became the holiday residence of King Louis-Philippe and Queen Victoria twice came to visit him to cement the 'Entente Cordiale'. The town has strong Irish connections, as Lawrence O'Toole, Archbishop of Dublin, crossed the channel in 1179 to challenge Henry II (of England) about the taxes imposed on Ireland. Henry refused to see him. When St. Lawrence (as he subsequently became) heard that Henry had moved towards the Belgian border he followed him and took up residence in the Collegiate Church at Eu, but Henry still refused to meet him. The aged Archbishop fell sick and died, and was buried in the church at Eu. His tomb became a place of pilgrimage.

The river forms the border between Normandy and Picardy, but the French, with their usual logic have theoretically moved the border so that the whole town lies in Seine-Maritime. In villages along the river there are factories producing the fancy scent bottles used by all the well-known perfumeries.

Mme. Demarquet. 'Manoir de Beaumont'
category: (M)
tel: 02.35.50.91.91.
B&B: 46.5€ for two. No Dinner

Situated high on the hill, which was once a Roman settlement, above the old town, this chambres d'hôtes is comprised of two different houses. The estate has been in the family for years. Madame was born here and is a mine of information about the surrounding area.

The rather austere red-brick building was an ancient *relais-de-chasse* and the long salon downstairs has a huge fireplace. Above are two guest rooms with private facilities; one for two, the *Entente-Cordiale* room comfortably furnished with a Louis XV bed; the other, a suite of two rooms for a family, has a small kitchen.

The Demarquets live in the lovely colombaged mansion next door and here have one luxurious guest room for four, most effectively furnished in red *toile de Jouy*, with adjoining bathroom and views over the garden. A charming room, with extra beds 8€. Breakfast is served in the family dining room, and there are comfortable chairs in the salon for guests.

LES LANDES. AUMALE. 76390.

46km SW of Amiens. 12 km W of Aumale. 12 Km E of Neufchâtel-en-Bray.
Turn north at L'Aventure on the N29 to the D16 and follow signs via La Caule, then take the D7 and the château is on the right.

M. & Mme. Simon-Lemettre.
'Château des Landes'
category: (M)
tel: 02.35.94.03.79.
B&B: 48/56€ for two. No Dinner

This lovely little château stands well back across a lawn from the entrance gates. It has passed through many hands, including English. Now your Parisian hosts have made their mark on it, redecorating throughout in pastel shades, creating a light and sunny aspect. In the dining room, woodwork is picked out in delicate green and white, two adjoining salons across the hall are pink and blue, one reserved for television.

Three rooms on the first floor are delightfully furnished, all in different matching colours, oak floors with large rugs, tall château windows, well draped, and armchairs beside the fireplaces. All have shower rooms. Bedside lamps lull you to sleep with dimmer switches. Furnished with comfort in mind.

Two rooms on the second floor are still light and airy though windows are shorter. Carpets in these, one for two, the other with three single beds.

A rear conservatory for breakfast is shaded in summer by a large fruiting vine. Recommended by a reader who thoroughly enjoyed his stay here.

Paris (Île-de-France)

PARIS (ILE de FRANCE)

Paris (Île-de-France)

Understandably dominated by its illustrious capital city, Paris, the Île-de-France tends to be a nonentity in most tourists' consciousness. Chambres-d'hôtes suggestions here are primarily intended as bases for visiting the city or Euro-Disney, letting the train take the strain.

This is not the place to extol the many virtues of Paris or list the attractions. Suffice to say that everyone should see for themselves where the magic lies, then return again and again.

Seine-et-Marne, the largest *département* of the region. lies on the eastern border of Paris, extending from just north of Charles-de-Gaulle airport to south of Fontainebleau, watered by the rivers Marne in the north and Seine in the south. The Seine turns north at Fontainebleau and heads for the centre of Paris. The closer to Paris one gets the more thickly populated it becomes, with ugly flats springing up, but most of the area is flat countryside, interspersed with small towns, villages and farm land. It is here on the fringe of Paris that you will find **Parc-Euro-Disneyland**, easily reached by skirting Paris by the north or south motorways.

Essonne is in the south-west of Paris, on the borders of the lovely forest of Fontainebleau, a much smaller *département* and more rural, with many farms among the small villages. Forests round Paris are of the huntin' shootin' fishin' variety, not just green-belt woods.

Yvelines. The *département* north-west of Paris, extends north to include part of the river Seine as it flows westwards and sea-wards from Paris. The beautiful palace of Versailles, built by Louis XIV, is the main attraction in this area. The forest of Rambouillet covers a vast area.

Val-d'Oise is a small narrow *département* in the valley of the river Oise, north of Paris, bordering lower Picardy.

SEINE-ET-MARNE

CHÂTILLON LA BORDE. 77820.

12 km E of Melun. 16 km NE of Fontainebleau.

From the Autoroute A5 take Sortie 'Châtillon-la-Borde', then follow signs to 'La Borde'

M. et Mme. Guerif. 'Labordière'.
16, Grande Rue, La Borde.
category: (M)
tel: 01.60.66.60.54.
B&B: 43€ for two
Evening meals 20.8€ each

A quiet little hamlet just a few km from the Seine and Fontainebleau. (Fontainebleau Château is open 9.30a.m. to 12.30p.m. and 2.30 to 5p.m.). Parking at Bois-le-Roi station is free and the train to Paris takes one hour. Come back to an evening meal prepared by Monsieur, who has retired from his *charcuterie* in Paris and enjoys cooking. He is now the Mayor of La Borde. No 16 is next to the *mairie*, where you park.

Restored by the owner, the village house has west-facing sunny bedrooms, one with a shower room as big as the bedroom, featuring a central dual vanitory unit. No ablutionary fights in the morning here. Two other rooms, united by a sitting area, would suit a family of four, sharing a shower room.

A sitting room downstairs opens on to a shady enclosed back garden. Evening meal with *aperitif* and red Burgundy wine *compris*, reserve ahead, well worth it

POMMEUSE 77515

20 km east of Disney land, by the N34. The mill is a restful place to return to after hectic hours in the theme park.

M. & Mme. Thomas. 'Le Moulin de Pommeuse'.
35 Ave. du Général Huerne.
category: (M)
tel: 01.64.75.29.45.
B&B: 47€ for two.
email: infos@moulin-de-pommeuse.com
www: le-moulin-depommeuse.com

The Thomases have moved from their original chambres d'hôtes the other side of the village and have spent two years enthusiastically converting a very old mill beside the river, into a large guest house, cleverly incorporating all the mill workings in the rustic decor. The mill is reputed to contain treasure hidden by Porthos, one of the Three Musketeers.

Pretty blue painted windows with colourful flower boxes are interspersed with the ivy hiding the slightly crumbling walls. Four guest rooms for two, and two family rooms, have names connected with the workings of the mill. Original *terre cuite* floors, painted iron bedsteads, country pretty bed linen, *crapaud* armchairs, and simple shower rooms in all. Ours was decorated with dressed dolls astride trapezes, all the handiwork of Mme. Thomas, everything so prettily arranged one can forgive the small towels and single bedside lamp.

Trees shade the extensive lawns on the river bank and small disused boats are bursting with summer blooms. Various receptions are held in the mill's spacious public rooms, so perhaps it would be wise to check on booking, if you want a quiet night.

Breakfast will set you up for the day. Evening meal in winter only, 18.28€.

Definitely a summer favourite for people returning from a day out in Paris or Disney land, when they can relax in the garden and try the local restaurants. The food at the 'Auberge de Moutier' in Faremoutiers is well worth the short drive.

VAUDROY-en-BRIE 77141.
21 km NW of Provins, on the N4.

Mme. Vandierendonk.
7, rue de Coulommiers.
category: (M)
tel: 01.64.07.51.38.
fax: 01.64.07.52.79.
B&B: 43€ for two.

The large cereal farm is at the entrance to this small village, from which buses leave for Paris. There are three rooms, furnished with family heirlooms. One for three has a balcony, another has a carved suite once belonging to a Russian ambassador. All have shower rooms. Extra beds 16€.

No evening meals and the café in the village didn't look too promising, however guests are welcome to picnic in the garden.

There is a large salon/dining room guests may use. This could be a hassle-free place to stay for a day in the city, leaving the car safely with your Belgiam hosts and catching the bus. Check buses with your hosts when you book.

ESSONNE

MILLY-la-FORÊT. 91490.

19 km W of Fontainebleau.

This small town proves to be more interesting than appears when first visiting it. Roman remains have been found, and the covered market in the centre dates back to the 15th century. The town has been noted for the production of medicinal herbs, grown in the surrounding forests, since the 12th century.

From Milly-la-Forêt take the D837 and turn off on the D1, Route de Gironville. The farm is on your right in 3 km.

M. & Mme. Desforges. 'Ferme de la Grange Rouge'
category: (M)
tel: 01.64.98.94.21.
fax: 01.64.98.99.91.
B&B: 40€ for two. No Dinner
Closed mid-December to end-January.

This lone cereal farm beside the main road is easy to find. It has a large courtyard surrounded by buildings. The neatly furnished guest rooms are on the first floor of a separate building. There is a dining salon and five bedrooms with smart new shower rooms. Beds vary from family carved bed-heads to wrought iron or modern divans, with a choice of singles and doubles, extra bed 9.5€. A nice straightforward sort of place but no great family contact. It is a busy farm and Mme. Desforges has young children, but a reasonable price for this area south of Paris.

No evening meals – restaurants in Milly-la-Forêt.

Picardy

PICARDY

Town

Chambres d'Hôtes

0   20km

Picardy

The battlefield of Europe bears many scars and memorials as lasting witness to its tribulations. Its rich and inoffensive farmland is where yeoman archers lined up, where horses were caparisoned for battle, where trenches were cut, where marching boots churned up the mud, where tanks rumbled, where treaties were signed, and where the victims of conflict fell, body upon body. It's such a short drive and such a long time between Crécy and the Somme. But Picardy is not all sadness and monotonous plains.

There is no other region that can rival the Gothic churches and châteaux of the region. In villages, cities, cross-roads throughout the *départements* you can trace the development of Gothic art, from the very first pointed arch at Morienval to the final expression of the Flamboyant. The cathedrals of Senlis, Amiens, Beauvais, the abbeys of St. Germer-de-Fly and St. Riquier are individual history lessons of the conception of religious architecture of the times. Some, like Amiens, are constructed with such industry that a young craftsman might live to see its completion; some, like St. Riquier, whose building was interrupted by war, and St. Germer, delayed by additions and reconstructions, explain, as no schoolteacher could, how fashions have changed in the intervals.

The little known area of **Aisne** receives few tourists, apart from those visiting the miracles of Laon and Soissons cathedrals. St. Quentin is a typical big provincial city, with attractive central square, and unusual art gallery. Vervins is completely different – ancient, fortified, self-contained, and hinting at the Ardennes next door.

In the south, less than 50km from Paris in the *département* of **Oise**, lies the incomparable Chantilly, whose château and stables, together with the neighbouring Senlis, alone would merit an excursion to this region.

For those who have already explored the Pas-de-Calais and are looking for a worthwhile extension to their experience of the accesssible North of France, I would suggest a drive down to the **Somme**. The capital, Amiens, well repays a visit. Look beyond its wartime devastation to the remarkable restoration in the St. Leu area, take a cruise on the waterways and allow plenty of time for the stunning cathedral. The battlefields of course are an abiding interest and sobering jolt. The lively port of St. Valery, with good market, superb walks and lots of fishing activity, would make a cheerful contrast.

AISNE

RESSONS-le-LONG. 02290
14 km W of Soissons 7 km E of Vic-sur-Aisne.

Take the N31 between Compiègne and Soissons and turn right to the village 3 km after Vic-sur-Aisne and continue right up the hill, left up the winding rue de la Villers then left again round a bend on to the rue de la Montagne, signed ahead through large gates.

M. & Mme. Ferté. 'Ferme de la Montagne'
category: (M)
tel: 03.23.74.23.71.
fax: 03.23.74.24.82.
B&B: 48€ for two. No Dinner

A rather incongruous address for this enormous conglomeration of buildings, high on a hill above the village. Originally this was an abbey, built by Charlemagne's daughter, a dependency of Soissons until the Revolution when it was closed. The land was let to tenant farmers until 1980 when grandparents of the present family bought it. Twice divided between sons the vast abbey buildings and some of the fields fell to the lot of the eldest son, the present owner. What an enormous undertaking the reconstruction of the main house has been, and is still going on. The views of the valley of the Aisne are riveting from all the rooms (unless you suffer from vertigo!).

There is one room for a family on the *rez-de-chaussée* and one on each floor above for three and for two with single beds. Very modern shower rooms adjoin each.

Our room had three windows on one side and another facing the hillside garden. Oak floors and cupboards and soft peach stone walls complemented the tapestry bed-heads and matching the curtains. Every comfort, including mineral water, the central heating and duvets, made this a pleasant cold weather stop. No evening meals; but Madame was waiting for us with a log fire when we returned from the small café/pub in the village, where a robust but interesting 'no choice' menu is on offer each night – 11€ including wine. Three new rooms are nearly ready, equally comfortable, and a new kitchen will be available for guests not wanting to drive out at night. A pathway down to the village is available, but it is a perpendicular climb back up – only for the fit.

M. & Mme. Ferté are charming, and a good breakfast of home-made jams, toast and croissants awaits you each morning with piping hot coffee.

There is a French billiard table in the dining room and other games for the tireless.

The main abbey and other buildings in various states of repair flank the huge courtyard when you drive in. No parking problems here.

VILLERS-AGRON. 02130

18 km SE of Fère-en-Tardenois on the D2. Just north of the A4 autoroute and only 23km SW of Reims but light years away in character.

This is deep, deep farming country.

If driving south from here spare a minute to visit the little village of Chatillon-sur-Marne 8 km away where a gigantic statue of Pope Urban II (1088-1099) stands on a hill, built in the style of the Statue of Liberty, it overlooks the surrounding vineyards for miles around.

☆ **M. et Mme. Ferry. 'Ferme du Château'**
category: (M)
tel: 03.23.71.60.67.
fax: 03.23.69.36.54.
B&B: 57.5/70€ for two.
Evening meal 30.5€. each.

If Xavier Ferry were not still an active *agriculteur* and his wife Christine an even more active mother of three children, one would be tempted to call this an hotel, so well equipped are the rooms, so well organised the comfort of the guests. But the sandpit on the terrace (among lots of expensive chairs and recliners), the child's desk, the homework on the piano, the board games on the table, all make it a home not a hotel and this is what chambres d'hôtes are all about.

That said, this is a quite exceptional representative of the genre. The old farmhouse starts off with two enormous advantages – a lovely stone building, a slope down to the river, a delightful setting – and Christine and Xavier have skilfully capitalised. Their four spacious rooms have delightful rural aspects and are furnished with style; all have colourful chintzes, and luxury bathrooms with fittings probably more refined than yours or mine back home. The salon is huge – raftered, log fire, piano – the dining room extremely elegant.

Evening meals are well worth reserving, Christine's cooking is way above average for a farmer's wife. If you haven't booked in time for an evening meal, there is an excellent choice of restaurants in nearby villages. The *Auberge du Postillon* at Ville-en-Tardenois does a very good *Menu du Marché*. There is only one snag – after a visit *chez* Ferry you will be spoilt for any other B&Bs. A ☆ for excellence.

OISE

SAINT JEAN aux BOIS 60350
9 km S of Compiègne.

Quite close to the ridiculously pretty château at Pierrefonds, right in the middle of the Forêt-de-Compiègne, this little village has the quiet opulence of commuter villages near Paris, where beautifully restored old houses hide behind high walls.

Mme. Langevin
2, rue du Parquet.
category: (M)
tel: 03.44.42.84.48.
B&B: 56€ for two

On a corner of the road at the entrance to the village, this rambling old house has a lovely walled garden, terraced down to a circular swimming pool. There is parking for two cars behind locked gates.

The guest rooms are well modernised in a restored barn across the garden. Two for a couple on the ground floor have independent entry with smart new shower rooms, simply furnished. Up an independent flight of stairs are two rooms for a family, one with double bed has a wash basin, the loo is shared on the landing; the other with three singles has shower and wash basin. Usually let together for a family – 80€; but they can be let independently.

Breakfast is in a room in the main house where the fireplace has a barbecue for guests who may also use the kitchen area.

No evening meals but a choice of two restaurants within easy walking distance, or the option of self catering.

Madame is away working in Paris some of the time; but there is always someone there to meet and greet and serve breakfast. A quiet hidey-hole in a delightful village with the advantage of a swimming pool in summer.

SOMME

CREUSE. 80480.

13 km SW of Amiens.

The village of Creuse is well placed for visiting Amiens, the ancient and historic capital of Picardy, home of the largest, most magnificent Gothic cathedral in France. Set in a unique water landscape, it must be on every Northern France itinerary. It does have its traffic problems and a maze of one way streets, so obey the Fenn No 1 city rule which is to head for the spire of the cathedral and dump the car as soon as possible. From here everything of interest is within walking distance. The newly restored area of St. Leu is now a delightful enclave of bars, restaurants and old houses, just behind the canal and always within sight of the glorious spire. Another good reason for a visit is to take a trip around the watery wonderland of the *hortillonages*, an hour's meander in a high-prowed punt that will give you a duck's eye view of the squares of gardens criss-crossed with mini-canals, all irrigated by the rivers Somme and Avre. (Not available November to March). Allow plenty of time to visit the magical cathedral, if possible early or late when the tourist crowds have gone. Market days are Wednesday and Saturday. Good shopping and restaurants are a cheer-up for a wet day.

Leave Amiens by the N29 then left on to D162. Signposted from Creuse.

☆ **Mme. Lemaître.**
26, rue Principale
category: (M)
tel/Fax.03.22.38.91.50.
B&B: 41.5/60.5€ for two. No Dinner
Closed 1 Nov. to 31 Mar.

As you turn in from the road under the archway you are likely to be greeted by a selection of residents. Two geese were being very protective about their territory, decorative bantams were pecking about and a shaggy dog lay soaking up the sun. More decorative fowl strutted on the lawns of the delightful garden, but although the 200-year-old building, whitewashed, dark beamed and brown shuttered, was indeed once a working *fermette* it has now been converted into an elegant and highly attractive home, with the stable block serving as chambres d'hôtes accommodation.

Doors lie open, white wrought-iron chairs dot the lawn and there is a charming feeling of outdoor living under the shady trees, on the well-kept grass. Chic, blonde Mme. Lemaître has decorated the four rooms with style, but always kept the rustic character. She loves white so a light and airy atmosphere predominates, helped by long French windows and in one room by a white canopy over the bed. All have private facilities, bath or shower, and one has a kitchenette.

I was not surprised to learn that Mme. Lemaître is a painter – her clever sense of decoration is evident again in her own house, where breakfast is served in winter by a huge log fire. A lovely place to stay, highly recommended.

FRANSU. 80620.
58 km SW of Arras. 25 km E of Abbeville.

Within easy reach of St. Riquier.

Turn off the D925 at Cramont on to the D130, then right on to the D46 then left again on to the D130 (SP Fransu). In the village, right when you reach the church and left opposite the road to Gorenflos.

Wind down a bumpy track to the gates of this pretty little château, delightfully situated in 20 hectares of farmland producing cereal and seed potatoes.

M. & Mme. de Franssu. 'Château de Houdencourt'
category: (M)
tel: 03.22.54.00.00.
fax: 03.22.54.77.79.
B&B: 56€ for two.

A complete ruin five years ago, the château is now totally restored. Step down from the wide, rose covered terrace to well-kept lawns sloping down to the meandering lake with a back-drop of trees – all quite lovely.

Inside is spacious and uncluttered, new wood stairs lead to a rear corridor off which three guest rooms on the first floor are simplicity itself, but the riveting view of the lake makes them extra special. All are white-walled with matching furniture. Just the carpets and covers and towels dictate the colour of the rooms. Bathrooms adjoin all three; 'Blue' is large, with an extra bed, and 'Green' is cosy for two, but 'Yellow' necessitates a visit downstairs for the loo.

Iron gates are locked at night. In the grounds are an attractive *gîte*, a converted stable hall for receptions and an old *colomberie* inhabited by white doves who pay you a morning call.

Breakfast is elegantly served in the dining room with delicious home-made jams.

No evening meals but there are restaurants in villages nearby at prices to suit everyone. At Gorenflos the cooking at the restaurant *Aux Deux Cygnes* is way above normal for such a small place.

The young de Franssus both work in the village where the farm headquarters are based but are always available to greet you if you reserve, and are very kind and helpful, suggesting places of interest to visit or restaurants for evening meals.

ST. RIQUIER. 80135
9 km E of Abbeville by D925.

Just a square full of plane trees, dominated by the abbey, impressive and strikingly beautiful – the centre of what is now a small town, but eleven centuries ago, was one of the most formidable strongholds in Picardy. Razed, rebuilt, razed, rebuilt, it never regained its former importance. Today's abbey is mostly 17th century, with only traces of its 13th-century origins. The local white stone has been delicately wrought into icicles of flowers and leaves and animals. Inside, don't miss the statues and glorious staircase. The *Centre Culturel* , in the monk's refectory and upstairs in their cells, is one of the best of regional museums.

Mme. Decayeux.
7, rue du Beffroi.
category: (M)
tel: 03.22.28.93.08.
fax: 03.22.28.93.10
B&B: 40/56€ for two.
Evening meal 17.5€.

Once a *Relais de Poste*, now a cereal/dairy farm of 40 hectares, deceptively hidden behind the house. Couldn't be more central – near the belfry, opposite the abbey – a nice old 18th-century house, now offering five bedrooms, colour coded, with bathroom apiece, *Jonquille* has a double bed, *Marguerite* is smaller again with a double bed, *Rose* has twins, *Lavande* is a single and *La Primevère* has one double and two singles, 12.5€ for extra beds.

Evening meal cooked by Madame (drinks not *compris*) is good value, and so is the excellent breakfast included in the price.

There is a pleasant *salle de séjour* with big, open fire, and TV everywhere – in the salon and in each bedroom. You can park the car in the locked, central courtyard at night, so there is no need to off-load everything.

Poitou-Charentes

POITOU-CHARENTES

Poitou-Charentes

South of the Loire, north of Bordeaux, this western region of France stretches from the Atlantic to the Limousin. Poitou-Charentes is divided into four *départements*, in the north Deux-Sèvres and Vienne lie side-by-side, as do Charente and Charente Maritime further south, the latter on the Atlantic coast.

Deux-Sèvres is so called because there are two river Sèvres flowing through the department – the Sèvre Nantaise heading for the Loire at Nantes on its way to the Atlantic at St. Nazaire in the north, and the Sèvre Niortaise in the south, which has given birth to the delightful little canals of the Marais Poitevin west of Niort. This area is usually attributed to the Vendée, but some of the prettiest parts actually lie in Deux-Sèvres. Niort, the *préfecture*, has a large central parking area in the Place-de-la-Brèche, when not taken up by the Saturday market.

Vienne again takes its name from the river, one of the prettiest in France. The large town of Poitiers is the *préfecture*, once the home of the English king Henry II and his wife, Eleanor of Aquitaine. Steeped in history and historic buildings, the town is well worth visiting. A few kilometres north at Jaunay Clan (exit 18 off the A10) is *Futuroscope*, a large theme park – a must for all visitors passing this way. It comprises a wonderful exhibition of cinemas and commerce of the future with ample entertainment for children. (See Avanton-Martigny p.360)

Travel down to **Charente**, named after another river, a lovely, tranquil, country area where the old town of Angoulême rules the *département*, – but the really famous name here is Cognac, where all the grapes grown in the warm countryside are turned into brandy. Such names as Hine, Courvoisier and Rémy Martin flash by as you drive along (see Lignières-Sonneville p348). Make sure you taste the *apéritif* of the region, *Pineau*, made from grape juice and brandy.

La Rochelle is the busy port of the **Charente-Maritime** where the river Charente finally finds its way to the sea. A very attractive town with the fortress and the harbour always coming into view as you wander through the main streets. This is a strong Protestant region and many Huguenot churches are still here. A colourful indoor market daily sells the fruit and vegetables from the countryside as well as the *produits de la mer*.

From here, you take the toll bridge to the attractive island of Île de Ré where the tiny ports are bursting with small craft in season and the tall lighthouse towers over the island.

Further south visit the old Roman town of Saintes where the large Arc de Triomphe still stands by the riverside and remains of old Roman baths are just outside the town.

CHARENTE

CONFOLENS 16500
57 km NW of Limoges

I still haven't discovered why this lovely little town is so attractive and conclude it is just its situation. The *sous-préfecture* of Charente, it straddles the confluence of the rivers Goire and the Vienne. Since the middle ages it has been at the centre of life in the area and still is, even more so each August when stands for the International music and dance festival take up most of the market place. Tangling with one way systems and full parking lots I have failed on two past occasions to stop. On a third attempt I booked into a chambres d'hôtes hoping to find it *centre ville*, with private parking.

From the one way system in *centre ville* take the left turn into rue Fontaine de Pommeau, pass in front of the *Eglise Saint-Maxime* into the rue du Vieux Château, then bear left in the Place du Dr. Defaut into the rue du Pont l'Ecuyer. The chambres d'hôtes is higher up on the left.

9, rue du Pont de l'Ecuyer
Confolens

M. & Mme. Valeyre et Loriette
9, rue du Pont l'Ecuyer
category: (M)
tel: 05 45 85 32 06
B&B: 46 €
Open in school holidays only.

Quite a surprise when this chambres d'hôtes hiding under a street number, turned out to be one of the prettiest 19th century Châteaux I have seen, not really *centre ville*, precipitously perched on the hillside above the town. Perhaps not for anyone averse to steps, a few up to the front door, more down to a delightful swimming pool tucked into a narrow terrace and even more to the shady car park below. Easy for the fit to walk into the town, uphill on the return. The best rooms with a superb view are for longer stays, but all are very comfortable with a mixture of antique and modern furniture and have good showers rooms. The salon has a floor to ceiling bay window affording an ariel view of the valley below. Your hosts are both teachers so opening times are restricted to school holidays. Breakfast is very good and helpful advice is given about local restaurants, some in Confolens, or in the next village, St Germaine de Confolens, the Auberge de la Tour is good value overlooking the R. Vienne.

LIGNIÈRES-SONNEVILLE 16130.
21 km S of Cognac

From Cognac take the D24 to Ségonzac, then the D1 to the cross-roads with the D699. Turn left here and the house is on your left.

M. Matignon has vast vineyards all around growing Ugny Blanc grapes and sells his produce to Rémy Martin, just up the road. First the grapes are pressed on the premises then left to ferment for one month before being collected by the Rémy Martin tanker as Grande Champagne wine for distillation. Most distilleries charge for visits but Mme. Matignon will give you free vouchers for a visit to Rémy Martin.

M. & Mme. Matignon. 'Les Collinauds'
category: (S)
tel: 05.45.80.51.23.
B&B: 40€ for two, and 48€ for four.
Evening meal 12.5€ each.

This huge three-storey house in the heart of the Grande Champagne region of Cognac is in a very large walled garden. Fast becoming restored to its former glory, overlooking an extensive view of hilly vineyards it has plenty of charm, and offers a peaceful retreat. The house, built in 1825, has been home to fifteen generations of this family. Since I first visited, the young owners have increased their guest rooms considerably. There is a sunny grass terrace the length of the house with steps down to the lawns.

Three new rooms for two, three or four, each with private facilities, are on the second floor; the only room for guests on the first floor also has a private bathroom but not adjoining. *Bateau* beds, polished wooden floors, beams and natural stone walls with old fireplaces give the rooms an authentic touch. The dining room has an enormous *Charentaise* sideboard dwarfing the small round breakfast table. Look out to the garden and the hills beyond as you enjoy an excellent breakfast with orange juice, fresh croissants and baguettes. Evening meals now on offer, if reserved ahead.

In a converted coach-house is a nicely equipped kitchen for self catering. The Matignons have small children and welcome others, and there is a large enclosed garden for them to play in. Very good value for a family

LUXÉ 16230.
28 km N of Angoulême.

Angoulême is near and well worth a visit; Cognac a little further south-west, has a good shopping precinct. If you like French pottery do visit the tiny village of La Chapelle-des-Pots just north-east of Saintes, where there is a factory and large showroom with an enormous range of products. English spoken.

From Mansle on the N10, south of Poitiers, take the D739 to Luxé-Gare. Turn right to Luxé and you will find the Ferme des Vignauds the other side of the village.

☆ **M. & Mme. Richard. 'Les Vignauds' Luxé-Bourg.**
category: (M)
tel/fax: 05.45.39.01.47.
B&B: 48€ for two.
Evening meal 12.5€ each.

One of the first chambres d'hôtes I ever stayed in and still going strong. Four well-furnished rooms, with baths or showers, occupy the first floor of this practically restored farmhouse. There is a terrace and large swimming pool, with pool-side barbecue and kitchen facilities. M. Richard is genial host and Mme. Richard an excellent cook; really copious meals, with wine included, are taken with the family. The last time I dined here someone mentioned it was their birthday and in seconds a bottle of champagne was produced. A ☆ for continued high standards.

CHARENTE-MARITIME

FOURAS. 17450.
22 km S of La Rochelle.

Right on the coast, the peninsula at Fouras extends like a nose into the sea. I was pleasantly surprised with this select little seaside resort. No crowds in September. A wide tree-lined promenade leads to Fort Vauban, housing the tourist office. It was at the tiny harbour of Port Sud that on 8 July 1815 Napoleon last stepped on French soil on his way to exile in St. Helena. No huge hotels on the front here, mostly three-storey apartments overlooking the sea, with the usual selection of cafés, restaurants and *pizzerias.*

From the N137 16 km south of La Rochelle turn on to the D937 to Fouras, branch right at next junction on to the Route des Valines, straight on along the Avenue Pierre Loti. At the next large intersection the rue des Courtineurs is on the right.

☆ **Mme. Lefèbvre**
4 ter, rue des Courtineurs.
category: (M)
tel/fax: 05.46.84.02.87.
B&B: 48/51€ for two. No Dinner
Closed 1 Oct. to 30 Apr.

This is proving to be a popular chambres d'hôtes for those who like to be beside the sea. Right on the coast, the rue des Courtineurs, a cul-de-sac on the fringe of the town, leads straight on to the beach, only 150 metres away so there is no traffic noise. This particular stretch of beach has many wooden fishing piers, where the fishermen hang their nets to be filled by the incoming tide.

This modern house has a wing on the ground floor with superb carpeted rooms, each with smart shower rooms, entered by French windows, the only ventilation on hot nights. The excellent breakfast, outside in summer or brought to your room in inclement weather, is elegantly served. A communal fridge for guests is an added asset. No evening meal, so take a trip out to the *Pointe-de-la-Fumée* where there are fish restaurants and you have views in all directions, or make for the sea-front where the choice is wider and watch the sun set as you dine.

M. Lefèbvre is an architect. Parking is in the garden with gate locked at midnight, so all is very safe.

MIRAMBEAU. 17150.
70 km N of Bordeaux. 45km S of Royan.

From the A10 (exit Mirambeau) head straight for the town centre and the château is on the right soon after the tourist office on the left.

M. Ventola. 'Le Parc Casamène'
95, Ave. de la République.
category: (L)
tel: 05.46.49.74.38.
B&B: 75/80/85€ for two
Evening meal 35€ each
Open all year by reservation only
Nov. to March.

What an easy place to find, just off the busy autoroute to Bordeaux. A very handy night stop for weary travellers. Shady parking and gates shut at night.

This neat château, built in 1877, has a park of five hectares containing some very interesting old trees. One cedar pre-dates the château. The present owner and his partner took six years restoring the building, opening as a chambres d'hôtes a few years ago, furnishing all the rooms in uncluttered 19th-century style.

The salon overlooks the park behind, as does the dining room where warm pink flowery walls are a backdrop for two identical polished sideboards, acquired with the château. Evening meals are prepared and served by your hosts who join you at table.

On arrival appropriate refreshment is always offered and I can vouch for the very nice home-made fruit cake.

One guest room on the ground floor has a fireplace, is pleasantly decorated in blue with matching Louis XV bed and wardrobe and has a large pale green bathroom adjoining. Luxury aubergine-coloured carpets are in all the guest rooms.

Three rooms all overlook the garden, each one entered by a vestibule dressing room, with space for suitcases. One, known as the cedar room, has dual aspect windows. Two more rooms have recently been added. There is a choice of single or double beds, well equipped bathrooms, bidets, dual washbasins and separate toilets in all.

Far too good for just a night stop, though prices are rising steeply for a chambres d'hôtes

SAINT-GEORGES-DES-AGOÛTS 17150
45 km south of Saintes. From the A10 exit 37 take direction Mirabeau after the roundabout continue past the supermarket 'Marché U' and take first

right opposite the notaire's with its gold sign, D254 to St-Georges-des-Agoûts. In St-Georges turn right at the church and follow signs 'chambres d'hôtes' to Font Maure.

Les Hauts de Font Maure
St. Georges-des-Agoûts

M. & Mme. Teulet. 'Les Hauts de Font Maure'
category: (M-L)
tel: 05.46.86.04.41.
fax: 05.46.49.67.18.
email: cteullet@aol.com
B&B: 58/66 €. for two.
Evening meals 21€ each.
Closed 1 Nov. to 1 Apr., except by special reservation.

Recommended by a reader, I hastened to visit and found this charming *Charentaise maison de maître* in a tiny farming hamlet close to the Gironde estuary, surrounded by fields of sunflowers and vineyards. The spaciousness of the house hits you as soon as you enter. Three rooms on the first floor are light and airy all with pristine new deluxe bathrooms. Furnished elegantly with carefully chosen antiques, leaving plenty of space to spread oneself about. Since I last visited, a new family suite, a double, and single room for one or two children sharing a bathroom is proving popular. M. Teulet is French, Madame is English, hence the vast bookshelves of French and English books on the wide landing which would keep one enthralled for weeks. A balustraded balcony at the rear of the long entrance hall, has steps down to the garden where hidden on a terrace is a swimming pool and white loungers on which to relax as you gaze at the countryside.

The salon, which guests may use at anytime, has a floor reconstructed from ancient *terre cuite* tiles discarded by a local church; impressions of animal foot prints can be found on some of the tiles when they were first dried out hundreds of years ago.

Dinner with your hosts or other guests in the high-ceilinged dining room is the highlight of the day, you consume four courses of Dinah's excellent cuisine. Wine included, a real party atmosphere prevails. Prices vary according to rooms. Extra beds 13€. Suite for three 76€

SAINT-SAVINIEN. 17350.
19 km N of Saintes. 15km SW of St. Jean-d'Angely.

From Saint-Savinien take the D114 and then the D124, SP 'Bord', to Pontreau and turn left at the sign to the chambres d'hôtes 200 metres up a lane. The house is on the right.

☆ **Mr. & Mrs. Elmes. 'Le Moulin de la Quine'**
Le Pontreau.
category: (M)
tel: 05.46.90.19.31
B&B: 41.5/48€ for two.
Evening meals 14.5€ each.

Everyone's dream cottage: white with green shutters, edible grapes cascading down one wall, hidden in four to five acres of fields and trees, not a house in sight. Only an English woman could have designed this peaceful garden, with well-kept lawns and interesting island beds.

Facing south, all rooms overlook the terrace, a veritable sun trap. Jeni and John have been here for many years now and are well used to entertaining. They have two large rooms for two or four guests, bathrooms in both. The tiled downstairs room has its own terrace, but upstairs is fully carpeted and has delightful low windows and extensive views. Tea-making facilities and hair dryers add to the many comforts in the room. Guests have come for a night and stayed a week.

Evening meals (by prior arrangement) with your hosts are most congenial and include all drinks. You won't be looking for restaurants here. The lovely old mill tower in the garden is now an unobtrusive *gîte*. Parking is in the shade of a large linden tree. Guests have applauded this one, so now a ☆. Lower price for longer stays.

SAINT-SORNIN. 17600.
27 km W of Saintes. 12 km E of Marennes.

A neat little village, with a *boulangerie* opposite the church. The countryside is flat here on the edge of the salt-pans. Within easy reach of the bridge to the Ile d'Oléron, one of the largest islands lying off the west coast of France. Also close to the unexpected isolated village of Brouage, known to many Canadians, as it was the birthplace (in about 1567) of Samuel de Champlain, the founder of Quebec. The small village is totally surrounded by a star-shaped wall. You can walk round the high ramparts and have an excellent view of the flat salt-pans stretching along the Havre de Brouage to the sea. As the salt-pans have declined, they are now used for storing shellfish. Aim to visit early in the day before the tourist buses. Enter the village by the old stone archway on the north side and wander round the quiet streets where the few restaurants serve really fresh fish. The church has a reredos looking like a piece of fine Wedgwood blue-and-white china, but it is actually wooden and was restored by the Canadians who have also put up the memorial to Samuel de Champlain. The most striking view of the village is from the air, so buy a card from the tourist office and see what I mean.

Return to St. Sornin for a night stop. From Saintes take the D782 (SP Marennes) for 27 km and turn right at the sign to the village. Turn left by the church and the entrance to the chambres d'hôtes is on the right.

☆ **M. & Mme. Pinel-Peschardière.**
'La Caussolière'
10, rue de Petit Moulin.
category: (M)
tel/fax: 05.46.85.44.62.
email: caussoliere@wanadoo.fr
B&B: 51/60.5€ for two.
Evening meals 24€ each.

It is not often I give a ☆ after a one-night stay; but this one is exceptionally nice. Monsieur is the local Mayor, and Madame modestly says she is a bit of an artist. Her work enhances all the rooms. Doors, lampshades, bathroom tiles and pictures are all tastefully painted to match the colour of the rooms. It doesn't stop there – the bed covers, table clothes and even mats are exquisitely made in matching patchwork.

One double-bedded room, in the main house has access to the garden; two much larger rooms are in the granary on the other side of the swimming pool. Sunflower-yellow on the ground floor has a double bed recessed behind dainty curtains and a settee which doubles for children in the salon area. The bathroom is very large and well furnished, including tea-making facilities and electric heating. Above, up an external stairway, the 'rose' room, with a double and single bed, is warmly decorated with appropriate flowery walls and the bathroom has all the same excellent facilities. There is a lounge in the main house, plus a restful garden where you can watch the fish and frogs in the pond, but in summer it is the terrace beside the swimming pool which will attract most. Convivial evening meals with your hosts include all drinks, but there are restaurants at Pont L'Abbé, 8 km, or Marennes 12 km. Breakfast, early in the year on the sheltered terrace, is copious. Madame Pinel-Peschardière has a workshop where guests may learn to paint on silk and where much of her unique work is on show. Superb value all round.

As in most seaside chambres d'hôtes, there is a small *taxe de séjour* in high season.

DEUX-SÈVRES

ARÇAIS 79210
30 km SE of Fontenay-le-Comte. 25 km W of Niort

The road beside the river Sèvre Niortaise is very pleasant from Arçais to Coulon and just at the border of Deux-Sèvres I was lucky to spot a newly-opened chambres d'hôtes beside the river at Les Bourdettes, 2 km east of Arçais.

M. & Mme. Pean
14, Chemin de la Foulée. Les Bourdettes.
category: (S-M)
tel: 05.49.35.88.95.
B&B: 43/48€ for two.
Evening meal 15€ each.

This is a particularly good address for visiting the Vendée and the delightful village of Arçais, where boats and bikes can be hired. The Peans seem to have thought of everything.

This typical long 'Vendée' house on the riverside backs on fields and woods, and now has four guest rooms. A. carpeted, simply-furnished family suite of two rooms, (extra beds 11€), shares a bathroom, and has the advantage of a large covered balcony overlooking the river. A room for two has river views and another overlooks the woods. another small room has single beds but shower room is on the landing.

There is a salon/dining room guests may use at all times. An evening meal, with *vin compris*, cooked by Monsieur, a Cordon Bleu chef, sounds promising. Alternatively walk across the bridge 200 yds away to an auberge the other side of the river. Parking is beside the house off the road, locked at night. A garage is available for bikes. Breakfast is served at separate tables in a pleasant conservatory.

COULON. 79510.
11 km W of Niort.

This small village beside the river Sèvre-Niortaise in the Marais Verte, though over the border in Poitou-Charentes, epitomises everything that is really the Vendée. With all its tourist attractions and plentiful restaurants, it remains unspoilt. Boats for hire at Coulon, or take a ride on the little train round the canals, or even a river trip with inclusive lunch or dinner down the Sèvre Niortaise.

Leave Coulon on the Vanneau road beside the river and turn right in 1 km at the sign to La Rigole.

☆ **Mme. Fabien. 'La Rigole'**
category: (S)
tel: 05.49.35.97.90.
B&B: 40€ for two. No Dinner
Closed Christmas and New Year.

On the edge of one of the prettiest villages in the Marais Poitevin, this colourful modernised cottage, well off the main road and right beside the canal, would be my choice for a holiday exploring the hidden waterways. On a second visit I liked it even more.

Youthful Mme. Fabien now has four delightful beamed rooms, including a family room with two double beds, one with a *ciel de lit*. The newest room overlooks the canal and is quite charming. All have excellent new showers rooms, no baths. and with extra beds 8€ are exceptional value. A large breakfast awaits you, but no evening meal – plenty of options in Coulon, where there are also bikes for hire. A ☆ as the best introduction to an under-appreciated area.

GERMOND-ROUVRE 79220
23km SW of Parthenay. 2 km west of the D743 between Parthenay and Niort.
Just off the route to La Rochelle and only 20 km from the Marais Poitevin.

☆ **M. & Mme. Blanchard.**
'Breilbon'
category: (S)
tel: 05.49.04.05.01.
B&B: 33.5€ for two.
Evening meals 11.2€

Readers have been unanimous in their praise for this little chambres d'hôtes and prices stay firmly low. The owners have diligently restored the lovely old house at the end of a hamlet near Germond-Rouvre. Peace and quiet is assured, and a very friendly welcome.

Better and better, there are now three well-furnished guest rooms, two in a restored outbuilding, and one on the first floor of the main house, all have shower rooms adjoining.

The Blanchards dine with their guests, Monsieur cooks superb evening meals using local produce and all drinks are included, making this exceptional value. Breakfast is well up to scratch, with fresh orange juice. We gave a ☆ in the last edition and this remains firmly in place. Superb value.

NANTEUIL 79400.
28 km S of Parthenay

Turn off the N11 at St. Maixent on to the D737; in 1 km signed to La Berlière on your left.

M. & Mme. Memeteau
2, Impasse de la Berlière.
category: (S)
tel: 05.49.05.60.71.
B&B: 38.5€ for two. No Dinner.
Closed 30 Sept. to 1 Apr.

Tucked away on a quiet hillside, this ancient farmhouse is only 6 km from the A10, with views over the valley and stream below. One pretty blue room, with warm carpeting, fluffy white towels and good reading lamps, is very comfortable. The suite is totally independent, and attractively decorated with beds for four and a kitchen area. A bargain stop for a family of four at 57.5€. Evening meals sadly no longer offered, but local restaurants are recommended. Try L'Orangerie at Soudan for interesting menus, 8 km away on the A10.

'*In terms of accueil, that provided by M. and Mme. Memeteau must take the honours*'. J Bryans. Such a pleasant family – Monsieur used to be in the French Air Force. Though closed in the winter, the Memeteaus will accept guests if reserved well ahead.

SAINT-LOUP-LAMARIÉ 79600
This pretty and prosperous little village in medieval times was within the château grounds, guarded by the Donjon. The Black Prince kept the French king John the Good a prisoner here in 1356, after the battle of Poitiers.

Comte de Bartillat. 'Château de
Saint-Loup-sur-Thouet'
category: (L)
tel: 05.49.64..81.73
fax: 05.49.64.82 06.
email: saint-loup@wfi.fr
Rooms 99/130/182.94€ for two.
Breakfast extra 11€ each.
Evening meals 56€ each.

The *Donjon* which still dominates the village was the original building on this site, the château was constructed later in the beginning of the 17th century by the wealthy Gouffier family in the style of Henry IV and Louis XIII. Passing through many families it fell into disrepair until it was rescued in 1992 by Comte Charles Henri de Bartillat, a distant relative of the original family. Since then much time and money has been spent restoring the château to its original style of the 17th/18th century, aided by the European Union and local authorities.

The château and the imposing *Donjon*, in the south east corner; are surrounded by a wide moat. The château itself is surprisingly compact with East and West wings, a bell tower tops the narrower central part. A huge *potager* and orchard lie alongside the river Thouet as it winds through the extensive grounds of 150 acres. A pavilion straddling a bridge, and an *orangerie* overlooking its own cultivated courtyard, can accommodate over 400 people for weddings and other celebrations.

The guest rooms maintain their privacy though the château and grounds are regularly open to the public. The Comte, (who speaks perfect English), and Comtesse are most entertaining hosts who work hard to make your stay a real pleasure.

The 18th century style of both rooms and garden is being carefully maintained. Each year one room is refurbished in the style relating to its name, with drapes and bed covers supplied by Pierre Frey who specialises in antique materials. Guest rooms are available in both the château and *donjon*. Eight in each vary from a small room for one, to a family suite of two rooms, all, with the exception of one, with adjoining large bathrooms. Named after previous occupants: Voltaire, the Black Prince and Perrault, who wrote the tale of 'Puss in Boots' inspired by the Marquis de Caravaz's title. Château rooms are high, light and airy often with triple aspect windows, all but one in the west wing. The Marquesses' room has a delicate original bed cover, perhaps not for trampolining toddlers! The 'Bishop's Room', a highly desirable room with couch in front of a log fire, is on the ground floor of the East wing. The *donjon* guest rooms are more robust, in medieval style with original stone window seats and *terre cuite* floors. One, very large, in the original kitchen has two huge fireplaces and two bathrooms, all are reached by climbing the tower. A compact family suite at the top of the *donjon* called 'The Eagles Nest' has good views and would be fun for children. All meals are served in the dining room in the *Donjon*. The more palatial dining room and library in the château are used only for special receptions.

It is a hugely expensive project restoring this historical château, so prices are understandably high. Evening meals (need 24 hours notice) wine included. Alternatively the village is on the doorstep.

VALLANS. 79270.
4km SW of Niort.

Take *Sortie* 33 from the A10 or from the N11 Epannes exit. Drive through Epannes and take the D1 to Vallans. Well signed in the village.

☆ **MM. Francis & Patric Guillot.** '**Le Logis d'Antan'**
140, rue Saint Louis.
category: (M)
tel: 05.49.04.91.50.
fax: 05.49.04.86.75. Open all year by reservation.
B&B: 56€ for two.
Evening meals 20.5€ each.

Close to the Venise Verte in the Vendée. Two brothers have converted this rustic *maison-de-maitre* into a first-rate chambres d'hôtes. All rooms have independent entry from outside, TV, phones, and are furnished with taste, combining modern amenities with interesting antiques. Hair dryers, tea-making facilities and a fridge are also supplied. Upstairs two rooms are carpeted. *La Salicorne* has a double bed and an attached room with bunks for three children. *L'Angélique* for two with a double bed has a charming *ciel de lit*. On the ground floor, for three, is *la Piballe* – large, with parquet floor and many windows plus a log fire in the winter. Another room overlooking the front garden has a tiled floor and ornamental fireplace.

Evening meals, on reservation, including all drinks, served in the dining room or pleasant sun lounge, feature local specialities cooked by Patric and should not be missed.

'Our *first port of call was Vallans. The accommodation is excellent and the evening meals were very good. Deserves an arrow without a doubt. The fact that Francis speaks a lot of English is a plus for anyone trying Chambres d'Hôtes for the first time'.* P. de la Haye.

VIENNE

AVANTON-MARTIGNY. 86170.

12 km N of Poitiers. 5 km west from exit 18 on the A10.

Avanton-Martigny is an excellent place to stay for those wishing to visit Futuroscope, a very large theme park just outside Poitiers with entertainment for all the family. The large futuristic buildings can be seen for miles around. You need stamina to spend a whole day looking at all the cinemas and the exhibitions. Entrance is free for the under fives. This fee covers one day but there is a two-day option. Just inside the entrance at the Vienne tourist office you can obtain free headsets which can be set to translate the French commentaries into English. You have to leave something like a driving licence as a deposit.

There are plenty of activities for children. 76 separate entertainments, of which only six carry an extra charge.

Take a picnic. Food in the numerous cafés and restaurants can be expensive for a family, and there are long queues at peak times. The grounds are ideal for al fresco eating with lovely lawns and lakes. A change of clothing or a swimsuit is useful for children; they won't be able to resist trying the water maze, tempting on a hot day. Don't miss the superb Magic Carpet cinema. Nor the 3D cinema, nor even the 360-degree one. Avoid the Simulator unless you adore the horrors of a roller coaster. Funnily enough, it attracted the largest queue of the day, parties of school children and the *Troisième âge*. I can't believe they knew what they were letting themselves in for – seven minutes of shuddering big dipper type film, with the floor and your seat moving, synchronised with it. Afterwards, calm yourself by taking a peaceful boat ride through the rural landscapes of Europe, or take the lift up the revolving tower for an aerial view of the whole of the park. There were some very weary people making their way to their cars and coaches after a full and happy day, so perhaps one should take advantage of the two-day option.

☆ Mme. Arrondeau. 'Ferme du Château', Martigny.
category: (M)
tel: 05.49.51.04.57
B&B: 46.5€ for two. No Dinner
Closed 1 Dec. to 14 Mar.

In this purely residential hamlet with no shops, you will find this delightful old house in a walled garden, once part of the château, where the stables have been modernised for comfort but keep all their old character. Two rooms on the first floor can each take an extra bed. On the ground floor is a family suite with double bed and two singles on a mezzanine. There is a really comfortable sitting-room, a dining alcove and smart kitchen area with all modern facilities, even a microwave. Coffee, tea and cold drinks are all provided and there's a patio for picnics in fine weather. Definitely my choice near Futuroscope, but book; always busy in holidays and at weekends. Locked parking in the garden beside the house. I couldn't fault this one; excellent *accueil* and the addition of a swimming pool has made it even more attractive.

'We were delighted with Mme. Arrondeau who is a charming hostess and ensured we had a memorable visit'. J & R Gay.

The ☆ stays firmly in place. Some English spoken. 10% discount for three nights. There is now a *taxe de séjour* here now.

LAVOUX 86800
12 km E of Poitiers. From A10 exit Poitiers. Nord, take N 10 direction Limoges, in 7 km, left to Bignoux, and follow signs to Bois Dousset.

Vicomte & Vicomtesse Hilaire de Villoutreys de Brignac. 'Logis du Château du Bois Dousset'.
category: (M)
tel/fax: 05.49.44.20.26.
B&B: 62€ for two.

A long drive from the D139 places the château well in the country. Dating from the 16th Century, the original owners departed for Germany during the Revolution and the State obtained the château. It was then bought by General Meunier, one of Napoleon's generals and great-great grandfather of the present Vicomte, who now occupies the converted Orangery, which is nearly as large as the château, in which his mother resides.

Chambres d'hôtes rooms are in the Orangery, and an adjoining building. Two rooms in the main house (one with four beds for a family) are large and well furnished with antiques, unfortunately they share a bathroom on the ground floor. As this is a listed building, permission has not yet been granted to alter this. However two rooms in the adjoining annexe, also furnished with antiques, have excellent modern bathrooms. Madame de Villoutreys' artistic nature has led her to paint the walls of the original stone staircase a warm orange and yellow and the *ciel-de-lits* are unusually artistic.

Gardens are formal in layout; but delightful carpets of cyclamen in Autumn spread under trees and across the lawns, cropping up in clusters in the gravel pathways.

The welcome is warm and friendly. M. le Vicomte whose English is very good, will fill you in with much history and Madame will keep the conversation flowing. As a rule no evening meal; but for English or American guests if you reserve ahead you might be lucky enough to be offered a light meal on your arrival. There is an Auberge at Bignoux, 5 km away

Two gîtes share the gardens. Prices, according to season, are very reasonable for a family château.

MOUTERRE-SILLY. 86200.
36 km SSE of Saumur.

From the D759 west of Loudon turn left to Mouterre-Silly. Silly is 1km further on.

☆ **M. & Mme. Pouit.**
Rue de la Fontaine.
category: (S)
tel: 05.49.22.46.41.
B&B: 36.5€ for two.
Evening meal 12.5€ each.

The tiny hamlet of Silly has neither *commerce* nor church; the Pouits' large farmhouse, once visited by Cardinal Richelieu, dominates the village with its two towers and extensive gardens of lawns and vegetables. Antique cartwheels decorate the large enclosed courtyard, outbuildings on all sides; a collection of fossils found in a neighbouring field is displayed on one wall.

If you have been château-bashing all day you will think you are still at it as you climb the stone staircase in the tower to one of the rooms here, and even more so as you open the very old door with a latch and an enormous 8-inch key. Two tall *armoires* and a huge fireplace dwarf the double bed and small single in the corner of the warm carpeted room. There are excellent modern shower and loo facilities in the adjoining tower. A second room, for three, has been created since my last visit, and very pretty it is too, with flowery wallpaper and blue predominating.

Madame Pouit is a splendid cook, and produces a feast nearly all home-produced, all drinks included. I shall always remember the meal I had when I stayed here. Soup, asparagus soufflé, roast duck, cheese and fresh strawberries – everything but the cheese from the garden.

Their youngest daughter speaks quite good English, and Madame Pouit understands more than she admits. Excellent value here.

NEUVILLE-de-POITOU. 86170.
15 km NW of Poitiers.
A small town on the D62, just off the N147. 10 minutes from Futuroscope.

The Sunday market in the town has been famous since the end of the 16th century, and if you are looking for wine go no further than the 'Cave du Haut-Poitou' at 32, rue Plault, available for *dégustations*, even on Sunday morning. There is an *Arboretum* nearby with examples of all the trees of the area.

Make for the Place Joffre in *centre ville* and take the road down to the church and water tower, bear right and then left to the rue Armand Caillard, a one-way street. Easy to find on foot, not so easy by car.

M. & Mme. Pray. 'La Roseraie'
78, rue Armand Caillard.
category: (S-M)
tel: 05.49.54.16.72.
B&B: 44€ for two
Evening meal 15€ each.

This rather lovely 18th-century house, with an even older orangery, is near the centre of the town. Parking in a locked courtyard is ideal, and the chance to visit all the shops on foot from a chambres d'hôtes is unusual.

A lot of thought has gone into the conversion of the orangery into five guest rooms and a downstairs sitting area. One room on the ground floor with a fireplace and wood floors has access to the garden; but you have to stay three days to qualify for this room. Two rooms on the first floor (I loved the blue one with a balcony), another two on the second floor have *velux* windows. All are light and airy and freshly painted in pastel shades and coordinating colours – very modern shower rooms and separate loos, carpets and comfortable *crapaud* armchairs in each make these rooms extremely pleasant.

Another suite for a family has two rooms, one with three singles, in the stables just off the rear parking area. There is also a *gîte*.

Ample room for children to play, with swings, and I hear the promised swimming pool is up and running.

Optional simple evening meals, *apéritif* and wine included, are served at an oval table, in the main house, sometimes seating twelve people. Restaurants within walking distance.

Provence

PROVENCE

Provence

Situated in the south-east corner of France, Provence since 600 BC has been colonised by Greeks, Celts and Romans, all leaving their imprint, mostly noticeable in names of towns. After the fall of the Roman Empire in the 4th century, Franks, Burgundians and Visigoths all descended on the area. It was a kingdom in its own right in the 9th century, became part of France in 1481, then came under the domination of the Italian kingdoms, and was eventually ceded to France by Sardinia in 1860. The modern autoroutes A8 and A9 follow the route of the old Roman roads from Italy through Nice, Aix and Arles then onwards to Narbonne and Spain.

The climate is hot in summer, mild in winter, except when the Mistral, the cold fierce northerly wind, is suddenly funnelled down the Rhône valley from the Alps.

In the north the **Hautes-Alpes** extend to Savoie and the Italian border in the east. The *préfecture* is Gap, a small town on the Route Napoléon, N85. The enormous *Parc National Des Ecrins* takes up a good part of this mountainous area, where Briançon is the highest town in Europe. Major roads like the N94 follow the river valleys. The river Durance was dammed 35 years ago to make the Lac de Serre Ponçon, now a popular holiday resort.

South-east, the **Alpes-de-Haute-Provence** *département* is sandwiched between the Vaucluse and the Alpes Maritimes, with a small Italian border in the east. The *préfecture* of Digne-les-Bains lies in the west of the *département*, also on the Route Napoléon. Due of course to the mountainous terrain, roads again skirt where they can. Covered with snow in the winter, it is a wild terrain with no famous ski resorts as in the Alps.

Descending into the **Alpes Maritimes**, the mountains are even more precipitous, reaching to the coastline in places, with many roads running through tunnels. Between Menton and Nice are three corniches tiering up from the Mediterranean coast, with pretty perched villages like Eze on the *Moyenne Corniche*. On the upper road are the striking remains of the Trophée des Alpes at La Turbie, built in the 6th century BC, to commemorate the final submission of the area's 44 tribes to obedience to Rome. There is a panoramic view over Monaco from the surrounding gardens. Now there is a higher motorway all the way from Nice to Italy, easier by far but lacking the excitement and the views of the three Corniches.

Nice, the *préfecture*, is right on the coast with the Promenade des Anglais overlooking the pebbly beach. Away from the coast, the old town is still very interesting and the port is just round a corner where the ferries leave for Corsica. This narrow coastline was once the loveliest in France, but it has been over-exposed and in summer the beaches are jam-packed. Better by far to venture up into the hills and find peace and quiet. High behind the coast is Grasse, the perfume capital of France. Busy with its own concerns, it seems detached from the tourist excesses of the coastal towns. A daily market and the added attraction of a visit to the perfume factories make this town a worth-while target. Vence and St. Paul de Vence are a bit too popular but you will regret it if you miss seeing them, too.

Napoleon landed at Golfe-Juan and marched up through France along what is now known as the Route Napoléon (N 85) through Grasse and on to Grenoble.

Further west the *département* of **Var** occupies a coastal position and stretches back into the hills as far as the Gorge du Verdon. Toulon, the *préfecture*, is the largest naval port in France. Near the coast the lesser hills of the Massif des Maures keep the north winds away from the beaches from Toulon to Fréjus, and the Massif de l'Esterel protrudes into the sea making many lovely coves. Inland, the Var is more penetrable than the Alpes Maritimes; roads straddle the plains, leading to the Lac de Ste. Croix, a large man-made lake at one end of the Gorge du Verdon. The gorge is a massive canyon made by the river cutting a winding course through the limestone rock, 21 km. long from Aiguines to Rougon and varying in depth from 250 to 700 metres. There are good roads on both sides, with viewing points (*belvédères*) at the best parts.

The most westerly *département* of **Bouches-du-Rhône** has the great Mediterranean port of Marseille as its *préfecture*. The flat salt marshy lands of the Camargue lie west of Marseille, cut by the delta of the river Rhône, where the white horses roam and the flamingos add their brilliance to the wildlife of the many lagoons. The infamous hill village of les Baux is on a peak of the Alpilles mountains. Now with its past well behind, it is a most attractive village.

The **Vaucluse** seems to be the most populated and most popular of the *départements*. Here the chambres d'hôtes come thick and fast. Small mountain ranges intersperse with valleys all producing the sun-kissed Rhône valley wines, particularly from the slopes of Mont Ventoux. The Lubéron is the most southerly range, a great favourite with climbers.

Avignon, the *préfecture*, on the river Rhône, is firmly tucked away in the north-west. The Popes made their home there in the 14th century when lawlessness broke out in Rome. Their old palace is open to the public. Don't forget to dance *under* the St. Bénézet bridge which is only half a bridge since a flood washed part away in the 17th century. The dancing was never *Sur le Pont d'Avignon* but on an island underneath. In the plains the perfume of the large lavender fields wafts through the air on a warm day.

There are many old Roman towns in the department. Orange with its well preserved theatre and glorious Arc-de-Triomphe dating back to 6 BC, simply mustn't be missed.

ALPES-DE-HAUTE-PROVENCE

LES MÉES. 04190.

16 km S of Sisteron.

An ideal place for an easy night stop off the Autoroute 51. Les Mées itself is far from exciting but the spectacular *rochers (Les Pénitents)* overhanging the town are. The story is that they are monks turned to stone. Rimbaud, Seigneur de Mées, took seven beautiful Moorish ladies into his château. The Prior of the monastery at Les Mées decided this was scandalous and threatened him with excommunication if he did not release them. He did, and while everyone was watching them emerge from the château Saint Donat, a hermit who lived at Lurs on the other side of the Durance thought the flock of monks watching were in moral danger so he petrified them on the spot. More realistically the weather has worn the rocks down to this shape, resembling a column of monks. The best view of the *Pénitents* is from the autoroute coming from Gap.

Some of the purest olive oil is produced in this valley – visit the co-operative for tastings.

From the A51 exit Les Mées, head for the town over the river Durance past the Intermarché supermarket, a useful place for refuelling both the car and picnic supplies. After you cross the river, branch right, SP Oraison D4, and the chambres d'hôtes is on the left at Bourelles, well signed.

M. & Mme. Verger. 'Le Mas des Oliviers', Les Bourelles.
category: (S)
tel: 04.92.34.36.99.
B&B: 38.5/41.5€ for two.
Evening meal 14.5€ each. (July & August there will be no evening meal, but guests will have full use of the summer kitchen.) Open all year. Reserve from Dec. to Feb.

A modern house, well designed to catch the sun, on the hillside just below the Canal-de-Durance.

There are four rooms: *La Lavande* upstairs has a bath and a private terrace. On the ground floor three others have shower rooms but two have their loos on the corridor. *Les Eglantines* has a private terrace. Parking is off the road in the hillside garden. Rooms are cosy in winter, with lots of small extras supplied – tissues, soap, sewing kit, etc. Evening meals, with wine *compris*, willingly offered, are simple and adequate and the welcome is warm and friendly.

NOYERS-sur-JABRON. 04200.
12 km SW of Sisteron. 48 km W of Digne.

Take the N85 (*Route Napoléon*) south from Sisteron, and in 4km turn right on to the D946. Noyers is 11 km along this road. Take the first right on leaving the village and follow the signs.

M. & Mme. Morel. 'Le Mas de la Caroline'
Chênebotte.
category: (M)
tel: 04.92.62.03.48.
fax: 04.92.62.03.46.
B&B: 48€ for two.
Evening meal 19€ each,
(reservation only).

A wonderfully peaceful retreat where you will be given a warm welcome by the owners, who on retirement bought this charming rustic house, which was once a sheep farm. The matured stone walls and vaulted ceilings are an interesting feature of the house.

There are two rooms on the ground floor with baths; they share a terrace and a south-facing salon, which is pleasantly decorated with some lovely antique furniture. A charming sunny suite is designed particularly for the disabled, with two single beds and a very pleasant salon opening on to a terrace. The shower room is kitted out with rails in all the right places and the floor gently slopes to facilitate the use of a wheelchair. It also has a little kitchen with a vaulted roof built on to the foundations of the house. I found the little suite utterly charming and well worth the 64€ for two.

Madame Morel will produce an evening meal for you, including wine. There is a reduction after the first night. All well worth a detour.

HAUTES-ALPES

ROSANS. 05150.
25 km W of Serres. 75 km from Bollène.

The ancient little hill village of Rosans in the Haute-Alpes, 700m high, is between Serres and Nyons on the D994, an alternative route to Provence.

It was once a fortified village. Celts, Saracens, Gallo-Romans have all played their part in its development; a few narrow streets and fortifications remain. Good parking in the little square by the bar. Take the D994 Nyons to Serres and in 1km after Rosans turn right on to the St. André-de-Rosans road D949 and L'Ensoleillée is just off the road on the right.

M. & Mme. Pacaud. 'L'Ensoleillée'
Le Béal Noir.
category: (M)
tel: 04.92.66.62.72.
fax: 04.92.66.62.87.
B&B: 43€ for two.
Evening meal 14.5€ each.

A purpose-built chambres d'hôtes, which looks like a motel, but the wonderful welcome assures you it isn't, though travellers cheques are accepted.

The Pacauds have been running it for a decade now and it still looks new. The six rooms are in a separate building. A very large family room on the *rez-de-chaussée* is divided into three sections, with two single beds in each, accommodating six people with a large bathroom. The extra beds are 12.5€, including breakfast. Above are five rooms accessible from the parking level. There is a choice of bath or shower. Two for three people have dual wash basins, others are for two. They are all prettily furnished in different colours and have private sunny terraces overlooking the mountains. Meals are served in the main house where the decor of the dining room is Provençal yellow. Evening meals cooked jointly by your hosts include wine.

An ideal spot for a night stop but book ahead and arrive early to enjoy the scenery, visit local villages and swim in the new pool which was being dug out when I was last there.

VENTEROL 05130.
20 km. S of Gap.

Just east of the Route Napoléon the high valleys are most attractive, surrounded by snow capped peaks; some like Céüse have ski pistes. Close by, the Lac de Serre-Ponçon has been formed by damming the powerful river Durance; there are extensive views as you drive round the lake which is well supplied with picnic sites.

From Gap take the D900B, turn left at the junction of the D942, continue for 3 km. towards Barcellonnette then fork right on the tiny D311 (signposted Venterol and Piégut and EASILY MISSED). Over a narrow bridge turn right to Venterol through the hamlet of Tournaires and keep on the Venterol road, winding uphill for 8 km. until you arrive in the tiny hamlet of Le Blanchet; the chambres d'hôtes is signed on the right.

M. & Mme. Boyer. 'La Méridienne'
Les Blanchets.
category: (S)
tel/fax: 04.92.54.18.51.
Demi-pension 35€ each

Panoramic mountain top views from this chambres d'hôtes which is once again a *ferme auberge*, offering demi-pension only (wine charged). There are five beamed rooms with all comforts, especially good lighting, and mezzanines for a third person in four of them. A comfortable lounge/dining room with log fire makes a winter stop a pleasure here. Mountain walks from the door, vast open garden, swings for children and delicious evening meals are well worth the drive up the hill and you will want to stay much more than one night. A very friendly place for a lone traveller. A little departing gift of lavender, honey and soap arrived on the breakfast table when I was there. If you want to be in the mountains, well away from towns, this is the place. Ask for a room with a valley view. Early booking is essential in summer. A really nice place, in an area short of chambres d'hôtes, and exceptional value.

ALPES-MARITIMES

BERRE-les-ALPES. 06390.

21 km N of Nice.

Take the autoroute from Nice to Menton and come off at exit 55 (La Trinité), then the D2204 to Sospel, dreary and industrial at first, then turn left on to the D215 to Berre-les-Alpes. The U bend turns eventually bring you to the clock in the centre of the village. If you think you have climbed to the top you have more in store, for Super Berre is even higher but flattens out into quite a wide residential area. A right fork by the clock will take you past the cemetery and over sleeping policemen to the villa on the right.

M. & Mme. Legras. 'Villa Benoît'
Super Berre.
category: (M)
tel: 04.93.91.81.07. or 04.93.91.84.30
fax: 04.93.91.85.47.
B&B: 53.5€ for two.

An interesting village with two hotels and various shops. Magnificent views from beside the post office.

This very large villa was once used as a recording studio (Super Bear), by the Beatles and other groups, the house was burnt down in 1986, bought and rebuilt by the Legras. Excellent parking in the garden which includes a swimming pool.

There are three pleasant rooms, 'Lavender' for two people, 'Rose' and 'Chestnuts' for three. Telephones and TV in all rooms. The walls of the salon/dining room are covered with exhibits from local artists, changed every two months. The chambres d'hôtes guests can be *en pension* or demi-pension, but Madame is extremely flexible about meals, Monsieur does the cooking and you can order full meals or snacks each evening. Accommodating and friendly hosts.

VALBONNE. 06560.

Situated 4km from the popular village of Valbonne, an attractive place large enough to boast an excellent choice of bistro-type restaurants and boutiques, and a large parking space to keep cars from choking the main roads, yet small enough to keep an intimate friendly character. Streets are narrow, winding, dripping with flowers; houses are old, photogenic. Altogether well worth an excursion or even better a longer stay.

This chambres d'hôtes is in an ideal position for visiting the coast, the mountains or the lovely old town of Grasse .

From Valbonne take the D3 towards Antibes and at a roundabout in 2 km take the third exit onto the D103, SP 'Antibes' (Route du Parc). Near a yellow bus stop on the left called 'La Petite Ferme', turn left up a little lane and the house is the one on the left.

M. & Mme. Ringenbach. 'Le Chéneau'
205, Route d'Antibes.
category: (M-L)
tel: 04.93.12.13.94.
fax: 04.93.12.91.85.
email: ringbach@club-internet.fr
B&B: 64/72€ for two (high season), 56/64€ (low season). No Dinner
Open all year.

A lovely upmarket chambres d'hôtes, where reservations are necessary, please, so don't just turn up or you will be disappointed. The beautifully appointed villa in a large park has three large, well-furnished guest rooms in different colours – blue, noisette, etc. – one on the ground floor and two on the first floor in a separate wing of the house, all with baths.

There is a very nice salon opening on to the garden (with a double-bed settee) and a smart modern kitchen which can be let together with any of the other rooms, as a suite, for 35€ extra. The suite then will not include breakfast. Good value for a family of four who wish to self-cater.

Other guests have the use of a salon where breakfast is served.

Prices vary from *Bleu*, the smallest, to *Noisette*, a lovely spacious room. Parking is excellent behind the house in the shade. Highly recommended.

BOUCHES-du-RHÔNE

AIX-EN-PROVENCE 13852.
16 km N of Marseille.

Aix-en-Provence, north of Marseille, is an attractive and dignified university town, with a cool shaded heart – the *Cours Mirabeau*, a tree-lined boulevard running through the centre of the town. where the restaurants and brasseries remind one of Paris. The Cathedral of St. Sauveur has a famous Triptych of the Burning Bush, viewing at certain times. Cézanne lived and painted here.

Leave Aix by the A51 SP Marseille, take exit 3 SP 'Bouc Bel Air'; then the D59 on the right. The Domaine du Frère is signed in 3 to 4 km on this road on the right. Easier to book ahead and receive a clear map of directions, as this one is definitely not in the town but 6 km to the south.

M. & Mme. Bouvant. 'Domaine du Frère'
495, rue Ampère, Pôle d'Activités des Milles.
category: (M)
tel: 04.42.24.24.62.
fax: 04.42.24.37.89.
email: bouvant@easynet.fr
B&B: 56/64€ for two. No Dinner

It is quite extraordinary to find such a pleasant house in a suburb, virtually surrounded by large office blocks. Built in 1735, it stands marooned in a large park. There is a sheltered garden, a swimming pool, tennis court and a huge parking area.

A reader tells me she was welcomed like a long-lost daughter. Certainly both M. and Mme. Bouvant have the knack of making you feel like truly private guests. The house still has the original stairs and floors and is a maze of passages and short steps to various rooms. The delightful mellowness will take you back years. Don't miss the family chapel off the salon, as I did on my first visit. Large bathrooms are not all en suite but usually private, even if on a different level. The rooms vary in size and price but are homely and comfortable and all have tea and coffee-making facilities and those irresistible little almond biscuits called *Calisson,* an Aix speciality.

Madame, who is Dutch and speaks fluent English, will cook you a delicious evening meal, if booked in advance, wine and coffee included. Her cooking is way above normal for most chambres d'hôtes.

I was right on my first visit, when I said the vibes were good here. Then

I hadn't met the owners. Monsieur now runs an Internet service on town chambres d'hôtes, an added interest for staying here.

LES BAUX-de-PROVENCE
13520. 15km NE of Arles.

Les Baux village (900m by 200m in area) is on a spur of rock detached from the Alpilles, with ravines on both sides. It gave its name to bauxite, a mineral discovered on its land in 1822.

In the middle ages the lords of les Baux were all warriors, who warred with their neighbours continuously.

The Turenne family controlled Les Baux at one time when Viscount Raymond de Turenne became guardian of his niece, Alix, the last Princess of Baux, in 1372. He was known as the 'Scourge of Provence', and delighted in throwing his un-ransomed prisoners over the rock face. The King of France joined Raymond's enemies and defeated him in 1399. When Alix died in 1426 the Domaine was incorporated into Provence and became a Barony.

In the 17th century Les Baux became a Marquisate under the Grimaldi family of Monaco, who still patronise the village.

There is only one approach road. In the summer when the car parks are full vehicles overflow down the hill.

The village is most attractive now, so compact and full of historical interest, with flowers cascading from the many delightful bijou boutiques, cafés and restaurants. It is a 'must' on everyone's itinerary.

M. & Mme. Fajardo-de-Livry. 'La Burlande'
Paradou.
category: (L)
tel: 04.90.54.32.32
B&B: 80/112€ for two.
Evening meal 22€ (reservation only).

Tucked away off the road from Paradou to Les Baux in the middle of the Alpilles mountains this pleasant modern villa has three elegant bedrooms in a separate wing on the ground floor, furnished with antiques, baths or showers, carpets and central heating for year-round occupancy. Two rooms can be adjoining for a family. All rooms have access through patio doors to the garden and pool. Evening meals offered but wine is not *compris*. Your hosts enjoy musical evenings round a grand piano or are equally happy to play bridge.

375

VERQUIÈRES. 13670.
10 km W of Cavaillon. 8 km NE of Saint-Rémy-de-Provence.
A neat village north of the Chaine-des-Apilles, which is central to many well-known towns. Avignon a few miles north, Cavaillon in the east where the largest fruit market in France is held daily, and St. Rémy-de-Provence a few miles south west where the painter Van Gogh once lived.

From the telephone box in the centre follow signs to this chambres d'hôtes past orchards for 3 km.

M. Pinet. 'Mas-de-Castellan'
category: (L)
tel: 04.90.95.08.22.
fax: 04.90.95.44.23.
B&B: 72€, reduced after four nights. No Dinner
Closed January.

'This was sensational – a beautiful, inspiring house. I stayed two nights and would have liked to stay longer'. G Harvey.

Hospitable M. Pinet is a semi-retired antique dealer who enjoys having guests. His lovely old house, dating from the 18th century is full of interesting furniture collected on his travels. You will be welcome to use the large comfortable salon with log fire.

Breakfast is served in the conservatory, full of greenery, overlooking the garden, which has a pool.

One of the five very comfortable rooms opens on to the garden; all are charming in different colours and tastefully furnished – I loved the blue one with the *baldaquin* and large windows.

No evening meals but restaurants nearby, many in Eyragues.

VAR

CARQUEIRANNE. 83320.
15km E of Toulon. 6 km W of Hyères

From the A570, finishing at Hyères take the road signed Carqueirrane and Almanarre. At Almanarre continue on the D559 to Carqueiranne, where at the first roundabout, with a fountain, go right round and back the way you came on the other side of the dual carriageway. Take the second turn on the right, Avenue de Font Brun and the house is on the right.

M. & Mme. Menard.
'L'Aumonerie'
620, Avenue de Font Brun.
category: (L)
tel: 04.94.58.53.56.
B&B: 64/80€ for two. 96€ for the Gîte.
Closed mid-July to end of August.

The Menards, now retired, allow you to share this idyllic position on the shore of the Med with them, but understandably not in the height of the summer holidays when their family take precedence.

This pretty pink house turned out to be exactly as depicted in the pictures I had seen. Easy turning and parking in the front garden, where there is a small detached first floor *gîte*. The rear garden is a mass of spring and summer flowers as early as March. White tables and chairs on the green lawn contrast with the blue Mediterranean. Steps lead down to a small sandy beach where the smooth rocks are washed by the tideless sea, tricky for swimmers, but a few yards out is a deep pool made by a bomb dropped during the war (American, not British!). The rocks have the advantage of keeping small boats away, so the beach is virtually private. Breakfast is served in this idyllic setting whenever warm enough, otherwise in your room. Access to the garden at all times; but no salon for guests.

One small double room is just inside the front door and has a private shower and loo across the hall. Upstairs are two rooms, one for three with a bath, and one for two with a shower room, but the loo is shared on the landing. These two have superb sea views over the garden and are comfortably furnished. Genteel hosts, with whom you would have limited contact. It is a lovely spot in hot weather, and the only chambres d'hôtes I could find with private access to a Mediterranean beach.

GINASSERVIS 83560.
26 km S of Manosque. 36 km N of St.Maximin-la-Ste-Baume.
From the village take the D25 south then after the *Lavoir* on the left take the D70. The chambres d'hôtes is signed on the left up a farm track in about 1 km.

M. & Mme. Perrier. 'La Rougeonne'
category: (M)
tel/fax: 04.94.80.11.31.
B&B: 60.5€ for two
Evening meal 20.8€ each.
Closed January and February.

This 14th-century farmhouse has been well restored, keeping much of its character. The modernised rooms have huge windows overlooking the Var countryside. In the main house is one large luxurious room with a modern shower room. Two others are in a detached building; one is a family suite on the ground floor, the other above.

Vivacious young Madame Perrier and her farmer husband, who speaks English, will make your stay a very pleasant one, offering *apéritifs* in their sun lounge before an evening meal *en famille*. You will be sure of an elegantly set table and farm produce, with all drinks included. Already gaining four stars from Gîtes de France, this looks like a winner. Book ahead. I liked the room in the main house best. A new swimming pool makes this one doubly attractive.

VAUCLUSE

CRILLON-le-BRAVE 84410.
15km NE of Carpentras

A tiny hill village on the south side of Mt. Ventoux. The statue of Crillon stands supreme by the *mairie*. He was a captain of Henry IV, and the village, which dates back to Grecian times, was in his wife's dowry. His descendants founded the famous Hotel Crillon in Paris.

Down the hill in the valley 3 km S of Bedoin on the D974 –

Mme. Ricquart. 'Moulin d'Antelon'
category: (M)
tel: 04.90.62.44.89.
fax: 04.90.62.44.90.
email: horisudp@imaginet.fr
B&B: 59€ for two.
Evening meal 20.8€.

There are views of Mont Ventoux from this ancient flour mill, set in a garden of 8 hectares; it has a stream running through it towards a very large solar heated swimming pool, It has been sympathetically restored, with the mill wheel incorporated in the decor of the salon/dining room. Three guest rooms overlook a sheltered courtyard where breakfast is served in summer; two others in the main house have baths and one has an extra room for a family. Madame Ricquart and her daughter now run this well-appointed chambres d'hôtes.

There is a restaurant just a few yards along the road, the only other building near, but evening meals *en famille* are often possible. You'll enjoy the quiet luxury here and bask in the attention and welcome of your kindly hostesses. Prices vary according to season.

ENTRECHAUX. 84340.
6 km SE of Vaison-la-Romaine.

You are spoilt for choice with places of interest in this part of the Vaucluse. There are two routes round Mont Ventoux, one taking you over the top by the observatory. *Dégustations* at many points on the way. The Roman theatre remains at Vaison-la-Romaine are worth a visit.

Leave Vaison-la-Romaine by the D938 bypass. Take the first left, D75, to St. Marcellin then bear right (SP Entrechaux) and you will pass the Auberge d'Anais on your left, and soon afterwards the chambres d'hôtes is on your left, opposite the hill village of Entrechaux.

M. & Mme. Subiat. 'L'Esclériade'
Route de St. Marcellin.
category: (M)
tel: 04.90.46.01.32.
fax: 04.90.46.03.71.
B&B: 64/72€ for two.
Evening meal 24€. each.
Closed 15 Oct. to 15 Mar.

New owners here who are now offering evening meals, there is locked parking, but otherwise little change. I would be grateful for any feedback, as I haven't yet been able to meet them. The modern rooms are quite superb, with choice of bath or shower, walk-in wardrobes, private patios, every convenience. It would be difficult to find a house in a nicer position – on the side of the hill, southerly views over Mont Ventoux and a swimming pool nestling below the terrace. All quite perfect, designed by a previous owner.

GORDES. 84220.
25 km E of Avignon 30 km W of Apt.

The hill village of Gordes, where artists flocked in the 1930s, was partially destroyed by the Germans in the last war; it has been rebuilt and is now a Mecca for artisans, whose shops line the hilly, narrow streets. The château dominates the village, where in the square coach-loads of tourists arrive constantly; the most prevalent accent is American. On a hot day take refuge in the simple cool church. Nearby is a small village of *bories* – old circular stone huts looking like giant beehives; once lived in by shepherds, now restored – a great attraction.

For a chambres d'hôtes my preference was at St. Pantaléon down the hill.

From the N100 at Coustellet take the D2 (direction Gordes) and turn left on to the D148, past the church, 200m. on the left.

M. & Mme. Lawrence. 'Villa-la-Lebre'
Près de St. Pantaléon.
category: (M)
tel/fax: 04.90.72.20.74.
B&B: 44.5€ for two. No Dinner

Only just outside the village, on a hill, this new house has been built from stones of an adjacent ruined farmhouse, giving it a rustic appearance but with large modern windows and terraces. A *gîte* on the ground floor elevates rooms to the first floor level, giving very good views over the vineyards to Bonnieux.

One very comfortable guest room with a mezzanine for a third person, has a bath, bidet, and an extra dressing room, and opens on to the terrace. Carpeted and well-furnished, with souvenirs of your hosts' life in the East. There is even air-conditioning for summer or winter stays.

Now retired, the Lawrences, who speak English, will welcome you warmly and give you a very good breakfast in their dining room along the terrace. No evening meals, plenty of restaurants in Gordes, and an especially good one in Goult.

GOULT. 84220.
38 km SE of Avignon.

A good place to stay for visiting many of the historical and interesting villages in this area west of Apt. The tourist trade has driven prices sky-high so you will be glad to find a less costly resting place on the fringe of a nearby hamlet.

From the N100 at Lumières take the D106 right, SP Lacoste, over the bridge, then take the D218, SP Ménerbes and the house is 500m on the left.

☆ **M. & Mme. Chabaud. 'Mas Marican'**
category: (M)
tel/fax: 04.90.72.28.09.
B&B: 46.5€ for two.
Evening meal 12.5€ each.
Closed 1 Jan. to 11 Feb.

Easy to find this old Provençal farmhouse which Peter Mayle once used for his guests; it is on a large agricultural estate of maize and vegetables and has an enormous courtyard for parking. You will receive a very cheerful welcome from Madame if you book ahead and let her know when to expect you; she works in the local *Cave Co-opérative* during the afternoon, but the above phone number will always find her.

There are five neat rooms with sunny aspects, tiled floors, good lighting and central heating – four on the first floor, including a very nice family room, and one on the ground floor suitable for the handicapped. You will be offered *apéritifs* before a generous evening meal *en famille*, when the wine flows freely. Lively Madame keeps the conversation flowing and you will soon become part of the family and asking to stay an extra night. A ☆ for welcome, food and all-round comfort and the price is right.

LACOSTE. 84710
20 km SW of Apt. 21 km E of Cavaillon

Lacoste is a tiny hill village, with narrow cobbled streets, dominated by the Marquis de Sade's château, now a ruin.

From the N 100 at Lumières take the D106 to La Coste.

Relais Du Procureur
La Coste   84

Mme. Court de Gebelin & Son.
'Relais de Procureur'
Rue Basse.
category: (L)
tel: 04.90.75.82.28.
fax: 04.90.75.86.94.
B&B: 96€ for two.
Open all year, but by reservation only from Jan. to March.

A chambres d'hôtes which is much nicer than outside impressions led me to believe. Built into the hillside, there is no lack of character here.

On the ground floor is a small vaulted salon for breakfast in winter; but as you climb the balustraded stone stairs in various directions you will find five very interesting well-modernised rooms, central heating, carpets, telephones and luxury en suite facilities with baths, though some of these are up a few steps. Room prices vary according to size. One with two double beds would suit a family. The higher you go, the better the view, but often windows are small and you look first over roof tops. However, on the fourth floor there is a secluded terrace for summer breakfasts beside the small swimming pool, which is enclosed by three walls, rather like a Roman bath, but nevertheless very acceptable in midsummer. From the terrace a door opens on to an outside lane, giving easy access to the top floor rooms. When reserving ask for these if you don't want to climb a lot of stairs.

Madame speaks good English. No evening meals but M. Gebelin has opened a restaurant a few doors away where I am assured prices will be *correct* from 19€ for an evening meal. Off-loading by the chambres d'hôtes; but parking at various spots in the village might be a problem in the daytime. Expensive, but full of character.

SEGURET 84110
10 km SW of Vaison-la- Romaine, 25 km N of Carpentras.
A small village on the wine route at the foot of the Dentelles mountains.

Take the D977 west from Vaison La Romaine and in 5 km turn at cross roads on to the D88 to Seguret. The chambres d'hôtes is well signed from here.

Mme. Augier. 'Saint-Jean'
category: (L)
tel: 04.90.46.91.76.
fax: 0 4.90.46.83.88.
B&B: 78/92.5€ for two. No Dinner

One of the prettiest houses I have encountered, with bright blue shutters. It once belonged to the Benedictine monks and the private church is still situated in the grounds.

A choice of rooms – for three *Chambre Bleue*, consists of is two adjoining rooms, sharing a bathroom, has tiled floors and a whole white-painted tree-trunk spans the ceiling. Up a spiral staircase, a small pretty pink room, overlooking the front garden has wood floors and a Louis XV bed. A third garden room, in what once must have been the *orangerie*, is now divided into a family suite. The lighter front area has three single beds and leads to a two-bedded room and bathroom. Extra bed 17€. TV, fridges in all rooms and prices vary according to size.

Breakfast in an elegant dining room. You will need no lunch. A delightful pool in the garden where you can laze all day has a view of the Dentelles. There is a restaurant in the village, and many more 10 kms away in Vaison-La-Romaine.

Rhône-Alpes

RHÔNE-ALPES / RHÔNE VALLEY

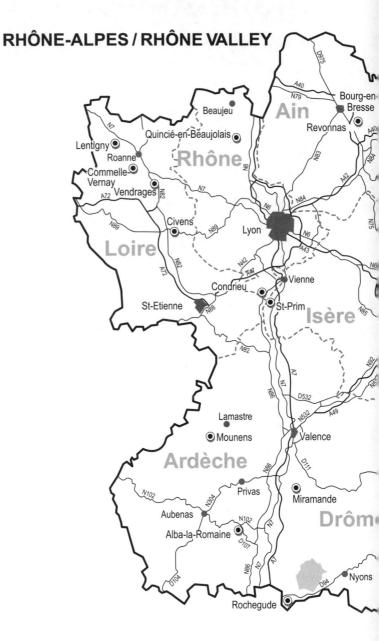

Town
◉ Chambres d'Hôtes
0 _____ 20km

Rhône-Alpes

Bordering on Switzerland in the east of France, this is the region with the highest mountains of France – the Alps, towered over by Mont Blanc (4807 metres).

There are two tourism seasons here; the longest is the winter ski season followed by a short spring in May, leading to the summer season.

The **Haute-Savoie** lies along the southern bank of Lac Léman and extends southwards into the mountains. Geneva in Switzerland takes nearly all the air traffic for this region, though the airport is actually at Ferney-Voltaire in France.

Drive down to Annecy and take the road to such places as Thônes and La Clusaz, then over the Col des Aravis to Megève, one of the oldest and most unspoilt ski resorts. Further east is Chamonix, the most famous name of all, a ski resort at the foot of Mont Blanc – pretty, crowded and expensive. In this direction further south are many purpose-built ski resorts such as La Plagne, packed and practical in winter but not always so attractive in summer. Stop a while in Annecy; nothing ever spoils this lovely old town situated on probably the most attractive lake in France – a chocolate-box picture at all times of the year.

Further south to **Savoie**, still mountainous; these two *départements* merge into each other. Visit the old Roman town of Aix-les-Bains on the longest lake in France, the Lac du Bourget. Chambéry is the *préfecture*.

South again is **Isère**, another mountainous département with skiing on high ground. Chartreuse, the liqueur, is produced in the mountains above Grenoble, which lies in a wide valley. This large university city, the *préfecture* of Isère, is bursting with commerce and traffic. Not easy to avoid if you wish to drive south, as the mountains are so high round it, but you can skirt the town and take the Route Napoléon N85 which takes you all the way to the Côte d'Azur. West, the autoroute 41 runs to the Rhône Valley.

ISÈRE

LES ABRETS. 38490.
30 km W of Chambéry.

From the A43 "Les Abrets" exit follow the signs to the town and to the chambres d'hôtes for 2 km.

Mme. Voifembert. 'La Bruyère'
category: (M-L)
tel: 04.76.32.01.66.
fax: 04.76.32.06.66,
email: carbone38@aol.com
B&B: 68.5/84€ for two.
No Dinner
Closed for 3 weeks in Nov.

Situated among fields and woods in a large garden, this old farmhouse, originally built in 1820, has had an unusual face-lift. Marble stairs now lead to six luxuriously furnished rooms in beautiful subtle colours; curtains and king-size beds are in matching materials. Separate bathrooms adjoin each room, some with smart corner baths, all with hair dryers. Luxurious thick carpets to step on and telephones by the bed. Two family rooms which extend across the second floor have convertible couches for children. Stay a few days and qualify for a bathrobe for your jaunt to the swimming pool.

A salon and dining room take up most of the ground floor with doors to the patio.

Breakfasts are copious. Do book ahead – such luxurious rooms attract the Parisians at all times of the year.

ST. PRIM. 38370.
40 Km S of Lyon. 10 km S of Vienne

Just across the bridge from Condrieu on the opposite side of the Rhône is St. Prim, Over the bridge turn immediately left and halfway up the hill is Pré Margot.

M. & Mme. Briot. 'Le Pré Margot'
Les Roches de Condrieu.
category: (S)
tel: 04.74.56.44.27.
fax: 04.74.56.30.93.
email: lamargotine@wanadoo.fr
website: wanadoo.fr/lamargotine
B&B: 41€ for two. Evening meals
14.5€ each.

A lovely situation on the hillside overlooking the river Rhône. An ever popular place to stay where the clientele return year after year. Prices have changed very little since I first visited years ago. All five rooms are modern, with TV, parquet floors and air conditioning. Pristine-clean, sanitised to suit the most fanatical. Flannels in sealed packets, to say nothing of plastic loo seat covers that move on at the touch of a button.

Strictly no smoking here. To emphasise this, there is a large ash tray fixed to the outside wall at the entrance. Had I been a smoker I should have felt compelled to empty all my packets of cigarettes into it!

The *pièce de résistance* is the enormous glassed-in veranda (full of tropical plants and gentle Muzak), which envelopes two sides of the house, all 80 feet of it, with a busy view of the river.

Evening meals, which include *apéritifs* but not wine, are perfectly served and cooked, by Madame. The food cannot be faulted. Everything, even the bread, as Madame expressly told us, was home-made. Perhaps this one is more like an English guest house than a true chambres d'hôtes, with Monsieur and Madame Briot as very pleasant patrons.

VILLARD DE LANS 38250.
30 km SW of Grenoble. A ski centre 1500m high.

This is quite a large town, with all commodities, but isolated. I am told it has the longest piste in Europe. Reached by the D531 from outside Grenoble or by the Gorge de la Bourne from Pont-en-Royans. The journey along the Gorge can be quite hazardous in wintry weather – snow, *chute-de-glaçons* (falling icicles), tunnels, etc., you name it.

Mme. Bon. 'Le Val Sainte-Marie'
Bois Barbu.
category: (M)
tel: 04.76.95.92.80.
B&B: 45.5€ for two.
Evening meals 14.5€ each.

Hotels seem to be more popular with serious skiers. Tired from the slopes, they don't often want to mix with strangers, but for anyone that does, this nice rustic farmhouse right beside the ski centre is 4 km outside Villard-le-Lans. It was quite the best I could find in this resort. Nicely situated on the mountainside, near the lifts, with a pleasant rustic lounge, a log fire, and excellent *accueil*. I couldn't see the rooms as all were occupied, which says something for its popularity. One of them has a velux window, they all have wood floors, beams and country decor with private facilities. An evening meal is also on offer at a reasonable price. I liked this one and would have stayed had it not been full. No smoking in the house. Book well ahead in the ski season.

SAVOIE

VIVIERS-DU-LAC. 73420.
2 Km S of Aix-les Bains On the D201 south.

Aix-les-Bains is a spa town on the longest lake in France; it was a favourite watering place of the Romans and is still a popular health resort in the modern world. Many people come to take the waters, which are said to cure rheumatism. The town, lying a little back from the lake, is busy and prosperous, with a good shopping arcade. The mountains tower above one side of the lake but there is a road right round. Mont Revard is to the east, and 2 km south is Viviers du Lac.

Mme. Montagnole.
516 Chemin de Boissy
Côteau de Boissy.
category: (S)
tel/fax: 04.79.35.31.26.
B&B: 35/38.5€ for two. No Dinner

A homely little chambres d'hôtes above the village, on a ridge between the Lac du Bourget and the N201. The Chemin de Boissy is a cul de sac on the north side of the village, not far from the church; stop and ask if you can't find it. No 516 is just opposite a vineyard on top of the ridge. Excellent views to Mont Revard, but only two minutes from the southern end of the Lac du Bourget.

The modern house, built into the hillside, has two rooms facing south, with patio doors on to a terrace, one double, one twin. A possible third room in the summer. No evening meals, but restaurants at 1km. Monsieur is a physiotherapist in Aix-les-Bains. Pleasant friendly hosts who join you for a chat and drinks on arrival.

HAUTE-SAVOIE

COPPONEX. 74350.
25 km S of Geneva. 20 km N of Annecy.

Very handy for visiting Geneva or Annecy, half-way between the two. Take the N201 from Annecy north to Cruseilles. In 2 km after the village take the D27 to Coppenex. Follow the signs to Châtillon after the cemetery.

M. & Mme. 'Gal. La Becassière'
Châtillon.
category: (M)
tel: 04.50.44.08.94.
B&B: 51€ for two. No Dinner
Closed 15 Nov. to 6 Feb.

A cheerful welcome here from jolly M. Gal and his wife. The old farmhouse is in the country and simple modern rooms have views, smart shower rooms with separate loos, and a choice of double or single beds. No longer evening meals. Restaurants nearby.

SAINT FÉLIX. 74540
A small village 12 km S of Annecy on the N201, renowned for its cheese, source of "La Vache qui Rit".

Just a kilometre out of the village in the hamlet of Mercy is the home of:

M. & Mme. Betts. 'Les Bruyères'
Mercy.
category: (L)
tel: 04.50.60.96.53.
fax: 04.50.60.94.65.
B&B: 112€ for two
Evening meals 36€ each.

Bernard and Denyse, on retiring from Canada, had always adored Annecy and after much searching in the area discovered this partly-converted farmhouse, once part of a large estate belonging to a *pied-noir* family (French returning from Algeria after independence). Situated on top of a hill, it looks down to a wooded bird sanctuary and has views both to the Jura and the Alps.

On the top floor the original hay-loft, with machinery, remains, but at one end of the house Bernard and Denyse have rebuilt the first floor, turning four small rooms into two luxurious suites for guests. Reached by a private external flight of steps, a colourful corridor leads first to *L'Albanaise*, a light and airy room freshly decorated in blue and white. Deep recessed windows hiding radiators overlook the front garden and tennis court. Sink into comfortable primrose armchairs while you look around at the elegantly-covered twin beds with matching *têtes de lits*, all made by Denyse. Ponder on the two doors, one a cupboard discreetly hiding a TV the other leading to a cute little 'powder room' with loo and wash basin, which complements a much larger modern shower room. Soft lights, restful prints and interesting pieces of carved furniture delight the eye. *L'Aixoise* suite at the rear of the house has warm red walls and matching decor, with a *tête de lit* and pretty floral bed cover. Thick carpets on polished wood floors, ample cupboard space, fresh flowers and plentiful reading material. This one has a brilliantly-lit bathroom, complete with bath and shower. Copious towels and toiletries dotted around.

In winter, breakfast, with freshly-squeezed orange juice, croissants and local breads just collected by Bernard, is elegantly served beside Napoleon's bust in the Betts' salon, partitioned from the dining room by a huge fireplace. In summer months the 'piggery', a more rustic room with a log fire and terrace, is used for meals.

Denyse, who writes cookery books, presents delicious dinners, including wine.

Parking is under cover, and a garage is available. Their full-time gardener keeps the *potager* and grounds in perfect order and fresh fruit and veg are delivered daily to the kitchen.

Your hosts, who are English and Canadian, will advise on places to visit in and around Annecy, produce picnics and even accompany you on occasions. Rooms don't come much more luxurious than these.

THORENS-GLIÈRES. 74570.
15km NE of Annecy.

From the A41 (sortie: Annecy Nord) take the N203 direction 'La Roche-sur-Foron'. In 15km turn right on to the D2 to Thorens-Glières, in 5 km go through the village and fork left in 800 metres to 'Plateau-des-Glières'. The house is signed on the left in Sales, where St Francis of Sales (1567-1622) the patron saint of writers, was born to a wealthy family in the château. He was ordained priest in 1593 and was distinguished for his service to the poor. He became Bishop of Geneva in 1602, and was canonised in 1665.

M. & Mme. Lavy
Hameau de Sales.
category: (S)
tel: 04.50.22.46.03.
B&B: 36.5€ for two.
Evening meals 14.5€ each.

Built in 1720 this farmhouse beside the road has a short drive, guarded by two goats and three chickens. You will receive a friendly welcome from M. or Mme. Lavy if their Yorkshire terrier doesn't make it first.

This is very much a family home. Two of the rooms on the first floor are for guests, with adjoining shower and loo. Both are carpeted and warmly heated. Walls throughout are drag-painted in bright pink and yellow colours and decorated with pretty flower frescos, particularly in the salon and kitchen where the four seasons are depicted.

Don't be deterred by the drum sets filling the entrance hall, played by their teenage son. The Lavys are a energetic family. Monsieur is an interior designer working in many countries, Madame makes curtains in her *atelier* but still finds time to entertain her guests and cook interesting Savoyard evening meals shared by all and accompanied by a drum recital – but only if requested.

Any noise of traffic is muted by double-glazing, but little passes at night. Freshly squeezed orange juice for breakfast, home-made cakes and jams and a *flûte* of fresh bread will set you up for the day.

No need to struggle in French here, Madame Lavy has spent some time in London as an 'au pair' and speaks English quite well.

Rhône Valley

RHÔNE-ALPES / RHÔNE VALLEY

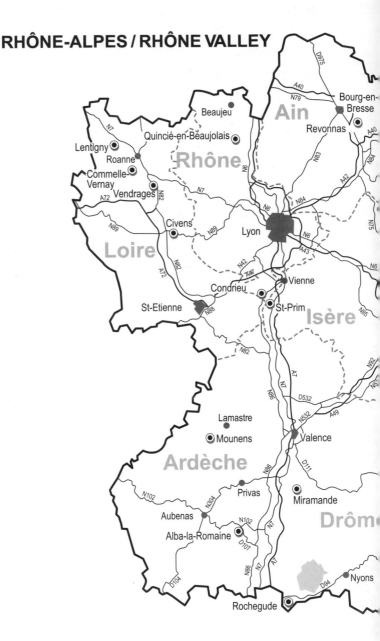

Town

Chambres d'Hôtes

0 —— 20km

Rhône Valley

To most people the Rhône Valley just seems to be one giant passageway from Lyon to Marseille, carrying roads and railways and dominated by the large river Rhône, but there is more to it. There are five very different *départements:* the Ain, Rhône and the Loire in the north, the Drôme and the Ardèche in the south.

Ain lies in the north-east of the region, sheltered by the mountain ranges of Franche-Comté. In the south it is bordered by the river Rhône. In the south west a low lying area is dotted with small lakes, bordering the river Saône. In summer the villages are bedecked with flowers, tier upon tier almost burying the cottages. Bourg-en-Bresse, the *préfecture*, which gives its name to the cheese *bresse bleu* and the succulent dish *poulet de Bresse*, has a compact shopping centre, but is especially noted for a famous monastery at Brou on the edge of the town.

Continuing west, the river Rhône passes through Lyon, the second largest town in France, and flows on through the **Rhône** *département*. The whole of this *département* is given over to the wine trade, notably the Beaujolais in the north and the Côtes-du-Rhône in the south.

The *Autoroute du Soleil*, the main route south from Paris to Marseille, comes through this valley with vineyards on every available slope. The climate is mild in winter except when the *Mistral* funnels down the valley, but in summer it can be very hot.

Further west is the department of **Loire**, taking its name from the upper reaches of this long river. Attractive hilly farming countryside. Use this as an alternative route for that long journey south, not so busy as the A6/A7 round Lyon and a much more pleasant run from Nevers past Roanne to St. Etienne on the N82, further south the road joins the river Rhône, where railways run parallel on both banks.

The southerly *départements* of this region are totally different. The **Drôme** in the east, is still fairly high, descending from the Alps. One interesting part is at Valréas where a small area belongs to the Vaucluse. In 1317 the Papacy was at Avignon in the Vaucluse and Pope John XXII bought the land round Valréas to extend his territory. Later he bought Richerenches (now a big truffle market) and Grillons; but at the end of the 18th century, when all new boundaries were established, the people of Valréas were offered the choice of living in the Drôme or staying with the Vaucluse. They opted for the latter and to this day a small piece of land surrounded by the Drôme still belongs to the Vaucluse.

On the right bank of the Rhône is the **Ardèche**. Turn up into the high rugged cliffs into a different world – probably the wildest area of France. Isolated farmsteads crop up in most unexpected places: no town planners have been round here! The main roads are good, but the smaller ones can be very narrow. Occasionally you run into high, flat areas in the south with rather pleasant little villages, giving strong reminders of the Roman occupation. The small hilly town of Privas is in the centre and a road runs across the *département* from here, the D102 on a high ridge; marvellous views on both sides and many small lanes lead off to hidden hamlets where there is sometimes a chambres d'hôtes. A lovely place for getting away from it all. Gorges and rivers, plenty of scope for canoeists and many holiday camp sites. High up in the Ardèche, on the D102, is the watershed for the Atlantic and the Mediterranean, and close by the source of the Loire. Wild flowers abound; in May the *genêt* (broom) covers all the hillsides, interspersed with tiny daffodils and narcissi. A walker's paradise. If you like it rough, rugged and rural choose the Ardèche; it has it all.

AIN

CHALLEX. 01630
6 km W of Geneva.

From Ferney-Voltaire take the D35 south. Join the D984 after St. Genis Pouilly. In 8 km turn left to Challex, then first right to Mucelle, a tiny hamlet where the house is on the road on the right.

M. & Mme. Dallemagne.
category: (S)
tel: 04. 50.56.31.30.
B&B: 38.5€ for two.
Evening meal 12.5€ each.

One of those nights when nothing goes right, thinking we would find a bed easily at Sergy, we hadn't reckoned with the Paris school holidays, and the international motor show in Geneva. After circling aimlessly around, we threw ourselves on the mercy of Mme. Moine at Sergy when she had finished her milking, knowing already her chambres d'hôtes was full. She immediately rang a friend at Challex and found us a bed for the night and M. Moine insisted on leading us halfway there.

Monsieur Dallemagne, the present Mayor of Challex was waiting outside the old farmhouse for us when we arrived and after installing us in a room led us to the Auberge Savoyarde at Pougny where he had previously booked a table (the Challex restaurant was closed). We were treated like royalty, given a table by a log fire and a five-course meal for 15.5 including wine.

Simple, sincere hospitality in this chambres d'hôtes. Rooms are as basic as they come, with skylight windows, but warm and carpeted and you will be spoilt by the kindly owners.

The first floor is assigned to guests. One suite of two rooms for a family has a private but not adjoining shower room with dual washbasins, the other has a double bed and shower but the private loo is on the landing; both share a large kitchen for self-catering. A comfortable sitting area on the landing has a desk with good lighting, and books and games. Best of all, if you are dining in, Mme. Dallemagne waltzes up to join you, clutching a tray of *apéritifs* before the evening meal, which is very reasonable with wine *compris*. If preferred, there is a Michelin-starred restaurant in Challex (closed on Mondays).

Breakfast here would put most hotels to shame – cereal, cheese, fruit, yoghurt and fresh baguettes, home-made jams and huge jugs of piping hot coffee and milk. Great value for your francs.

REVONNAS. 01250. CEYZERIAT
10 km SE of Bourg-en-Bresse.

Close to Bourg-en-Bresse, the *préfecture* of Ain, noted for its cheese and chicken dishes. It is a busy, interesting city with a good ring road, on which you will find the famous Église-de-Brou well signed. Founded on the site of an old priory by Marguerite of Austria early in the 16th century, in memory of her husband Philibert Le Beau, the Duke of Savoy, it is the only monastery in France to have three cloisters. No sooner had she commissioned the church, than her brother died and she became Regent of Holland and had to leave Bresse. The building went ahead as planned, but unfortunately she died in 1530, six years before completion, and her body was brought to Bresse two years later to be buried at Brou. The nave is simple and unadorned contrasting with the chancel behind the rood screen where lie the ornate tombs of Marguerite, Philibert and her mother-in-law, Marguerite of Anjou. Do visit the monks' comfortable cells on the first floor, some furnished. Wander round the cloisters, the one beside the refectory has the well in the centre of it.

Take the D979 from the by-pass at Brou SP 'Ceyzériat' then the D52 to Journans for 2 km and the house is on the left, or from A40 exit 7 and take the signs to Montagnat-Revonnas. Through the village on the D52.

M. & Mme. Assier de Pompignan.
'Grillerin'
category: (S-M)
tel: 04.74.30.02.68.
B&B: 48/56€ for two
Evening meal 16€ each.

Iron railings and pedestal gate posts lead to this faded pink mansion flanked by two stable blocks, occupied, by monks in the 18th century. The de Pompignans bought it many years ago, a great change from working in Paris. The large rear lawn is dotted with wild flowers in March.

Genteel Mme. de Pompignan offered us a room and evening meal late one afternoon, after a short drive from *l'Église* at Brou. Little has changed since this house was built in the 17th century. An original stone passage leads to a room for three on the ground floor which stretches the width of the house, with handy access to one's car outside. Old books line one wall, dual brass lamps hang from the ceiling, dark blue moquette walls tone with tapestry bed covers, there are plentiful well polished chairs, and even a piano. The writing table has real inkwells, and a pale blue carpet takes the chill off the terra-cotta floor. The adjoining shower room is down one step, converted, I would guess, from a possible cloakroom.

Other rooms on the first floor are smaller. Your hosts entertain you well over a sustaining evening meal, wine included. Plenty of interesting history to be researched here. Madame believes she may be related to our royal family as she is descended from the Brunswick line.

SERGY. 01630.
10 km W of Geneva.

Just west of Geneva under the Mont Jura is the peaceful little backwater of Sergy, one of the many tiny villages which dot the D89. It's a straggly village with old and new houses and farms all mixed up. Little vegetable gardens come right up to the roadside. A bus or train ferry service runs directly from Sergy to Geneva, saving all the hassle of driving and parking in that city.

Mme. Moine. 'La Forge'
Chemin de la Charrière.
category: (S)
tel: 04.50.42.18.03.
fax: 04.50.42. 11.34.
B&B: 35€ for two.
Evening meal 11.2€ each.

No shops in this village. Make for the Chemin de la Charrière just behind the *Logis* and beware of running over ducks; it is more of a farmyard than a through road, Mme. Moine's house is the second on the right.

The original chambres d'hôtes down the road is now for long-staying guests. The newly-built *La Forge* opposite the farmhouse has four guest rooms. Light and sunny rooms with central heating, self-contained with a kitchen corner. First floor rooms have small balconies, simple but practical, these are popular year round. Children welcome, cots supplied. Book well ahead.

Mme. Moine, a busy farmer's wife, is so obliging and friendly, and speaks more English every time I see her. There is now an evening meal ¼ *vin compris*. Excellent value, close to one of the busiest cities in Europe.

ARDÈCHE

ALBA-LA-ROMAINE. 07400.
15km W of Montélimar.

Turn off the N86 at le Teil near Montélimar on to the N102.

Climbing up into the Ardèche mountains the scene changes dramatically; the old houses made of small round stones are dotted sporadically around the countryside. Good, fast, winding roads bring you to Alba-la-Romaine just off the N102. An attractive little village, surprisingly lively and sporting many old Roman ruins, including a well-preserved little theatre only 1 km from the village. No turnstiles here; you can park beside it and even picnic on the theatre seats. The village has shops, restaurants and is not far from the much-photographed Gorges-de-l'Ardèche.

M. & Mme. Arlaud. 'Le Jeu du Mail'
category: (M)
tel/fax: 04.75.52.41.59:
email: lejeudumail@free.fr
B&B: 48/59€ for two. No Dinner

Down a cul de sac leading to the cemetery only 100 metres from the village centre is a large old family house with three guest rooms for two and a couple of adjoining rooms for a family, all with private facilities. No evening meal, but restaurants within walking distance. There is a garden kitchen for guests to use in summer by the pool.

Ex air-hostess Mme. Arlaud speaks perfect English and knows how to pamper her guests. You will want to stay here more than one night – so many places to visit.

M. Arlaud makes his own wine, calling it 'Le Jeu du Mail', like their house, after a ball game played in the Middle Ages.

LAMASTRE . 07270.
5 km S of Lamastre. 30 km W of Valence.

Take the D578 from Lamastre towards Le Cheyland. In 5 km at Lapras turn left just after the end of the village up a small hill to Mounens. Well signed in the hamlet.

M. & Mme. Moncuit-Dejour
Mounens
category: (M)
tel: 04.75.06.47.59.
email: max.dejour@wanadoo.fr
website: www.perso.wanadoo.fr/
mounens/index.htm
B&B: 59/62.5€ for two.
Evening meals 19€ each.
Closed 11 Nov. to 30 Apr.

566 metres high in the Haut Viverais of the Ardèche, this 18th century farmhouse has been in the family for many years. Once the grange was for the animals below and the hay above, but now there are two very pleasant rustic guest rooms above, each with a mezzanine for two children, and private facilities with baths, fully carpeted and electrically heated. Below is a pleasant salon where meals are prepared by Madame, and eaten on the terrace overlooking the pool in summer. A third room on the first floor of the main house across the garden has a double bed and bunks for children. A startlingly bright green carpet adorns the large shower room. This really is a pleasant rural place to stay for a few days and well worth the price. Wine is included in the evening meals, which are cooked by Madame who is renowned for her menus of local specialities.

Book ahead – could be busy in summer.

DRÔME

MIRMANDE. 26270.
20 km from Montélimar.

From the A7 sortie Loriol-sur-Drôme, take the N 304 to the N7 SP Montélimar, in about 7 km turn on to the D204 at Saulce-sur-Rhône to Mirmande. The chambres d'hôtes is through the village, bearing right. Recommended by a reader who enjoyed his stay here.

M. & Mme. Goriou.
category: (M)
tel: 04.75.63.01.15.
fax: 04.75.63.14.06.
B&B: 48€ for two. No Dinner
Closed January.

The Goriou's bought this establishment as a ruin and have gradually built a very interesting home, tucked away on the hillside but still within walking distance of the village. Monsieur is a sculptor and much of his work is dotted about the garden.

Two rooms have been built on the first floor of a separate wing overlooking a secluded swimming pool. One large room has two single beds; another has a double bed, and both have very nice modern showers. The double room is smaller but has a terrace. Electric heating, original quarry-tiled floors, pretty *provençale* covers and curtains and TV in both. Breakfast is taken in a very pleasant corner of your hosts' dining room with a vast window overlooking the garden. No evening meals. The village at hand.

Loire

The Loire department, not to be confused with the Loire Valley region, is part of the Rhône Valley. It lies as a narrow wedge south of Burgundy and east of the Auvergne, and is so-called because the river Loire flows north right through the middle, wending its way from its source in the Ardèche. As soon as you enter this *département,* skirting the large town of Roanne in the north, the landscape changes: really high hills and pitched valleys make it quite picturesque. This part of the Loire has its own elegant Château-de-la-Roche, almost an island, dating from the 13th century, and finally restored at the beginning of this century. Wonderful sightseeing tours and walks, ancient villages and churches, without having to drive too far each day. It is an attractive area not often penetrated by the British.

COMMELLE-VERNAY 42120
3 km SW of Roanne.

Roanne, on the banks of the upper part of the Loire is one of those tucked away towns that only come to light when travelling a *Bis* route to the south of France. Just a few kms outside is this surprisingly lovely place to stay.

M. & Mme. Noirard. 'Château de Bachelard'
category: (L)
tel: 04.77.71.93.67.
fax: 04.77.78.10.20.
email: Bachelard@worldonline.fr
B&B: 88.42€ for two. Suite for 6 is 213€
Evening meals 23€. each

What a find! Great gates from the driveway lead to locked parking for this 17th century château which has been superbly renovated between 1957 and 1988 when it was inherited by M. Noirard from his father. The rooms have been elegantly decorated with great charm by chic little Madame Noirard.

Prepare to meet a life sized tiger in the entrance hall. The large dining room has enormous patio doors to the terrace an equally large swimming pool, and plentiful luxury armchairs in the adjoining lounge.

Worn stone stairs in the tower lead to five luxurious bedrooms, adjoining bathrooms or shower rooms contain all necessary toiletries. One family suite in a private corridor has two bathrooms and four single beds in a large yellow room plus a double room for parents in warm red colours which overlooks the pool. The blue and orange rooms are spacious, but the smaller green room with its own salon is exceptionally pretty with walls artistically decorated by Madame. A choice of rooms would be difficult here, come back again and again and try them all.

A small cosy bar with fireplace is used for winter breakfasts.

16 hectares of land include a lake and paths to ramble round almost on the banks of the Loire.

Evening meals contain vegetables from the *potager* all cooked by your most accommodating young hosts, wine and coffee included in the deal. Prices are very reasonable for such luxury.

LENTIGNY 42155
8 km W of Roanne

Mme. Gaume. 'Domaine de Champfleury'.
category: (M)
tel: 04.77. 63. 31. 43
B&B: 63€. for two

The proximity to the tiny village centre, containing all necessities, makes this an exceptionally useful place to rest awhile. The solid little *Maison de Maître* is charmingly furnished to complement the year it was built, 1866, and gentille Mme. Gaume is the perfect hostess for such a place. The long drive and large garden with tennis court cut off all noise from the village.

There are two rooms, one for two with a luxury shower room is furnished with repro. Louis XV among genuine antiques and overlooks the well-manicured rear lawn and flower beds. A family suite for three divided by a charmingly tiled bathroom with claw-footed bath has a small double in the a children's room. The stables is being converted into a gîte.

No need for evening meals as the village has a restaurant within easy walking distance, or Roanne is close by for greater variety.

VENDRANGES 42590
14 km S of Roanne

From the N82, south of Roanne, turn right at Vendranges on to the D42 to Saint-Priest-la-Roche and in 1km you will see a farmhouse on the right in a dip with its own lakes. (There is another chambres d'hôtes in the vicinity, so make sure it is the *Ferme de Montissut.)*

☆ M. & Mme. Deloire. 'Ferme de Montissut'
category: (S)
tel: 04.77.64.90.96.
B&B: 36.5€ for two.
Evening meal 12€ each.

A charming welcome to this dairy farm from Madame, a busy farmer's wife. Two rooms each have an adjoining room for two children, cosy and prettily furnished with duvets and fresh flowery wallpaper. The whole house has warm central heating in winter and is immaculately kept.

Evening meals, not obligatory, are well presented country-fare with all drinks *compris*. You may picnic in the garden in summer if you have a family and need to budget more tightly.

A really delightful place. Even at the end of November I found this a most comfortable refuge. Children will enjoy watching the milking in the pristine parlour beside the house. A ☆ for such pretty rooms and all round comfort, again at such good prices

RHÔNE

CONDRIEU 69420
40 km S of Lyon. On the N86 13km S of Vienne.

South of Lyon at le Rosay, high up above Condrieu on the west bank of the Rhône. Take the Rosay road out of Condrieu by the *Mairie*, climb the winding hill and in about 2 km at the top, the sign is on the left.

Cote de Chatillon

Mme. Font. 'Côte Châtillon'
category: (S-M)
tel: 04.74.87.88.27.
B&B: 43€ for two.

The view from this house is breath-taking. Far below the busy river Rhône wends its way south. Hospitable little Mme. Font has three rooms on the first floor. Two adjoining share a shower room, have superb views and are well heated for winter months, another without the view is for two. Breakfast in summer served on the terrace would be a real treat. Highly recommend, especially for situation.

QUINCIÉ-en-BEAUJOLAIS. 69430.
33 km SW of Macon. 19 km NW of Villefranche-sur-Saône.

This is Beaujolais land with a vengeance. Not a field escapes the vines, however hilly.

From Macon take the A6 south to Belleville, then the D37 towards Beaujeu, in about 12 km take the D9 left through the village of Quincié and you will pick up signs to 'Romarand', which lies 3 km the other side of the village.

Quincié-en-Beaujolais

M. & Mme. Berthelot. 'Domaine de Romarand'
category: (M)
tel/fax: 04.74.04.34.49.
B&B: 48/52€ for two.
Evening meal 16/19€ each.

High above the village, among the sloping vineyards, this extensive old farmhouse has three modernised rooms in the first-floor granary wing, but the entrance through the salon is level with the garden behind where there is an inviting swimming pool on a sheltered terrace. Locked parking is behind gates in front of the house.

A charming friendly welcome from Madame, who was busy in the garden when we arrived, but not too busy to give us tea and home-made cakes. We enjoyed an evening meal with both Monsieur and Madame: egg salad from the garden, sausage and new potatoes, cheese and a wonderful orange tart – all washed down with Beaujolais of various vintages, one from vines which are over 125 years old! Well worth the long drive up the hill to find this place.

Over dinner Monsieur Berthelot, who is a true *Vigneron*, selling his wine privately all over France, explained the difference between a *'Viticulteur'* and a *'Vigneron'*. The former cultivates and harvests the grapes then sends them off to a *'Coopérative'* to be made into wine, the latter makes his own at home, bottles and sells it himself.

Wines and spirits
by John Doxat

Bonne cuisine et bons vins, c'est le paradis sur terre.
(Good cooking and good wines, that is earthly paradise.)
KING HENRI IV

Outline of French wine regions

Bordeaux
Divided into a score of districts, and sub-divided into very many communes (parishes). The big district names are Médoc, St Emilion, Pomerol, Graves and Sauternes. Prices for the great reds (châteaux Pétrus, Mouton-Rothschild, etc.) or the finest sweet whites (especially the miraculous Yquem) have become stratospheric. Yet 'château' in itself means little and the classification of various rankings of châteaux is not easily understood. Some tiny vineyards are entitled to be called château, which has led to disputes about what have been dubbed 'phantom châteaux'. Visitors are advised, unless wine-wise, to stick to the simpler designations.

Bourgogne (Burgundy)
Topographically a large region, stretching from Chablis (on the east end of the Loire), noted for its steely dry whites, to Lyons. It is particularly associated with fairly powerful red wines and very dry whites, which tend to acidity except for the costlier styles. Almost to Bordeaux excesses, the prices for really top Burgundies have gone through the roof. For value, stick to simpler local wines.
Technically Burgundies, but often separately listed, are the Beaujolais wines. The young red Beaujolais (not necessarily the over-publicised nouveau) are delicious when mildly chilled. There are several rather neglected Beaujolais wines (Moulin-à-Vent, Morgon, St Amour, for instance) that improve for several years: they represent good value as a rule. The Mâconnais and Chalonnais also produce sound Burgundies (red and white) that are usually priced within reason.

Rhône
Continuation south of Burgundy. The Rhône is particularly associated with very robust reds, notably Châteauneuf-du-Pape; also Tavel, to my mind the finest of all still rosé wines. Lirac rosé is nearly as good. Hermitage and Gigondas are names to respect for reds, whites and rosés. Rhône has well earned its modern reputation – no longer Burgundy's poorer brother. From the extreme south comes the newly 'smart' dessert vin doux naturel, ultrasweet Muscat des Beaumes-de-Venise, once despised by British wine-drinkers. There are fashions in wine just like anything else.

Alsace

Producer of attractive, light white wines, mostly medium-dry, widely used as carafe wines in middle-range French restaurants. Alsace wines are not greatly appreciated overseas and thus remain comparatively inexpensive for their quality; they are well placed to compete with popular German varieties. Alsace wines are designated by grape – principally Sylvaner for lightest styles, the widespread and reliable Riesling for a large part of the total, and Gerwürtztraminer for slightly fruitier wines.

Loire

Prolific producer of very reliable, if rarely great, white wines, notably Muscadet, Sancerre, Anjou (its rosé is famous), Vouvray (sparkling and semi-sparkling), and Saumur (particularly its 'champagne styles'). Touraine makes excellent whites and also reds of some distinction – Bourgueil and Chinon. It used to be widely believed – a rumour put out by rivals? – that Loire wines 'did not travel': nonsense. They are a successful export.

Champagne

So important is Champagne that, alone of French wines, it carries no AC: its name is sufficient guarantee. (It shares this distinction with the brandies Cognac and Armagnac.) Vintage Champagnes from the grandes marques – a limited number of 'great brands' – tend to be as expensive in France as in Britain. You can find unknown brands of high quality (often off-shoots of grandes marques) at attractive prices, especially in the Champagne country itself. However, you need information to discover these, and there are true Champagnes for the home market that are doux (sweet) or demi-sec (medium sweet) that are pleasing to few non-French tastes. Champagne is very closely controlled as to region, quantities, grape types, and is made only by secondary fermentation in the bottle. From 1993, it is prohibited (under EU law) to state that other wines are made by the 'champagne method' – even if they are.

Minor regions (very briefly)

Jura – Virtually unknown outside France. Try local speciality wines such as vin jaune if in the region.

Jurançon – Remote area; sound, unimportant white wines, sweet styles being the better.

Cahors – Noted for its powerful vin de pays 'black wine', darkest red made.

Gaillac – Little known; once celebrated for dessert wines.

Savoy – Good enough table wines for local consumption. Best product of the region is delicious Chambéry vermouth: as an aperitif, do try the well distributed Chambéryzette, a unique vermouth with a hint of wild strawberries.

Bergerac – Attractive basic reds; also sweet Monbazillac, relished in France but not easily obtained outside: aged examples can be superb.

Provence – Large wine region of immense antiquity. Many and varied vins de pays of little distinction. Best known for rosé, usually on the sweet side; all inexpensive and totally drinkable.

Midi – Stretches from Marseilles to the Spanish border. Outstandingly prolific contributor to the 'EU wine lake' and producer of some 80 per cent of French vins de table, white and red. Sweet whites dominate, and there is major production of vins doux naturels (fortified sugary wines).

Corsica – Roughish wines of more antiquity than breeding, but by all means drink local reds – and try the wine-based aperitif Cap Corse – if visiting this remarkable island.

Paris – Yes, there is a vineyard – in Montmartre! Don't ask for a bottle: the tiny production is sold by auction, for charity, to rich collectors of curiosities.

Hints on spirits

The great French spirit is brandy. Cognac, commercially the leader, must come from the closely controlled region of that name. Of various quality designations, the commonest is VSOP (very special old pale): it will be a cognac worth drinking neat. Remember, champagne in a cognac connotation has absolutely no connection with the wine. It is a topographical term, grande champagne being the most prestigious cognac area: fine champagne is a blend of brandy from the two top cognac sub-divisions. Armagnac has become better known lately outside France, and rightly so. As a brandy it has a much longer history than cognac: some connoisseurs rate old armagnac (the quality designations are roughly similar) above cognac.

Be cautious of French brandy without a cognac or armagnac title, regardless of how many meaningless 'stars' the label carries or even the magic word 'Napoleon' (which has no legal significance).

Little appreciated in Britain is the splendid 'apple brandy', Calvados, mainly associated with Normandy but also made in Brittany and the Marne. The best is Calvados du Pays d'Auge. Do taste well-aged Calvados, but avoid any suspiciously cheap.

Contrary to popular belief, true Calvados is not distilled from cider – but an inferior imitation is: French cider (cidre) is excellent.

Though most French proprietary aperitifs, like Dubonnet, are fairly low in alcohol, the extremely popular Pernod/Ricard pastis-style brands are highly spirituous. Eau-de-vie is the generic term for all spirits, but colloquially tends to refer to local, often rough, distillates. Exceptions are the better alcools blancs (white spirits), which are not inexpensive, made from fresh fruits and not sweetened as crèmes are.

Bringing back those bottles

When thinking of what to bring back from France in the way of wines and spirits, apart from considerations of weight and bulk, there are a few other matters to bear in mind. Within the theoretically unlimited import for personal consumption of products which have paid any national taxes in the country of origin, there are manifest practical as well as some semi-official restrictions.

Wine: to choose sensibly is not inevitably to go for the least expensive. Unless you envisage having to entertain a lot of relatives, beware the very cheapest of French table wines! Though France produces many of the world's greatest, her prolific vineyards also make wines to which no British supermarket would allocate shelf-space. Quality does count along with value. Primarily what you are saving by purchasing in France is the comparatively high excise duties imposed in Britain against the minimal ones in France. However, the British tax is just the same on a bottle of the most ordinary vin ordinaire as on the rarest of vintage claret. When it comes to the latter, buying fine vintage wines in France does not automatically mean obtaining a bargain, unless you are an expert. There are not that many specialist wine merchants in France, a commerce in which Britain excels.

To summarise: it is undoubtedly sound, middle range wines that are the most sensible buy.

If you like those famous liqueurs, such as Bénédictine, Chartreuse, the versatile Cointreau, which are so expensive in Britain, shop around for them: prices seem to vary markedly.

I have briefly dealt elsewhere with French spirits. If you are buying Scotch whisky, gin or vodka, you may find unfamiliar names and labels offering apparent bargains. None will harm you but some may have low, even unpleasant, taste characteristics. It is worth paying a trifle more for well-known brands, especially de-luxe styles. Though they are little sold in Britain, former French colonies distill several excellent types of rum (rhum).

I deem it a good idea to make an outline list of intended purchases, after deciding what you can carry and how much you wish to spend. As to wines, do you want mainly red, or only white, or what proportion of both types? Can you afford champagne? Best to buy that in visiting the region where you should have the opportunity to taste and possibly find a bargain. What about other sparklers? What do you require in dessert wines, vermouths, liqueurs, spirits? Does your list work out at more cases (12 bottles) than you can easily transport? A conspicuously overloaded vehicle may be stopped by police as a traffic hazard. Now you have a list of sorts. What about cost? For essential comparisons, I would put against each item the maximum (per bottle) I would be prepared to pay in Britain.

Basic glossary of French wine terms

Alsace – See Wine Regions (page 417)

Abricotine – Generic apricot liqueur: look for known brands.

Alcool blanc – Spirit distilled from various fruits (not wine); not fruit-flavoured cordials.

Aligoté – Light dry Burgundy.

Anis – Aniseed, much favoured in pastis (Ricard/Pernod) type aperitifs.

Anjou – See Loire, Wine Regions (page 417)

Aperitif – Literally 'opener': any drink taken as an appetiser.

Appellation (d'origine) Contrôllée – or AC wine, whose label will give you a good deal of information, will usually be costlier – but not necessarily better – than one that is a VDQS 'designated (regional) wine of superior quality'. A newer, marginally lesser category is VQPRD: 'quality wine from a specified district'. Hundreds of wines bear AC descriptions: you require knowledge and/or a wine guide to find your way around. The intention of the AC laws was to protect consumers and ensure wine was not falsely labelled – and also to prevent over-production. Only wines of reasonable standards should achieve AC status: new ones (some rather suspect) are being regularly admitted to the list.

Armagnac – See Hints on Spirits (page 418)

Barsac – Very sweet Sauternes of varying quality.

Basserau – A bit of an oddity: sparkling red Burgundy.

Beaumes-de-Venise – Well-known vin doux naturel; see Provence, Minor Regions (page 417)

Beaune – Famed red Burgundy; costly.

Bergerac – Sound red wine from south-west France.

Blanc de Blancs – White wine from white grapes alone. Sometimes confers extra quality but by no means always. White wine made from black grapes (the skins removed before fermentation) is Blanc de Noirs – Carries no special quality connotation in itself.

Bordeaux – See Wine Regions (page 416).

Bourgeuil – Reliable red Loire wine.

Bourgogne – Burgundy; see Wine Regions (page 416).

Brut – Very dry; description particularly applicable to best sparkling wines.

Brut Sauvage – Dry to the point of displeasing acidness to most palates; very rare though a few good wines carry the description.

Cabernet – Noble grape, especially Cabernet-Sauvignon for excellent, if not absolutely top grade, red wines.

Cacao – Cocoa; basis of a popular crème.

Calvados – See Hints on Spirits (page 418).

Cassis – Blackcurrant; notably in crème de cassis (see Kir).

Cave – Cellar.

Cépage – Indicates grape variety; e.g. Cépage Cabernet-Sauvignon.

Chablis – See Burgundy, Wine Regions (page 416). Fine Chablis are expensive.

Chai – Ground-level storehouse, wholly employed in Cognac and sometimes in Bordeaux and other districts.

Champagne – See Wine Regions (page 417). Also specialty note Méthode Traditionelle below.

Château(x) – See Wine Regions, Bordeaux (page 417).

Châteaneuf-du-Pape – Best known of powerful Rhône red wines.

Chenin-blanc – Grape variety associated with many fine Loire wines.

Clairet – Unimportant Bordeaux wine, its distinction being probable origin of English word Claret.

Clos – Mainly a Burgundian term for a vineyard formerly (rarely now) enclosed by a wall.

Cognac – See Hints on Spirits (page 418).

Corbières – Usually a sound south of France red wine.

Côte – Indicates vineyard on a hillside; no quality connotation necessarily.

Côteau(x) – Much the same as above.

Crème – Many sweet, sometimes sickly, mildly alcoholic cordials with many local specialities. Nearer to true liqueurs are top makes of crème de menthe and crème de Grand Marnier (q.v.). Crème de Cassis is mixed with white wine to produce kir or a sparkling white wine to produce kir royale.

Crémant – Sparkling wine with strong but rather brief effervescence.

Cru – Literally 'growth'; somewhat complicated and occasionally misleading term: e.g. grand cru may be only grower's estimation; cru classé just means the wine is officially recognised, but grand cru classé is most likely to be something special.

Cuve close – Literally 'sealed vat'. Describes production of sparkling wines by bulk as opposed to individual bottle fermentation. Can produce satisfactory wines and certainly much superior to cheap carbonated styles.

Cuvée – Should mean unblended wine from single vat, but cuvée spéciale may not be particularly special: only taste will tell.

Demi-sec – Linguistically misleading, as it does not mean 'half-dry' but 'medium sweet'.

Domaine – Broadly, Burgundian equivalent to Bordeaux château.

Doux – Very sweet.

Eau-de-vie – Generic term for all distilled spirits but usually only applied in practice to roughish marc (q.v.) and the like.

Entre-deux-Mers – Undistinguished but fairly popular white Bordeaux.

Frappé – Drink served with crushed ice; viz. crème de menthe frappée.

Fleurie – One of several superior Beaujolais wines.

Glacé – Drink chilled by immersion of bottle in ice or in refrigerator, as distinct from frappé above.

Goût – Taste; also colloquial term in some regions for local eau-de-vie (q.v.).

Grand Marnier – Distinguished orange-flavoured liqueur. See also crème.

Haut – 'High'. It indicates upper part of wine district, not necessarily the best, though Haut-Médoc produces much better wines than other areas.

Hermitage – Several excellent Rhône red wines carry this title.

Izarra – Ancient Armagnac-based liqueur much favoured by its Basque originators.

Juliénas – Notable Beaujolais wine.

Kir – Well-chilled dry white wine (should be Bourgogne Aligoté) plus a teaspoon of crème de cassis (q.v.). Made with champagne (or good dry sparkling wine) it is Kir Royal.

Liqueur – From old liqueur de dessert, denoting postprandial digestive. Always very sweet.

'Liqueur' has become misused as indication of superior quality: to speak of 'liqueur cognac' is contradictory – yet some very fine true liqueurs are based on cognac.

Loire – See Wine Regions (page 417).

Méthode Traditionnelle – Most widely-used description of superior sparkling wine made as is champagne, by fermentation in bottle, now that any labelling association such as 'champagne method' is banned.

Marc – Mostly coarse distillations from wine residue with strong local popularity. A few marcs ('mar') – de Champagne, de Bourgogne especially – have achieved a certain cult status.

Marque – Brand or company name.

Meurseult – Splendid white Burgundy for those who can afford it.

Minervoise – Respectable southern red wine: can be good value as are many such.

Mise – As in mise en bouteilles au château ('château-bottled'), or ... dans nos caves ('in our cellars') and variations.

Montrachet – Very fine white Burgundy.

Moulin-à-Vent – One of the rather special Beaujolais wines.

Muscadet – Arguably the most popular light dry Loire white wine.

Muscat – Though used for some dry whites, this grape is mainly associated with succulent dessert-style wines.

Nouveau – New wine, for drinking fresh; particularly associated with now tiring vogue for Beaujolais Nouveau.

Pastis – General term for powerful anis/liquorice aperitifs originally evolved to replace banned absinthe and particularly associated with Marseilles area through the great firm of Ricard.

Pétillant – Gently, naturally effervescent.

Pineau – Unfermented grape juice lightly fortified with grape spirit; attractive aperitif widely made in France and under-appreciated abroad.

Pouilly-Fuissé – Dry white Burgundy (Macon); sometimes over-valued.

Pouilly-Fumé – Easily confused with above; a very dry fine Loire white.

Porto – Port wine: usually lighter in France than the type preferred in Britain and popular, chilled, as an aperitif.

Primeur – More or less the same as nouveau, but more often used for fine vintage wine sold en primeur for laying down to mature.

Rosé – 'Pink wine', best made by allowing temporary contact of juice and black grapes during fermentation; also by mixing red and white wine.

Sauvignon – Notable white grape; see also Cabernet.

Sec – 'Dry', but a wine so marked will be sweetish, even very sweet. Extra Sec may actually mean on the dry side.

Sirop – Syrup; e.g. sugar-syrup used in mixed drinks, also some flavoured proprietary non-alcoholic cordials.

Supérieur(e) – Much the same as Haut (q.v.) except in VDQS.

VQRPD. – See AC above.

Vin de Xeres – Sherry ('vin de 'ereth').

Glossary of cooking terms and dishes

This basic glossary provides an introduction to the terms you are most likely to encounter. For a more complete guide, see the companion pocket-sized book French Entrée to Food and Drink Companion (ISBN 1-904012-05-1) that provides a comprehensive bilingual menu dictionary together with all the useful phrases that will help you make the most of French food and restaurants.

Aigre-doux	bittersweet	Béchamel	white sauce flavoured with infusion of herbs
Aiguillette	thin slice (aiguille – needle)		
Aile	wing	Beignets	fritters
Aiolli	garlic mayonnaise	Bercy	sauce with white wine and shallots
Allemande (à l')	German style, i.e.: with sausages and sauerkraut	Beurre blanc	sauce from Nantes, with butter, reduction of shallot-flavoured vinegar or wine
Amuse-gueules	appetisers		
Andouille	large uncooked sausage, served cold after boiling	Beurre noir	browned butter with Seville oranges
Andouillettes	(as per Andouille) but made from smaller intestines, usually served hot after grilling	Bigarade	
		Billy By	mussel soup
		Bisque	creamy shellfish soup
Anglaise (à l')	plain boiled. Crème Anglaise – egg and cream sauce	Blanquette	stew with thick, white creamy sauce, usually veal
		Boeuf à la mode	braised beef
Anis	aniseed	Bombe	ice-cream mould
Argenteuil	with asparagus	Bonne femme	with root vegetables
Assiette Anglaise	plate of cold meats	Bordelais	Bordeaux-style, with red or white wine, marrowbone fat
Baba au rhum	yeast-based sponge macerated in rum	Bouchée	mouthful, e.g. vol-au-vent
Baguette	long, thin loaf	Boudin	sausage, white or black
Ballotine	boned, stuffed and rolled meat or poultry, usually cold	Bourride	thick fish-soup
		Braisé	braised
		Brandade (de morue)	dried salt-cod pounded into mousse
Béarnaise	sauce made from egg yolks, butter, tarragon, wine, shallots	Broche	spit
		Brochette	skewer

Brouillade	stew, using oil	Coque (à la)	e.g. oeufs –
Brouillé	scrambled		boiled eggs
Brûlé	burnt, e.g. crème	Cou	neck
	brûlée	Coulis	juice, purée (of
Campagne	country style		vegetables or
Cannelle	cinnamon		fruit)
Carbonnade	braised in beer	Court-bouillon	aromatic liquor
Cardinal	red-coloured		for cooking meat,
	sauce, e.g. with		fish, vegetables
	lobster, or in	Couscous	N. African dish
	pâtisserie with		with boiled
	redcurrants		grains of millet,
Cassolette or cassoulette	small pan		served with
Cassoulet	rich stew with		chicken or
	goose, pork and		vegetables
	haricot beans	Crapaudine	involving fowl,
Cervelas	pork garlic		particularly
	sausage		pigeon, trussed
Cervelles	brains	Crécy	with carrots
Chantilly	whipped	Crème pâtissière	thick custard
	sweetened cream		filling
Charcuterie	cold pork-	Crêpe	pancake
	butcher's meats	Crépinette	little flat
Charlotte	mould, as dessert		sausage, encased
	lined with		in caul
	sponge-fingers,	Croque-Monsieur	toasted cheese-
	as savoury lined		and-ham
	with vegetables		sandwich
Chasseur	with mushrooms,	Croustade	pastry or baked
	shallots, wine		bread shell
Chausson	pastry turnover	Croûte	pastry crust
Chemise	covering, i.e.	Croûton	cube of fried or
	pastry		toasted bread
Chiffonnade	thinly-cut, e.g.	Cru	raw
	lettuce	Crudités	raw vegetables
Choron	tomato	Demi-glâce	basic brown
	Béarnaise		sauce
Choucroute	Alsatian stew	Doria	with cucumber
	with sauerkraut	Émincé	thinly sliced
	and sausages	Entremets	sweets
Civet	stew	Étuvé	stewed, e.g.
Clafoutis	batter dessert,		vegetables in
	usually with		butter
	cherries	Farci	stuffed
Clamart	with peas	Feuilleté	leaves of flaky
Cocotte	covered casserole		pastry
Compôte	cooked fruit	Fines herbes	parsley, thyme,
Concassé	e.g. tomates		bayleaf
	concassées-	Flamande	Flemish style,
	skinned,		with beer
	chopped, juice	Flambé	flamed in spirit
	extracted	Flamiche	flan
Confit	preserved	Florentine	with spinach
Confiture	jam	Flûte	thinnest bread
Consommé	clear soup		loaf

Foie gras	goose liver	Gratinée	browned under grill
Fond (d'artichaut)	heart (of artichoke)	Grecque (à la)	cold vegetables served in oil
Fondu	melted	Grenadin	nugget of meat, usually of veal
Forestière	with mushrooms, bacon and potatoes	Grenouilles	frogs: cuisses de grenouille – frogs' legs
Four (au)	baked in the oven	Grillé	grilled
Fourré	stuffed, usually sweets	Gros sel	coarse salt
Frais, fraîche	fresh and cool	Hachis	minced or chopped
Frangipane	almond-cream pâtisserie	Haricot	slow cooked stew
Fricadelle	Swedish meat ball	Haricots	beans
		Hochepot	hotpot
Fricandeau	veal, usually topside	Hollandaise	sauce with egg, butter, lemon
Fricassé	stew (usually of veal) in creamy sauce	Hongroise	Hungarian, i.e. spiced with paprika
Frit	fried	Hors-d'oeuvre	assorted starters
Frites	chips	Huile	oil
Friture	assorted small fish, fried in batter	Île flottante	floating island – soft meringue on egg-custard sauce
Froid	cold		
Fumé	smoked	Indienne	Indian, i.e. with hot spices
Galantine	loaf-shaped chopped meat, fish or vegetable, set in natural jelly	Jambon	ham
		Jardinière	from the garden, i.e. with vegetables
Galette	Breton pancake, flat cake	Jarret	shin, e.g. jarret de veau
Garbure	thick country soup	Julienne	matchstick vegetables
Garni	garnished, usually with vegetables	Jus	natural juice
		Lait	milk
		Langue	tongue
Gaufre	waffle	Lard	bacon
Gelée	aspic	Longe	loin
Gésier	gizzard	Macédoine	diced fruits or vegetables
Gibier	game		
Gigot	leg	Madeleine	small sponge cake
Glacé	iced		
Gougère	choux pastry, large base	Magret	breast (of duck)
		Maïs	sweetcom
Goujons	fried strips, usually of fish	Maître d'hôtel	sauce with butter, lemon, parsley
Graine	seed		
Gratin	baked dish of vegetables cooked in cream and eggs	Marchand de vin	sauce with red wine, shallots
		Marengo	sauce with tomatoes, olive oil, white wine

Marinière	seamens' style e.g. moules marinière (mussels in white wine)	*Pavé*	thick slice
		Paysan	country style
		Périgueux	with truffles
		Persillade	chopped parsley and garlic topping
Marmite	deep casserole		
Matelote	fish stew, e.g. of eel	*Petit pain*	bread roll
		Petits fours	tiny cakes, sweetmeats
Médaillon	round slice		
Mélange	mixture	*Piperade*	peppers, onions, tomatoes in scrambled egg
Meunière	sauce with butter, lemon		
Miel	honey	*Poché*	poached
Mille-feuille	flaky pastry, (lit. 1,000 leaves)	*Poêlé*	fried
		Poitrine	breast
Mirepoix	cubed carrot, onion etc. used for sauces	*Poivre*	pepper
		Pommade	paste
		Potage	thick soup
Moëlle	beef marrow	*Pot-au-four*	broth with meat and vegetables
Mornay	cheese sauce		
Mouclade	mussel stew	*Potée*	country soup with cabbage
Mousseline	Hollandaise sauce, lightened with egg whites		
		Pralines	caramelised almonds
Moutarde	mustard	*Primeurs*	young veg
Nage (à la)	poached in flavoured liquor (fish)	*Printanier (printanière)*	garnished with early vegatables
		Profiteroles	choux pastry balls
Nature	plain		
Navarin (d'agneau)	stew of lamb with spring vegetables	*Provençale*	with garlic, tomatoes, olive oil, peppers
Noisette	nut-brown, burned butter	*Pureé*	mashed and sieved
Noix de veau	nut (leg) of veal	*Quenelle*	pounded fish or meat bound with egg, poached
Normande	Normandy style, i.e. with cream, apple, cider, Calvados		
		Queue	tail
		Quiche	pastry flan, e.g. quiche Lorraine – egg, bacon, cream
Nouilles	noodles		
Onglet	beef cut from flank		
Os	bone	*Râble*	saddle, e.g. râble de lièvre
Paillettes	straws (of pastry)		
Panaché	mixed	*Ragoût*	stew
Panade	flour crust	*Ramequin*	little pot
Papillote (en)	cooked in paper case	*Râpé*	grated
		Ratatouille	Provençale stew of onions, garlic, peppers, tomatoes
Parmentier	with potatoes		
Pâté	paste, of meat or fish		
Pâte	pastry	*Ravigote*	highly seasoned white sauce
Pâte brisée	rich short-crust pastry		
		Rémoulade	mayonnaise with gherkins, capers, herbs and shallots
Pâtisserie	pastries		
Paupiettes	paper-thin slice		

Rillettes	potted shredded meat, usually fat pork or goose		(according to size)
Riz	rice	Smitane	with sour cream, white wine, onion
Robert	sauce with mustard, vinegar, onion	Soissons	with dried white beans
Roquefort	ewe's milk blue cheese	Sorbet	water ice
Rossini	garnished with foie gras and truffle	Soubise	with creamed onions
		Soufflé	puffed, i.e. mixed with egg-white and baked
Rôti	roast		
Rouelle	nugget	St-Germain	with peas
Rouille	hot garlicky sauce for soupe de poisson	Sucre	sugar (sucre – sugared)
Roulade	roll	Suprême	fillet of poultry breast or fish
Roux	sauce base -flour and butter	Tartare (sauce)	mayonnaise with capers, herbs, onions
Sabayon	sweet fluffy sauce, with eggs and wine	Tartare	raw minced beef, flavoured with onions etc. and bound with raw egg
Safran	saffron		
Sagou	sago		
Salade niçoise	salad with tuna-fish, anchovies, tomatoes, beans, black olives	Tarte Tatin	upside down (apple) pie
		Terrine	pottery dish/baked minced, chopped meat, veg., chicken, fish or fruit
Salé	salted		
Salmis	dish of game or fowl, with red wine		
Salpicon	meat, fowl, vegetables, chopped fine, bound with sauce and used as fillings	Thé	tea
		Tiède	luke warm
		Timbale	steamed mould
		Tisane	infusion
		Tourte	pie
Sang	blood	Tranche	thick slice
Santé	lit. healthy, i.e. with spinach and potato	Truffes	truffles
		Tuile	tile, i.e. thin biscuit
Saucisse	fresh sausage	Vacherin	meringue confection
Saucisson	dried sausage		
Sauté	cooked in fat in open pan	Vallée d'Auge	with cream, apple, Calvados
Sauvage	wild	Vapeur (au)	steamed
Savarin	ring of yeast-sponge, soaked in syrup and liquor	Velouté	white sauce, bouillon-flavoured
		Véronique	with grapes
Sel	salt	Vert(e)	green, e.g. sauce verte, with herbs
Selle	saddle		
Selon	according to, e.g. selon grosseur	Vessie	pig's bladder

Vichysoisse	chilled creamy leek and potato soup
Vierge	prime (virgin) olive oil
Vinaigre	vinegar (lit. bitter wine)
Vinaigrette	wine vinegar and oil dressing
Volaille	poultry
Vol-au-vent	puff-pastry case
Xérès	sherry
Yaourt	yoghurt

FISH – Les Poissons

SHELLFISH – Les Coquillages

Alose	shad
Anchois	anchovy
Anguille	eel
Araignée de mer	spider crab
Bar	sea bass
Barbue	brill
Baudroie	monkfish, anglerfish
Belon	flat-shelled oyster
Bigomeau	winkle
Blanchaille	whitebait
Brochet	pike
Cabillaud	cod
Calamar	squid
Carpe	carp
Carrelet	plaice
Chapon de mer	scorpion fish
Claire	oyster
Coquille St-Jacques	scallop
Crabe	crab
Crevette grise	shrimp
Crevette rose	prawn
Daurade	sea bream
Écrevisse	crayfish
Éperlan	smelt
Espadon	swordfish
Étrille	baby crab
Favouille	spider crab
Flétan	halibut
Fruits de mer	seafood
Grondin	red gurnet
Hareng	herring
Homard	lobster
Huître	oyster
Julienne	ling
Laitance	soft herring-roe
Lamproie	lamprey

Langouste	Dublin Bay prawn
Lieu	ling
Limande	lemon sole
Lotte de mer	monkfish
Loup de mer	sea bass
Maquereau	mackerel
Merlan	whiting
Morue	salt cod
Moule	mussel
Mulet	grey mullet
Ombre	grayling
Oursin	sea urchin
Palourde	clam
Pétoncle	small scallop
Plie	plaice
Portugaise	oyster
Poulpe	octopus
Praire	large clam
Raie	skate
Rascasse	scorpion-fish
Rouget	red mullet
Sandre	zander
Saumon	salmon
Saumonette	rock salmon
Seiche	squid
Sole	sole
Soupion	inkfish
St-Pierre	John Dory
Thon	tuna/tunny
Tourteau	large crab
Tortue	turtle
Truite	trout
Turbot	turbot
Turbotin	chicken turbot

FRUITS – Les Fruit

VEGETABLES – Les Légumes

NUTS – Les Noix

HERBS – Les Herbes

SPICES – Les Épices

Abricot	apricot
Ail	garlic
Algue	seaweed
Amande	almond
Ananas	pineapple
Aneth	dill
Arachide	peanut
Artichaut	globe artichoke
Asperge	asparagus
Avocat	avocado
Banane	banana
Basilic	basil

Betterave	beetroot		fungus
Blette	Swiss chard	Mûre	blackberry
Brugnon	nectarine	Muscade	nutmeg
Cassis	blackcurrant	Myrtille	bilberry,
Céléri	celery		blueberry
Céléri-rave	celeriac	Navet	turnip
Cêpe	edible fungus	Noisette	hazelnut
Cerfeuil	chervil	Oignon	onion
Cerise	cherry	Oseille	sorrel
Champignon	mushroom	Palmier	palm
Chanterelle	edible fungus	Pamplemousse	grapefruit
Châtaigne	chestnut	Panais	parsnip
Chicorée	endive	Passe-Pierre	seaweed
Chou	cabbage	Pastèque	water melon
Chou-fleur	caulliflower	Pêche	peach
Choux de Bruxelles	Brussels sprouts	Persil	parsley
Ciboulette	chive	Petit pois	pea
Citron	lemon	Piment doux	sweet pepper
Citron vert	lime	Pissenlit	dandelion
Coing	quince	Pistache	pistachio
Concombre	cucumber	Pleurote	edible fungi
Coriandre	coriander	Poire	pear
Cornichon	gherkin	Poireau	leek
Courge	pumpkin	Poivre	pepper
Courgette	courgette	Poivron	green, red and
Cresson	watercress		yellow peppers
Échalote	shallot	Pomme	apple
Endive	chicory	Pomme de terre	potato
Épinard	spinach	Prune	plum
Escarole	salad leaves	Pruneau	prune
Estragon	tarragon	Quetsch	small dark plum
Fenouil	fennel	Radis	radish
Fève	broad bean	Raifort	horseradish
Flageolet	dried bean	Raisin	grape
Fraise	strawberry	Reine Claude	greengage
Framboise	raspberry	Romarin	rosemary
Genièvre	juniper	Safran	saffron
Gingembre	ginger	Salsifis	salsify
Girofle	clove	Thym	thyme
Girolle	edible fungus	Tilleul	lime blossom
Grenade	pomegranate	Tomate	tomato
Griotte	bitter red cherry	Topinambour	Jerusalem
Groseille	gooseberry		artichoke
Groseille noire	blackcurrant	Truffe	truffle
Groseille rouge	redcurrant		
Haricot	dried white bean		
Haricot vert	French bean		
Laitue	lettuce		
Mandarine	tangerine, mandarin		
Mangetout	sugar pea		
Marron	chestnut		
Menthe	mint		
Mirabelle	tiny gold plum		
Morille	dark brown crinkly edible		

MEAT – Les Viandes

Le Boeuf	Beef
Charolais	is the best
Chateaubriand	double fillet steak
Contrefilet	sirloin
Entrecôte	rib steak
Faux Filet	sirloin steak
Filet	fillet
L'Agneau	Lamb

GLOSSARY OF GASTRONOMIC TERMS

Pré-Salé	is the best	Bécassine	snipe
Carré	neck cutlets	Caille	quail
Côte	chump chop	Canard	duck
Epaule	shoulder	Caneton	duckling
Gigot	leg	Chapon	capon
Le Porc	Pork	Chevreuil	roe deer
Jambon	ham	Dinde	young hen
Jambon cru	raw smoked ham		turkeyΩ
Porcelet	suckling pig	Dindon	turkey
Le Veau	Veal	Dindonneau	young turkey
Escalope	thin slice cut	Faisan	pheasant
	from fillet	Grive	thrush
Les Abats	Offal	Lièvre	hare
Foie	liver	Oie	goose
Foie gras	goose liver	Perdreau	partridge
Cervelles	brains	Pigeon	pigeon
Langue	tongue	Pintade	guineafowl
Ris	sweetbreads	Pluvier	plover
Rognons	kidneys	Poularde	chicken (boiling)
Tripes	tripe	Poulet	chicken
			(roasting)

POULTRY – Volaille

GAME – Gibier

		Poussin	spring chicken
		Sanglier	wild boar
		Sarcelle	teal
Abatis	giblets	Venaison	venison
Bécasse	woodcock		

Index